ADDISON WESLEY

# Math
## Makes Sense

**7**

## Author Team

Jason Johnston

Mary Doucette

Steve Thomas

Trevor Brown

Don Jones

Jennifer Paziuk

Ken Harper

Bryn Keyes

Antonietta Lenjosek

Margaret Sinclair

Cathy Heideman

Michael Davis

Sharon Jeroski

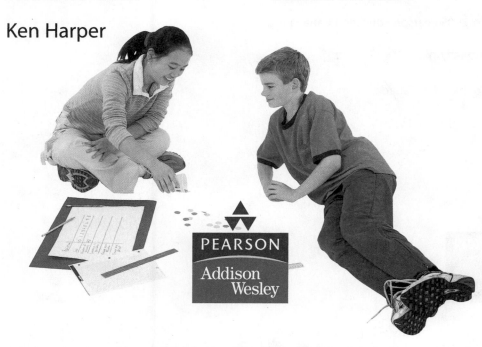

PEARSON

Addison
Wesley

**Publishing Team**
Lesley Haynes
Enid Haley
Lynne Gulliver
Ingrid D'Silva
Cristina Gulesiu
Stephanie Cox
Judy Wilson
Nicole Argyropoulos

**Editorial Contributors**
John Burnett
Jim Mennie
Janine Leblanc
Christina Yu

**Publisher**
Claire Burnett

**Elementary Math Team Leader**
Anne-Marie Scullion

**Product Manager**
Nishaant Sanghavi

**Photo Research**
Karen Hunter

**Design**
Word & Image Design Studio Inc.

Copyright © 2005 Pearson Education Canada Inc.

ISBN 0-321-23577-0

Printed and bound in Canada.

9 10 11 12    17 16 15 14

The information and activities presented in this book have been carefully edited and reviewed. However, the publisher shall not be liable for any damages resulting, in whole or in part, from the reader's use of this material.

Brand names that appear in photographs of products in this textbook are intended to provide students with a sense of the real-world applications of mathematics and are in no way intended to endorse specific products.

The publisher has taken every care to meet or exceed industry specifications for the manufacturing of textbooks. The spine and the endpapers of this sewn book have been reinforced with special fabric for extra binding strength. The cover is a premium, polymer-reinforced material designed to provide long life and withstand rugged use. Mylar gloss lamination has been applied for further durability.

# Program Consultants and Advisers

## Program Consultants

Craig Featherstone
Maggie Martin Connell
Trevor Brown

*Assessment Consultant*
Sharon Jeroski

*Elementary Mathematics Adviser*
John A. Van de Walle

## Program Advisers

Pearson Education thanks its Program Advisers, who helped shape the vision for *Addison Wesley Mathematics Makes Sense* through discussions and reviews of prototype materials and manuscript.

Anthony Azzopardi
Sandra Ball
Victoria Barlow
Lorraine Baron
Bob Belcher
Judy Blake
Steve Cairns
Christina Chambers
Daryl M. J. Chichak
Lynda Colgan
Marg Craig
Elizabeth Fothergill
Jennifer Gardner
Florence Glanfield

Linden Gray
Pamela Hagen
Dennis Hamaguchi
Angie Harding
Andrea Helmer
Peggy Hill
Auriana Kowalchuk
Gordon Li
Werner Liedtke
Jodi Mackie
Lois Marchand
Becky Matthews
Betty Milne
Cathy Molinski

Cynthia Pratt Nicolson
Bill Nimigon
Stephen Parks
Eileen Phillips
Carole Saundry
Evelyn Sawicki
Leyton Schnellert
Shannon Sharp
Michelle Skene
Lynn Strangway
Laura Weatherhead
Mignonne Wood

## Program Reviewers

### Field Testers

Pearson Education would like to thank the teachers and students who field-tested *Addison Wesley Math Makes Sense 7* prior to publication. Their feedback and constructive recommendations have helped us to develop a quality mathematics program.

### Aboriginal Content Reviewers

Early Childhood and School Services Division
Department of Education, Culture, and Employment
Government of Northwest Territories:

**Steven Daniel**, Coordinator, Mathematics, Science, and Secondary Education
**Liz Fowler**, Coordinator, Culture Based Education
**Margaret Erasmus**, Coordinator, Aboriginal Languages

### Grade 7 Reviewers

**Judy Blaney**
OISE/University of Toronto, ON

**Michaela Clancy**
Simcoe Muskoka Catholic District School Board, ON

**Tina Conlon**
Niagara Catholic District School Board, ON

**Kelly Denholme**
School District #43 (Coquitlam), BC

**Gwen Emery**
Toronto District School Board, ON

**Thomas Falkenberg**
School District #44 (North Vancouver), BC

**Norma Fraser**
School District #83 (North Okanagan/Shuswap), BC

**Rob D'Ilario**
Niagara Catholic District School Board, ON

**AJ Keene**
Lakehead District School Board, ON

**Linda LoFaro**
Ottawa-Carleton Catholic School Board, ON

**David MacLean**
School District #43 (Coquitlam), BC

**Becky Matthews**
Victoria, BC

**Jim McCann**
Simcoe County District School Board, ON

**Timothy T. Millan**
Toronto District School Board, ON

**Mark Moorhouse**
Lakehead District School Board, ON

**Walter Rogoza**
Rainy River District School Board, ON

**Wendy Swonnell**
School District #61 (Greater Victoria), BC

**James Tremblay**
Durham Catholic District School Board, ON

**Gregg Williamson**
Hamilton-Wentworth District School Board, ON

# Table of Contents

Cross Strand Investigation: Making a Booklet     2

## UNIT 1   Patterns in Whole Numbers

**Strand** • Number Sense and Numeration
         • Patterning and Algebra

| | |
|---|---|
| Skills You'll Need | 6 |
| **1.1** Numbers All Around Us | 10 |
| **1.2** Factors and Multiples | 14 |
| **Game:** The Factor Game | 18 |
| **1.3** Squares and Square Roots | 19 |
| Mid-Unit Review | 22 |
| **1.4** Exponents | 23 |
| **The World of Work:** Hospital Administrator | 27 |
| **1.5** Number Patterns | 28 |
| **Reading and Writing in Math:** Using Different Strategies | 32 |
| Unit Review | 34 |
| Practice Test | 37 |
| **Unit Problem:** Fibonacci Numbers | 38 |

## UNIT 2   Ratio and Rate

**Strand** | • Number Sense and Numeration

| | |
|---|---|
| Skills You'll Need | 42 |
| **2.1** What Is a Ratio? | 45 |
| **2.2** Equivalent Ratios | 49 |
| **2.3** Comparing Ratios | 53 |
| Mid-Unit Review | 57 |
| **2.4** Applications of Ratios | 58 |
| **2.5** What Is a Rate? | 62 |
| **Reading and Writing in Math:** Organizing a Math Notebook | 66 |
| **The World of Work:** Race Engineer | 68 |
| Unit Review | 69 |
| Practice Test | 71 |
| **Unit Problem:** Who's the Smartest? | 72 |

# UNIT 3

## Geometry and Measurement

**Strand** • Geometry and Spatial Sense
• Measurement

| | |
|---|---|
| **Skills You'll Need** | **76** |
| **3.1** Sketching Views of Solids | **78** |
|  **Technology:** Using a Computer to Draw Views of Solids | **82** |
| **3.2** Sketching Solids | **84** |
| **The World of Work:** Forensic Graphics Specialist | **88** |
| **3.3** Building Objects from Nets | **89** |
| **Mid-Unit Review** | **93** |
| **3.4** Using Variables in Measurement Formulas | **94** |
| **3.5** Surface Area of a Rectangular Prism | **97** |
| **3.6** Volume of a Rectangular Prism | **101** |
| **Reading and Writing in Math:** Decoding Word Problems | **104** |
| **Unit Review** | **106** |
| **Practice Test** | **109** |
| **Unit Problem:** Making Food for a Bake Sale | **110** |
| **Cross Strand Investigation: Ratios in Scale Drawings** | **112** |

# UNIT 4

## Fractions and Decimals

**Strand** • Number Sense and Numeration

| | |
|---|---|
| **Skills You'll Need** | **116** |
| **4.1** Combining Fractions | **120** |
| **Game:** Join the Dots | **123** |
| **4.2** Adding Fractions Using Models | **124** |
| **4.3** Adding Fractions | **128** |
| **4.4** Subtracting Fractions Using Models | **132** |
| **4.5** Subtracting Fractions | **136** |
| **Game:** Shade One | **139** |
| **Mid-Unit Review** | **140** |
| **4.6** Exploring Repeated Addition | **141** |
| **Technology:** Fractions to Decimals | **144** |
| **4.7** Multiplying Decimals | **145** |
| **4.8** Dividing Decimals | **149** |
| **The World of Work:** Advertising Sales Representative | **153** |
| **4.9** Order of Operations with Decimals | **154** |
| **Reading and Writing in Math:** Writing a Math Journal Entry | **156** |
| **Unit Review** | **158** |
| **Practice Test** | **161** |
| **Unit Problem:** Publishing a Book | **162** |
| **Cumulative Review Units 1-4** | **164** |

# UNIT 5

## Data Management

**Strand** • Data Management and Probability

| | |
|---|---|
| **Skills You'll Need** | 168 |
| **5.1** Collecting Data | 169 |
| **Technology:** Using Databases to Find Data | 172 |
| **5.2** Recording Data | 174 |
| **5.3** Stem-and-Leaf Plots | 179 |
| **The World of Work:** Meteorologist | 183 |
| **Mid-Unit Review** | 184 |
| **Technology:** Using *Fathom* to Investigate Scatter Plots | 185 |
| **5.4** Line Graphs | 188 |
| **Technology:** Using Spreadsheets to Record and Graph Data | 193 |
| **5.5** Applications of Mean, Median, and Mode | 198 |
| **5.6** Evaluating Data Analysis | 202 |
| **Reading and Writing in Math:** Making a Study Sheet | 206 |
| **Unit Review** | 208 |
| **Practice Test** | 211 |
| **Unit Problem:** Organizing a Winter Carnival | 212 |

# UNIT 6

## Measuring Perimeter and Area

**Strand** • Measurement
• Patterning and Algebra

| | |
|---|---|
| **Skills You'll Need** | 216 |
| **6.1** Area of a Parallelogram | 217 |
| **6.2** Area of a Triangle | 221 |
| **Mid-Unit Review** | 225 |
| **6.3** Area and Perimeter of a Trapezoid | 226 |
| **The World of Work:** Measuring for Construction | 231 |
| **Reading and Writing in Math:** Interpreting a Problem | 232 |
| **6.4** Measuring Irregular Figures | 234 |
| **Game:** Trapezoid Challenge | 238 |
| **Unit Review** | 239 |
| **Practice Test** | 241 |
| **Unit Problem:** Designing a Patio | 242 |

# UNIT 7

## Geometry

Strand • Geometry and Spatial Sense

| | |
|---|---|
| Skills You'll Need | 246 |
| 7.1 Classifying Figures | 250 |
| 7.2 Congruent Figures | 255 |
| Mid-Unit Review | 260 |
| 7.3 Transformations | 261 |
| 7.4 Tiling Patterns | 266 |
| 7.5 Using Transformations to Make Designs | 270 |
| Technology: Using a Computer to Transform Figures | 274 |
| Reading and Writing in Math: Choosing a Strategy | 278 |
| The World of Work: Office Space Planner | 280 |
| Unit Review | 281 |
| Practice Test | 283 |
| Unit Problem: Tessellations | 284 |
| Cross Strand Investigation: Pick's Theorem | 286 |

# UNIT 8

## Working with Percents

Strand • Number Sense and Numeration
• Data Management and Probability

| | |
|---|---|
| Skills You'll Need | 290 |
| 8.1 Relating Fractions, Decimals, and Percents | 292 |
| Game: Showdown | 296 |
| 8.2 Estimating and Calculating Percents | 297 |
| 8.3 Multiplying to Find Percents | 302 |
| Mid-Unit Review | 305 |
| 8.4 Drawing Circle Graphs | 306 |
| 8.5 Dividing to Find Percents | 311 |
| Reading and Writing in Math: Choosing a Strategy | 314 |
| The World of Work: Sports Trainer | 316 |
| Unit Review | 317 |
| Practice Test | 319 |
| Unit Problem: At the Shopping Mall | 320 |
| Cumulative Review Units 1-8 | 322 |

# UNIT 9 — Integers

**Strand** • Number Sense and Numeration

| | |
|---|---|
| **Skills You'll Need** | **326** |
| **9.1** What Is an Integer? | **327** |
| **9.2** Comparing and Ordering Integers | **330** |
| **9.3** Representing Integers | **334** |
| **9.4** Adding Integers with Tiles | **337** |
| **9.5** Adding Integers | **341** |
| **Mid-Unit Review** | **345** |
| **9.6** Subtracting Integers with Tiles | **346** |
| **9.7** Subtracting Integers | **351** |
| **Reading and Writing in Math:** Choosing a Strategy | **356** |
| **The World of Work:** Historian | **358** |
| **Unit Review** | **359** |
| **Practice Test** | **361** |
| **Unit Problem:** What Time Is It? | **362** |

# UNIT 10 — Patterning and Algebra

**Strand** • Patterning and Algebra

| | |
|---|---|
| **Skills You'll Need** | **366** |
| **10.1** Number Patterns | **368** |
| **10.2** Graphing Patterns | **373** |
| **10.3** Variables in Expressions | **378** |
| **Mid-Unit Review** | **382** |
| **10.4** Evaluating Algebraic Expressions | **383** |
| **10.5** Reading and Writing Equations | **387** |
| **10.6** Solving Equations | **390** |
| **The World of Work:** Clothes Buyer | **395** |
| **Reading and Writing in Math:** Choosing a Strategy | **396** |
| **Unit Review** | **398** |
| **Practice Test** | **401** |
| **Unit Problem:** Fund Raising | **402** |

**Strand** • Data Management and Probability

| | |
|---|---|
| **Skills You'll Need** | **406** |
| **11.1** Listing Outcomes | **407** |
| **11.2** Experimental Probability | **411** |
| **Mid-Unit Review** | **415** |
| **11.3** Theoretical Probability | **416** |
| **11.4** Applications of Probability | **420** |
| **Reading and Writing in Math:** Choosing a Strategy | **424** |
| **Game:** Empty the Rectangles | **426** |
| **Unit Review** | **427** |
| **Practice Test** | **429** |
| **Unit Problem:** Games of Chance | **430** |
| **Cross Strand Investigation: A Population Simulation** | **432** |
| **Cumulative Review Units 1-11** | **434** |
| **Extra Practice** | **438** |
| **Illustrated Glossary** | **451** |
| **Index** | **458** |
| **Acknowledgments** | **462** |

# Welcome to
## *Addison Wesley Math Makes Sense 7*

Math helps you understand your world.

This book will help you improve your problem-solving skills and show you how you can use your math now, and in your future career.

The opening pages of **each unit** are designed to help you prepare for success.

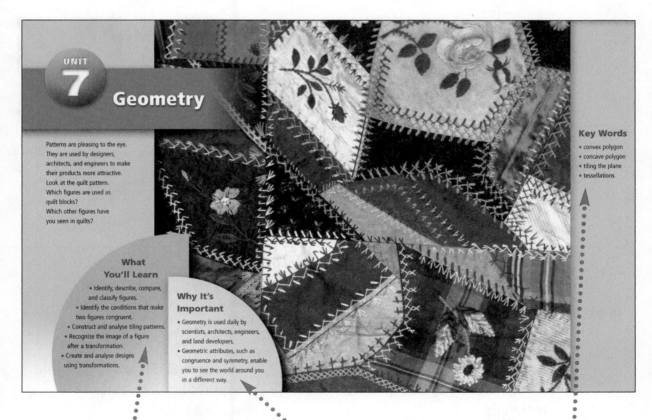

UNIT **7** **Geometry**

Patterns are pleasing to the eye. They are used by designers, architects, and engineers to make their products more attractive. Look at the quilt pattern. Which figures are used as quilt blocks? Which other figures have you seen in quilts?

**Key Words**
- convex polygon
- concave polygon
- tiling the plane
- tessellations

### What You'll Learn
- Identify, describe, compare, and classify figures.
- Identify the conditions that make two figures congruent.
- Construct and analyse tiling patterns.
- Recognize the image of a figure after a transformation.
- Create and analyse designs using transformations.

### Why It's Important
- Geometry is used daily by scientists, architects, engineers, and land developers.
- Geometric attributes, such as congruence and symmetry, enable you to see the world around you in a different way.

Find out **What You'll Learn** and **Why It's Important**. Check the list of **Key Words**.

Review some of the math concepts you've already met.

**Study the Example.**

**Then try the Check questions to review your skills.**

---

**UNIT 6**

## Skills You'll Need

### Perimeter and Area of a Rectangle

**Perimeter** is the distance around a figure.
**Area** is the amount of surface a figure covers.

#### Example 1

a) Find the perimeter of each figure.

i)

5 cm

ii)

7 m

4 m

b) Find the area of each figure in part a.

#### Solution

a) i) The figure is a square.
The perimeter of a square is: $P = 4s$
Substitute $s = 5$.
$P = 4 \times 5$
  $= 20$
The perimeter is 20 cm.

ii) The figure is a rectangle.
The perimeter of a rectangle is: $P = 2(b + h)$
Substitute $b = 7$ and $h = 4$.
$P = 2(7 + 4)$
  $= 2 \times 11$
  $= 22$
The perimeter is 22 m.

b) i) The area of a square is: $A = s^2$
Substitute $s = 5$.
$A = 5^2$
  $= 5 \times 5$
  $= 25$
The area is 25 cm².

ii) The area of a rectangle is: $A = bh$
Substitute $b = 7$ and $h = 4$.
$A = 7 \times 4$
  $= 28$
The area is 28 m².

#### ✓ Check

1. Find the perimeter and area of each figure.

a) 3 cm / 12 cm

b) 8 m / 5 m

c) 4.5 cm

d) 3.0 cm / 1.2 cm

216   UNIT 6: Measuring Perimeter and Area

---

### 6.1   Area of a Parallelogram

**Focus** Use a formula to find the area of a parallelogram.

This is a **parallelogram**.
How would you describe it?

height
base

Here is the same parallelogram.
Any side of the parallelogram is a base.
The height is perpendicular to the base.

height
base

#### Explore

Work with a partner.

You will need a tangram and grid paper.
➤ One tan is a parallelogram. Find its area.
➤ Make another parallelogram by combining tans. Find the area of the parallelogram.
➤ Continue to combine tans to make different parallelograms. Find the area of each parallelogram you make.
➤ Record your work. Draw each parallelogram on grid paper.
➤ Use variables. Write a formula to find the area of a parallelogram.

#### Reflect & Share

How did you find the area of each parallelogram?
Which different strategies did you use?
Which strategy helped you write the formula for the area?

6.1 Area of a Parallelogram   217

---

## In each Lesson:

**Explore** an idea or problem. You may use materials.

**Reflect & Share** your results with other students.

**Examples** show you how to use the ideas.

**Connect** summarizes the math.

Stay sharp with **Number Strategies**, **Mental Math**, and **Calculator Skills**.

**Practice** questions reinforce the math.

**Take It Further** questions offer enrichment and extension.

**Reflect** on the big ideas of the lesson.

Use the **Mid-Unit Review** to refresh
your memory of key concepts.

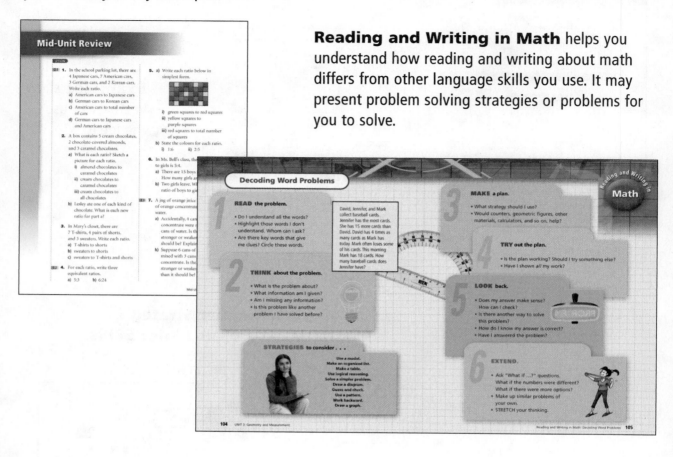

**Reading and Writing in Math** helps you
understand how reading and writing about math
differs from other language skills you use. It may
present problem solving strategies or problems for
you to solve.

**What Do I Need to Know?** summarizes
key ideas from the unit.

**What Should I Be Able to Do?** allows
you to find out if you are
ready to move on. The
on-line tutorial **etext**
provides additional
support.

The **Practice Test** models the kind of test your teacher might give.

The **Unit Problem** presents problems to solve, or a project to do, using the math of the unit.

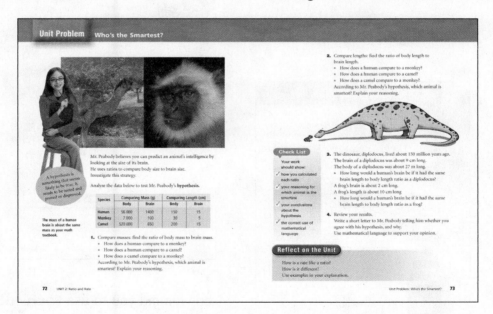

Keep your skills sharp with **Cumulative Review** and **Extra Practice.**

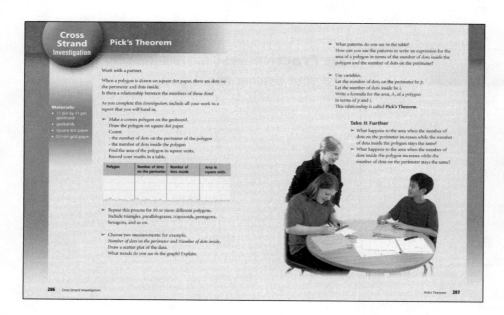

Explore some interesting math when you do the **Cross Strand Investigations**.

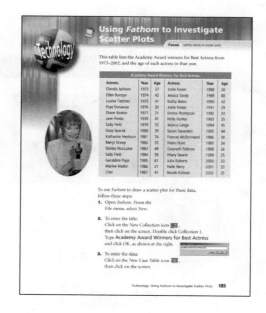

Icons remind you to use **technology**. Follow the step-by-step instructions for using a computer or calculator to do math.

Play a **Game** with your classmates or at home to reinforce your skills.

**The World of Work** describes how people use mathematics in their careers.

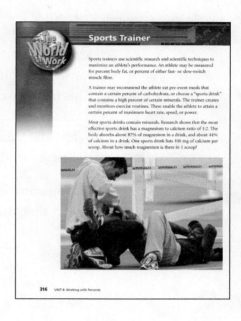

The **Illustrated Glossary** is a dictionary of important math words.

# Making a Booklet

Work with a partner.

A book is made up of **signatures**. A signature has 16 or 32 pages. A signature is a sheet of paper printed on both sides, in a special arrangement. The sheet is measured in inches. The dimensions for the sheet in this *Investigation* are 25 inches by 38 inches. This is approximately 64 cm by 97 cm.

This sheet of paper is then folded into sections of 16 or 32 pages. When the sheet of paper is folded and cut in some places, the pages read in the correct numerical order.

As you complete this *Investigation*, include all your work in a report that you will hand in.

**Materials:**
- sheets of newsprint measuring 25 inches by 38 inches

## Part 1

Here are both sides of a 16-page signature.
The pages are from 1 to 16.

There are patterns in the numbers on a signature. These patterns help the printer decide which page numbers go on each side of a sheet when it goes on press.

Your challenge will be to find the patterns in the numbers on a signature. How would knowing these patterns help you create a book with more than 32 pages?

➤ How many folds are needed to make a 16-page signature? Fold a 25-inch by 38-inch piece of paper in half, several times, to find out.

Write the page numbers consecutively on the pages.

Open the sheet of paper.

Where are all the even numbers?

Where are all the odd numbers?

What else do you notice about the page numbers?

What patterns do you see in the page numbers?

➤ The 2nd signature has pages 17 to 32.
Draw a sketch. Show both sides of this signature with page numbers in place.

➤ Look for patterns in the numbers.
How do these patterns compare with those in the 1st signature?

## Part 2

Here are both sides of a 32-page signature.

➤ Repeat the steps in *Part 1* for this 32-page signature.
Describe all the patterns you discover.

➤ Find some books in the school or class library.
Calculate how many signatures each book might have.

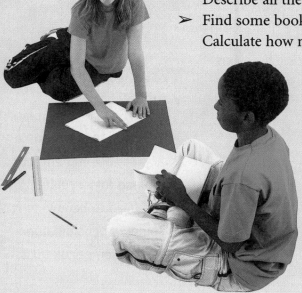

### Take It Further

Suppose you have to create a 64-page signature.

How can you use the number patterns in *Parts 1* and *2* to help you create a 64-page signature?

# Patterns in Whole Numbers

There are many patterns you can see in nature. You can use numbers to describe many of these patterns.

At the end of this unit, you will investigate a famous set of numbers, the Fibonacci Numbers. You will explore these numbers, and find how they can be used to describe the breeding of animals, such as rabbits.

Think about the different patterns you learned in earlier grades. Give an example of each type of pattern.

## What You'll Learn

- Use mental math, paper and pencil, calculators, and estimation to solve problems.
- Justify your choice of method for calculations.
- Find factors and multiples of numbers.
- Find the greatest common factor and lowest common multiple of two numbers.
- Identify prime and composite numbers.
- Use exponents to represent repeated multiplication.
- Identify and extend number patterns.
- Choose and justify strategies for solving problems.

## Why It's Important

- You need to know an appropriate and efficient method for calculations.
- You need to be able to find common denominators for fraction calculations.

## Key Words

- factor
- prime number
- composite number
- greatest common factor (GCF)
- multiple
- lowest common multiple (LCM)
- square number
- square root
- exponent form
- base
- exponent
- power
- cube number
- perfect square
- perfect cube

# Skills You'll Need

## Rounding

The place-value chart below shows the number 1 234 567.

| Millions | Hundred thousands | Ten thousands | Thousands | Hundreds | Tens | Ones |
|----------|-------------------|---------------|-----------|----------|------|------|
| 1 | 2 | 3 | 4 | 5 | 6 | 7 |

To round:

Look at the digit to the right of the place to which you are rounding.

Is this digit 5 or greater?

If it is, add 1 to the place digit.

If it is not, leave the place digit as it is.

Change all the digits to the right of the place digit to 0.

### Example 1

a) Round 425 to the nearest ten.

b) Round to the nearest thousand.

   i) 2471        ii) 13 999

### Solution

a)

425 rounded to the nearest ten is 430.

b) i)

2471 rounded to the nearest thousand is 2000.

ii)

| Ten thousands | Thousands | Hundreds | Tens | Ones |
|:---:|:---:|:---:|:---:|:---:|
| 1 | 3 | 9 | 9 | 9 |

This number is greater than 5.

So, add 1 thousand to this number to get 4 thousands.
Replace each number to the right of 4 with 0.

13 999 rounded to the nearest thousand is 14 000.

## ✓ Check

**1.** Round to the nearest ten.

   **a)** 36               **b)** 42              **c)** 75              **d)** 361

**2.** Round to the nearest hundred.

   **a)** 311            **b)** 789           **c)** 625            **d)** 2356

## Multiplying by 10, 100, 1000

To multiply a whole number:
– by 10, write 0 after the number.
– by 100, write 00 after the number.
– by 1000, write 000 after the number.

### Example 2

Multiply.

**a)** $32 \times 10$          **b)** $478 \times 100$          **c)** $51 \times 1000$
**d)** $32 \times 20$          **e)** $47 \times 300$

### Solution

**a)** $32 \times 10 = 320$      **b)** $478 \times 100 = 47\ 800$      **c)** $51 \times 1000 = 51\ 000$

**d)** $32 \times 20 = 32 \times 2 \times 10$      **e)** $47 \times 300 = 47 \times 3 \times 100$

$$= 64 \times 10$$
$$= 640$$

$$= 141 \times 100$$
$$= 14\ 100$$

**3.** Find.

a) $3 \times 10$  b) $1000 \times 5$  c) $131 \times 10$  d) $100 \times 63$

**4.** Use a place-value chart. Explain why we can write zeros after a number when we multiply by 10, 100, or 1000.

**5.** Multiply.

a) $50 \times 72$  b) $18 \times 600$  c) $4000 \times 33$

## Mental Math

### Example 3

Use mental math.

a) $53 \times 6$  b) $308 + 56 - 6$  c) $197 + 452$

**Solution**

a) $53 \times 6$

Think:

$50 \times 6 + 3 \times 6$
$= 300 + 18$
$= 318$

b) $308 + 56 - 6$

Think:

$56 - 6 = 50$
Then: $308 + 50 = 358$

c) $197 + 452$

Think:

$197 = 200 - 3$
Then: $200 + 452 - 3 = 652 - 3$   Count back to subtract.
$= 649$

**Check**

**6.** Use mental math.

a) $4 + 17$  b) $9 + 8$  c) $12 + 6$
d) $20 + 6$  e) $40 + 30$  f) $17 - 2$
g) $22 - 4$  h) $70 - 20$  i) $20 - 15$

**7.** Use mental math. Explain your strategy.

a) $28 + 13 + 12$  b) $2 \times 29 \times 5$  c) $98 + 327$
d) $4 \times 981 \times 25$  e) $99 \times 21$  f) $62 \times 8$

# Divisibility Rules

A number is divisible by:
- 2 if the number is even
- 3 if the sum of its digits is divisible by 3
- 4 if the number represented by the last 2 digits is divisible by 4
- 5 if the last digit is 0 or 5
- 6 if the number is divisible by 2 and 3
- 8 if the number represented by the last 3 digits is divisible by 8
- 9 if the sum of the digits is divisible by 9
- 10 if the last digit is 0

## Example 4

Which of these numbers is 1792 divisible by?

a) 2          b) 3          c) 4          d) 5          e) 6

### Solution

a) 1792 is divisible by 2 because 1792 is an even number.
b) $1 + 7 + 9 + 2 = 19$
   19 is not divisible by 3, so 1792 is not divisible by 3.
c) The last 2 digits are 92.
   $92 \div 4 = 23$
   Since the last 2 digits are divisible by 4, 1792 is divisible by 4.
d) 1792 is not divisible by 5 because the last digit is not 0 or 5.
e) Since 1792 is not divisible by 3, 1792 is also not divisible by 6.

## ✓ Check

8. Which numbers are divisible by 3?
   a) 490          b) 492          c) 12 345

9. Write 4 other numbers greater than 400 that are divisible by 3.

10. Which numbers are divisible by 6?
    a) 870          b) 232          c) 681

11. Which numbers from 1 to 10 is:
    a) 660 divisible by?   b) 1001 divisible by?

We use numbers to understand and describe our world.

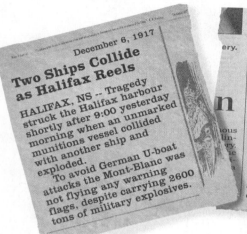

**December 6, 1917**

### Two Ships Collide as Halifax Reels

HALIFAX, NS -- Tragedy struck the Halifax harbour shortly after 9:00 yesterday morning when an unmarked munitions vessel collided with another ship and exploded.

To avoid German U-boat attacks the Mont-Blanc was not flying any warning flags, despite carrying 2600 tons of military explosives.

### The Halifax Explosion

**Did You Know?**
At the time of the explosion, the Mont-Blanc was carrying
- 226 797 kg of TNT
- 2 146 830 kg of picric acid
- 56 301 kg of guncotton
- 223 188 kg of benzol
— all highly explosive and dangerous chemicals.

The 1917 explosion was 1/7 the strength of the atomic bomb dropped on Hiroshima.

**Saturday, August 23, 2003**

### Southern BC Fires Approach City

KELOWNA, BC – Police with bullhorns ordered a staggering 20,000 Kelowna residents to evacuate their homes as fast-moving wildfires moved closer.

Thick smoke choked Kelowna's 100,000 residents and at times clouded the view of nearby Okanagan Lake.

The fire prompted the closure of Route 97, between Okanagan Falls and Penticton, and brought the total number of evacuees driven out by the fire to 30,000.

More than 3,000 firefighters from British Columbia and elsewhere in Canada are battling over 825 fires in the province.

## Explore

**January, 1998**

### Five Day Ice Storm Cripples Quebec and Eastern Ontario

*The 1998 Ice Storm*

Did You Know?
- The ice storm of 1998 was Canada's most expensive natural disaster, and cost approximately $1.6 billion, including $500 million in private property damage.
- When the ice storm ended on Jan 10, 23,000 hydro poles and 80 km of power lines were destroyed on the south shore of Montreal.
- A wooden hydro pole costs $3000.
- Hydro towers are built to withstand 15 mm of freezing rain. Montreal received over 100 mm during the storm.

Work on your own.
Read the articles above and at the left.

➤ Which numbers do you think are exact?
Which numbers are estimates? Explain your thinking.
➤ Use the numbers in the articles.
Write a problem you would solve each way:
- using mental math
- by estimating
- using pencil and paper
- using a calculator
➤ Solve your problem.
➤ Trade problems with a classmate.
Solve your classmate's problem.

### Reflect & Share

Compare the strategies you used to solve the problems.
- Explain why some strategies work while others may not.
- Is one strategy more effective? Why?

- When the numbers are easy to handle, use mental math.
- When the problem has too many steps, use a paper and pencil.
- When an approximate answer is appropriate and to check reasonableness, estimate.
- When a more accurate answer is needed and the numbers are large, use a calculator.

## Example

The population of Canada was 30 750 000 in July 2000. Statistics Canada (Stats Can) data show that there were 6367 telephones per 10 000 people in that year.
a) About how many telephones were there in Canada in 2000?
b) Find the exact number of telephones in Canada in 2000.
c) How did Stats Can know there were 6367 phones per 10 000 people? Explain how this answer affects the answer to part b.

## Solution

a) Estimate.
Round 30 750 000 to the nearest ten million: 30 000 000
Round 6367 to the nearest thousand: 6000
10 000 people use about 6000 phones.
10 000 000 people use about 6000 × 1000, or 6 000 000 phones.
30 000 000 people use about 6 000 000 × 3, or 18 000 000 phones.
There were about 18 million phones in Canada in 2000.

b) Find how many groups of 10 000 people there are in 30 750 000.
That is, 30 750 000 ÷ 10 000 = 3075
For each group of 10 000 people, there were 6367 phones.

 **Use a calculator.**
The number of phones: 3075 × 6367 = 19 578 525
So, there were 19 578 525 phones in Canada in 2000.

c) Stats Can conducted a survey of about 40 000 people.
It asked how many phones each person had.
Stats Can then calculated how many phones per 10 000 people.

To find out exactly how many phones there are in Canada, Stats Can would have to survey the entire population. This is impractical. So, the number of phones in part b is an estimate.

1. Solve without a calculator.
   a) 72 + 43
   b) 123 + 85
   c) 672 + 189
   d) 97 − 24
   e) 195 − 71
   f) 821 − 485
   g) 65 × 100
   h) 14 × 75
   i) 83 × 25
   j) 780 ÷ 10
   k) 724 ÷ 4
   l) 245 ÷ 7

2. Use pencil and paper to find each answer.
   a) 6825 + 127
   b) 7928 − 815
   c) 3614 − 278
   d) 138 × 21
   e) 651 ÷ 21
   f) 6045 ÷ 15

3. Estimate each answer. Explain the strategy you used each time.
   a) 103 + 89
   b) 123 − 19
   c) 72 × 9
   d) 418 ÷ 71

**Mental Math**

Multiply.

3.6 × 1000   3.6 × 100
3.6 × 10     3.6 × 1
3.6 × 0.1    3.6 × 0.01

What patterns do you see in the questions and the answers?

Questions 4 to 7 pose problems about the 1997 Red River Flood in Manitoba. Use mental math, estimation, pencil and paper, or a calculator. Justify your strategy.

4. The 1997 Red River Flood caused over $815 036 000 in damages.
   a) Write this amount in words.
   b) How close to $1 billion were the damages?

5. Pauline Thiessen and fellow volunteers made an average of 10 000 sandwiches every day for 2 weeks to feed the flood relief workers. How many sandwiches did they make?

6. Winnipeg used 6.5 million sandbags to hold back the flood. Each sandbag was about 10 cm thick. About how high would a stack of 6.5 million sandbags be in centimetres? Metres? Kilometres?

7. To help with the flood relief, Joe Morena of St. Viateur Bagels in Montreal trucked 300 dozen of his famous bagels to Manitoba.
   a) How many bagels did he send?
   b) Joe sells bagels for $4.80 a dozen. What was the value of his donation?

8. The Monarch butterfly migrates from Toronto to El Rosario, Mexico. This is a distance of 3300 km.
   A monarch butterfly can fly at an average speed of 15 km/h. How long does the migration flight take?

9. Estimate each answer. Is each estimate high or low?
How do you know?
a) 583 + 702  b) 3815 − 576  c) 821 ÷ 193  d) 695 ÷ 310

For questions 10 and 11: Make up a problem using the given data.
Have a classmate solve your problems.

10. Sunil earns $7 per hour. He works 4 h per day during the week
and 6 h per day on the weekends.

11. In October 1954, Hurricane Hazel blew through Toronto,
Ontario. Winds reached 124 km/h, 111 mm of rain fell in 12 h,
and over 210 mm of rain fell over 2 days.

12. **Assessment Focus**  The table shows the populations
of some Canadian provinces in 1999.

| Province | Population |
|----------|-----------|
| NF and Labrador | 541 000 |
| PEI | 138 000 |
| Nova Scotia | 939 800 |
| New Brunswick | 755 000 |
| Ontario | 11 513 800 |

The **mean** of a set of
numbers is the sum of the
numbers divided by how
many numbers there are.

a) Do you think these numbers are exact? Explain.
b) Find the total population of the 4 Atlantic provinces.
c) Find the mean population of the Atlantic provinces.
d) Approximately how many times as many people are in
Ontario as are in the Atlantic provinces?
e) Make up your own problem about these data. Solve it.

**Take It Further**

13. Find 2 whole numbers that:
a) have a sum of 10 and a product of 24
b) have a difference of 4 and a product of 77
c) have a sum of 77 when added to 3
Which of parts a to c have more than one answer? Explain.

**Reflect**

Write an example of a problem you would solve:
• by estimation     • by using a calculator
Justify your choice.

Just as numbers can describe our world, we can use numbers to describe other numbers. We can describe a number by its factors, by the number of its factors, and by the sum of its factors.

**Explore**

Work with a partner.

➤ Analyse the numbers in the circles.

**Abundant** 18 12 20

**Deficient** 15 8 7

**Perfect** 6

Use a table to record the factors of each number.
Cross out the number itself.
Find the sum of the remaining factors.

| Number | Factors | Sum of Factors |
|--------|---------|----------------|
|        |         |                |

➤ Look for patterns among your results.
Why do you think a number is called "Abundant," "Deficient," or "Perfect"?
➤ Copy the 3 circles. Based on your ideas, place each number from 2 to 30 in the appropriate circle. What do you notice?
➤ Use your observations to predict where 36 and 56 belong. Check your predictions.

**Reflect & Share**

Share your results with another pair of students.
What relationships did you see?
How did you describe each type of number?

## Connect

> Recall that a factor is a number that divides exactly into another number.
> For example, 1, 2, 3, and 6 are the factors of 6.
> Each number divides into 6 with no remainder.
>
> A **prime number** has only 2 factors, itself and 1.
> 2, 3, and 5 are prime numbers.
> All prime numbers are deficient.
>
> A **composite number** has more than 2 factors.
> 8 is a composite number because its factors are 1, 2, 4, and 8.
> Composite numbers can be deficient, abundant, or perfect.
>
> 1 has only one factor, so 1 is neither prime nor composite.
>
> When we find the factors that are the same for 2 numbers, we find **common factors**.

### Example 1

Show the factors of 12 and 30 in a Venn diagram.
What is the **greatest common factor** (**GCF**) of 12 and 30?

**Solution**

Find pairs of numbers that divide into 12 exactly.

**Use the divisibility rules.**

| | |
|---|---|
| $12 \div 1 = 12$ | 1 and 12 are factors. |
| $12 \div 2 = 6$ | 2 and 6 are factors. |
| $12 \div 3 = 4$ | 3 and 4 are factors. |

Stop at 3 because the next number, 4, is already a factor.
The factors of 12 are 1, 2, 3, 4, 6, and 12.

Find the factors of 30.

| | |
|---|---|
| $30 \div 1 = 30$ | 1 and 30 are factors. |
| $30 \div 2 = 15$ | 2 and 15 are factors. |
| $30 \div 3 = 10$ | 3 and 10 are factors. |
| $30 \div 5 = 6$ | 5 and 6 are factors. |

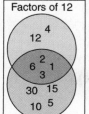

Mark the factors on the Venn diagram.
Place the common factors in the overlapping region.
The GCF of 12 and 30 is 6.

➤ The **multiples** of a number are found by multiplying the number by 1, by 2, by 3, by 4, and so on, or by skip counting.
When we find multiples that are the same for 2 numbers, we find **common multiples**.
We can use a 100 chart to find multiples and common multiples.

**Example 2**

a) Use a 100 chart to find the common multiples of 12 and 21.
b) Find the **lowest common multiple (LCM)** of 12 and 21.

**Solution**

a)

| 1 | 2 | 3 | 4 | 5 | 6 | 7 | 8 | 9 | 10 |
|---|---|---|---|---|---|---|---|---|---|
| 11 | 12 | 13 | 14 | 15 | 16 | 17 | 18 | 19 | 20 |
| 21 | 22 | 23 | 24 | 25 | 26 | 27 | 28 | 29 | 30 |
| 31 | 32 | 33 | 34 | 35 | 36 | 37 | 38 | 39 | 40 |
| 41 | 42 | 43 | 44 | 45 | 46 | 47 | 48 | 49 | 50 |
| 51 | 52 | 53 | 54 | 55 | 56 | 57 | 58 | 59 | 60 |
| 61 | 62 | 63 | 64 | 65 | 66 | 67 | 68 | 69 | 70 |
| 71 | 72 | 73 | 74 | 75 | 76 | 77 | 78 | 79 | 80 |
| 81 | 82 | 83 | 84 | 85 | 86 | 87 | 88 | 89 | 90 |
| 91 | 92 | 93 | 94 | 95 | 96 | 97 | 98 | 99 | 100 |

The multiples of 12 are blue.
The multiples of 21 are shaded green.
The common multiple is blue and shaded green.

b) Multiples of 12 are 12, 24, 36, 48, 60, 72, **84**, 96, …
Multiples of 21 are 21, 42, 63, **84**, …
The LCM is 84.

## Practice

1. List 4 multiples of each number.
   a) 5      b) 7      c) 8

2. Find the factors of each number. Explain how you did it.
   a) 18    b) 20    c) 28    d) 36    e) 37    f) 45

3. Find the factors of each number.
   a) 50    b) 51    c) 67    d) 75    e) 84    f) 120

**4.** Is each number prime or composite? How do you know?
   **a)** 18      **b)** 13      **c)** 9      **d)** 19      **e)** 61      **f)** 2

**5.** Find the GCF of each pair of numbers.
   Which strategy did you use?
   **a)** 10, 5      **b)** 12, 8      **c)** 15, 25      **d)** 9, 12      **e)** 18, 15

**6.** Use a 100 chart. Find the LCM of each pair of numbers.
   **a)** 3, 4      **b)** 2, 5      **c)** 12, 18      **d)** 10, 25      **e)** 27, 18

**7.** Can a pair of numbers have:
   **a)** more than one common multiple?
   **b)** more than one common factor?
   Use a diagram to explain your thinking.

**8.** Julia and Sandhu bought packages of granola bars.
   **a)** Julia had 15 bars in total. Sandhu had 12 bars in total.
      How many bars could there be in one package?
   **b)** What if Julia had 24 bars and Sandhu had 18 bars?
      How many bars could there be in one package?
   Draw a diagram to explain your thinking.

**9.** **Assessment Focus**  Kevin, Alison, and Fred work
   part-time. Kevin works every second day. Alison works every
   third day. Fred works every fourth day. Today they all worked
   together. When will they work together again?
   Explain how you know.

**10.** The numbers 4 and 16 could
   be called "near-perfect".
   Why do you think this name
   is appropriate?
   Find another example of a
   near-perfect number.
   What strategy did you use?

What is the difference between a factor and a multiple?
Is a factor ever a multiple? Is a multiple ever a factor?
Use diagrams, pictures, or a 100 chart to explain.

# The Factor Game

## HOW TO PLAY THE GAME:

1. Roll a number cube. The person with the greater number goes first.

2. Player A circles a number on the game board and scores that number. Player B uses a different colour to circle all the factors of that number not already circled. She scores the sum of the numbers she circles.

   **For example,** suppose Player A circles 18. Player B circles 1, 2, 3, 6, and 9 (18 is already circled) to score $1 + 2 + 3 + 6 + 9 = 21$ points

3. Player B circles a new number. Player A circles all the factors of that number not already circled. Record the scores.

4. Continue playing. If a player chooses a number with no factors left to circle, the number is crossed out. The player loses her or his turn, and scores no points.

**For example,** if player A circled 16, but 1, 2, 4, and 8 have already been circled, he would lose his turn and score no points.

5. The game continues until all numbers have been circled or crossed out. The player with the higher score wins.

| A | B |
|---|---|
| 18 | 21 |

|    |    |    |    |    |    |    |    |
|----|----|----|----|----|----|----|----|
| ① | ② | ③ | 4  | 5  | ⑥ | 7  | 8  |
| ⑨ | 10 | 11 | 12 | 13 | 14 | 15 | 16 |
| 17 | ⑱ | 19 | 20 | 21 | 22 | 23 | 24 |
| 25 | 26 | 27 | 28 | 29 | 30 | 31 | 32 |
| 33 | 34 | 35 | 36 | 37 | 38 | 39 | 40 |
| 41 | 42 | 43 | 44 | 45 | 46 | 47 | 48 |
| 49 | 50 | 51 | 52 | 53 | 54 | 55 | 56 |
| 57 | 58 | 59 | 60 | 61 | 62 | 63 | 64 |

**What is the best first move? What is the worst first move? Why? How does this game involve factors, multiples, and prime numbers?**

# 1.3 Squares and Square Roots

ocus Find the squares and square roots of whole numbers.

## Explore

Work with a partner.
This chart shows the number of factors of each whole number.

| 1 | 2 | 3 | 4 | 5 | 6 | 7 | 8 | 9 | 10 | 11 | 12 | 13 | 14 | 15 | 16 | 17 | 18 | 19 | 20 | 21 | 22 | 23 | 24 | 25 | 26 | 27 | 28 | 29 | 30 |
|---|---|---|---|---|---|---|---|---|----|----|----|----|----|----|----|----|----|----|----|----|----|----|----|----|----|----|----|----|----|
|   |   |   |   |   |   |   |   |   |    |    |    |    |    |    |    |    |    |    |    |    |    |    | X  |    |    |    |    |    | X  |
|   |   |   |   |   |   |   |   |   |    |    |    |    |    |    |    |    |    |    |    |    |    |    | X  |    |    |    |    |    | X  |
|   |   |   |   |   |   |   |   |   |    |    | X  |    |    |    |    |    | X  |    | X  |    |    |    | X  |    |    |    | X  |    | X  |
|   |   |   |   |   |   |   |   |   |    |    | X  |    |    |    | X  |    | X  |    | X  |    |    |    | X  |    |    |    | X  |    | X  |
|   |   |   |   |   | X |   | X |   | X  |    | X  |    | X  | X  | X  |    | X  |    | X  | X  | X  |    | X  |    | X  | X  | X  |    | X  |
|   |   |   | X |   | X |   | X | X | X  |    | X  |    | X  | X  | X  |    | X  |    | X  | X  | X  |    | X  | X  | X  | X  | X  |    | X  |
|   | X | X | X | X | X | X | X | X | X  | X  | X  | X  | X  | X  | X  | X  | X  | X  | X  | X  | X  | X  | X  | X  | X  | X  | X  | X  | X  |
| X | X | X | X | X | X | X | X | X | X  | X  | X  | X  | X  | X  | X  | X  | X  | X  | X  | X  | X  | X  | X  | X  | X  | X  | X  | X  | X  |

Look for patterns and relationships in this chart.
Find the factors of the numbers with two factors.
What do you notice?
Describe the numbers with four or more factors.
Describe the numbers that have an odd number of factors.

### Reflect & Share

One way to describe a number with an odd number of factors is to call it a **square number**.
Why do you think this name is used?
Draw pictures to support your explanation.

## Connect

The factors of a composite number occur in pairs.
For example, 48 ÷ 2 = 24          2 and 24 are factors of 48.
When the quotient is equal to the divisor, the dividend is a square number.
For example, 49 ÷ 7 = 7, so 49 is a square number.

dividend  divisor  quotient

We can get 49 by multiplying the whole number, 7, by itself.

$49 = 7 \times 7$

We write: $7 \times 7 = 7^2$

We say: 7 squared

- One way to model a square number
  is to draw a square.
  This square has area 9 square units.
  The side length is $\sqrt{9}$, or 3 units.
  We say: A **square root** of 9 is 3.

9 square units

*Other inverse operations are addition and subtraction, multiplication and division*

- When we multiply a number by itself, we square the number.
  Squaring and taking a square root are inverse operations.
  That is, they undo each other.

$7 \times 7 = 49$                         $\sqrt{49} = \sqrt{7^2}$

so, $7^2 = 49$                              $= 7$

## Example 1

Find the square of each number.

a)  5                    b)  15                    c)  32

**Solution**

a) $5^2 = 5 \times 5$        b) $15^2 = 15 \times 15$        c) $32^2 = 32 \times 32$
   $= 25$                        $= 225$                          $= 1024$

Use a calculator.

## Example 2

Draw a diagram to find a square root of each number.

a)  16                    b)  36

**Solution**

a) On grid paper, draw a square
   with area 16 square units.
   The side length of
   the square is 4 units.
   So, $\sqrt{16} = 4$

16 square units

b) On grid paper, draw a square
   with area 36 square units.
   The side length of
   the square is 6 units.
   So, $\sqrt{36} = 6$

36 square units

1. Find.
   a) $8^2$      b) $16^2$      c) $1^2$      d) $29^2$

2. Find the square of each number.
   a) 4      b) 17      c) 13      d) 52

3. a) Find the square of each number.
   i) 1      ii) 10      iii) 100      iv) 1000

   b) Use the results of part a. Predict the square of each number.
   i) 10 000      ii) 1 000 000

4. Use grid paper. Find a square root of each number.
   a) 16      b) 4      c) 900      d) 144

5. Calculate the side length of a square with each area.
   a) 100 m²      b) 64 cm²      c) 81 m²

6. Order from least to greatest.
   a) $\sqrt{36}$, 36, 4, $\sqrt{9}$      b) $\sqrt{400}$, $\sqrt{100}$, 19, 15

7. Which whole numbers have squares between 50 and 200?

8. **Assessment Focus**   Which whole numbers have square roots between 1 and 20? How do you know?

9. A large square room has an area of 144 m².
   a) Find the length of a side of the room.
   b) How much baseboard is needed to go around the room?
   c) Each piece of baseboard is 2.5 m long. How many pieces of baseboard are needed?

10. A garden has an area of 400 m².
    The garden is divided into 16 congruent square plots.
    What is the side length of each plot?

**Reflect**

How can you find the perimeter of a square when you know its area? Use an example to explain.

# Mid-Unit Review

**1.1** **1.** The table shows the most common surnames for adults in the United Kingdom.

| Surname | Number |
|---------|--------|
| Smith | 538 369 |
| Jones | 402 489 |
| Williams | 279 150 |

a) Approximately how many adults have one of these three names?
To which place value did you estimate? Explain your choice.

b) Exactly how many more Smiths are there than Jones? Explain.

c) Write your own problem about these data. Solve your problem. Justify your strategy.

**2.** In one week, Joe worked 23 h cutting grass. He was paid $9/h. From this money, Joe bought 5 tickets for a football game, at $15 per ticket, and 2 DVDs for $21 each, including tax. How much money did Joe have left?

**1.2** **3.** Find all the factors of each number.
a) 35         b) 24

**4.** Find 2 factors of each number.
a) 6         b) 10
c) 14       d) 15
e) 9        f) 21

**5.** Organize the first 8 multiples of 6 and 8 in a Venn diagram.

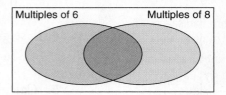

**6.** For the numbers 15 and 6, find:
a) the GCF      b) the LCM

**7.** a) Why is 7 a prime number?
b) Why is 8 not a prime number?

**1.3** **8.** Can three consecutive whole numbers all be primes? Justify your answer.

**9.** A square patio has an area of 81 m². How long is each side?

**10.** Find.
a) $\sqrt{49}$      b) $8^2$
c) $\sqrt{100}$    d) the square of 9

**11.** Find two squares with a sum of 100.

**12.** Write 100 as a square number and as a square root of a number.

**13.** Explain why:
$\sqrt{1} = 1$

# 1.4 Exponents

Focus Use exponents to represent repeated multiplication.

## Explore

Work with a small group.
You will need 65 interlocking cubes.
The edge length of each cube is 1 unit.
The volume of each cube is 1 cubic unit.

➤ How many different ways can you make a larger cube?
➤ What is the volume of each larger cube you make?
  What is its edge length?
➤ Use factors to write the volume of each cube.
➤ Record your results in a table.

| Number of Cubes | Volume (cubic units) | Edge Length (units) | Volume As a Product |
|---|---|---|---|
| 1 | 1 | 1 | $1 \times 1 \times 1$ |

### Reflect & Share

Observe how the volume grows. Describe the growth using pictures or numbers. What other patterns do you see in the table?
Use these patterns to help you write the volumes of the next 3 cubes in the pattern.

## Connect

When numbers are repeated in multiplication, we can write them in **exponent form**.

For example, we can write $2 \times 2 \times 2 \times 2$ as $2^4$.
2 is the **base**.
4 is the **exponent**.
$2^4$ is the **power**.

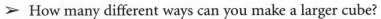

base $2^4$ exponent
power

We say: 2 to the power of 4, or
        2 to the 4th
$2^4$ is a power of 2.

If we graph the power against the exponent, we see how quickly the power gets very large.

| Exponent | Power |
|:---:|:---:|
| 1 | $2^1 = 2$ |
| 2 | $2^2 = 4$ |
| 3 | $2^3 = 8$ |
| 4 | $2^4 = 16$ |
| 5 | $2^5 = 32$ |

Square numbers and cube numbers are special powers.

➤ A power with exponent 2 is a **square number**.
  The area of a square is side length × side length.
  This square has side length 4 cm.
  Area = 4 cm × 4 cm
      = 16 cm²

  Here are 3 ways to write 16:
     Standard form:   16
     Expanded form:  4 × 4
     Exponent form:  $4^2$
  $4^2$ is a power of 4.
  16 is called a **perfect square**.

➤ A power with exponent 3 is a **cube number**.
  The volume of a cube is edge length × edge length × edge length.
  This cube has edge length 4 cm.
  Volume = 4 cm × 4 cm × 4 cm
        = 64 cm³

  Here are 3 ways to write 64:
     Standard form:   64
     Expanded form:  4 × 4 × 4
     Exponent form:  $4^3$
  $4^3$ is a power of 4.
  64 is called a **perfect cube**.

Example 1

Write in exponent form.

a)  $6 \times 6$        b)  $5 \times 5 \times 5$        c)  32

**Solution**        a)  $6 \times 6 = 6^2$        b)  $5 \times 5 \times 5 = 5^3$

c)  $32 = 2 \times 2 \times 2 \times 2 \times 2 = 2^5$

**Example 2**

Write in expanded form and standard form.

a)  $3^5$                          b)  $7^4$

**Solution**        a)      $3^5$                          b)      $7^4$

$= 3 \times 3 \times 3 \times 3 \times 3$        $= 7 \times 7 \times 7 \times 7$

$= 243$                          $= 2401$

A calculator can be used to simplify a power such as $3^5$.
For a scientific calculator, the keystrokes are:

$\boxed{3}$ $\boxed{\wedge}$ $\boxed{5}$ $\boxed{\text{ENTER}}$  or  $\boxed{3}$ $\boxed{y^x}$ $\boxed{5}$ $\boxed{\text{ENTER}}$  to display 243

For a non-scientific calculator, use repeated multiplication.
The keystrokes are:

$\boxed{3}$ $\boxed{\times}$ $\boxed{=}$ $\boxed{=}$ $\boxed{=}$ $\boxed{=}$  to display 243

## Practice

1.  Write the base of each power.
    a) $2^4$      b) $3^2$      c) $7^3$      d) $10^5$      e) $6^9$      f) $8^3$

2.  Write the exponent of each power.
    a) $2^5$      b) $3^2$      c) $7^1$      d) $9^5$      e) $8^{10}$      f) $10^4$

3.  Write in expanded form.
    a) $2^4$      b) $10^3$      c) $6^5$      d) $4^2$      e) $2^1$      f) $5^4$

4.  Write in exponent form.
    a) $3 \times 3 \times 3 \times 3$   b) $2 \times 2 \times 2$  c) $5 \times 5 \times 5 \times 5 \times 5 \times 5$
    d) $10 \times 10 \times 10$   e) $79 \times 79$   f) $2 \times 2 \times 2 \times 2 \times 2 \times 2 \times 2 \times 2$

5. Write in exponent form, then in standard form.
   a) $5 \times 5$
   b) $3 \times 3 \times 3 \times 3$
   c) $10 \times 10 \times 10 \times 10 \times 10$
   d) $2 \times 2 \times 2$
   e) $9 \times 9 \times 9$
   f) $2 \times 2 \times 2 \times 2 \times 2 \times 2 \times 2$

6. Write in standard form.
   a) $2^4$  b) $10^3$  c) $3^5$  d) $7^3$  e) $2^8$  f) $4^1$

7. Write as a power of 10. How did you do it?
   a) 100
   b) 10 000
   c) 100 000
   d) 10
   e) 1000
   f) 1 000 000

8. Write as a power of 2. Explain your method.
   a) 4  b) 16  c) 64  d) 256  e) 32  f) 2

9. What patterns do you see in the pairs of numbers? Which is the greater number in each pair? Explain how you know.
   a) $2^3$ or $3^2$  b) $2^5$ or $5^2$  c) $3^4$ or $4^3$  d) $5^4$ or $4^5$

10. Write these numbers in order from least to greatest: $3^5, 5^2, 3^4, 6^3$. How did you do this?

 11. Simplify.
   a) $3^{12}$  b) $7^3$  c) $5^6$  d) $4^8$  e) $9^8$  f) $2^{23}$

12. **Assessment Focus**
   a) Express each number in exponent form in as many different ways as you can.
      i) 16  ii) 81  iii) 64
   b) Find other numbers that can be written in exponent form, in more than one way. Show your work.

13. Write in exponent form:
   a) the number of small squares on a checkerboard
   b) the area of a square with side length 5 units
   c) the volume of a cube with edge length 9 units

**Reflect**

When you see a number, how can you find out if it is a perfect square, or a perfect cube, or neither? Give examples.

# Hospital Administrator

The administrator of a busy hospital makes hundreds of decisions every day, many of which involve whole number computations and conversions. Should she purchase more 'standard' 24-tray carts for the orderlies to deliver meals to the new 84-bed hospital wing? The administrator calculates she would need four of these carts to take enough meals to the new wing. In the cart supplier's catalogue, there are also 32-tray carts which are more expensive, but priced within budget. Only three of the 32-tray carts would deliver all the meals, and they would cost less than four of the standard carts.

When the orderlies look at the catalogue picture of the 32-tray cart, they tell the administrator that the cart is too low. It is tiring and slower to bend so far down, so they wouldn't use the lowest eight tray bins. So, it's back to the calculator for the administrator. Which cart would *you* choose now? Give reasons for your answer.

**Your World**

Carpet and tile prices are given per square unit. A paint can label tells the area the paint will cover in square units. Wallpaper is sold in rolls with area in square units.

## Explore

Work on your own.
Blaise Pascal lived in France in the 17th century.
He was 13 years old when he constructed the triangle below.
This triangle is called Pascal's Triangle.

```
                1                        row 1
              1   1                      row 2
            1   2   1                    row 3
          1   3   3   1                  row 4
        1   4   6   4   1                row 5
      1   5  10  10   5   1              row 6
```

➤ What patterns do you see in the triangle?
➤ What symmetry do you see in the triangle?

### Reflect & Share

Compare your patterns with those of a classmate.
Together, write about three different patterns you see in the triangle.

## Connect

Here are some of the patterns in Pascal's Triangle.

|  |  | Sum |
|---|---|---|
| ➤ Each row begins and ends with 1. | 1 | 1 |
| After the second row, each number | 1 1 | 2 |
| is the sum of the 2 numbers above it. | 1 2 1 | 4 |
| To write row 7: | 1 3 3 1 | 8 |
| Start with 1. | 1 4 6 4 1 | 16 |
| Add: $1 + 5 = 6$ | 1+5+10+10+5+1 | 32 |
| Add: $5 + 10 = 15$ | 1 6 15 20 15 6 1 | 64 |
| Add: $10 + 10 = 20$, and so on |  |  |

➤ The sum of the numbers in each row is shown above,
and in the table on the next page.
From the 2nd row on, the sums can be written as powers.

| Row | 2 | 3 | 4 | 5 | 6 | 7 |
|---|---|---|---|---|---|---|
| Sum in standard form | 2 | 4 | 8 | 16 | 32 | 64 |
| Sum in exponent from | $2^1$ | $2^2$ | $2^3$ | $2^4$ | $2^5$ | $2^6$ |

We can use this table to predict the sum of the numbers in any row. All sums are powers of 2.

The exponent is 1 less than the row number.

So, the 10th row has sum: $2^9 = 512$

And the 19th row has sum: $2^{18} = 262\ 144$

➤ The 3rd numbers in each row have this pattern: 1, 3, 6, 10, 15, ...
To get each term in the pattern, we add 1 more than we added before. We can use this to extend the pattern.

The 5th term: 15

The 6th term: $15 + 6 = 21$

The 7th term: $21 + 7 = 28$, and so on

**Example**

Describe each pattern in words. Write the next 3 terms.

a) 4, 9, 14, 19, ...  b) 1, 3, 9, 27, ...  c) 1, 3, 7, 13, 21, ...

**Solution**

a) 4, 9, 14, 19, ...
Start at 4.
Add 5 to get the next number.
The next 3 terms are 24, 29, 34.

b) 1, 3, 9, 27, ...
Start at 1.
Multiply by 3 to get the next number.
The next 3 terms are 81, 243, 729.

c) 1, 3, 7, 13, 21, ...
Start at 1.
Add 2.
Increase the number added by 2 each time.
The next 3 terms are 31, 43, 57.

1. Write the next 3 terms in each pattern.
   a) 7, 9, 11, 13, …                   b) 1, 5, 25, 125, …
   c) 4, 7, 10, 13, …                   d) 1, 10, 100, 1000, …
   e) 20, 19, 18, 17, …                 f) 79, 77, 75, 73, …

2. Write the next 3 terms in each pattern.
   a) 3, 4, 6, 9, …                     b) 1, 4, 9, 16, …
   c) 101, 111, 121, 131, …             d) 1, 12, 123, 1234, …
   e) 1, 4, 16, 64, …                   f) 256, 128, 64, 32, …

3. Describe each pattern in words.
   Write the next 3 terms.
   a) 200, 199, 201, 198, …             b) 4, 7, 12, 19, …
   c) 100, 99, 97, 94, …                d) 2, 6, 12, 20, …
   e) 50, 48, 44, 38, …                 f) 2, 6, 18, 54, …

4. Create your own number pattern. Trade patterns with a
   classmate. Describe your classmate's pattern.
   Write the next 3 terms.

5. a) Copy this pattern.  Find each product.

| 99 × 11 = ☐ | 99 × 111 = ☐ | … |
| 99 × 22 = ☐ | 99 × 222 = ☐ | … |
| 99 × 33 = ☐ | 99 × 333 = ☐ | … |
| ⋮ | ⋮ | |

   b) Extend this pattern sideways and down.
      Predict the next 6 terms in each row and column.
   c) Check your predictions with a calculator.

6. This pattern shows the first 3 triangular numbers.

1        3          6

   a) Draw the next 3 terms in the pattern.
   b) List the first 6 triangular numbers.
   c) Find the next 2 triangular numbers without drawing pictures.
      Explain how you did this.

**d)** Add consecutive triangular numbers;
that is, Term 1 + Term 2; Term 2 + Term 3; and so on.
What pattern do you see?
Write the next 3 terms in this pattern.

**e)** Subtract consecutive triangular numbers;
that is, Term 2 − Term 1; Term 3 − Term 2; and so on.
What pattern do you see?
Write the next 3 terms in this pattern.

**7.** This pattern shows the first 3 cube numbers.

**a)** Sketch the next 3 cube numbers in the pattern.
Use interlocking cubes if they help.

**b)** Write the next 3 cube numbers without drawing pictures.
Explain how you did this.

**8. Assessment Focus**

**a)** Write the first 10 powers of 2; that is, $2^1$ to $2^{10}$,
in standard form.

**b)** What pattern do you see in the units digits?

**c)** How can you use this pattern to find the units digit of $2^{40}$?

**d)** Investigate powers of other numbers.
Look for patterns in the units digits.
Explain how you can use these patterns to find units digits
for powers too large to display on the calculator.

**Take It Further**

**9.** Some sequences of numbers may represent different patterns.
Extend each pattern in as many different ways as you can.
Write the pattern rule for each pattern.

**a)** 1, 2, 4, …    **b)** 1, 4, 9, …    **c)** 5, 25, …

**Reflect**

Choose 3 different types of patterns from this section.
Describe each pattern.
Explain how you can use the pattern to predict the next term.

# Using Different Strategies

## Problem

There are 8 people at a party.
Each person shakes hands with everyone else.
How many handshakes are there?

## Think of a strategy

*Strategy 1:* **Draw a diagram and count.**

Draw 8 dots. Join every dot to every other dot.
Count the line segments.

8

5 + 5 + 4 + 3 + 2 + 1

Number of line segments
= 8 + 5 + 5 + 4 + 3 + 2 + 1
= 28

There are 28 handshakes.

*Strategy 2:* **Solve simpler problems, then look for a pattern.**

2 people    3 people    4 people    5 people
1 handshake    3 handshakes    6 handshakes    10 handshakes

Make a table.
Each time you add a person,
you add one more
handshake than the time before.
So, 6 people: 10 + 5, or 15 handshakes
7 people: 15 + 6, or 21 handshakes
8 people: 21 + 7, or 28 handshakes

| Number of People | Number of Handshakes | |
|---|---|---|
| 2 | 1 | |
| 3 | 3 | +2 |
| 4 | 6 | +3 |
| 5 | 10 | +4 |

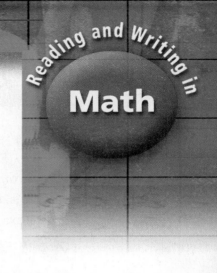

*Strategy 3:* **Use reasoning.**

Each of 8 people shakes hands with
7 other people.
That is, 8 × 7, or 56 handshakes
But we have counted each handshake twice.
We have said that A shaking hands with B is
different from B shaking hands with A.
So, we divide by 2: $\frac{56}{2} = 28$
There are 28 handshakes.

## Look back

- Look at the numbers of handshakes for 2 to 8 people.
  Where have you seen this pattern before?
- What if there were 9 people at the party?
  How many handshakes would there be?
  How do you know?

## Problems

Solve each problem. Try to use more than one strategy.

**1.** A ball is dropped from a height of 16 m.
Each time it hits the ground, the ball bounces to one-half its
previous height. The ball is caught when its greatest height for that
bounce is 1 m. How far has the ball travelled?

**2.** A rectangular garden is 100 m long and 44 m wide.
A fence encloses the garden.
The fence posts are 2 m apart.
How many posts are needed?

**3.** Here is a 5 by 5 square.
How many squares of each different
size can you find in this large square?

**Reflect**

Why might you want to solve a problem more than one way?

# Unit Review

Review any lesson with

## What Do I Need to Know?

☑ A *factor* of a number divides into the number exactly;
that is, there is no remainder.
For example, $6 \div 2 = 3$, so 2 is a factor of 6.

☑ A *prime number* has only 2 factors, itself and 1.
For example, the only factors of 17 are 17 and 1, so 17 is a prime number.

☑ A *composite number* has more than 2 factors.
For example, 12 has factors 1, 2, 3, 4, 6, and 12, so 12 is a composite number.

☑ A *square number*, or *perfect square*, has an odd number of factors.
It can also written as a power with exponent 2.
For example, the factors of 9 are 1, 3, and 9, so 9 is a perfect square.
We write $9 = 3^2$.

☑ A *square root* of a number is a factor that is squared to get the number.
For example, 9 is a square root of 81 because $9^2 = 81$.
We write $\sqrt{81} = 9$.

☑ When a number is written in *exponent form*, it is written as a *power*.
For example, for the power $5^3$:
5 is the *base*.
3 is the *exponent*.
$5 \times 5 \times 5$ is the *expanded form*.
125 is the *standard form*.

☑ A *cube number*, or *perfect cube*, is a power with exponent 3.
For example, $1^3 = 1$, $2^3 = 8$, $3^3 = 27$, $4^3 = 64$,
so 1, 8, 27, and 64 are perfect cubes.

For extra practice, go to page 438.

**LESSON**

**1.1**
**1.** Find each answer.
Use pencil and paper.
a) 3621 + 8921
b) 5123 − 4123
c) 35 × 12
d) 125 × 27
e) 815 + 642 − 85
f) 1638 ÷ 21

**2.** This table shows the highest all-time scorers at the end of the 2000–2001 NBA season.

| Kareem Abdul-Jabbar | 38 387 |
| Karl Malone | 32 919 |
| Wilt Chamberlain | 31 419 |
| Michael Jordan | 29 277 |

a) What is the total number of points?
b) Write a problem about these data. Solve your problem. Justify the strategy you used.

**3.** a) Write the number 300 as the sum of 2 or more consecutive whole numbers. Find as many ways to do this as you can.
b) What patterns do you see in the numbers added?
c) Suppose you started with another 3-digit number. Will you see similar patterns? Investigate to find out.

**4.** Solve each problem. State any assumption you made.
a) Armin's house is 3 km from a mall. He walks 1 km in 15 min. How long does it take Armin to walk to the mall?
b) Tana makes $15, $21, and $19 for baby-sitting one weekend. How much will Tana make in a month?

**5.** The table shows the ticket prices and number of tickets sold for a popular movie.

|  | Ticket Price ($) | Number of Tickets Sold |
|---|---|---|
| Adults | 12 | 125 |
| Seniors | 10 | 34 |
| Youths | 8 | 61 |

Calculate the total cost of the ticket sales.

**1.2**
**6.** Find all the factors of each number.
a) 36          b) 50
c) 75          d) 77

**7.** Find the first 10 multiples of each number.
a) 9          b) 7
c) 12          d) 15

**8.** For the numbers 18 and 60, find:
a) the GCF          b) the LCM
Draw a Venn diagram to illustrate part a.

**9.** How many prime numbers
are even?
Justify your answer.

1.3 **10.** Find a square root of
each number.
**a)** 121    **b)** 169    **c)** 225

**11.** Find each square root.
Draw a picture if it helps.
**a)** $\sqrt{25}$    **b)** $\sqrt{100}$    **c)** $\sqrt{81}$

**12.** Calculate the area of a square
with each side length.
**a)** 7 cm    **b)** 17 cm    **c)** 93 m

**13.** The area of a square is 81 m². 
What is the perimeter of the
square? How do you know?

**14.** Raquel cooks 8-cm square
hamburgers on a grill.
The grill is a rectangle with
dimensions 40 cm by 40 cm.
How many hamburgers can
be grilled at one time?
Justify your answer.

1.4 **15.** Copy and complete this table.

|  | Exponent Form | Base | Exponent | Expanded Form | Standard Form |
|---|---|---|---|---|---|
| **a)** | 3⁴ |  |  |  |  |
| **b)** | 2⁵ |  |  |  |  |
| **c)** | 10⁷ |  |  |  |  |
| **d)** |  | 5 | 4 |  |  |
| **e)** |  |  |  | 4×4×4×4 |  |

1.5 **16.** A perfume formula requires 4 g
of an essential oil per bottle.
**a)** How many grams are needed
for 2500 bottles?
**b)** Write this number in exponent
form.

**17.** Write these numbers in order
from greatest to least.
$3^4, 4^4, 5^3, 2^6$

**18. a)** Write the next 3 terms in
each pattern.
**i)** 3, 5, 6, 8, 9, …
**ii)** 1, 2, 4, 8, …
**iii)** 1, 4, 9, 16, …
**iv)** 3, 4, 6, 9, …
**b)** Describe each pattern in
part a.

**19. a)** Copy and complete
this pattern.
$1^2 + 2^2 = \square$
$2^2 + 3^2 = \square$
$3^2 + 4^2 = \square$
$4^2 + 5^2 = \square$
**b)** Write the next two rows
in the pattern.
**c)** Describe the pattern.

**20.** $1^2 = 1$
$1^2 + 2^2 = 5$
$1^2 + 2^2 + 3^2 = 14$
$1^2 + 2^2 + 3^2 + 4^2 = 30$
**a)** Write the next two lines
in the pattern.
**b)** What pattern do you see?

# Practice Test

1. Estimate. Describe your strategy.
   a) $624 + 1353$   b) $897 \div 23$   c) $752 \times 36$

2. Use mental math to evaluate $2 \times 395 \times 5$. Explain your strategy.

3. Use a Venn diagram
   to show the factors of 48 and 18.
   Circle the GCF.

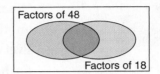

Factors of 48

Factors of 18

4. Use patterns to find the first
   6 common multiples of 15 and 6.

5. Use the clues below to find the mystery
   number. Explain your strategy and reasoning.
   Clue 1:   I am a 2-digit number.
   Clue 2:   I am less than $9^2$.
   Clue 3:   I have 26 and 6 as factors.

6. Sharma plays basketball every third day of the month.
   She baby-sits her little brother every seventh day of the
   month. How many times in a month will Sharma have a conflict
   between basketball and baby-sitting? Explain your thinking.

7. Write these numbers in order from least to greatest.
   a) $5^2, 2^5, \sqrt{25}, 10^2, 3^3$   b) $10 \times 10 \times 10, 2^3, \sqrt{400}, 3^2, 17$

8. The perimeter of a square is 32 cm.
   What is the area of the square? Explain your thinking.
   Include a diagram.

9. Write the next 3 terms in each pattern. Describe each pattern.
   a) $1, 3, 6, 10, \ldots$   b) $23, 25, 27, \ldots$   c) $100, 81, 64, 49, \ldots$

10. Write the number 35 as:
    a) the sum of 3 squares
    b) the difference between 2 squares
    c) the sum of a prime number and a square

One of greatest mathematicians of the Middle Ages was an Italian, Leonardo Fibonacci.

Fibonacci is remembered for this problem:

A pair of rabbits is placed in a large pen.
When the rabbits are two months old, they produce
another pair of rabbits.
Every month after that, they produce another pair of rabbits.
Each new pair of rabbits does the same.
None of the rabbits dies.
How many rabbits are there at the beginning of each month?

This table shows the rabbits at the beginning of the first 5 months.

| Beginning of Month | Number of Pairs | Number of Rabbits |
|:---:|:---:|:---|
| 1 | 1 | 🐰 |
| 2 | 1 | 🐰 |
| 3 | 2 | 🐰 🐰 |
| 4 | 3 | 🐰 🐰 🐰 |
| 5 | 5 | 🐰 🐰 🐰 🐰 🐰 |

1. a) Continue the pattern for two more months.
      Use different colours to show the new rabbits.
   b) Write the number of pairs of rabbits at the beginning of
      each month, for the first 7 months.
      These are the Fibonacci numbers.
      What pattern do you see?
      Explain how to find the next number in the pattern.

2. The Fibonacci sequence appears in the family tree of the drone,
   or male bee.
   The drone has a mother, but no father.
   Female bees are worker bees or queens.
   They have a mother and a father.
   The family tree of a male bee back to its grandparents is
   shown on the next page.

queen     drone

a) Copy the diagram. Trace the male bee's ancestors back 5 more generations.
b) Explain how you can use this pattern to find the Fibonacci numbers.

There are many patterns you can find in the Fibonacci sequence.

**3.** Write the first 15 Fibonacci numbers.
   a) What type of number is every third number?
   b) Which number is a factor of every fourth number?
   c) Which number is a factor of every fifth number?

**4.** Add the squares of the:
2nd and 3rd terms
3rd and 4th terms
4th and 5th terms
What do you notice?
Write the next two lines of
this pattern.

**5.** Research Fibonacci
numbers. Make a poster
to show your work.

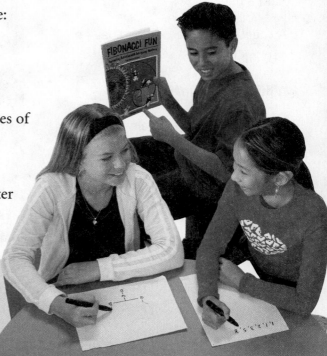

## Reflect on the Unit

What have you learned about whole numbers?
What have you learned about number patterns?
Write about some of the things you have learned.

The animal kingdom provides much interesting information. We use information to make comparisons. What comparisons can you make from these facts?

A sea otter eats about $\frac{1}{3}$ of its body mass a day.

A Great Dane can eat up to 4 kg of food a day.

A cheetah can reach a top speed of 110 km/h.

A human can run at 18 km/h.

The heart of a blue whale is the size of a small car.

One in 5000 North Atlantic lobsters is born bright blue.

## What You'll Learn

- Understand what a ratio is.
- Find equivalent ratios.
- Compare ratios and use them to solve problems.
- Understand what a rate is.
- Find unit rates.
- Compare rates and use them to solve problems.

## Why It's Important

You use ratios and rates to compare numbers and quantities; and to compare prices when you shop.

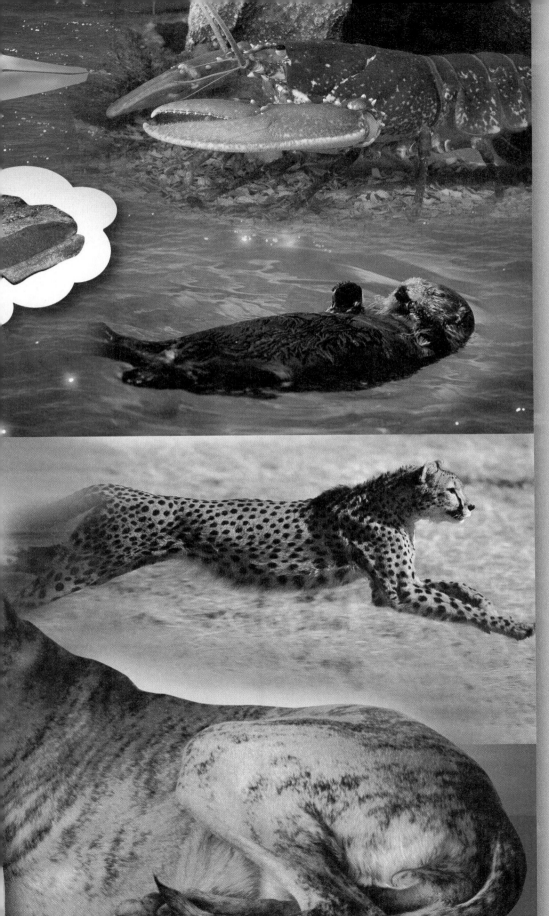

## Key Words

- ratio
- part-to-whole ratio
- part-to-part ratio
- terms of a ratio
- equivalent ratios
- simplest form
- rate
- unit rate
- average speed

# Skills You'll Need

## Greatest Common Factor

Recall that the greatest common factor (GCF) of a set of numbers is the greatest number that will divide exactly into the given numbers.
For example, 6 is the greatest common factor of 18 and 24.

### Example 1

Find the GCF of 24 and 30.

### Solution

Draw a factor tree for each number.

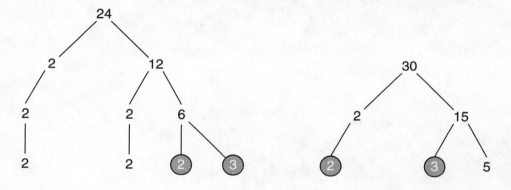

Circle the numbers that appear in the bottom row of both factor trees.
2 and 3 are common to both factor trees.
The GCF of 24 and 30 is $2 \times 3 = 6$.

✓ **Check**

**1.** Find the GCF of the numbers in each set.
   **a)** 30, 75
   **b)** 27, 63
   **c)** 42, 56
   **d)** 12, 18, 42

# Lowest Common Multiple

Recall that the lowest common multiple (LCM) of a set of numbers is the least number that is a multiple of each number in the set. This also means that each number in the set is a factor of the lowest common multiple.

## Example 2

Find the LCM of 18 and 32.

### Solution

Draw a factor tree for each number.

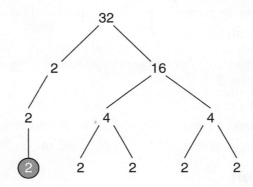

Circle the numbers that appear in the bottom row of both factor trees. Multiply the numbers not circled and one each of the circled numbers:
$3 \times 3 \times 2 \times 2 \times 2 \times 2 \times 2 = 288$
The LCM of 18 and 32 is 288.

## ✓ Check

**2.** Write the first 6 multiples of each number.
   **a)** 4          **b)** 7          **c)** 9          **d)** 12

**3.** Find the LCM of the numbers in each pair.
   **a)** 9, 12          **b)** 14, 35          **c)** 16, 40

**4.** Find the LCM of the numbers in each set.
   **a)** 36, 45          **b)** 3, 4, 6          **c)** 12, 15, 20

# Converting among Metric Units

100 cm = 1 m                    1000 m = 1 km
1000 g = 1 kg                   1000 mL = 1 L

- To convert centimetres to metres, divide by 100.
- To convert:

  metres to kilometres ⎫
  grams to kilograms   ⎬  Divide by 1000.      **Divide to convert to a**
  millilitres to litres ⎭                       **larger unit.**

- To convert metres to centimetres, multiply by 100.
- To convert:

  kilometres to metres ⎫
  kilograms to grams   ⎬  Multiply by 1000.    **Multiply to convert to a**
  litres to millilitres ⎭                       **smaller unit.**

## Example 3

Convert.

**a)** 650 cm to metres          **b)** 82 km to metres
**c)** 2.4 kg to grams           **d)** 2840 mL to litres

## Solution

**a)** $650 \text{ cm} = \frac{650}{100} \text{ m}$       **b)** $82 \text{ km} = 82 \times 1000 \text{ m}$
$= 6.5 \text{ m}$                           $= 82\,000 \text{ m}$
**c)** $2.4 \text{ kg} = 2.4 \times 1000 \text{ g}$    **d)** $2840 \text{ mL} = \frac{2840}{1000} \text{ L}$
$= 2400 \text{ g}$                          $= 2.84 \text{ L}$

## ✓ Check

**5.** Convert.
  **a)** 1280 cm to metres          **b)** 680 m to kilometres
  **c)** 2454 g to kilograms        **d)** 1987 mL to litres
  **e)** 8.2 m to centimetres       **f)** 1.25 km to metres
  **g)** 0.45 kg to grams           **h)** 2.3 L to millilitres

**Focus** | Use models and diagrams to investigate ratios.

There are different ways to compare numbers.
Look at these advertisements.

How are the numbers in each advertisement compared?
Which advertisement is most effective? Explain.

## Explore

Work with a partner.

How can you compare the number of blue counters to the number of yellow counters?
How many different ways can you compare the counters?
Write each way you find.

## Reflect & Share

Share your list with another pair of classmates.
Add any new comparisons to your list.
Talk about the different ways you compared the counters.

## Connect

Here is a collection of models.

**This is a part-to-whole ratio.**

➤ We can use a **ratio** to compare one part of the collection to the whole collection.
There are 9 cars compared to 13 models.
The ratio of cars to models is written as 9 to 13 or 9:13.

**This is a part-to-part ratio.**

➤ We can use a ratio to compare one part of the collection to another part.
There are 9 cars compared to 4 planes.
The ratio of cars to planes is written as 9 to 4 or 9:4.
**9** and **4** are called the **terms** of the ratio.
9 is the first term and 4 is the second term.

### Example

At a class party, there are 16 boys, 15 girls, and 4 adults.
What is each ratio?
a) boys to girls          b) girls to adults
c) adults to total number of people at the party

### Solution

a) There are 16 boys and 15 girls.
So, the ratio of boys to girls is 16:15.
b) There are 15 girls and 4 adults.
So, the ratio of girls to adults is 15:4.
c) The total number of people is 16 + 15 + 4 = 35.
So, the ratio of adults to total number of people is 4:35.

1. Look at the crayons below. Write each ratio.
   a) red crayons to the total number of crayons
   b) yellow to the total number of crayons
   c) blue crayons to green crayons

2. Use words, numbers, or pictures.
   Write a ratio to compare the items in each sentence.
   a) A student had 9 green counters and 7 red counters on his desk.
   b) In a dance team, there were 8 girls and 3 boys.
   c) The teacher had 2 fiction and 5 non-fiction books on her desk.

3. The ratio of T-shirts to shorts in Frank's closet is 5:2.
   Write the ratio of T-shirts to the total number of garments.

4. a) What is the ratio of boys to girls in your class?
   b) What is the ratio of girls to boys?
   c) What is the ratio of boys to the total number of students in your class?
   d) What if two boys leave the room?
      What is the ratio in part c now?

5. a) Draw two different diagrams to show the ratio 3:5.
   b) Draw a diagram to show the ratio 7:1.

6. Maria shares some seashells with Jeff.
   Maria says, "Two for you, three for me, two for you, three for me …"
   Tonya watches.
   At the end, she says, "So Jeff got $\frac{2}{3}$ of the shells."
   Do you agree with Tonya? Give reasons for your answer.

What is the sum of
all the prime numbers
between 1 and 30?

**7.** A box contains 8 red, 5 green, 2 brown, 3 purple, 1 blue,
and 6 yellow candles.
   **a)** Write each ratio.
   **i)** red:purple          **ii)** green:blue
   **iii)** purple:green     **iv)** brown and yellow:total candles
   **b)** What if 3 red, 2 green, and 4 yellow candles were burned?
   Write the new ratios for part a.

**8.** **Assessment Focus**   Patrick plans to make salad. The recipe
calls for 3 cups of cooked macaroni, 3 cups of sliced oranges,
2 cups of chopped apple, 1 cup of chopped celery, and 2 cups
of mayonnaise.
   **a)** What is the total amount of ingredients?
   **b)** What is the ratio of oranges to apples?
   Mayonnaise to macaroni?
   **c)** What is the ratio of apples and oranges to the total amount
   of ingredients?
   **d)** Patrick makes a mistake. He uses 2 cups of oranges instead of 3.
   What are the new ratios in parts b and c?
   **e)** Write your own ratio problem about this salad.
   Solve your problem.

**Take It Further**

**9.** **a)** Create four different ratios using these figures.

   **b)** How can you change one figure to create ratios of 2:5 and
   7:3? Explain.

**Reflect**

Look in newspapers and magazines for examples of ratios.
Cut out the examples. Paste them in your notebook.
Explain how the ratios are used.
What information can you get from them?

## Explore

Work on your own.
Which cards have the same ratio of pepperoni pieces to pizzas?

### Reflect & Share

Share your answers with a classmate.
Why do you think your answers are correct?
What patterns do you see?

A ratio of 4:3 means that, for every 4 triangles, there are 3 squares.

A ratio of 8:6 means that, for every 8 triangles, there are 6 squares.

The ratios 8:6 and 4:3 are called **equivalent ratios**.
Equivalent ratios are equal. 8:6 = 4:3

➤ An equivalent ratio can be formed by multiplying or dividing
the terms of a ratio by the same number.

**Note that**
$3 \div 2$ is $\frac{3}{2} = 1.5$
and
$3 \div 4$ is $\frac{3}{4} = 0.75$

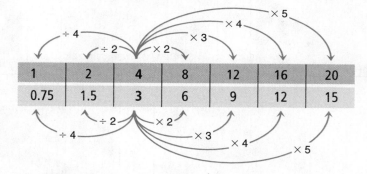

The equivalent ratios are:
1:0.75; 2:1.5; 4:3; 8:6; 12:9; 16:12; 20:15

➤ The equivalent ratios can be shown on a grid.

| 1st term | 1 | 2 | 4 | 8 | 12 | 16 | 20 |
|----------|------|-----|---|---|----|----|----|
| 2nd term | 0.75 | 1.5 | 3 | 6 | 9 | 12 | 15 |

The points representing the ratios lie on a straight line.

**Graph of Equivalent Ratios**

A ratio is in simplest form when its terms have no common factors.

➤ When we divide the terms in a ratio by their greatest common factor, we write the ratio in **simplest form**.
To write 24:16 in simplest form:

$$24:16 \qquad \text{The GCF is 8. Divide by 8.}$$
$$= (24 \div 8):(16 \div 8)$$
$$= \qquad 3:2$$

So, 24:16 and 3:2 are equivalent ratios.
The ratio 3:2 is in simplest form.

## Example

Construction kits come in different sizes.
The Regular Kit contains 120 long rods, 80 short rods, and 40 connectors.

**a)** What other kits could be created with the same ratio of rods and connectors?

**b)** One kit has 10 connectors. How many short and long rods does it have?

**Solution**

**a)** Use a table to find equivalent ratios.
Label each new kit.

| Component | Kit A | Kit B | Kit C | Kit D | Kit E | Regular Kit | Kit F |
|-----------|-------|-------|-------|-------|-------|-------------|-------|
| Long Rods | 3 | 6 | 15 | 30 | 60 | 120 | 240 |
| Short Rods | 2 | 4 | 10 | 20 | 40 | 80 | 160 |
| Connectors | 1 | 2 | 5 | 10 | 20 | 40 | 80 |

**b)** Use the table in part a.
The kit with 10 connectors is Kit D.
It has 20 short rods and 30 long rods.

**1.** Write three ratios equivalent to each ratio.
Use tables to show your work.
a) 3:4                          b) 14:4

**2.** Rewrite each sentence as a ratio statement in simplest form.
a) In a class, there are 15 girls and 12 boys.
b) In a parking lot, there were 4 American cars and 12 Japanese cars.
c) A paint mixture is made up of 6 L of blue paint and 2 L of white paint.
d) A stamp collection contains 12 Canadian stamps and 24 American stamps.

**3.** Name the pairs of equivalent ratios:
2:3, 9:12, 8:5, 1:2, 2:1, 16:10, 3:6, 6:9, 5:8, 3:4
Tell how you know they are equivalent.

**4.** In a class library, 3 out of 4 books are non-fiction.
The rest are fiction.
a) How many non-fiction books could there be?
How many fiction books?
b) How many different answers can you find for part a?
Which answers are reasonable? Explain.

**5.** The official Canadian flag has a length to width ratio of 2:1.
Doreen has a sheet of paper that measures 30 cm by 20 cm.
What are the length and width of the largest Canadian flag
Doreen can draw? Sketch a picture of the flag.

**6.** (**Assessment Focus**)   Use red, blue, and green counters.
Make a set of counters with these two ratios:
red:blue = 5:6        blue:green = 3:4
How many different ways can you do this?
Record each way you find.

**Reflect**

Choose a ratio. Use pictures, numbers, or words to show how to find
two equivalent ratios.

**Focus** Use equivalent ratios to compare ratios.

## Explore

Work with a partner.
Recipe A for punch calls for 2 cans of concentrate and 3 cans of water.

Recipe B for punch calls for 3 cans of concentrate and 4 cans of water.

In which recipe is the punch stronger?
Or are the drinks the same?
Explain how you know.

### Reflect & Share

Compare your answer with that of another pair of classmates.
Compare strategies.
If your answers are the same, which strategy do you prefer? Would there be a situation when the other strategy would be better? Explain.
If your answers are different, find out which is correct.

## Connect

Erica makes her coffee with 2 scoops of coffee to 5 cups of water.

Jim makes his coffee with 3 scoops of coffee to 7 cups of water.

Here are two ways to find out which coffee is stronger.

➤ Find how much water is used for 1 scoop of coffee.

**Erica**                                    **Jim**

1 scoop of coffee to
$2\frac{1}{2}$ cups of water.

1 scoop of coffee to
$2\frac{1}{3}$ cups of water.

Since $2\frac{1}{3}$ is less than $2\frac{1}{2}$,
Jim uses less water to 1 scoop of coffee.
So, Jim's coffee is stronger.

➤ Find how much coffee is used for the same amount of water.
Write each mixture as a ratio.
Write each ratio with the same second term,
then compare the first terms.
Use equivalent ratios.

**Erica**                                    **Jim**

Since 2:5 = 14:35,          Since 3:7 = 15:35,
Erica uses 14 scoops of     Jim uses 15 scoops of
coffee to 35 cups of water. coffee to 35 cups of water.

Jim uses more coffee. So, Jim's coffee is stronger.
Notice that, as we multiply to get equivalent ratios,
we get multiples of the terms of the ratios.
That is, the first terms in Erica's equivalent ratios are multiples of 2;
the second terms are multiples of 5.

A quicker way to write each ratio with the same second term is to find the lowest common multiple of the second terms.
That is, the lowest common multiple of 5 and 7 is 35.

## Example

At the outdoor centre, there were the same numbers of boys and girls. Five out of every 8 boys wanted to kayak. Two out of every 3 girls wanted to kayak. Do more boys than girls want to kayak? Explain.

## Solution

Five out of every 8 boys want to kayak.
This is a ratio of 5:8.
Two out of every 3 girls want to kayak.
This is a ratio of 2:3.
To compare the ratios, write them with the second terms the same.
The lowest common multiple of 8 and 3 is 24.
Multiply to make the second term of each ratio 24.

| Boys | Girls |
|------|-------|
| 5:8 | 2:3 |
| $= (5 \times 3):(8 \times 3)$ | $= (2 \times 8):(3 \times 8)$ |
| $=$ 15:24 | $=$ 16:24 |
| 15 out of 24 boys want to kayak | 16 out of 24 girls want to kayak |

Since 16 is greater than 15, more girls want to kayak.

## Practice

A

B

**1.** The concentrate and water in each picture are mixed.
Which mixture is stronger: A or B?
Draw a picture to show your answer.

**2.** Two boxes contain pictures of hockey and basketball players.
In one box, the ratio of hockey players to basketball players is 4:3.
In the other box, the ratio is 3:2.
The boxes contain the same number of pictures.
**a)** What could the total number of pictures be?
**b)** Which box contains more pictures of hockey players?
Draw a picture to show your answer.

There are 10 coins
that total $0.60.
What are the coins?

3. In a basketball game, Alison made 6 of 13 free shots.
Madhu made 5 of 9 free shots. Who played better? Explain.

4. The principal is deciding which shade of blue to have the
classrooms painted. One shade of blue requires 3 cans of white
paint mixed with 4 cans of blue paint. Another shade of blue
requires 5 cans of white paint mixed with 7 cans of blue paint.
   a) Which mixture will give the darker shade of blue? Explain.
   b) Which mixture will require more white paint?

5. Look at the two mixtures.
   a) What is the ratio of concentrate to water in A and in B?

   b) Explain how you could add concentrate or water
      to make both ratios the same.
      Draw a picture to show your answer.

6. **Assessment Focus**  The ratio of fiction to non-fiction books
   in Ms. Arbuckle's class library is 7:5.
   The ratio of fiction to non-fiction books in Mr. Albright's class
   library is 4:3.
   Each classroom has 30 non-fiction books.
   a) Which room has more fiction books? How many more?
   b) Mr. Albright added two non-fiction books to his class library.
      Does this make the ratio the same in both classes? Explain.

7. At Ria's party, there were 2 pizzas for every 3 people.
   At Amin's party, there were 5 pizzas for every 7 people.
   At which party did each person get more pizza? Explain.

### Reflect

In one store, the ratio of DVDs to videos is 7:5.
In another store, the ratio of DVDs to videos is 4:3.
Explain why you cannot say which store has more DVDs.

# Mid-Unit Review

LESSON

2.1 **1.** In the school parking lot, there are 4 Japanese cars, 7 American cars, 3 German cars, and 2 Korean cars. Write each ratio.

   **a)** American cars to Japanese cars

   **b)** German cars to Korean cars

   **c)** American cars to total number of cars

   **d)** German cars to Japanese cars and American cars

**2.** A box contains 5 cream chocolates, 2 chocolate-covered almonds, and 3 caramel chocolates.

   **a)** What is each ratio? Sketch a picture for each ratio.

   **i)** almond chocolates to caramel chocolates

   **ii)** cream chocolates to caramel chocolates

   **iii)** cream chocolates to all chocolates

   **b)** Lesley ate one of each kind of chocolate. What is each new ratio for part a?

**3.** In Mary's closet, there are 7 T-shirts, 4 pairs of shorts, and 3 sweaters. Write each ratio.

   **a)** T-shirts to shorts

   **b)** sweaters to shorts

   **c)** sweaters to T-shirts and shorts

2.2 **4.** For each ratio, write three equivalent ratios.

   **a)** 5:3    **b)** 6:24

**5. a)** Write each ratio below in simplest form.

   **i)** green squares to red squares

   **ii)** yellow squares to purple squares

   **iii)** red squares to total number of squares

   **b)** State the colours for each ratio.

   **i)** 1:6    **ii)** 2:5

**6.** In Ms. Bell's class, the ratio of boys to girls is 5:4.

   **a)** There are 15 boys in the class. How many girls are there?

   **b)** Two girls leave. What is the new ratio of boys to girls?

2.3 **7.** A jug of orange juice requires 3 cans of orange concentrate and 5 cans of water.

   **a)** Accidentally, 4 cans of concentrate were mixed with 5 cans of water. Is the mixture stronger or weaker than it should be? Explain.

   **b)** Suppose 6 cans of water were mixed with 3 cans of concentrate. Is the mixture stronger or weaker than it should be? Explain.

# Applications of Ratios

## Explore

Work on your own.

In the book *Gulliver's Travels*, Gulliver meets little people who are only 15 cm tall, and giants who are 18 m tall.

Gulliver is 1.80 m tall.

How many times as big as a little person is Gulliver?

How many times as big as Gulliver is a giant?

Write these comparisons as ratios.

### Reflect & Share

Compare your answers with those of a classmate.

Work together to find the ratio of the height of the giants to the height of the little people.

How many times as big as a little person is a giant?

## Connect

You can use diagrams and tables to model and solve ratio problems.

### Example 1

Jolene makes a scale drawing of her home.

She uses a scale of 5 cm to represent 1.5 m.

a)  What is the ratio of a length in the drawing to the actual length? What does this ratio mean?

b)  Jolene measures her bedroom on the drawing. It is 16 cm long. What is the actual length of Jolene's bedroom?

c)  The house measures 18 m by 12 m. What are the dimensions of the scale drawing?

**Solution**

a)  Length in the drawing:actual length

$$= \quad 5 \text{ cm}:1.50 \text{ m}$$
$$= \quad 5 \text{ cm}:150 \text{ cm}$$
$$= \quad (5 \text{ cm} \div 5 \text{ cm}):(150 \text{ cm} \div 5 \text{ cm})$$
$$= \quad 1:30$$

> When you write ratios of measurements, the units must be the same. Multiply 1.50 m by 100 to change metres to centimetres.

Each 1 cm in the drawing represents 30 cm in the home.

**b)** Draw a diagram.

The length in the drawing is 16 cm.
Each 1 cm in the drawing represents 30 cm in the bedroom.
So, the length of the bedroom is 16 × 30 cm = 480 cm
= 4.8 m

**c)** Draw a diagram.

1 cm in the drawing represents 30 cm in the house.
Divide each measurement in the house to find the measurement
on the drawing.

Length in the drawing $= \frac{1800 \text{ cm}}{30}$
$= 60$ cm

Width in the drawing $= \frac{1200 \text{ cm}}{30}$
$= 40$ cm

The dimensions of the scale drawing are 60 cm by 40 cm.

**Example 2**

Wallpaper paste can be made by mixing flour and water.
The table shows the volume of water to be mixed with flour to make
different quantities of paste.

| Water (mL) | 16 | 32 | 48 |
|---|---|---|---|
| Flour (mL) | 3 | 6 | 9 |

**a)** What is the ratio of the volume of water to the volume of flour?
**b)** How much water is required for 15 mL of flour?

**Solution**

a) Volume of water:volume of flour = 16:3

b) Use a pattern to continue the table in part a.
   For the water, the pattern rule is: Start at 16, then add 16.
   The next three terms are 64, 80, 96.
   For the flour, the pattern rule is: Start at 3, then add 3.
   The next three terms are 12, 15, 18.
   Extend the table to include these numbers.

| Water (mL) | 16 | 32 | 48 | 64 | 80 | 96 |
|---|---|---|---|---|---|---|
| Flour (mL) | 3 | 6 | 9 | 12 | 15 | 18 |

From the table, 80 mL of water are needed for 15 mL of flour.

# Practice

1. This table shows the quantities of concentrate and water needed to make punch.

| Orange concentrate (cans) | 2 | 4 | 6 | | |
|---|---|---|---|---|---|
| Cranberry concentrate (cans) | 1 | 2 | 3 | | |
| Water (cans) | 3 | 6 | 9 | | |
| Punch (L) | 1.5 | 3 | 4.5 | | |

   a) What are the next two numbers in each row of the table?
   b) What is the ratio of cranberry concentrate to water?
   c) Suppose you use 10 cans of orange concentrate.
      How much punch would you get?
   d) Suppose you use 12 cans of concentrate in total.
      How much punch would you get?
   e) How much of each ingredient would you need to make 15 L of punch? Explain your reasoning.

Remember to convert the units so you work with all measurements in the same units.

2. Jenny makes models of Canadian Coast Guard ships.
   She uses a scale of 3 cm to 1.5 m.
   a) What is the ratio of a length on the model to a length on the ship?
   b) The Terry Fox ship is 88 m long. How long is the model?
   c) The model of the Otter Bay is 27 cm long.
      What is the actual length of the Otter Bay?
      Draw diagrams to show your answers.

**3.** A set designer builds a model of the stage and the different pieces of furniture on it. He uses a scale of 5 cm to 1 m.
  a) What is the ratio of a length on the model to a length on the stage?
  b) The length of a table is 1.4 m. What is the length of the model?
  c) The height of the model of a lamp is 3 cm. What is the actual height of the lamp?
  d) The height of the model of an ornament is 0.5 cm. What is the actual height of the ornament? How did you find out?
  Draw diagrams to show your answers.

**4.** Janice builds a model using a scale of 2 cm to represent 3 m. Her friend William says she is using a ratio of 2:3. Is William correct? Explain.

**5.** This table shows the quantities of salt and water needed to make salt solutions.

| Water (L) | 2 | 4 | 6 | 8 |
|-----------|----|----|----|----|
| Salt (g) | 18 | 36 | 54 | 72 |

  a) How much salt would be needed for 7 L of water?
  b) How much water would be needed for 90 g of salt?

**6.** **Assessment Focus**   Aston challenges his father to a 100-m race.
  Aston runs 4 m for every 5 m his father runs.
  a) Who wins the race? Draw a diagram to show your answer.
  b) How far will Aston have run when his father crosses the finish line?
  c) Aston asks to race again but wants to be given a head start. How much of a start should Aston's father give him to make it a close race? Explain your answer.

**Social Studies**

A scale on a provincial map is 1:1 500 000. This means that 1 cm on the map represents 1 500 000 cm on the ground, which is $\frac{1\,500\,000}{100}$ m, or 15 000 m on the ground.
And, 15 000 m is $\frac{15\,000}{1000}$ km, or 15 km.
So, a scale of 1:1 500 000 is 1 cm to 15 km.

**Reflect**

Make up your own ratio problem.
Solve your problem. Show your work.

## Explore

Work with a partner.
You will need a stopwatch.
One person is the "blinker." The other person is the timekeeper.
The blinker blinks as many times as possible.
Count the number of times the blinker blinks in 20 s.
Reverse roles.
Count the number of times the blinker blinks in 30 s.

➤ Who was the faster blinker?
How do you know?

➤ Estimate how many times each person would blink in 1 h.
What assumptions do you make?
Are these assumptions reasonable?

### Reflect & Share

Compare your results with those of another pair of classmates.
How can you decide who is the fastest blinker?

## Connect

When we compare two different things, we have a **rate**.
Here are some rates.

- We need 5 sandwiches for every 2 people.
- Oranges are on sale at $1.49 for 12.
- Gina earns $4.75 per hour for baby-sitting.
- There are 500 sheets on one roll of paper towels.

The last two rates above are **unit rates**.
Each rate compares a quantity to 1 unit.

Jamal skipped rope 80 times in 1 min.
We say that Jamal's rate of skipping is 80 skips per minute.
We write this as 80 skips/min.

To find unit rates, we can use diagrams, tables, and graphs.

## Example 1

The doctor took Marjorie's pulse. He counted 25 beats in 20 s.
What was Marjorie's heart rate in beats per minute?

**Solution**

Draw a diagram.
There are 25 beats in 20 s.
There are 60 s in 1 min.
We multiply 20 s by 3 to get 60 s.
So, multiply the number of beats
in 20 s by 3 to get the number of
beats per minute.

25 beats × 3 = 75 beats

Marjorie's heart rate is 75 beats/min.

## Example 2

A printing press prints 120 sheets in 3 min.
a) Express the printing as a rate.
b) How many sheets are printed in 1 h?
c) How long will it take to print 1000 sheets?

**Solution**

a) Draw a diagram.
The press prints 120 sheets in 3 min.
So, in 1 min, the press prints:
120 sheets ÷ 3 = 40 sheets
The rate of printing is 40 sheets/min.

b) In 1 min, the press prints 40 sheets.
One hour is 60 min.
So, in 60 min, the press prints:
60 × 40 sheets = 2400 sheets
The press prints 2400 sheets in 1 h.

c) *Method 1*
In 1 min, the press prints 40 sheets.
So, in 5 min, the press prints: 5 × 40 = 200 sheets
Make a table. Every 5 min, 200 more sheets are printed.
Extend the table until you get 1000 sheets.

| Time (min) | 5 | 10 | 15 | 20 | 25 |
|---|---|---|---|---|---|
| Sheets printed | 200 | 400 | 600 | 800 | 1000 |

*Method 2*

The press prints 40 sheets in 1 min.
Think: What do we multiply
40 by to get 1000?
Use division: 1000 ÷ 40 = 25
So, 40 × 25 = 1000
We multiply the time by the same number.
1 min × 25 = 25 min
The press takes 25 min to print 1000 sheets.

The rate at which a car travels is its **average speed**.
When a car travels at an average speed of 80 km/h, it travels:

    80 km in 1 h
    160 km in 2 h
    240 km in 3 h
    320 km in 4 h
    400 km in 5 h … and so on

We can show this motion on a graph.
An average speed of 80 km/h is a unit rate.

## Practice

1. Express as a unit rate.
   a) Morag typed 60 words in one minute.
   b) Peter swam 25 m in one minute.
   c) Abdu read 20 pages in one hour.

2. Express as a unit rate.
   a) June cycled 30 km in 2 h.
   b) An elephant travelled 18 km in 30 min.
   c) A plane flew 150 km in 15 min.

3. Before running in a 100-m race, Gaalen's heart rate was
   70 beats/min. Which do you think is more likely after the race:
   60 beats/min or 120 beats/min? Explain.

4. Ribbon costs $1.44 for 3 m.
   a) What is the cost per metre?
   b) How much would 5 m of ribbon cost?
   c) How much ribbon could you buy for $12?

5. The graph shows the distance
   travelled by a cyclist in 3 h.
   a) How far did the cyclist
      travel in 1 h?
   b) What is the average speed
      of the cyclist?
      How do you know?

How a Cyclist Travels

6. James and Lucinda came to Canada on holiday from England.
   The rate of exchange for their money was $2.50 Can to £1.
   a) How many Canadian dollars would James get for £20?
   b) What is the value in English pounds of a gift
      Lucinda bought for $30 Can?

7. When a person runs a long-distance race, she thinks of the
   time she takes to run 1 km (min/km), rather than the
   distance run in 1 min (km/min).
   On a training run, Judy took 3 h 20 min to run 25 km.
   What was Judy's rate in minutes per kilometre?

8. **Assessment Focus**    Scott trained for the marathon.
   On day 1, he took 70 min to run 10 km.
   On day 10, he took 2 h 40 min to run 20 km.
   On day 20, he took 4 h 15 min to run 30 km.
   a) What was Scott's running rate, in minutes per kilometre,
      for each day?
      i) Day 1              ii) Day 10              iii) Day 20
   b) What do you think Scott's running rate, in minutes per
      kilometre, might be for the 44 km of the marathon?
      How long do you think it will take him? Explain.

**Reflect**

Look through newspapers and magazines to find three different
examples of rates. Explain how the rates are used.

# Organizing a Math Notebook

**1** You must include the date for each new note taken or activity performed.

**2** You must include a title for each new note or activity.

**3** All dates and titles must be underlined with a ruler.

**4** All tables must be neat.
Use a ruler to draw a table.

For example:
_Section 2.5, question 8._

_April 13, 2005_

| Day | Time (min) | Distance (km) | Rate (min/km) |
|-----|-----------|---------------|---------------|
| 1   |           |               |               |

**5** Your daily work must be legible, complete, and well-organized.

You must make corrections where necessary.

To organize a math problem:

- Restate the problem in your own words.
  For example, "This problem is about..."

- Think about a strategy you will use
  and tell about it.
  For example, "The strategy I will use
  is..._____ because..."

- Solve the problem. Show all your work.

- State the answer to your problem, and explain how you
  know it is reasonable and correct.
  For example, "I found the answer to be...
  I know my answer is reasonable because...
  I know my answer is correct because..."

- Extend your thinking. Make up a similar problem by
  asking "What if?" questions.
  For example, "What if all the numbers in this question
  were doubled? How would the answer change?"

# Race Engineer

The equivalent of the 100-m sprint in the world of cars is the $\frac{1}{4}$-mile drag race. One-quarter of one mile is about 400 m. The race engineers (men and women who help design, build, and tune the cars) are an important part of the racing team. Theirs is a world filled with gear ratios, cylinder compression ratios, fuel mixture ratios, acceleration, and speed. It's a constant cycle of theory, real-world application, testing, and evaluating. And, sometimes, all these take place during a few hours between race runs! Helping the dragster team driver get to the finish line $\frac{1}{1000}$ th of a second faster than a previous run could mean the difference between winning and losing the race.

In October, 2003, a top fuel dragster recorded a new "fastest time" of 4.441 s for the $\frac{1}{4}$-mile drag race. But another car and driver continued to hold the record for the fastest recorded speed achieved during a race—an incredible 536 km/h! Why do you suppose the second car doesn't hold the record for fastest time?

# Unit Review

## What Do I Need to Know?

☑ A ratio is a comparison of quantities.
For example, 3 dogs to 7 cats is 3:7.

☑ An equivalent ratio can be formed by multiplying or dividing the terms of a ratio by the same number.

For example:

|  |  |
|---|---|
| 5:8 | and | 36:30 |
| = (5 × 3):(8 × 3) | = (36 ÷ 6):(30 ÷ 6) |
| = 15:24 | = 6:5 |
| 5:8 and 15:24 | 36:30 and 6:5 |
| are equivalent ratios. | are equivalent ratios. |

☑ Two ratios can be compared when the second terms are the same.
For example, Scott's scoring record was 16:5.
Brittany's scoring record was 10:3.
To find who had the better record, use equivalent ratios to make the second term of each ratio 15.

|  **Scott**  |  **Brittany**  |
|---|---|
| 16:5 | 10:3 |
| = (16 × 3):(5 × 3) | = (10 × 5):(3 × 5) |
| = 48:15 | = 50:15 |

Brittany had the better record.

☑ A rate is a comparison of two quantities with different units.
For example:
Heart rate is measured in beats per minute (beats/min).
Average speed is measured in kilometres per hour (km/h).
Fuel consumption of an aircraft is measured in litres per hour (L/h).

LESSON

**2.1**

**1.** On a school trip, there are 9 boys, 10 girls, and 4 adults.
Write each ratio.
   a) girls to boys
   b) boys and girls to adults
   c) adults to boys and girls

**2.2**

**2.** Write four ratios to describe the coloured squares.

**3.** Explain two different ways to get ratios equivalent to 25:10.

**4.** Jake has to draw a flag with a length to width ratio of 3 to 2. What is the largest flag Jake can draw on a 25-cm by 20-cm sheet of paper?

**2.3**

**5.** The ratio of computers to students in Ms. Beveridge's class is 2:3. The ratio of computers to students in Mr. Walker's class is 3:5. Each class has the same number of students.
Which room has more computers? Explain.

**2.4**

**6.** Ali builds model planes. He uses a scale of 8 cm to represent 1.8 m.
   a) What is the ratio of a length on the model to the actual length on the plane?
   b) A plane has a length of 72 m. What is the length of the model?
   c) A model has a length of 60 cm. What is the actual length of the plane?
Draw pictures to show your answers.

**7.** Red and white paint is mixed in the ratio of 3 to 2.
   a) How many cans of red paint would be needed with 6 cans of white paint?
   b) How many cans of each colour are needed to make 20 cans of mixture?

**2.5**  **8.** Express as a unit rate.
   a) A bus travelled 120 km in 3 h.
   b) An athlete ran 1500 m in 6 min.
   c) A student earned $16 for 2 h work.

**9.** A lion can run 550 m in 25 s. A zebra can run 270 m in 15 s.
   a) Which animal is faster?
   b) What is the ratio of their average speeds?

# Practice Test

1. a) Write each ratio in simplest form.
   i) red squares to blue squares
   ii) blue squares to green squares
   iii) red squares and blue squares to total numbers of squares
   b) Suppose the grid is increased to a rectangle measuring 9 units by 4 units. The ratios of the colours remain the same. How many red squares will there be in the new rectangle?

2. In the league, the Leos play 8 games. Their win to loss ratio is 5:3. The Tigers play 11 games. Their win to loss ratio is 7:4.
   a) Which team has the better record? Explain.
   b) Suppose the Leos win their next game and the Tigers lose theirs. Which team would have the better record? Explain.

3. Hessa is building a scale model of a park. She uses a scale of 12 cm to represent 1.5 m.
   a) The actual length of the bridge is 20 m. What is the length of the model bridge?
   b) In the model, the height of the climbing frame is 10 cm. What is the actual height of the frame?

4. Look at this graph.
   a) What is the speed of each car?
   b) How far apart are the cars after 4 s?

5. Trevor's mark on a math test was 10 out of 15. Anne's mark on another test was 15 out of 20. Trevor said, "Each of us got 5 wrong. So, our marks are equal." Do you agree? Give reasons for your answer.

Mr. Peabody believes you can predict an animal's intelligence by looking at the size of its brain.

He uses ratios to compare body size to brain size. Investigate this strategy.

Analyse the data below to test Mr. Peabody's **hypothesis**.

A **hypothesis** is something that seems likely to be true. It needs to be tested and proved or disproved.

The mass of a human brain is about the same mass as your math textbook.

| Species | Comparing Mass (g) | | Comparing Length (cm) | |
|---------|------|-------|------|-------|
| | **Body** | **Brain** | **Body** | **Brain** |
| **Human** | 56 000 | 1400 | 150 | 15 |
| **Monkey** | 7 000 | 100 | 30 | 5 |
| **Camel** | 520 000 | 650 | 200 | 15 |

**1.** Compare masses: find the ratio of body mass to brain mass.
  • How does a human compare to a monkey?
  • How does a human compare to a camel?
  • How does a camel compare to a monkey?
According to Mr. Peabody's hypothesis, which animal is smartest? Explain your reasoning.

**2.** Compare lengths: find the ratio of body length to brain length.

- How does a human compare to a monkey?
- How does a human compare to a camel?
- How does a camel compare to a monkey?

According to Mr. Peabody's hypothesis, which animal is smartest? Explain your reasoning.

**Check List**

Your work should show:

✓ how you calculated each ratio

✓ your reasoning for which animal is the smartest

✓ your conclusions about the hypothesis

✓ the correct use of mathematical language

**3.** The dinosaur, diplodocus, lived about 150 million years ago.
The brain of a diplodocus was about 9 cm long.
The body of a diplodocus was about 27 m long.

- How long would a human's brain be if it had the same brain length to body length ratio as a diplodocus?

A frog's brain is about 2 cm long.
A frog's length is about 10 cm long

- How long would a human's brain be if it had the same brain length to body length ratio as a frog?

**4.** Review your results.
Write a short letter to Mr. Peabody telling him whether you agree with his hypothesis, and why.
Use mathematical language to support your opinion.

**Reflect on the Unit**

How is a rate like a ratio?
How is it different?
Use examples in your explanation.

# Geometry and Measurement

Most products are packaged
in boxes or cans.
How is a package made?
How do you think the manufacturer
chooses the shape and style of
package? What things need to
be considered?

Look at the packages on this page.
Choose one package.
Why do you think the manufacturer
chose that form of packaging?

CRABTREE & EVELYN

## What You'll Learn

- Recognize different views of an object.
- Sketch different views of an object.
- Sketch an object.
- Build an object from a net.
- Develop and use a formula for the surface area of a rectangular prism.
- Develop and use a formula for the volume of a rectangular prism.

## Why It's Important

- Drawing a picture is one way to help solve a problem or explain a solution.
- Calculating the volume and surface area of a prism is an extension of the measuring you did in earlier grades.

## Key Words

- polyhedron (polyhedra)
- prism
- pyramid
- regular polyhedron
- cube
- tetrahedron
- isometric
- pictorial diagram
- icosahedron
- octahedron
- dodecahedron
- frustum
- variable
- surface area

# Skills You'll Need

## Identifying Polyhedra

A **polyhedron** is a solid with faces that are polygons.
Two faces meet at an edge.
Three or more edges meet at a vertex.

A **prism** has 2 congruent bases, and is named for its bases.
Its other faces are parallelograms.

A pentagonal prism

A triangular prism

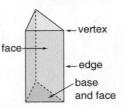

A **pyramid** has 1 base and is named for that base.
Its other faces are triangles.

A square
pyramid

A hexagonal
pyramid

A **regular polyhedron** has all faces congruent.
The same number of faces meet at each vertex.
The same number of edges meet at each vertex.

A **cube** is a
regular
rectangular
prism.

A **regular
tetrahedron**
is a regular
triangular
pyramid.

 **Check**

Use the pictures of the solids above. Use the solids if you have them.
**1. a)** How are the solids alike? How are they different?
  **b)** Name a real-life object that has the shape of each solid.

# Using Isometric Dot Paper to Draw a Cube

To draw this cube:

 Join 2 dots for one vertical edge.

 Join pairs of dots diagonally for the front horizontal edges, top and bottom.

 Join the dots for the other 2 vertical edges.

 Complete the cube. Join dots diagonally for the back horizontal edges at the top.

Shade visible faces differently to get a three-dimensional (3-D) look.

Isometric means "equal measure." On isometric dot paper, the line segments joining 2 adjacent dots in any direction are equal.

## ✓ Check

**2.** Use isometric dot paper. Draw each object. Use linking cubes when they help.

a)    b)    c)

Which objects do you see in this picture?

Choose an object. What does it look like from the top? From the side? From the back?

## Explore

Work on your own.
Choose a classroom object.

Sketch the object from every view possible. Label each view.
Use dot paper or grid paper if it helps.
Describe each sketch.

### Reflect & Share

Trade sketches with a classmate.
Try to identify the object your classmate drew.

## Connect

We can use square dot paper to draw each view of the object at the left. We ignore the holes in each face.

**Left side view**

**Front view**

Back view

Front view

Left side view

Right side view

Top view

## Example

A triangular prism fits
on top of a rectangular prism.
The bases of the triangular prism
are right isosceles triangles.
The rectangular prism has
two square faces.
Sketch the front, back,
side, and top views.

**A right isosceles triangle has a 90° angle and two equal sides.**

## Solution

The front view and back
view are the same.
Sketch a right isosceles
triangle on top of a rectangle.

Front view

Side view

The two side views are the same.
The side face of the triangular
prism is a rectangle. Sketch a
rectangle on top of a square.

Top view

The top view is two
congruent rectangles.

## Practice

Use linking cubes when they help.

**1.** Many signs are views of objects.
Identify the view (front, back, side, or top) and the object on
each sign.
**a)** Child care  **b)** Airport transportation  **c)** Fully accessible

**2.** Use linking cubes. Make each object A to E. Figures J to Q are views of objects A to E. Match each view (J to Q) to each object (A to E), in as many ways as you can.

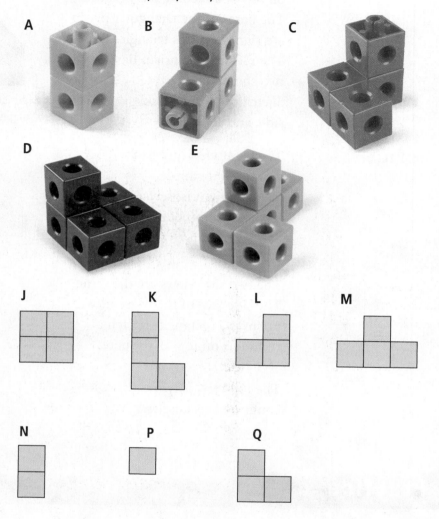

**3.** Use linking cubes. Make each object. Use square dot paper. Draw the front, back, side, and top views of each object.

a)                    b)                    c)

**4.** Sketch the top, front, side, and back views of the birdhouse at the left. Label each view.

**5.** Design a road safety or information sign for each situation. Tell which view you used. Explain how each sign shows the information.

    **a)** playground ahead     **b)** tennis court

    **c)** skateboarding allowed     **d)** no flash cameras allowed

**6.** Find each object in the classroom. Sketch the front, back, top, and side views of each object.

    **a)** filing cabinet     **b)** vase     **c)** teacher's desk

**Mental Math**

How many:
• days in a year?
• months in a year?
• days in a week?
• hours in a day?
• minutes in an hour?
• seconds in a minute?

**7.** **Assessment Focus** Use 4 linking cubes. Make as many different objects as possible. Draw the front, back, top, and side views for each object. Label each view. Use your sketches to explain how you know all the objects you made are different.

**8.** All 5 views of a cube are the same. Use the solids in the classroom.

    **a)** Are there any other prisms with all views the same? Explain.

    **b)** Which solid has 4 views the same?

    **c)** Which solid has only 3 views the same?

    **d)** Which solid has no views the same?

    If you cannot name a solid for parts b to d, use linking cubes to make a solid.

**9.** Here is one view of an object. Sketch a possible different view of the object.

    **a)**      **b)**      **c)**

**Reflect**

Choose an object. How many views do you need to sketch, so someone else can identify it? Explain. Sketch the views you describe.

# Using a Computer to Draw Views of Solids

Software, such as *The Geometer's Sketchpad*, can be used to draw different views of solids.

Follow these steps.
1. Open *The Geometer's Sketchpad*.

To make a "dot paper" screen:

2. From the **Edit** menu, choose **Preferences**.
   Select the Units tab. Check the Distance units are cm.
   Click **OK**.

3. From the **Graph** menu, choose **Define Coordinate System**.
   Click on a point where the grid lines intersect.
   The grid is now highlighted in pink.

4. From the **Display** menu, choose **Line Width**, then **Dotted**.
   There are dots at the grid intersections.
   Click anywhere on the screen other than the dots.
   The dots are no longer highlighted. Hold down the shift key.
   Click on each numbered axis and the two red dots.
   Release the shift key.
   The axes and the dots are now highlighted.

5. From the **Display** menu, choose **Hide Objects**.
   The axes and dots disappear.
   The screen now appears like a piece of dot paper.
   From the **Graph** menu, choose **Snap Points**.

Make this object with linking cubes.
Follow the steps below to create
views of this object.

Front view

6. From the **Toolbox** menu, choose **A** (Text Tool).
   Move the cursor to the screen and a finger appears.
   Click and drag to make a box at the top left.
   Inside the box, type: Front View

7. From the **Toolbox** menu, choose  (Straightedge Tool).

Move to a dot on the screen below the title.
Click and drag to draw a line segment.
Release the mouse button.
Continue to draw line segments to draw
the front view.
Click to select each line segment.
From the **Display** menu, choose **Line Width**, then **Dashed**.
This draws the line segments as broken lines.

Front View

8. From the **Toolbox** menu, click on ⬉ (Selection Arrow Tool).

Click to select the four corners of the top square,
in clockwise order.
From the **Construct** menu, choose **Quadrilateral Interior**.
From the **Display** menu, choose **Color**, then choose blue.

Front View

9. Repeat *Step 8* to make
the bottom squares
red and green.

Front View

10. Repeat *Step 6* to *9* to draw and label the left side view and
the back view.

Front View    Left Side View    Back View

11. Draw the top view and right side view.

1. Open a new sketch. Draw different views of objects from
*Section 3.1, Practice* question 3. Compare the hand-drawn
views with the computer-drawn views.

**Focus**   Sketch pictures of objects from models and drawings.

## Explore

Work with a partner.
You will need isometric dot paper and 4 linking cubes.
Make an object so its front, top, and side views are all different.
Draw the object on isometric dot paper so all 4 cubes are visible.

### Reflect & Share

Trade isometric drawings with another pair of classmates.
Make your classmates' object.
Was it easy to make the object? Explain.
Compare objects. If they are different, find out why.

## Connect

An object has 3 dimensions: length, height, and width or depth.
A drawing is a picture of an object on paper.
It has 2 dimensions: length and width.

➤ We use isometric dot paper to show the 3 dimensions of an object. Parallel edges on an object are drawn as parallel line segments. An object made with 5 linking cubes is shown at the left.

When we draw the object from the front or the top, we see only 4 cubes.

Front view

Top view

Place the object so that all 5 cubes are seen.

Draw the edges in this order:
- vertical edges (red)
- horizontal edges that appear to go down to the right (blue)
- horizontal edges that appear to go up to the right (green)

Shade faces to produce a 3-D effect.

**Number Strategies**

Simplify.
Use order of operations.
- $17 - 7 \times 2 + 3$
- $15 - 6 \div 2$
- $14 \div 2 \times 3$
- $8 \times 2 + 21 - 6$
- $15 + 3 \times 5$

➤ We can use translations to draw a **pictorial diagram**.

A pictorial diagram shows the shape of an object in 2 dimensions.
It gives the impression of 3 dimensions.
To sketch the rectangular prism above right:

Draw a rectangle 4 cm by 2 cm.

Draw another rectangle that is the image of the first rectangle after a translation up and to the right.

Join corresponding vertices for a sketch of a rectangular prism.
Label the dimensions.

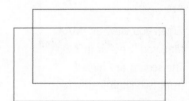

Note that the depth of the prism is 3 cm but, on the drawing, this distance is less than 3 cm. In a pictorial drawing, the depth of an object is drawn to a smaller scale than the length and width. This gives the appearance of 3 dimensions.

We can use similar ideas to sketch a 3-D picture of any object.

## Example

Sketch this mug.

## Solution

The mug is an open cylinder
with a handle.
Draw an oval for the circular top.
Draw vertical lines for the
curved surface (blue).
Draw half an oval for the
circular base (red).
Draw 2 overlapping curves
for the handle (green).

**In a pictorial drawing, a circle is drawn as an oval.**

## Practice

### Art

When you view an IMAX film, you "see" it in 3-D. The scenes are filmed from two slightly different angles. This imitates how our eyes view the world. Both films are projected onto the screen to give you the feeling of depth.

Use linking cubes when they help.

**1.** Make each object. Draw it on isometric dot paper.

a)
b)

**2.** Turn each object in question 1.
Draw it a different way on isometric dot paper.

**3.** Use linking cubes. Make each object.
Draw it on plain paper or isometric dot paper.

a)
b)

**4.** Here are different views of an object made with linking cubes.

Front

Back

Top

Left Side

Right Side

Make the object.
Draw it on isometric dot paper or plain paper.

**5.** Sketch a 3-D picture of each object on plain paper.

a)

b)

c)

**6.** Square pieces of shelving snap together to make cube-shaped stacking shelves. All the faces are square and measure 30 cm by 30 cm. A side face costs $1.50.
A top or bottom face costs $1.30. The back face costs $1.10. Kate built shelves using 9 side faces, 6 back faces, and 9 top/bottom faces.

  a) Use linking cubes to build a possible design.
  b) Draw a picture of your design on isometric dot paper.
  c) How much did the shelving cost?
  d) Is it possible to have the same number of cubes but use fewer pieces? Explain.
  e) If your answer to part d is yes, what is the new cost of shelving? Explain.

**7.** (Assessment Focus)  Use 5 linking cubes. Make a solid.
  a) Sketch the solid on isometric dot paper.
  b) Sketch a 3-D picture of the solid on plain paper.
  c) How is sketching a solid on isometric paper different from sketching it on plain paper? How are the methods alike? Use your sketches to explain.

**Reflect**

How do you draw an object to show its 3 dimensions?
Use words and pictures to explain.

# Forensic Graphics Specialist

A forensic investigator collects information from a crime scene to find out who was involved and exactly what happened. The forensic investigator also presents evidence in court as required by law.

The forensic graphics specialist visits the crime scene to take photographs and measurements. She may research to compose technical drawings to help with the investigation. When she prepares these drawings, the graphics specialist pays attention to shading and relative line thickness. It is important that she does not present optical illusions such as an object appearing to be "inside out."

# **Building Objects from Nets**

In earlier grades, you designed nets for prisms and pyramids.
Now, you will fold nets to make prisms, pyramids, and other polyhedra.

## Explore

Work with a partner.
You will need scissors and tape.
Your teacher will give you large copies of the nets below.

➤ Identify the polyhedron for each net above.
➤ Use a copy of each net.
  Cut it out. Fold, then tape it to make a polyhedron.
➤ Identify congruent faces on each polyhedron.

### **Reflect & Share**

Look at each polyhedron from the top, front, back, and sides.
Which views are the same? Explain.

## Connect

There are 5 regular polyhedra.
You reviewed 2 of them, the cube and the tetrahedron,
in *Skills You'll Need*, page 76.

One regular polyhedron is
an **icosahedron**.
Here is a net for one-half
of an icosahedron.

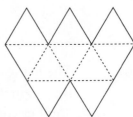

This net can be cut out and folded.
The net has 10 congruent triangles.

Two of these pieces are taped
together to make an icosahedron.

An icosahedron has
20 congruent faces.
Each face is an equilateral triangle.
In the *Practice* questions, you will
make the other 2 regular polyhedra.

A regular **octahedron**          A regular **dodecahedron**

In previous grades, you designed and sketched
nets of prisms and pyramids.
In the *Example* that follows, and in *Practice* questions,
you will investigate nets for other objects.

**Example**

Fold this net to make
an object.
Describe the object.

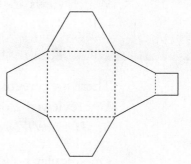

**Solution**

The net is folded along the broken
line segments. Each edge touches
another edge. The edges are taped.

The object looks like the bottom of a pyramid; that is, a pyramid with the top part removed. The object is called a **frustum** of a pyramid.

The object has 2 non-congruent square faces, and 4 congruent trapezoid faces. The 2 square faces are parallel.

## Practice

Your teacher will give you a large copy of each net.

1. Fold this net to make a polyhedron.
   a) Identify the polyhedron.
   b) Describe the polyhedron.

2. Fold this net.
   a) Is the object a polyhedron? If so, what are the attributes that make it a polyhedron?
   b) Identify parallel faces and perpendicular faces.

**Calculator Skills**

Find three prime numbers that have a sum of 43 and a product of 1085.

3. Fold two of these nets to make two square pyramids with no base. Tape the two pyramids together at their missing bases. You have made a regular octahedron.
   a) Why does it have this name?
   b) Describe the octahedron. How do you know it is regular?

4. Fold each net. Describe each object. How are the objects the same? How are they different?

   a)

   b)

**5.** Fold two of these nets. Put the open parts together. Tape the pieces to make a regular dodecahedron. Describe the dodecahedron.

**6.** A soccer ball is not a sphere. It is a polyhedron. Look at a soccer ball. Explain which polygons are joined to make the ball. How are the polygons joined?

**7.** (Assessment Focus)   Fold the net shown.

   **a)** Describe the object formed.
   **b)** Name the object. Justify your answer.

**8.** All the nets you have used fold to make objects. Which features must be true for this to happen?

**Take It Further**

**9.** Use isometric dot paper or plain paper. Draw the object that has this net. Explain your thinking.

**Reflect**

Choose a product that has a package in the shape of a polyhedron. Sketch the package. Include appropriate dimensions. Cut along the edges to make the net. Why do you think the manufacturer used this shape for the package? Can you find a better shape for the packaging? Explain.

# Mid-Unit Review

LESSON

3.1 **1.** Sketch the front, back, top, and side views of each object. Label each view.

**a)** Television

**b)** Baseball mitt

**c)** Chair

3.2 **2.** Make each object. Sketch a 3-D view of the object on isometric dot paper.

**a)**

**b)**

**3.** Sketch a 3-D view of each object on plain paper.

**a)**  **b)**

**4.** Suppose you had to construct an object from linking cubes. Which would you prefer to use: a drawing of the object on isometric dot paper, or 5 different views on plain paper? Justify your choice. Use diagrams to support your choice.

3.3 **5.** Use a large copy of this net. Fold the net to make an object. Name the object. List its attributes.

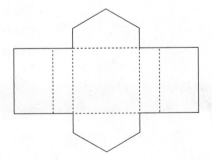

**6.** Which polyhedra could have each view shown below? Find as many polyhedra as you can for each view.

**a)**  **b)**

**Focus** Use measurement formulas to introduce the concept of a variable.

## Explore

Work with a partner.

➤ Find the area of each rectangle below, in square units.

➤ Find the perimeter of each rectangle above, in units.

### Reflect & Share

Compare your results with those of another pair of classmates.
How did you find the area when you did not know:
- the base?
- the height?
- the base and height?

How did you find the perimeter in each case?

## Connect

When we do not know the dimensions of a figure,
we use letters to represent them.
For a rectangle, we use *b* to represent the length of the base,
and *h* to represent the height.

One way to find the area of a rectangle is to use a formula.
The formula for the area of a rectangle is:

$$A = \text{base} \times \text{height}$$

Then $A = b \times h$

We write $A = b \times h$ as $A = bh$.

The formula for the perimeter of a rectangle is:
$P = 2 \times (\text{base} + \text{height})$
Then $P = 2 \times (b + h)$
We write $P = 2 \times (b + h)$ as $P = 2(b + h)$.

The letters we use to represent the base and height are called **variables**. Variables in a formula can represent different numbers. When we know the values of the variables, we **substitute** for the variables. That is, we replace each variable with a number.

A square is a rectangle with all sides equal.
The formula for the area of a square is:
$A = \text{side length} \times \text{side length}$
Use the variable $s$ for the side length.
Then, $A = s \times s$
    or $A = s^2$

**We use exponents to represent repeated multiplication.**

The formula for the perimeter of a square is:
    $P = 4 \times \text{side length}$
or $P = 4 \times s$

We write $P = 4 \times s$ as $P = 4s$.

## Example

A rectangle has base 15 cm and height 3 cm. Use formulas to find its area and perimeter.

**Solution**

Area, $A = bh$
$b = 15$ and $h = 3$
Substitute for $b$ and $h$ in the formula.
$A = 15 \times 3$
$A = 45$
The area is 45 cm².

Perimeter, $P = 2(b + h)$
Substitute for $b$ and $h$.
$P = 2(15 + 3)$          Use order of operations.
$P = 2(18)$              Do the operation in
$P = 36$                 brackets first. Then multiply.
The perimeter is 36 cm.

**1.** Use the formula: $P = 4s$
Find the perimeter of the square with each side length.
a) 5 cm  b) 9 cm  c) 2 cm  d) 8 cm

**2.** Use the formula for the area of a rectangle: $A = bh$
Find the area of each rectangle.
a) base: 6 cm; height: 3 cm  b) base: 11 cm; height: 2 cm

**3. a)** For each rectangle, what is the value of $b$ and the value of $h$?

i)   ii)   iii)

**b)** Use your answers to part a to explain why
we call $b$ and $h$ variables.
**c)** What is true about $b$ and $h$ in part a, iii?

**4.** Find the area and perimeter of each rectangle.
a) base: 12 cm; height: 4 cm  b) base: 10.5 cm; height: 3.0 cm

**5.** Find the perimeter and area of each square.
a) side length: 2.8 cm  b) side length: 3.1 cm

**6.** **Assessment Focus**
Here is another formula for the perimeter of a rectangle:
$P = 2b + 2h$
Write this formula in words.
Explain why there are two formulas for the perimeter
of a rectangle.

**Take It Further**

**7. a)** How could you use the formula for the perimeter of a
rectangle to get the formula for the perimeter of a square?
**b)** How could you use the formula for the area of a rectangle to
get the formula for the area of a square?

**Reflect**

What is a variable?
Why do we use variables to write measurement formulas?

**Focus** | Use a formula to calculate the surface area of a rectangular prism.

## Explore

Work in a group.
You will need several different empty cereal boxes, scissors, and a ruler.

➤ Cut along the edges of a box to make a net.
What is the area of the surface of the box?
➤ Repeat the activity above for 2 other boxes.
➤ Write a formula to find the area of the surface
of a rectangular prism.

### Reflect & Share

Compare your formula with that of another group.
Did you write the same formula?
If not, do both formulas work? Explain.

## Connect

Here is a rectangular prism, and its net.

In the net, there are 3 pairs of
congruent rectangles.
The area of the net is the sum of
the areas of the rectangles.

The area of the net $= 2(8 \times 3) + 2(8 \times 5) + 2(3 \times 5)$
$\qquad\qquad\quad = 2(24) + 2(40) + 2(15)$  Multiply.
$\qquad\qquad\quad = 48 + 80 + 30$  Add.
$\qquad\qquad\quad = 158$

**Use order of operations, with brackets first.**

The area of the net is 158 cm².
We say that the **surface area** of the rectangular prism is 158 cm².

We can use the net of a rectangular prism to write a formula for its surface area.
We use a variable to label each dimension.
The prism has length *l*, width *w*, and height *h*.

In the net, there are 3 pairs of congruent rectangles.
The surface area of the prism is the sum of the areas of the rectangles.

**Remember that *lw* means *l* × *w*.**

The surface area of the prism = $2lh + 2lw + 2hw$
We write: $SA = 2lh + 2lw + 2hw$

We can use this formula to find the surface area of a rectangular prism, without drawing a net first.

## Example

Find the surface area of this rectangular prism.

## Solution

Use the formula:
$SA = 2lh + 2lw + 2hw$
Substitute: $l = 15$, $h = 8$, and $w = 10$

$SA = 2(15 \times 8) + 2(15 \times 10) + 2(8 \times 10)$
$= 2(120) + 2(150) + 2(80)$
$= 240 + 300 + 160$
$= 700$

The surface area of the rectangular prism is 700 cm².

# Practice

**Visualize the net. How does that help to find the surface area?**

**1.** Find the surface area of each rectangular prism.

a)  4 cm   4 cm   8 cm

b)  6 cm   6 cm   6 cm

c)  2 cm   3 cm   7 cm

**2.** Use isometric dot paper or plain paper.
Sketch a rectangular prism with these dimensions:
6 cm by 3 cm by 2 cm.
Find the surface area of the prism.

**3.** Find the surface area of each rectangular prism.

a)  3.6 cm   5.5 cm   2.0 cm

b)  4.5 cm   7.2 cm   3.0 cm

c)  5.8 cm   5.0 cm   3.5 cm

## Mental Math

Estimate each product.
What strategies did you use?

Order the products from least to greatest.

- 24.8 × 3.2
- 35.2 × 2.8
- 13.2 × 5.7
- 5.5 × 15.5

**4.** Use linking cubes.
   **a)** Find the surface area of a cube with edge length 1 unit.
   **b)** What if the edge length is doubled?
   What happens to the surface area?
   Make a new cube to find out.
   **c)** What if the edge length is tripled?
   What happens to the surface area?
   Make a new cube to find out.
   **d)** Predict the surface area of a cube with edge length 4 units.
   Explain your prediction. Make a new cube to check.

**5.** **a)** Find a rectangular prism in the classroom.
   Measure its length, width, and height.
   Find its surface area.
   **b)** Suppose each dimension of
   the prism is halved.
   What happens to the
   surface area? Explain.

3.5 Surface Area of a Rectangular Prism    **99**

**6.** Tanya paints the walls of her family room.
The room measures 3 m by 4 m by 7 m.
The walls need 2 coats of paint. A 4-L can of paint covers 40 m².
a) How much paint should Tanya buy?
b) What assumptions do you make? Explain.

**7.** **Assessment Focus**  Sketch a rectangular prism. Label its
dimensions. What do you think happens to the surface area of a
prism when its length is doubled? Its length is halved?
Investigate to find out. Show your thinking.

**8.** Each object has the shape of a rectangular prism, but one
face or parts of faces are missing. Find each surface area.

a)

10 cm
4 cm   14 cm   7 cm
22 cm

b)

10 cm   10 cm
10 cm   4 cm
4 cm

c)

25 cm
10 cm
18 cm

**9.** The surface area of a cube is 54 cm².
a) What is the area of one face of the cube?
b) What is the length of one edge of the cube?

**Take It Further**

**10.** A 400-g cereal box measures 20 cm by 7 cm by 31 cm.
A 750-g cereal box measures 24 cm by 9 cm by 33 cm.
a) Find the surface area of each box.
b) What is an approximate ratio of surface areas?
What is an approximate ratio of masses?
c) Compare the ratios in part b.
Do you expect the ratios to be equal? Explain.

**11.** A rectangular prism has a square base with area 4 m².
The surface area of the prism is 48 m².
What are the dimensions of the prism?

**12.** A rectangular prism has faces with these areas: 12 cm², 24 cm²,
and 18 cm². What are the dimensions of the prism? Explain.

**Reflect**

Explain how to find the surface area of a rectangular prism
using a formula. Include an example in your explanation.

# 3.6 Volume of a Rectangular Prism

Focus Use a formula to calculate the volume of
a rectangular prism.

## Explore

Work in a group.
You will need several empty cereal boxes and a ruler.

➤ Find the volumes of 3 cereal boxes.
➤ Write a formula you can use to find the volume of a
rectangular prism.
➤ Measure a 4th cereal box. Substitute its dimensions in your
formula to check that your formula is correct.

### Reflect & Share

Compare the formulas for the volume of a rectangular prism and
the area of a rectangle. What do you notice? Explain.

## Connect

Recall that the volume of a
rectangular prism is:
Volume = base area × height

**The base of a rectangular prism can be any face of the prism.**

The base of the prism is a rectangle.
Label the length $l$ and the width $w$.
Then, the area of the base is $l \times w$,
or $lw$.

**The height is measured from the base to the opposite face. The height is perpendicular to the base.**

Label the height $h$.
Volume = base area × height
$$V = lw \times h$$
$$V = lwh$$
The volume of a rectangular prism is: $V = lwh$

If we let $A$ represent the area of the base,
then $A = lw$.

Another way to write the volume is: $V = A \times h$,
or $V = Ah$

3.6 Volume of a Rectangular Prism **101**

## Example

A deck of 54 cards fits in a box with dimensions 6.5 cm by 9.0 cm by 1.6 cm. What is the volume of the box? Give the answer to the nearest cubic centimetre.

**Solution**

Recall that, when the dimensions are measured in centimetres (cm), the volume is measured in cubic centimetres (cm³).

Draw a diagram.
The box is a rectangular prism.
Label each dimension.
Use the formula: $V = lwh$
Substitute: $l = 9.0$, $w = 6.5$, and $h = 1.6$
$V = 9.0 \times 6.5 \times 1.6$  Use a calculator.
   $= 93.6$
The volume is 93.6 cm³, or about 94 cm³.

# Practice

Use a calculator when it helps.

**1.** For each rectangular prism: find the area of its base, then find its volume.

a)

b)

c)

**2.** Find the volume of each rectangular prism.

a)

b)

c)

**3.** Use linking cubes.
Make all possible rectangular prisms with volume 36 units³.
Sketch each prism you make.
Label each prism with its dimensions in units.
How do you know you have found all possible prisms?

**4.** Philip made fudge that filled a 20-cm by 21-cm by 3-cm pan.
   **a)** What is the volume of the fudge?
   **b)** Philip shares the fudge with his classmates. There are 30 people in the class. How much fudge will each person get?
   **c)** How should Philip cut the fudge so each person gets the same size piece? Sketch the cuts he should make.
   **d)** What are the dimensions of each piece of fudge?

**5.** Sketch a rectangular prism. Label its dimensions.
   What do you think happens to the volume of the prism when:
   **a)** its length is doubled?
   **b)** its length and width are doubled?
   **c)** its length, width, and height are doubled?
   Investigate to find out. Show your work.
   Will the results be true for all rectangular prisms?
   How do you know?

**6.** How can you double the volume of a rectangular prism?
   Does its surface area double, too? Explain.

**7.** **Assessment Focus**   Use linking cubes.
   **a)** How many rectangular prisms can you make with 2 cubes? 3 cubes? 4 cubes? 5 cubes? 6 cubes? and so on, up to 20 cubes?
   **b)** How many cubes do you need to make exactly 1 prism? Exactly 2 prisms? Exactly 3 prisms? Exactly 4 prisms?
   **c)** What patterns do you see in your answers to part b?

**8. a)** Sketch 3 different rectangular prisms with volume 24 cm³.
   **b)** Which prism has the greatest surface area? The least surface area?
   **c)** Try to find a prism with a greater surface area. Describe the shape of this prism.
   **d)** Try to find a prism with a lesser surface area. Describe the shape of this prism.

**Reflect**

Suppose you know the volume of a rectangular prism.
How can you find its dimensions? Use words and pictures to explain.

# Decoding Word Problems

## 1 READ the problem.

- Do I understand all the words?
- Highlight those words I don't understand. Whom can I ask?
- Are there key words that give me clues? Circle these words.

David, Jennifer, and Mark collect baseball cards. Jennifer has the most cards. She has 15 more cards than David. David has 4 times as many cards as Mark has today. Mark often loses some of his cards. This morning Mark has 18 cards. How many baseball cards does Jennifer have?

## 2 THINK about the problem.

- What is the problem about?
- What information am I given?
- Am I missing any information?
- Is this problem like another problem I have solved before?

## STRATEGIES to consider . . .

Use a model.
Make an organized list.
Make a table.
Use logical reasoning.
Solve a simpler problem.
Draw a diagram.
Guess and check.
Use a pattern.
Work backward.
Draw a graph.

## 3 MAKE a plan.

- What strategy should I use?
- Would counters, geometric figures, other materials, calculators, and so on, help?

## 4 TRY out the plan.

- Is the plan working? Should I try something else?
- Have I shown *all* my work?

## 5 LOOK back.

- Does my answer make sense? How can I check?
- Is there another way to solve this problem?
- How do I know my answer is correct?
- Have I answered the problem?

## 6 EXTEND.

- Ask "What if …?" questions. What if the numbers were different? What if there were more options?
- Make up similar problems of your own.
- STRETCH your thinking.

Review any lesson with

online tutorial

## What Do I Need to Know?

✓ Perimeter of a rectangle:
$P = 2(b + h)$

✓ Area of a rectangle:
$A = bh$

✓ Perimeter of a square:
$P = 4s$

✓ Area of a square:
$A = s^2$

✓ Volume of a cube:
$V = c^3$

✓ Surface area of a cube:
$SA = 6c^2$

✓ Surface area of a rectangular prism:
$SA = 2lh + 2lw + 2hw$

✓ Volume of a rectangular prism:
$V = lwh$
or $V = Ah$, where $A = lw$

**LESSON**

**3.1** **1.** Sketch the front, back, side, and top views of each object. Use square dot paper, plain paper, or *The Geometer's Sketchpad*.

**a)**

**b)**

**c)**

**3.2** **2. a)** Identify the view and the objects on each sign.

**i)** Railway Crossing Ahead

**ii)** Fishing Area

**b)** Design a new sign from a different view. Sketch your design.

**3.3** **3.** This is a net for an octahedron.

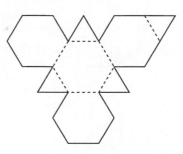

**a)** Fold a large copy of the net. Describe the object. Why do you think it is called an octahedron?

**b)** How is the object you built different from a regular octahedron?

**3.4** **4.** Find the area of each figure.
**a)** a square with side length 7 cm
**b)** a rectangle with base 12 m and height 3 m

**5.** A cube has edge length $c$.
**a)** Write a formula for the surface area of the cube.
**b)** Use the formula to find the surface area when $c$ is 4 cm.

**6.** A children's play area is 90 m long and 44 m wide. A fence will enclose the area.
**a)** How much fencing is needed?
**b)** Fencing comes in 12-m bundles. Each bundle costs $35. How much will the fence cost? Justify your answer.

3.5
3.6

**7.** Find the surface area and volume of each rectangular prism.

a)

6 m
2 m
3 m

b)

8 cm
3 cm
3 cm

c)

50 cm
50 cm
50 cm

**8.** Elizabeth pastes wallpaper on 3 walls of her bedroom. She paints the 4th wall. This is one of the smaller walls. The dimensions of the room are 3 m by 5 m by 6 m. A roll of wallpaper covers about 5 m². A 4-L can of paint covers about 40 m².

a) How much wallpaper and paint should Elizabeth buy?

b) What assumptions do you make?

**9.** The surface area and volume of a cube have the same numerical value. Find the dimensions of this cube. How many answers can you find?

**10.** Sketch all possible rectangular prisms with a volume of 28 m³. Each edge length is a whole number of metres. Label each prism with its dimensions. Calculate the surface area of each prism.

**11.** In *Gulliver's Travels* by Jonathan Swift, Gulliver visits a land where each of his dimensions is 12 times as large as that of the inhabitants.

a) Assume you can be modelled as a rectangular prism. Measure your height, width, and thickness.

b) Suppose you were one of the inhabitants. What would Gulliver's dimensions be?

c) Use your dimensions. Calculate your surface area and volume.

d) Calculate Gulliver's surface area and volume.

**12.** The volume, V, and base area, A, of a rectangular prism are given. Find the height of each prism. Sketch the prism. What are possible dimensions for the prism? Explain.

a) $V = 18$ m³, $A = 6$ m²

b) $V = 60$ cm³, $A = 15$ cm²

**13.** Samya is making candles. She uses a 1-L milk carton as a mould. Its base is a 7-cm square. Samya pours 500 mL of wax into the carton. Recall that 1 mL = 1 cm³. Approximately how tall will the candle be? Justify your answer.

# Practice Test

1. Build the letter H with linking cubes.
   Draw the front, back, side, and top views.

2. Fold a copy of this net.
   a) Describe the object.
      What name could
      you give it?
      Justify your answer.
   b) Sketch the object.

3. Find the surface area and volume of this rectangular prism.

4. Each edge length of a rectangular prism is 7 cm.
   a) Sketch the prism.
   b) Use formulas to find its volume and surface area.

5. Here are the dimensions of two designs for a sandbox for the
   primary playground. Each sandbox is a rectangular prism.
   One design is 3 m by 3 m by 30 cm.
   A second design is 3.25 m by 3.25 m by 25 cm.
   a) Sketch each sandbox. Include its dimensions.
   b) Compare the designs. For each design, calculate the area
      of material needed to build it and the volume of sand
      it will hold.
   c) Which sandbox should be built? Justify your answer.

6. Think about the nets you have folded and the solids
   you have made.
   Suppose you are a tent manufacturer.
   Which net would you use to make a tent?
   Explain why it would be a good tent design.

Suppose you are planning to sell baked goods at the
local charity bake sale.
You have to decide the selling price for your baked goods.
You want to make sure that the price covers the cost of the
ingredients and the packaging.

Decide on the baked goods you will sell.
For example, here is a recipe for Rice Krispies Treats.

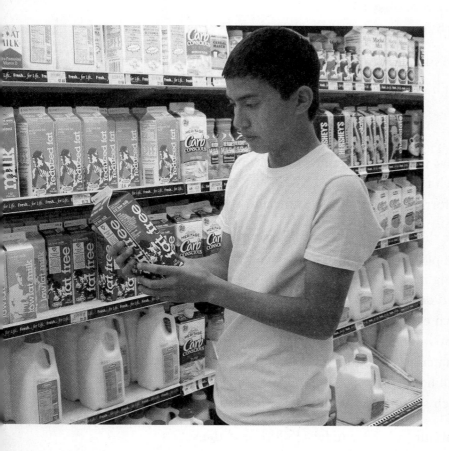

### Rice Krispies Treats

50 mL margarine
250 g marshmallows
1.5 L Rice Krispies

Melt the margarine.
Add marshmallows and
stir until melted.
Remove from heat.
Add Rice Krispies.
Stir until the Rice Krispies
are coated.
Press mixture into
greased 32-cm
by 23-cm pan.
When mixture is cool,
cut into squares.

Use this recipe or find your own recipe for treats.
How many batches of treats will you make?
Calculate how much of each ingredient you need.
Use grocery flyers to find how much the ingredients will cost.

1. Calculate the cost of 1 batch of treats.

2. How many treats will you sell in 1 package?
   Design a box as the package for your treats.
   Decide if the box is open and covered with plastic wrap,
   or if the box is closed.
   Draw a 3-D picture of your box.
   Sketch a net for your box.

3. Calculate the surface area and volume of your box.
   Suppose the cost of cardboard is 50¢/m².
   How many boxes can you make from 1 m² of cardboard?
   How much does each box cost?
   What other costs are incurred to make the boxes?
   What assumptions do you make?

4. Draw the top, front, back,
   and side views of your box.

5. How much will you sell
   1 box of treats for?
   Justify your answer.
   Show how the selling
   price of the treats covers
   the cost of all the
   things you bought.

## Check List

Your work
should show:

✓ all calculations
  in detail

✓ all sketches clearly
  labelled

✓ a clear explanation
  of your results

✓ how you decided the
  selling price of 1 box
  of treats

## Reflect on the Unit

Write a paragraph to tell what you have learned about polyhedra in this unit.
Try to include something from each lesson in the unit.

## Ratios in Scale Drawings

Work with a partner.

A **scale drawing** is larger or smaller than the original drawing or object, but has the same shape. The scale of the drawing is the ratio of a length on the scale drawing to the same length on the original drawing or object.

**Materials:**
- 1-cm grid paper
  2-cm grid paper
  0.5-cm grid paper
- a ruler

Polygons that have the same shape but different sizes are **similar**.

As you complete this *Investigation*, include all your work in a report that you will hand in.

### Part 1

How are the ratios of corresponding sides in similar polygons related?

➤ Use grid paper.
  Draw a polygon with vertices where the grid lines meet.
  Trade drawings with your partner.

- Draw a similar polygon that is larger or smaller than the polygon drawn by your partner. You can use the same sheet of grid paper or a sheet with different grid dimensions. Your drawing is a scale drawing of the polygon.
- Measure and record the lengths of the sides of the two polygons.
- Compare the lengths of corresponding sides of the two polygons. What are the ratios? Are the ratios the same for each pair? Explain.
- Predict the ratio of the perimeters of the polygons. Check your prediction.
- Compare your findings with those of your partner. Explain any differences.

## Part 2

How are the ratios of corresponding sides related to the ratios of the areas of the polygons?

- Draw a polygon with vertices where grid lines meet. Draw a similar polygon that is larger. What is the ratio of the corresponding sides?
- Predict the ratio of the area of the original polygon to the area of the second polygon. Explain your reasoning for making this prediction.
- Find the area of each polygon. What is the ratio of the two areas?
- How does your prediction compare to your findings? Explain any differences.
- How is the ratio of the corresponding sides of the polygons related to the ratio of the areas of the polygons?

## Take It Further

- Suppose you have to enlarge a polygon so that its area is doubled. Should you double the length of each side? Explain. Use an example in your explanation.
- Suppose you have to enlarge a polygon so that its area is four times its original area. How would you do that?
- What patterns do you see? How could you use these patterns to enlarge a polygon even more?

# Fractions and Decimals

Many newspapers and magazines sell advertising space. Why do small companies run small advertisements?

Selling advertising space is a good way to raise funds. Students at Garden Avenue School plan to sell advertising space in their yearbook.

How can fractions and decimals be used in advertising space and advertising rates?

## What You'll Learn

- Add and subtract fractions.
- Multiply a fraction by a whole number.
- Compare and order decimals.
- Multiply and divide decimals.
- Use order of operations with decimals.
- Solve problems using fractions and decimals.

## Why It's Important

- You use fractions when you share or divide.
- You use decimals when you shop and when you measure.

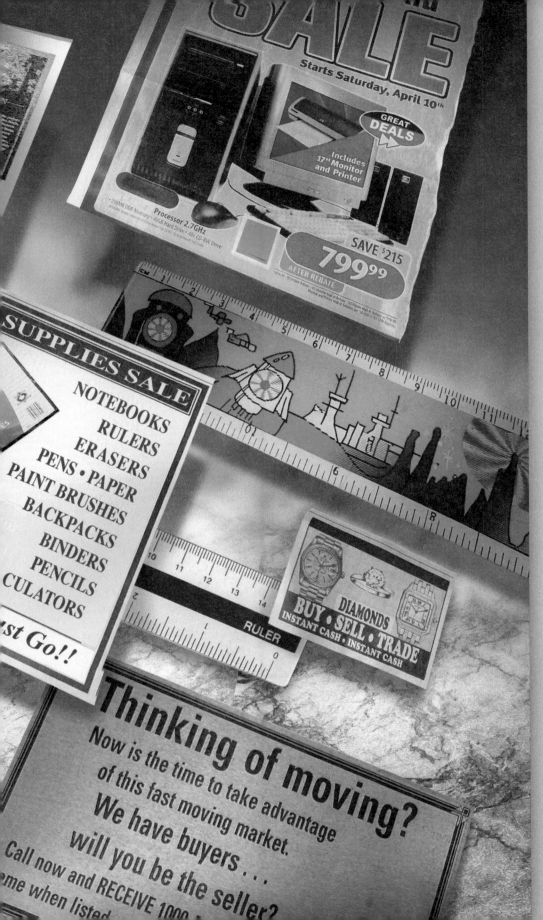

## Key Words

- fraction strips
- equivalent fractions
- related denominators
- unrelated denominators
- common denominator
- lowest common denominator
- unit fraction
- terminating decimal
- repeating decimal

# Skills You'll Need

## Adding and Subtracting Fractions with Pattern Blocks

Let the yellow hexagon represent 1:

Then the red trapezoid
represents $\frac{1}{2}$:

the blue rhombus
represents $\frac{1}{3}$:

and the green triangle
represents $\frac{1}{6}$:

### Example 1

Use Pattern Blocks to add and subtract.

a) $\frac{1}{3} + \frac{1}{2}$

b) $\frac{1}{2} - \frac{1}{3}$

### Solution

a) $\frac{1}{3} + \frac{1}{2}$

b) $\frac{1}{2} - \frac{1}{3}$

Show $\frac{1}{2}$.    Cover $\frac{1}{3}$.

$\frac{1}{3}$     +     $\frac{1}{2}$     =     $\frac{5}{6}$

$\frac{1}{2} - \frac{1}{3} = \frac{1}{6}$    $\frac{1}{6}$ is not covered.

## ✓ Check

**1.** Use Pattern Blocks to add.

a) $\frac{1}{3} + \frac{2}{3}$          b) $\frac{4}{6} + \frac{1}{6}$          c) $\frac{7}{6} + \frac{1}{2}$          d) $\frac{5}{6} + \frac{2}{3}$

**2.** Use Pattern Blocks to subtract.

a) $\frac{5}{6} - \frac{2}{6}$          b) $\frac{2}{3} - \frac{1}{6}$          c) $\frac{3}{2} - \frac{2}{3}$          d) $\frac{5}{6} - \frac{2}{3}$

# Multiplying by 0.1, 0.01, and 0.001

We can use patterns to multiply by 0.1, 0.01, and 0.001.
We can show products on a place-value chart.

|  | Thousands | Hundreds | Tens | Ones • | Tenths | Hundredths | Thousandths |
|---|---|---|---|---|---|---|---|
| 24 × 100 | 2 | 4 | 0 | 0 • | | | |
| 24 × 10 | | 2 | 4 | 0 • | | | |
| 24 × 1 | | | 2 | 4 • | | | |
| 24 × 0.1 | | | | 2 • | 4 | | |
| 24 × 0.01 | | | | 0 • | 2 | 4 | |
| 24 × 0.001 | | | | 0 • | 0 | 2 | 4 |

On the chart:
- To multiply by 0.1, move each digit 1 place to the right.
- To multiply by 0.01, move each digit 2 places to the right.
- To multiply by 0.001, move each digit 3 places to the right.

To get the product:
- Move the decimal point 1 place to the left.
- Move the decimal point 2 places to the left.
- Move the decimal point 3 places to the left.

## Example 2

Multiply.
**a)** $372 \times 0.1$　　　　**b)** $56 \times 0.01$　　　　**c)** $41 \times 0.001$

### Solution

Mark the decimal point in the whole number.
**a)** $372. \times 0.1 = 37.2$　　　　The decimal point moves 1 place to the left.
**b)** $56. \times 0.01 = 0.56$　　　　The decimal point moves 2 places to the left.
**c)** $41. \times 0.001 = 0.041$　　　Write zeros as placeholders. Then move the decimal point 3 places to the left.

## ✓ Check

**3.** Multiply.
　**a)** $5 \times 0.1$　　　　**b)** $98 \times 0.1$　　　　**c)** $124 \times 0.1$
　**d)** $326 \times 0.01$　　**e)** $72 \times 0.01$　　**f)** $6 \times 0.01$
　**g)** $56 \times 0.001$　　**h)** $276 \times 0.001$　**i)** $8 \times 0.001$

## Operations with Decimals

### Example 3

Evaluate.

**a)** $82.34 + 4.7$     **b)** $79.1 - 43.8$     **c)** $426.31 \times 2$     **d)** $9.47 \div 2$

### Solution

**a)** $82.34 + 4.7$

Add the hundredths.
Add the tenths: 10 tenths = 1 whole
Add the ones. Add the tens.

Estimate: $80 + 5 = 85$

$$\begin{array}{r} \overset{1}{8}2.34 \\ + \;4.7 \\ \hline 87.04 \end{array}$$

**b)** $79.1 - 43.8$

To subtract the tenths, trade 1 whole for 10 tenths.
Subtract the ones. Subtract the tens.

Estimate: $80 - 40 = 40$

$$\begin{array}{r} 7\overset{8}{9}.\overset{11}{1} \\ - \;43.8 \\ \hline 35.3 \end{array}$$

**c)** $426.31 \times 2$

Ignore the decimal point.
Multiply as you would with whole numbers.
Place the decimal point in the answer by estimation:
$426.31 \times 2$ is about $400 \times 2 = 800$
So, $426.31 \times 2 = 852.62$

Estimate: $400 \times 2 = 800$

$$\begin{array}{r} 426.31 \\ \times \quad\; 2 \\ \hline 852.62 \end{array}$$

**d)** $9.47 \div 2$

Use short division.
Divide 9 ones by 2. There is 1 whole left.
Trade 1 whole for 10 tenths.
Divide 14 tenths by 2.
Divide 7 hundredths by 2. There is 1 hundredth left.
Trade 1 hundredth for 10 thousandths. Divide 10 thousandths by 2.
So, $9.47 \div 2 = 4.735$

Estimate: $10 \div 2 = 5$

$$2 \,\overline{\left)\, 9.^{1}47^{1}0 \right.}$$
$$4.\,73\,5$$

---

✓ **Check**

**4.** Evaluate.

**a)** $12.3 + 3.5$     **b)** $21.41 - 13.8$     **c)** $31.47 \times 4$     **d)** $7.44 \div 2$

**e)** $182.34 \times 7$     **f)** $52.103 + 71.81$     **g)** $49.35 \div 3$     **h)** $138.97 \times 6$

# Comparing and Ordering Decimals

Here are two ways to order these decimals from least to greatest: 1.84, 2.10, 1.80, 1.89
➤ Use a number line.
   Mark each decimal on a number line in hundredths from 1.75 to 2.15.
   1.84 is between 1.80 and 1.85, but closer to 1.85.
   1.89 is between 1.85 and 1.90, but closer to 1.90.

➤ Use place value.
   **1.84, 2.10, 1.80, 1.89**
   In the ones place, the least digit is 1.
   Three decimals have 1 as a ones digit.
   Compare these 3 decimals: 1.8**4**, 1.8**0**, 1.8**9**
   In the tenths place, each decimal has the digit 8.
   So, look in the hundredths place:
   The least hundredths digit is 0; so, 1.80 is the least decimal.
   The next hundredths digit is 4; so, 1.84 is the next largest decimal.
   The next hundredths digit is 9; so, 1.89 is the next largest decimal.
So, from least to greatest: 1.80, 1.84, 1.89, 2.10

## Example 4

Compare each pair of decimals. Place > or < between each pair.
**a)** 0.5 and 0.08                    **b)** 47.305 and 47.5

### Solution

**a)** 0.5 and 0.08
   Both decimals have 0 ones.
   In the tenths place, 5 > 0
   So, 0.5 > 0.08

**b)** 47.305 and 47.**5**
   Both decimals have 4 tens and 7 ones.
   In the tenths place, 3 < 5
   So, 47.305 < 47.5

## ✓ Check

**5.** Order the numbers in each set from least to greatest.
   **a)** 7.32, 4.116, 3.79, 4.12, 3.1        **b)** 4.4, 0.62, 2.591, 0.65, 4.15
   **c)** 1.25, 3.62, 1.43, 2.81, 2.55        **d)** 3.669, 1.752, 3.68, 2.67, 1.8

We can use an area model to show fractions of one whole.

## Explore

Work with a partner.

Your teacher will give you a copy of the map.

The map shows a section of land owned by 8 families.

- What fraction of the land did each family own?
  What strategies did you use?

Four families sold land to the other 4 families.

- Use the clues below to draw the new map.
- Write addition equations, such as $\frac{1}{2} + \frac{1}{4} = \frac{3}{4}$, to keep track of the land sales.

**CLUES**

**1:** When all the sales were finished, four families owned all the land – Smith, Perry, Haynes, and Chan.

**2:** Each owner can walk on her or his land without having to cross someone else's property.

**3:** Smith now owns $\frac{1}{2}$ of the land.

**4:** Perry kept $\frac{1}{2}$ of her land, and sold the other half to Chan.

**5:** Haynes bought land from two other people. He now owns $\frac{3}{16}$ of the land.

**6:** Chan now owns the same amount of land as Haynes.

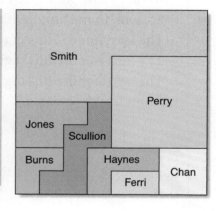

### Reflect & Share

Did you find any equivalent fractions? How do you know?
Which clues helped you most to draw the new map?
Explain how they helped.

## Connect

This circle shows equivalent fractions.

$\frac{2}{5} = \frac{4}{10}$

The circle also shows:
$\frac{1}{2} + \frac{2}{5} + \frac{1}{10} = 1$

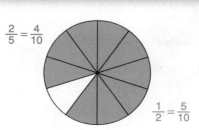

$\frac{1}{2} = \frac{5}{10}$

You can model fractions with strips of paper called **fraction strips**.

Here are more fraction strips and some equivalent fractions they show.

$$\frac{1}{4} = \frac{2}{8}$$

$$\frac{1}{2} = \frac{2}{4} = \frac{4}{8}$$

To add $\frac{1}{4} + \frac{1}{2}$, estimate first.

You know that $\frac{1}{2} + \frac{1}{2} = 1$. Since $\frac{1}{4} < \frac{1}{2}$, then $\frac{1}{4} + \frac{1}{2} < 1$

Use fraction strips to add. Align the strips for $\frac{1}{4}$ and $\frac{1}{2}$.

Find a single strip that has the same length as the two strips.

There are 2 single strips: $\frac{6}{8}$ and $\frac{3}{4}$.

So, $\frac{1}{4} + \frac{1}{2} = \frac{6}{8}$

And, $\frac{1}{4} + \frac{1}{2} = \frac{3}{4}$

$\frac{3}{4}$ and $\frac{6}{8}$ are

**equivalent fractions.**

They represent the
same amount.

The strip on the left, labeled **1**:

**This strip represents 1 whole.**

---

**Example**

Use fraction strips to add.

$\frac{1}{3} + \frac{2}{4}$

Estimate: $\frac{1}{3} < \frac{1}{2}$; $\frac{2}{4} = \frac{1}{2}$
So, $\frac{1}{3} + \frac{2}{4} < 1$

**Solution**

$\frac{1}{3} + \frac{2}{4}$

Use the $\frac{1}{3}$- and $\frac{2}{4}$-
fraction strips.

These strips align with
the $\frac{5}{6}$-strip.

$\frac{1}{3} + \frac{2}{4} = \frac{5}{6}$

Use models.

**1.** Which fraction is greater? How do you know?

a) $\frac{2}{3}, \frac{2}{5}$      b) $\frac{3}{4}, \frac{2}{3}$      c) $\frac{5}{8}, \frac{3}{5}$      d) $\frac{3}{4}, \frac{5}{6}$

**2. a)** Add.

i) $\frac{1}{5} + \frac{1}{5}$      ii) $\frac{2}{3} + \frac{1}{3}$      iii) $\frac{4}{10} + \frac{3}{10}$      iv) $\frac{1}{4} + \frac{2}{4}$

**b)** Look at your work in part a.
How else could you add fractions with the same denominator?

**3.** Add. Estimate first.

a) $\frac{1}{5} + \frac{1}{10}$      b) $\frac{1}{2} + \frac{1}{3}$      c) $\frac{1}{6} + \frac{1}{3}$      d) $\frac{1}{4} + \frac{1}{8}$

**4.** Add. Estimate first.

a) $\frac{2}{4} + \frac{3}{8}$      b) $\frac{2}{3} + \frac{1}{6}$      c) $\frac{2}{5} + \frac{2}{10}$      d) $\frac{3}{6} + \frac{4}{8}$

**5.** Find 2 fractions that have a sum of 1.
Try to do this as many ways as you can.

**6.** Meena's family had a pizza for dinner. The pizza was cut into
8 equal pieces. Meena ate 1 piece, her brother ate 2 pieces,
and her mother ate 3 pieces.

**a)** What fraction of the pizza did Meena eat? Her brother eat?
Her mother eat?

**b)** Which person's fraction can you write in more than one way?
Explain.

**c)** What fraction of the pizza was eaten? What fraction was left?

**7.** Find the missing number that makes both sides equal.

a) $\frac{1}{5} + \frac{1}{2} = \frac{\square}{10}$      b) $\frac{\square}{10} + \frac{2}{5} = \frac{6}{10}$      c) $\frac{1}{2} + \frac{3}{\square} = \frac{7}{8}$

**8.** **Assessment Focus**   Boris added 2 fractions. Their sum was $\frac{5}{6}$.
Which 2 fractions might Boris have added?
Find as many pairs of fractions as you can.

---

**Number Strategies**

A loonie has a
diameter of about
25 mm. About how
many loonies, laid
side by side, would
there be in 1 km?

---

**Reflect**

Write 4 equivalent fractions.
How are these fractions the same? How are they different? Explain.

# Join the Dots

**HOW TO PLAY THE GAME:**

**1.** Use dot paper. Mark an array of 49 dots.

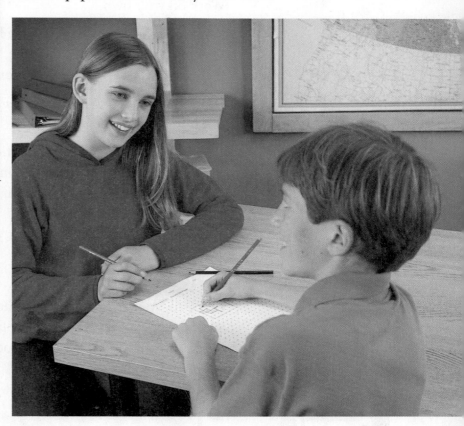

**YOU WILL NEED**

Square dot paper

**NUMBER OF PLAYERS**

2 or more

**GOAL OF THE GAME**

To write the greatest number of equivalent fractions

**What if you used a square array of 81 dots. How would this affect the game?**

**2.** Take turns to join 2 dots.

**3.** The player who completes a square claims that square by writing her initials in it.

**4.** Continue playing until all squares are claimed.

**5.** Each player writes the squares he has as a fraction of the whole.

**6.** The winner is the player who can write the greatest number of equivalent fractions for her share.

**Focus** | Add fractions using circles or fraction strips.

## Explore

Work on your own.

Baljit trains for cross-country one hour a day.
One day, she ran for $\frac{1}{3}$ of the time, walked for 25 minutes,
then got a second wind and ran for the rest of the time.

How long did Baljit run altogether?
What fraction of the hour is this?

- Use fractions to write an addition equation to show how Baljit spent her hour. Baljit never runs for the whole hour.
- Write another possible training schedule for Baljit. Share it with a classmate.
- Write an additon equation for your classmate's training schedule.

### Reflect & Share

Compare your equations with your classmate's equation.
Were the equations the same? Explain.
When might a clock be a good model for thinking about adding fractions?
When is a clock not a good model?

## Connect

There are many models that help us add fractions.

- We could use clocks to model halves, thirds, fourths, sixths, and twelfths.

$$\frac{1}{2} + \frac{1}{3} + \frac{1}{12} = \frac{11}{12}$$

Circle models are useful when the sum is less than 1.

- When the sum is greater than 1, we could use fraction strips and a number line.

$$\frac{3}{4} + \frac{2}{3} = \frac{17}{12}$$

## Example

Add. $\frac{1}{2} + \frac{4}{5}$

## Solution

$\frac{1}{2} + \frac{4}{5}$

> Estimate:
> $\frac{4}{5}$ is close to 1; so, $\frac{1}{2} + \frac{4}{5} > 1$

Place both strips end-to-end on the halves line.

The right end of the $\frac{4}{5}$-strip does not line up with a fraction on the halves line.

Place both strips on the fifths line.

The right end of the $\frac{4}{5}$-strip does not line up with a fraction on the fifths line.

Find a line on which to place both strips so the end of the $\frac{4}{5}$-strip lines up with a fraction.

The end of the $\frac{4}{5}$-strip lines up with a fraction on the tenths line.

The strips end at $\frac{13}{10}$.

So, $\frac{1}{2} + \frac{4}{5} = \frac{13}{10}$

Use models.

**1.** Write 2 equivalent fractions for each fraction shown.

**a)**
**b)**

**2.** Add.

**a)** $\frac{2}{4} + \frac{3}{4}$     **b)** $\frac{8}{10} + \frac{9}{10}$     **c)** $\frac{3}{5} + \frac{4}{5}$     **d)** $\frac{7}{8} + \frac{7}{8}$

**3.** Find 2 fractions with a sum of $\frac{3}{2}$.
Try to do this as many ways as you can.
Record each way you find.

**4.** Add. Estimate first.

**a)** $\frac{7}{8} + \frac{1}{2}$     **b)** $\frac{7}{10} + \frac{3}{5}$     **c)** $\frac{1}{2} + \frac{3}{4}$     **d)** $\frac{5}{6} + \frac{2}{3}$

**5.** Add. Estimate first.

**a)** $\frac{3}{8} + \frac{3}{4}$     **b)** $\frac{4}{4} + \frac{1}{2}$     **c)** $\frac{2}{2} + \frac{4}{6}$     **d)** $\frac{1}{2} + \frac{9}{10}$

**6.** Use your answers to questions 4 and 5.
**a)** Look at the denominators in each part, and the number line you used to get the answer. What patterns do you see?
**b)** The denominators in each part of questions 4 and 5 are **related denominators**.
Why do you think they have this name?

**7.** Add.

**a)** $\frac{1}{2} + \frac{2}{3}$     **b)** $\frac{1}{2} + \frac{2}{5}$     **c)** $\frac{1}{3} + \frac{3}{4}$     **d)** $\frac{2}{2} + \frac{3}{5}$

**8.** Look at your answers to question 7.
**a)** Look at the denominators in each part, and the number line you used to get the answer. What patterns do you see?
**b)** The denominators in each part of question 7 are called **unrelated denominators**.
Why do you think they have this name?
**c)** When you add 2 fractions with unrelated denominators, how do you decide which number line to use?

**Calculator Skills**

How many days are there in one million seconds?

9. One day Ryan ran for 30 min, rested for 20 min, and then ran for another 45 min. Use fractions of one hour. Write an addition equation that represents his training session.

10. A jug holds 2 cups of liquid. A recipe for punch is $\frac{1}{2}$ cup of orange juice, $\frac{1}{4}$ cup of raspberry juice, $\frac{3}{8}$ cup of grapefruit juice, and $\frac{5}{8}$ cup of lemonade. Is the jug big enough for the punch? Explain.

11. **Assessment Focus**    Use any of the digits 1, 2, 3, 4, 5, 6 only once. Copy and complete. Replace each □ with a number.

$$\frac{□}{□} + \frac{□}{□}$$

   a)  Find as many sums as you can that are between 1 and 2.
   b) Find the least sum that is greater than 1.
   Show your work.

12. Abey and Anoki are eating chocolate bars.
   The bars are the same size.
   Abey has $\frac{3}{4}$ left. Anoki has $\frac{7}{8}$ left.
   How much chocolate is left altogether?

**Take It Further**

13. A pitcher of juice is half empty.
   After $\frac{1}{2}$ cup of juice is added, the pitcher is $\frac{3}{4}$ full.
   How much juice does the pitcher hold when it is full?
   Show your thinking.

14. Which number line would you need to add each pair of fractions? Explain.
   a) $\frac{1}{3} + \frac{1}{8}$      b) $\frac{1}{3} + \frac{1}{5}$      c) $\frac{1}{4} + \frac{1}{5}$      d) $\frac{1}{4} + \frac{1}{6}$

**Reflect**

Which strategies do you use to add 2 fractions?
Include 3 different examples in your answer.

In *Section 4.2*, you used models to add fractions.
A clock model only works with certain fractions.
You may not always have suitable fraction strips.

We need a new strategy we can use to add fractions
without using a model.

## Explore

Work with a partner.

A cookie recipe calls for $\frac{3}{8}$ cup of brown sugar and
$\frac{1}{3}$ cup of white sugar.
How much sugar is needed altogether?
How can you find out?
Show your work.

### Reflect & Share

Describe your strategy.
Will your strategy work with all fractions?

Test it with $\frac{4}{5} + \frac{2}{3}$.

Use models to justify your strategy.

## Connect

We can use equivalent fractions to add $\frac{1}{4} + \frac{1}{3}$.

Use equivalent fractions that have the same denominators.
12 is a multiple of 3 and 4.
12 is a **common denominator**.

$\frac{1}{4} = \frac{3}{12}$ and $\frac{1}{3} = \frac{4}{12}$

So, $\frac{1}{4} + \frac{1}{3} = \frac{3}{12} + \frac{4}{12}$

$= \frac{7}{12}$

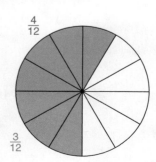

**Both fractions are written
with the same denominator.**

A fraction is in **simplest form** when the numerator and denominator have no common factors.

Look at the pattern in the equivalent fractions below.

$$\frac{1}{4} \;\overset{\times 3}{\underset{\times 3}{=}}\; \frac{3}{12} \qquad\qquad \frac{1}{3} \;\overset{\times 4}{\underset{\times 4}{=}}\; \frac{4}{12}$$

So, to get an equivalent fraction, multiply numerator and denominator by the same number.

We may also get equivalent fractions by dividing.

For example, $\frac{8}{10}$ can be written $\frac{8 \div 2}{10 \div 2} = \frac{4}{5}$  **This fraction is in simplest form.**

## Example 1

Add. $\frac{5}{6} + \frac{2}{9}$

**Solution**

$\frac{5}{6} + \frac{2}{9}$

The common denominator is a multiple of 6 and 9.

List the multiples of 6: 6, 12, **18**, 24, …

List the multiples of 9: 9, **18**, 27, 36, …

18 is the lowest common multiple of 6 and 9.

So, choose 18 as the common denominator.

Estimate:
$\frac{5}{6}$ is close to 1; $\frac{2}{9} < \frac{1}{2}$
So, $\frac{5}{6} + \frac{2}{9}$ is less than $1\frac{1}{2}$.

$$\frac{5}{6} \;\overset{\times 3}{\underset{\times 3}{=}}\; \frac{15}{18} \qquad\qquad \frac{2}{9} \;\overset{\times 2}{\underset{\times 2}{=}}\; \frac{4}{18}$$

**We say that 18 is the lowest common denominator.**

$\frac{5}{6} + \frac{2}{9} = \frac{15}{18} + \frac{4}{18}$

$\qquad\qquad = \frac{19}{18}$  **We can write $\frac{19}{18}$ as a mixed number: $1\frac{1}{18}$**

## Example 2

Add. $\frac{1}{2} + \frac{2}{3} + \frac{3}{4}$

**Solution**

$\frac{1}{2} + \frac{2}{3} + \frac{3}{4}$

2 is a multiple of 4.

Estimate:
$\frac{2}{3} > \frac{1}{2}$ and $\frac{3}{4} > \frac{1}{2}$
So, $\frac{1}{2} + \frac{2}{3} + \frac{3}{4}$ is greater than $1\frac{1}{2}$.

So, the common denominator is a multiple of 3 and 4.

List the multiples of 3: 3, 6, 9, **12**, 15, 18, …

List the multiples of 4: 4, 8, **12**, 16, 20, 24, …

12 is the lowest common multiple of 3 and 4.

So, 12 is the lowest common denominator.

$$\frac{1}{2} + \frac{2}{3} + \frac{3}{4} = \frac{6}{12} + \frac{8}{12} + \frac{9}{12}$$

$$= \frac{23}{12}$$

We can write $\frac{23}{12}$ as a mixed number: $1\frac{11}{12}$

## Practice

A fraction with numerator 1 is a **unit fraction**.

**1.** Add. Use grid paper. Draw a picture to show each sum.

a) $\frac{1}{2} + \frac{1}{3}$     b) $\frac{1}{3} + \frac{1}{5}$     c) $\frac{1}{4} + \frac{1}{5}$     d) $\frac{1}{5} + \frac{1}{6}$

**2.** Copy and complete. Replace each ☐ with a number to make a true sentence.

a) $\frac{3}{12} = \frac{\square}{4}$     b) $\frac{3}{4} = \frac{6}{\square}$     c) $\frac{3}{6} = \frac{\square}{4}$     d) $\frac{6}{8} = \frac{15}{\square}$

**3.** Add. Estimate first.

a) $\frac{4}{5} + \frac{1}{2}$     b) $\frac{3}{4} + \frac{1}{3}$     c) $\frac{2}{3} + \frac{4}{5}$     d) $\frac{2}{3} + \frac{3}{4}$

**4.** Add.

a) $\frac{2}{3} + \frac{2}{9}$     b) $\frac{1}{6} + \frac{5}{12}$     c) $\frac{3}{8} + \frac{1}{2}$     d) $\frac{3}{4} + \frac{7}{8}$

**5.** Add.

a) $\frac{5}{6} + \frac{1}{4}$     b) $\frac{1}{6} + \frac{4}{9}$     c) $\frac{7}{10} + \frac{4}{6}$     d) $\frac{3}{4} + \frac{3}{10}$

**6.** One page of a magazine had 2 advertisements. One was $\frac{1}{8}$ of the page, the other $\frac{1}{16}$. What fraction of the page did these occupy?

**7.** Which sum is greater? How do you know?

$$\frac{2}{3} + \frac{5}{6} \qquad \text{or} \qquad \frac{3}{4} + \frac{4}{5}$$

**8.** Add.

a) $\frac{3}{8} + \frac{1}{2} + \frac{3}{4}$     b) $\frac{1}{4} + \frac{3}{2} + \frac{2}{5}$     c) $\frac{2}{3} + \frac{5}{6} + \frac{4}{9}$

### Mental Math

Multiply.
- $5 \times 27 \times 2$
- $10 \times 3 \times 31$
- $4 \times 9 \times 25$
- $6 \times 20 \times 5$

Which mental math strategies did you use?

**To add 2 mixed numbers:**
Add the whole numbers.
Add the fractions.
Write the sum as a
mixed number.

**9.** Add.

a) $1\frac{1}{6} + 2\frac{1}{2}$     b) $3\frac{1}{3} + 1\frac{1}{2}$     c) $4\frac{1}{6} + 2\frac{3}{8}$

**10.** A recipe for punch calls for $2\frac{2}{3}$ cups of fruit concentrate and $6\frac{3}{4}$ cups of water.

How many cups of punch will the recipe make?

**11.** **Assessment Focus**    Three people shared a pie.
Which statement is true? Can both statements be true?
Use diagrams to show your thinking.

a) Edna ate $\frac{1}{10}$, Farrah ate $\frac{3}{5}$, and Fran ate $\frac{1}{2}$.

b) Edna ate $\frac{3}{10}$, Farrah ate $\frac{1}{5}$, and Fran ate $\frac{1}{2}$.

**Take It Further**    **12.** $\frac{1}{2} + \frac{1}{3} + \frac{1}{6} = 1$

Find 3 other fractions with different denominators
that add to 1.
Explain your strategy.

**13.** Copy this sum. Replace □ with the correct digit.
$2\frac{1}{4} + 1\frac{\square}{3} = 3\frac{7}{12}$

Explain your strategy.

**Reflect**

When you add fractions, and the denominators are different,
how do you add?
Give 2 different examples. Use pictures to show your thinking.

## Explore

Work with a partner.
You will need fraction strips and number lines.

Find 2 fractions with a difference of $\frac{1}{2}$.

How many different pairs of fractions can you find?
Record each pair.

### Reflect & Share

Discuss with your partner.
How are your strategies for subtracting fractions the same as your strategies for adding fractions? How are they different?

## Connect

To subtract $\frac{3}{5} - \frac{1}{2}$, think addition: What do we add to $\frac{1}{2}$ to get $\frac{3}{5}$?
Try the fifths number line.
Place the $\frac{1}{2}$-strip with its right end at $\frac{3}{5}$.

Estimate:
$\frac{3}{5} < 1$ ; so, $\frac{3}{5} - \frac{1}{2} < \frac{1}{2}$

**Equivalent fractions:**
$\frac{3}{5} = \frac{6}{10}$
$\frac{1}{2} = \frac{5}{10}$

The left end of the strip does not line up with a fraction on the line.
Use a number line that has equivalent fractions for halves and fifths.
Put the $\frac{1}{2}$-strip on the tenths number line, with its right end at $\frac{6}{10}$.

The left end of the strip is at $\frac{1}{10}$.
So, $\frac{3}{5} - \frac{1}{2} = \frac{1}{10}$

## Example

Use fraction strips and number lines to subtract.

**a)** $\frac{6}{5} - \frac{4}{5}$          **b)** $\frac{5}{8} - \frac{1}{4}$

## Solution

**a)** $\frac{6}{5} - \frac{4}{5}$

Think addition.

What do we add to $\frac{4}{5}$ to get $\frac{6}{5}$?

Use the fifths number line because
both denominators are 5.

Place the $\frac{4}{5}$-strip on the fifths number line with its right end at $\frac{6}{5}$.

> **Estimate:**
> $\frac{6}{5} > 1, \frac{4}{5} < 1;$
> so, $\frac{6}{5} - \frac{4}{5} < 1$

The left end of the strip is at $\frac{2}{5}$.

So, $\frac{6}{5} - \frac{4}{5} = \frac{2}{5}$

**b)** $\frac{5}{8} - \frac{1}{4}$

Think addition.

What do we add to $\frac{1}{4}$ to get $\frac{5}{8}$?

> **Estimate:**
> $\frac{5}{8}$ is between $\frac{1}{2}$ and 1,
> $\frac{1}{4} < \frac{1}{2}$; so , $\frac{5}{8} - \frac{1}{4} < \frac{1}{2}$

Use a number line that shows equivalent fractions for
eighths and fourths.

That is, use the eighths number line.

Place the $\frac{1}{4}$-strip on the eighths number line with its right
end at $\frac{5}{8}$.

The left end of the strip is at $\frac{3}{8}$.

So, $\frac{5}{8} - \frac{1}{4} = \frac{3}{8}$

Use models.

**1.** Subtract.

a) $\frac{3}{4} - \frac{2}{4}$      b) $\frac{4}{5} - \frac{1}{5}$      c) $\frac{2}{3} - \frac{1}{3}$      d) $\frac{5}{8} - \frac{3}{8}$

**2.** a) Write a rule you could use to subtract fractions with like denominators without using number lines or fraction strips.

b) Write 3 subtraction questions with like denominators.
Use your rule to subtract the fractions.
Use fraction strips and number lines to check your answers.

**3.** Write the subtraction equation that each number line and fraction strip represent.

a)

b)

c)

**Number Strategies**

Find:

• 8 tenths less than 22.23

• 9 hundredths more than 94.43

• 36 hundredths more than 48.425

• 36 thousandths more than 48.425

**4.** Subtract. Estimate first.

a) $\frac{3}{8} - \frac{1}{4}$      b) $\frac{5}{6} - \frac{2}{3}$      c) $\frac{5}{4} - \frac{1}{2}$      d) $\frac{7}{10} - \frac{3}{5}$

**5.** Subtract. Estimate first.

a) $\frac{3}{4} - \frac{1}{2}$      b) $\frac{3}{4} - \frac{3}{8}$      c) $\frac{2}{3} - \frac{1}{6}$      d) $\frac{5}{6} - \frac{1}{2}$

**6.** Aaron has $\frac{2}{3}$ cup of raisins. He gives Raj $\frac{1}{2}$ cup.
How much does Aaron have left?

**7.** Subtract.

a) $\frac{2}{3} - \frac{1}{4}$      b) $\frac{5}{3} - \frac{1}{2}$      c) $\frac{1}{2} - \frac{1}{5}$      d) $\frac{3}{2} - \frac{1}{3}$

**8.** Subtract.

a) $\frac{11}{8} - \frac{3}{4}$  b) $\frac{3}{2} - \frac{2}{3}$  c) $\frac{9}{5} - \frac{3}{2}$  d) $\frac{5}{3} - \frac{5}{6}$

**9.** Subtract.

a) $2 - \frac{1}{2}$  b) $1 - \frac{3}{5}$  c) $2 - \frac{5}{4}$  d) $1 - \frac{2}{3}$

**10.** A cookie recipe calls for $\frac{3}{4}$ cup of chocolate chips.
Spencer has $\frac{2}{3}$ cup. Does he have enough?
If your answer is yes, explain.
If your answer is no, how much more does Spencer need?

**11.** Copy and replace each □ with a number, to make each
statement correct.
Try to do this more than one way.

a) $\frac{3}{4} - \frac{\square}{\square} = \frac{1}{4}$  b) $\frac{\square}{\square} - \frac{1}{5} = \frac{3}{5}$  c) $\frac{\square}{6} - \frac{2}{\square} = \frac{1}{6}$

**12.** **Assessment Focus**  Kelly had $\frac{3}{4}$ of a tank of gas at the
beginning of the week.
At the end of the week, Kelly had $\frac{1}{8}$ of a tank left.

a) Did Kelly use more or less than $\frac{1}{2}$ of a tank? Explain.

b) How much more or less than $\frac{1}{2}$ of a tank did Kelly use?

**13.** a) Which of these differences is greater than $\frac{1}{2}$ ?
How do you know?

i) $\frac{5}{6} - \frac{2}{3}$  ii) $\frac{5}{6} - \frac{1}{2}$  iii) $\frac{5}{6} - \frac{1}{6}$

b) Explain how you found your answers to part a.
Which other way can you find the fractions with
a difference greater than $\frac{1}{2}$? Explain.

**Reflect**

Which pairs of fractions can you *not* subtract using the number
lines and fraction strips you have? Give 3 examples.

# 4.5 Subtracting Fractions

Addition and subtraction are related operations.
You can use what you know about adding fractions to subtract them.

## Explore

Work with a partner.
Use any of the digits 1, 2, 3, 4, 5, 6 only once.
Copy and complete. Replace each □ with a number.

$$\frac{\Box}{\Box} - \frac{\Box}{\Box}$$

Find the least difference greater than 0.
Which strategies did you use?

### Reflect & Share

Compare your least difference with that of another pair of classmates.
Are the differences the same?
If your answer is no, what is the least difference?

## Connect

To subtract $\frac{3}{4} - \frac{1}{6}$, estimate first.
$\frac{3}{4}$ is between $\frac{1}{2}$ and 1, and $\frac{1}{6} < \frac{1}{4}$.
So, $\frac{3}{4} - \frac{1}{6}$ is about $\frac{1}{2}$.
Use equivalent fractions to subtract.
Express $\frac{3}{4}$ and $\frac{1}{6}$ with a common denominator.
Find the lowest common denominator.
List the multiples of 4: 4, 8, **12**, 16, 20, …
List the multiples of 6: 6, **12**, 18, 24, 30, …
The lowest common denominator is 12.

$$\overset{\times 3}{\frac{3}{4}} = \underset{\times 3}{\frac{9}{12}} \qquad \overset{\times 2}{\frac{1}{6}} = \underset{\times 2}{\frac{2}{12}}$$

$$\frac{3}{4} - \frac{1}{6} = \frac{9}{12} - \frac{2}{12}$$
$$= \frac{7}{12}$$

**Think:** 9 twelfths minus 2 twelfths is 7 twelfths.

**Example**

Subtract.

a) $\frac{3}{4} - \frac{5}{8}$                        b) $\frac{3}{2} - \frac{2}{5}$

**Solution**

a) $\frac{3}{4} - \frac{5}{8}$

Since 8 is a multiple of 4, use 8 as the lowest common denominator.

> **Estimate:**
> Both $\frac{3}{4}$ and $\frac{5}{8}$ are between $\frac{1}{2}$ and 1; so, $\frac{3}{4} - \frac{5}{8} < \frac{1}{2}$

$$\frac{3}{4} \overset{\times 2}{=} \frac{6}{8}$$
$$\scriptstyle \times 2$$

$$\frac{3}{4} - \frac{5}{8} = \frac{6}{8} - \frac{5}{8}$$
$$= \frac{1}{8}$$

b) $\frac{3}{2} - \frac{2}{5}$

List the multiples of 2:
2, 4, 6, 8, **10**, 12, …
List the multiples of 5:
5, **10**, 15, 20, …
The lowest common denominator is 10.
Write each fraction with a denominator of 10.

> **Estimate:**
> $\frac{2}{5} < \frac{1}{2}$ ; so, $\frac{3}{2} - \frac{2}{5} > 1$

$$\frac{3}{2} \overset{\times 5}{\underset{\times 5}{=}} \frac{15}{10} \qquad \frac{2}{5} \overset{\times 2}{\underset{\times 2}{=}} \frac{4}{10}$$

$$\frac{3}{2} - \frac{2}{5} = \frac{15}{10} - \frac{4}{10}$$
$$= \frac{11}{10}$$

**We can write $\frac{11}{10}$ as the mixed number $1\frac{1}{10}$.**

---

## Practice

**1.** Subtract.

a) $\frac{4}{5} - \frac{2}{5}$       b) $\frac{2}{3} - \frac{1}{3}$       c) $\frac{7}{9} - \frac{4}{9}$       d) $\frac{5}{7} - \frac{3}{7}$

**2.** Subtract. Estimate first.

a) $\frac{5}{8} - \frac{1}{2}$       b) $\frac{4}{9} - \frac{1}{3}$       c) $\frac{3}{2} - \frac{4}{10}$       d) $\frac{5}{3} - \frac{5}{6}$

**3.** Subtract.

a) $\frac{5}{6} - \frac{2}{9}$  b) $\frac{5}{6} - \frac{2}{4}$  c) $\frac{5}{8} - \frac{3}{12}$  d) $\frac{7}{10} - \frac{4}{15}$

**4.** Subtract. Estimate first.

a) $\frac{3}{4} - \frac{2}{3}$  b) $\frac{5}{2} - \frac{3}{4}$  c) $\frac{4}{5} - \frac{2}{3}$  d) $\frac{5}{4} - \frac{4}{5}$

**5.** Subtract.

a) $\frac{4}{6} - \frac{1}{2}$  b) $\frac{5}{3} - \frac{3}{4}$  c) $\frac{7}{2} - \frac{3}{2}$  d) $\frac{5}{6} - \frac{3}{4}$

**6.** Subtract.

a) $5\frac{5}{7} - 1\frac{2}{7}$  b) $3\frac{4}{9} - 2\frac{1}{6}$  c) $4\frac{3}{10} - 2\frac{1}{5}$  d) $4\frac{3}{5} - 2\frac{1}{2}$

To subtract 2 mixed numbers: Subtract the whole numbers. Subtract the fractions. Write the difference as a mixed number.

**7.** **Assessment Focus**  Terri biked $2\frac{1}{4}$ h on Sunday.
Terri increased the time she biked by $\frac{1}{4}$ h every day.
Sam biked $\frac{1}{2}$ h on Sunday.
Sam increased the time he biked by $\frac{1}{2}$ h every day.

a) Who will bike longer the next Saturday? Explain.
b) For how much longer will this person bike?
c) What did you need to know about fractions to answer these questions?

**Calculator Skills**

Suppose the $\boxed{8}$ key on your calculator is broken. How would you use your calculator to find each answer?

• 18 + 27
• 118 − 85
• 18 × 27
• 225 ÷ 8

**8.** A recipe calls for $\frac{3}{4}$ cup of walnuts and $\frac{2}{3}$ cup of pecans. Which type of nut is used more in the recipe? How much more?

**9.** Write as many different subtraction questions as you can where the answer is $\frac{3}{4}$.

**10.** The difference of 2 fractions is $\frac{1}{2}$.
The lesser fraction is between 0 and $\frac{1}{4}$.
What do you know about the other fraction?

**Reflect**

When you subtract fractions, and the denominators are different, how do you subtract? Give 2 different examples.
Explain your steps.

# Shade One

## HOW TO PLAY THE GAME:

1. Each player chooses a different colour marker.

2. Place the set of fraction cards face down.

3. Player A turns over a card. This is his *target fraction*.

4. Player A could shade the target fraction on one fraction strip, or share the fraction among several fraction strips. However, the total fraction shaded must equal the target fraction.

**For example:** If your target fraction is $\frac{3}{4}$, you could shade from 0 to $\frac{3}{4}$ on the fourths strip, or 0 to $\frac{6}{8}$ on the eighths strip. Or you could shade several fractions that add up to $\frac{3}{4}$. For example, you could shade $\frac{3}{12}$, $\frac{2}{8}$, and $\frac{1}{4}$; or you could shade $\frac{2}{5}$, $\frac{1}{10}$, and $\frac{1}{4}$.

5. Player B turns over the next fraction card. He repeats *Step 4* for his fraction.

6. Play continues with players taking turns to shade the target fraction. If there is not enough of a fraction strip left, and it is impossible to shade the target fraction, that player forfeits his turn. When a player is not able to shade any more fractions, the game is over.

7. The player who shades to complete 1 whole gets 1 point.

8. The person with the most points wins.

## YOU WILL NEED

One gameboard; coloured markers; 1 set of 42 fraction cards

## NUMBER OF PLAYERS

2 or more

## GOAL OF THE GAME

To shade 1 whole on each fraction strip

# Mid-Unit Review

**4.1** **1.** Add. Use fraction strips to help you.

a) $\frac{2}{3} + \frac{1}{6}$  b) $\frac{2}{4} + \frac{1}{3}$

c) $\frac{2}{8} + \frac{2}{4}$  d) $\frac{2}{10} + \frac{3}{5}$

**4.2** **2.** We know that $\frac{1}{2} + \frac{4}{5} = \frac{13}{10}$. Use this result to find each sum.

a) $1\frac{1}{2} + \frac{4}{5}$  b) $5\frac{1}{2} + 2\frac{4}{5}$

**3.** Use models to add.

a) $\frac{4}{5} + \frac{3}{5}$  b) $\frac{2}{3} + \frac{1}{2}$

c) $\frac{1}{2} + \frac{5}{6}$  d) $\frac{3}{2} + \frac{1}{3}$

**4.3** **4.** Add. Estimate first.

a) $\frac{3}{4} + \frac{5}{6}$  b) $\frac{3}{2} + \frac{2}{3}$

c) $\frac{7}{10} + \frac{2}{5}$  d) $\frac{5}{9} + \frac{5}{6}$

**5.** Add.

a) $\frac{2}{5} + \frac{3}{2} + \frac{3}{10}$

b) $\frac{3}{8} + \frac{3}{4} + \frac{1}{2}$

c) $\frac{1}{3} + \frac{5}{6} + \frac{2}{9}$

**6.** Add.

a) $2\frac{1}{3} + 3\frac{1}{3}$

b) $2\frac{1}{4} + 1\frac{1}{3}$

c) $1\frac{3}{4} + 3\frac{3}{8}$

**4.4** **7.** Use models to subtract.

a) $\frac{7}{8} - \frac{3}{4}$  b) $\frac{3}{2} - \frac{3}{5}$

c) $\frac{4}{3} - \frac{5}{6}$  d) $\frac{11}{6} - \frac{2}{3}$

**8.** Peter put $\frac{4}{5}$ cup of chocolate chips into his cookie batter. Samantha put $\frac{7}{8}$ cup into hers. Whose batter contains more chips? How do you know?

**9.** Alex delivered flyers to $\frac{1}{4}$ of her route on Saturday morning. She delivered to $\frac{2}{3}$ of the route on Saturday afternoon, and the remainder on Sunday.

a) What fraction of her route did Alex deliver on Saturday?

b) What fraction did she deliver on Sunday?

**4.5** **10.** Subtract. Estimate first.

a) $\frac{3}{2} - \frac{1}{5}$  b) $\frac{7}{6} - \frac{2}{3}$

c) $\frac{11}{6} - \frac{3}{4}$  d) $\frac{13}{10} - \frac{3}{5}$

**11.** We know that $\frac{9}{8} - \frac{1}{4} = \frac{7}{8}$. Use this result to find each difference. Explain how you did this.

a) $\frac{12}{8} - \frac{1}{4}$  b) $\frac{5}{8} - \frac{1}{4}$

**12.** Subtract.

a) $3\frac{5}{8} - 2\frac{3}{8}$  b) $2\frac{1}{2} - 1\frac{1}{4}$

How many ways can you find this sum?

$2 + 2 + 2 + 2 + 2 + 2 + 2 + 2 + 2$

You can use the same strategies in *Explore*.

## Explore

Work with a partner.

Jan takes $\frac{3}{4}$ h to walk to her music lesson.

Jan has a music lesson once a week, for 9 weeks.

How much time does Jan spend walking to her music lessons?

### Reflect & Share

Compare your strategy for solving the problem with that of another pair of classmates.

Did you get the same answers?

If not, who is correct? Explain.

## Connect

$\frac{1}{5} + \frac{1}{5} + \frac{1}{5} + \frac{1}{5} = \frac{4}{5}$

All the fractions added are $\frac{1}{5}$.

Repeated addition can be written as multiplication.

$\frac{1}{5} + \frac{1}{5} + \frac{1}{5} + \frac{1}{5} = 4 \times \frac{1}{5} = \frac{4}{5}$

We can show this as a picture.

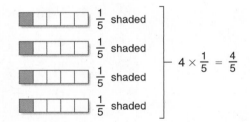

Similarly: $\frac{3}{4} + \frac{3}{4} + \frac{3}{4} + \frac{3}{4} + \frac{3}{4}$

$= 5 \times \frac{3}{4}$

$= \frac{15}{4}$

We can show this as a picture.

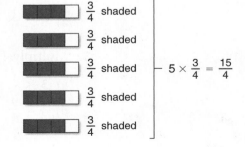

## Example 1

Use multiplication to find this sum.

$$\frac{3}{8} + \frac{3}{8} + \frac{3}{8} + \frac{3}{8} + \frac{3}{8} + \frac{3}{8} + \frac{3}{8} + \frac{3}{8} + \frac{3}{8}$$

**Solution**

$$\frac{3}{8} + \frac{3}{8} + \frac{3}{8} + \frac{3}{8} + \frac{3}{8} + \frac{3}{8} + \frac{3}{8} + \frac{3}{8} + \frac{3}{8} = 9 \times \frac{3}{8}$$

$$= \frac{27}{8}$$

**Think:**
9 times 3 eighths is 27 eighths.

## Example 2

Multiply.

**a)** $\frac{3}{5} \times 5$

**b)** $7 \times \frac{5}{6}$

**Solution**

**a)** $\frac{3}{5} \times 5 = \frac{15}{5}$

$\qquad = 3$

**Think:** $\frac{15}{5}$ means $15 \div 5$, which is 3.

**b)** $7 \times \frac{5}{6} = \frac{35}{6}$

**Think:** 7 times 5 sixths is 35 sixths.

## Practice

1. Write each repeated addition as a multiplication question.

   **a)** $\frac{1}{4} + \frac{1}{4} + \frac{1}{4}$

   **b)** $\frac{2}{7} + \frac{2}{7} + \frac{2}{7} + \frac{2}{7} + \frac{2}{7}$

   **c)** $\frac{3}{10} + \frac{3}{10} + \frac{3}{10} + \frac{3}{10}$

2. Write each multiplication question as repeated addition.
   Draw a picture to show each answer.

   **a)** $5 \times \frac{1}{8}$      **b)** $\frac{2}{5} \times 3$      **c)** $4 \times \frac{5}{12}$

3. Multiply. Draw a picture to show each answer.

   **a)** $3 \times \frac{4}{7}$      **b)** $5 \times \frac{1}{12}$      **c)** $\frac{2}{15} \times 10$

   **d)** $4 \times \frac{9}{4}$      **e)** $\frac{2}{5} \times 7$      **f)** $9 \times \frac{1}{2}$

**4.** Multiply.

a) $3 \times \frac{4}{5}$      b) $5 \times \frac{7}{10}$      c) $\frac{5}{6} \times 6$

d) $\frac{1}{2} \times 5$      e) $12 \times \frac{7}{12}$      f) $\frac{2}{3} \times 9$

**5.** It takes $\frac{2}{3}$ h to pick all the apples on one tree at
Springwater Farms. There are 24 trees.
How long will it take to pick all the apples?
Show your work.

**6. a)** Draw a picture to show each product. What is each answer?

     **i)** $4 \times \frac{3}{10}$      **ii)** $3 \times \frac{4}{10}$

**b)** How are the questions in part a related?
Write 2 more questions like these.
Find each product. What do you notice?

**7.** A cookie recipe calls for $\frac{3}{4}$ cup of oatmeal.
How much oatmeal is needed to make 3 batches of cookies?

**8. Assessment Focus**

     **a)** Draw a picture to show $5 \times \frac{1}{2}$.

     **b)** What meaning can you give to $\frac{1}{2} \times 5$?
     Draw a picture to show your thinking.

**Take It Further**

**9.** Jacob takes $\frac{3}{4}$ h to fill one shelf at the supermarket.
Henry can fill the shelves in half Jacob's time.
There are 15 shelves. Henry and Jacob work together.
How long will it take to fill the shelves? Justify your answer.

---

**Number Strategies**

Calculate each answer.

$6000 \div 10$    $6000 \times 0.1$

$600 \div 10$    $600 \times 0.1$

$60 \div 10$    $60 \times 0.1$

$6 \div 10$    $6 \times 0.1$

What patterns
do you see in
the questions
and answers?

---

**Reflect**

Draw a picture to show why $4 \times \frac{2}{5}$ is the same as $\frac{2}{5} + \frac{2}{5} + \frac{2}{5} + \frac{2}{5}$.
Explain your picture.
Draw a different picture to show the same answer.

# Fractions to Decimals

 Recall that $\frac{1}{10}$ means $1 \div 10$, which is 0.1 as a decimal.

Similarly, $\frac{1}{2}$ means $1 \div 2$, which is 0.5 as a decimal.

0.1 and 0.5 are **terminating decimals**, because each has a definite number of decimal places.

On a calculator, press: $\boxed{1}$ $\boxed{\div}$ $\boxed{11}$ $\boxed{=}$ to display 0.090909091

The calculator rounds up the last digit.
The fraction $\frac{1}{11}$ is a **repeating decimal**.

The decimal for $\frac{1}{11}$ is $0.\overline{09}$, with a bar above the 0 and 9 to show they repeat.

**A period above an equal sign shows the answer is approximate.**

We can round $0.\overline{09}$ to an approximate decimal.
- $0.\overline{09} \doteq 0.1$ to 1 decimal place
- $0.\overline{09} \doteq 0.09$ to 2 decimal places
- $0.\overline{09} \doteq 0.091$ to 3 decimal places

**✓ Check**

1. Investigate other unit fractions; that is, fractions with numerator 1.
   a) Which unit fractions from $\frac{1}{3}$ to $\frac{1}{20}$ produce terminating decimals?
      Which produce repeating decimals? Explain why.
   b) Investigate other fractions.
      For example, how are the decimals for $\frac{1}{6}, \frac{2}{6}, ..., \frac{5}{6}$ related?

2. Investigate fractions with greater denominators.
   For example, how are the decimals for $\frac{1}{9}, \frac{1}{99}, \frac{1}{999}, ...$ related?

3. Which is greater in each case? Justify your answer.
   a) $0.\overline{3}$ or 0.3
   b) $\frac{1}{9}$ or 0.11

To multiply 2 whole numbers, we can use Base Ten Blocks. This picture shows the product

$20 \times 16 = 100 + 100 + 60 + 60$
$\qquad\qquad = 320$

We can also use Base Ten Blocks to multiply a decimal and a whole number.

The flat represents 1.

The rod represents 0.1.

The small cube represents 0.01.

This picture shows the product

$2 \times 1.6 = 1 + 1 + 0.6 + 0.6$
$\qquad\qquad = 3.2$

In *Explore*, you will use Base Ten Blocks to multiply 2 decimals.

## Explore

Work with a partner.
A rectangular tabletop measures 2.4 m by 1.8 m.
Use Base Ten Blocks to find the area of the tabletop.
Record your work on grid paper.

### Reflect & Share

Compare your answer with that of another pair of classmates.
Did you draw the same picture? Explain.
Did you get the same area? Explain.

A rectangular park measures 1.7 km by 2.5 km.

Here are 2 ways to find the area of the park.

➤ Use Base Ten Blocks.

There are 2 flats: $2 \times 1 = 2$
There are 19 rods: $19 \times 0.1 = 1.9$
There are 35 small cubes: $35 \times 0.01 = 0.35$
The total area is $2 + 1.9 + 0.35 = 4.25$
The area of the park is 4.25 km².

➤ Use the method for multiplying 2 whole numbers.
The area, in square kilometres, is $1.7 \times 2.5$.

Multiply: $17 \times 25$

$$\begin{array}{r} 17 \\ \times\ 25 \\ \hline 85 \\ 340 \\ \hline 425 \end{array}$$

Estimate to place the decimal point in the answer.
$1.7 \times 2.5$ is about $2 \times 3 = 6$
So, the product is 4.25.
The area of the park is 4.25 km².

**Example 1**

Multiply. $5.8 \times 9.7$

**Solution**

$5.8 \times 9.7$
Multiply: $58 \times 97$

Estimate to place the decimal point.
$5.8 \times 9.7$ is about $6 \times 10 = 60$.
So, the product is 56.26.

$$\begin{array}{r} 58 \\ \times\ 97 \\ \hline 406 \\ 5220 \\ \hline 5626 \end{array}$$

## Example 2

Multiply.
**a)** $0.9 \times 6.8$   **b)** $0.5 \times 0.4$

**Solution**

**a)** $0.9 \times 6.8$

Multiply: $9 \times 68$

$$\begin{array}{r} 68 \\ \times\ 9 \\ \hline 612 \end{array}$$

Estimate to place the decimal point.
$0.9 \times 6.8$ is about $1 \times 7 = 7$.
So, the product is 6.12.

**b)** $0.5 \times 0.4$

Multiply: $5 \times 4 = 20$

Estimate to place the decimal point.
$0.5 \times 0.4$ is about $1 \times 0.4 = 0.4$.
So, the product is 0.20.

## Practice

**1.** Write a multiplication equation for each picture.
Each small square represents 0.01.

**a)**    **b)**

**2.** Use Base Ten Blocks to find each product.
**a)** $2.6 \times 1.5$   **b)** $1.4 \times 2.8$   **c)** $2.7 \times 1.6$

**3.** Use Base Ten Blocks to find each product.
Record your work on grid paper.
**a)** $2.3 \times 0.4$   **b)** $0.6 \times 1.9$   **c)** $0.8 \times 0.7$

**4.** Multiply: $36 \times 24$
Use this to find each product. Explain your work.
**a)** $36 \times 2.4$   **b)** $3.6 \times 24$   **c)** $3.6 \times 2.4$

**5.** Multiply.
**a)** $4.2 \times 3.7$   **b)** $8.9 \times 0.3$   **c)** $0.6 \times 0.9$

**6.** Carla drives 7.6 km to work. She drives the same distance home. How many kilometres does Carla drive in a 5-day workweek?

**7.** A rectangular plot of land measures 30.5 m by 5.3 m. What is the area of the plot?

**8. a)** Multiply.

    **i)** $6.3 \times 1.8$       **ii)** $4.2 \times 0.7$       **iii)** $0.8 \times 0.5$

  **b)** Look at the questions and products in part a. What patterns do you see in the numbers of decimal places in the question and the product? How could you use this pattern to place the decimal point in a product without estimating?

**9.** The product of 2 decimals is 0.36. What might the decimals be? Find as many answers as possible.

**10.** Recall that dividing by 10 is the same as multiplying by 0.1. Multiply to find:

  **a)** $\frac{1}{10}$ of 25.2       **b)** $\frac{2}{10}$ of 37.3       **c)** $\frac{6}{10}$ of 58.7

**11.** **Assessment Focus** An area rug is rectangular. Its dimensions are 3.4 m by 2.7 m. Show different strategies you can use to find the area of the rug. Which strategy is best? Justify your answer.

**12. a)** Find each product.

    **i)** $4.8 \times 5.3$       **ii)** $4.8 \times 0.6$       **iii)** $0.4 \times 0.6$

  **b)** When you multiply 2 decimals, how does the product compare with the numbers you multiplied? Explain your reasoning.

**Take It Further**

**13.** Explain why the sum of the number of digits to the right of the decimal point in the factors of a product equals the number of digits to the right of the decimal point in the product.

**Reflect**

When you multiply 2 decimals, how do you know where to place the decimal point in the product? Use examples to explain.

Recall that we can use the same Base Ten Blocks to multiply:

$14 \times 18 = 252$         and         $1.4 \times 1.8 = 2.52$

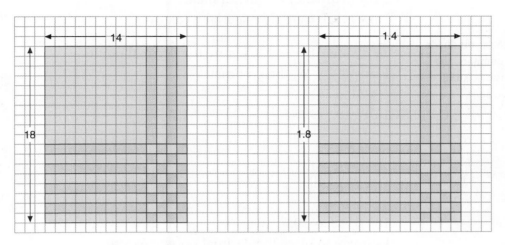

The only difference is the values we assign to the flat, the rod, and the small cube.

In a similar way, we can divide 2 decimals by thinking about whole numbers instead.

So, $252 \div 18 = 14$         and         $2.52 \div 1.8 = 1.4$

To divide 2 decimals, ignore the decimal points.
Divide as you would whole numbers, then estimate to place the decimal point in the answer.

## Explore

Work with a partner.
Mark bought 19.5 m of fabric to make costumes for a play.
Each costume needs 2.6 m of fabric.
How many costumes can Mark make?
How much material is left over?
Show your work.

### Reflect & Share

How did you use division of whole numbers to find your answer?

Jan bought 18.9 m of framing to make picture frames.
Each picture needs 1.8 m of frame.
How many frames can Jan make?
How much framing material is left over?

**When you divide 2 numbers, the answer is the quotient.** ⟶

To divide: 18.9 ÷ 1.8, ignore the decimal points.
Find 189 ÷ 18, then estimate.

$$
\begin{array}{r}
10.5 \\
18\overline{)189.0} \\
180\phantom{.0} \\
\hline
90 \\
90 \\
\hline
0
\end{array}
$$

189 ÷ 18 = 10.5
Estimate to place the decimal point correctly.
18.9 ÷ 1.8 is about 20 ÷ 2, which is 10.
So, 18.9 ÷ 1.8 is 10.5.

Jan can make 10 frames.
10 frames use 10 × 1.8 m = 18 m.
So, the framing material left is 18.9 m − 18 m = 0.9 m.

Sometimes when we divide 2 decimals, the quotient is not a terminating decimal.

## Example

Divide.

**a)** 12.5 ÷ 0.6 **b)** 25.2 ÷ 4.7

## Solution

**a)** 12.5 ÷ 0.6

$$
6\overline{)125.^50^20^20}
$$
$$
20.\,8\;3\;3
$$

**Think:** Use short division to find 125 ÷ 6.

If we continue to divide, the 3 in the quotient repeats.
So, 125 ÷ 6 = 20.8$\overline{3}$
To estimate: 12.5 ÷ 0.6 is about 13 ÷ 1 = 13.
So, the quotient is 20.8$\overline{3}$.

**b)** 25.2 ÷ 4.7

> **Think:** Use long division to find 252 ÷ 47.

$$
\begin{array}{r}
5.36 \\
47\overline{)252.00} \\
235 \\
\hline
17\ 0 \\
14\ 1 \\
\hline
2\ 90 \\
2\ 82 \\
\hline
8
\end{array}
$$

There is 1 decimal place in each number in the question. Continue to divide until there are 2 decimal places in the quotient. That is, calculate the quotient to 1 more decimal place than in the question. Then, round the quotient to 1 decimal place.

Round the quotient to 5.4.
To estimate: 25.2 ÷ 4.7 is about 25 ÷ 5 = 5.
So, the quotient is approximately 5.4.

## Practice

**1.** Look at each division equation on the left.
Use it to write each quotient on the right.
  **a)** 234 ÷ 13 = 18        23.4 ÷ 1.3
  **b)** 133 ÷ 7 = 19         13.3 ÷ 7
  **c)** 714 ÷ 34 = 21        71.4 ÷ 3.4
  **d)** 450 ÷ 18 = 25        4.5 ÷ 1.8
  **e)** 51 ÷ 17 = 3          5.1 ÷ 1.7

**2.** Choose the correct quotient for each division question.
Explain how you know.

| Question | Possible Quotients | | |
|---|---|---|---|
| **a)** 5.95 ÷ 3.5 | 17 | 1.7 | 0.17 |
| **b)** 195.3 ÷ 6.2 | 315 | 31.5 | 3.15 |
| **c)** 31.32 ÷ 1.8 | 174 | 17.4 | 1.74 |
| **d)** 1.44 ÷ 0.12 | 12 | 1.2 | 0.12 |

**Number Strategies**

A rectangular prism has dimensions 6 cm by 4 cm by 8 cm. Find the surface area and volume of this rectangular prism.

**3.** Divide.
  **a)** 8.7 ÷ 0.3        **b)** 2.24 ÷ 0.7        **c)** 10.3 ÷ 0.6

**4.** Divide.
  **a)** 10.92 ÷ 0.6        **b)** 30.42 ÷ 1.3        **c)** 18.56 ÷ 5.8

**Measurement**

The prefixes in units of length less than 1 m show fractions or decimals of 1 m.

One decimetre is $\frac{1}{10}$ or 0.1 m.

One centimetre is $\frac{1}{100}$ or 0.01 m.

One millimetre is $\frac{1}{1000}$ or 0.001 m.

One micrometre is $\frac{1}{1\,000\,000}$ or 0.000 001 m.

**5.** Divide. Round the quotient to the nearest tenth.
   **a)** $172.5 \div 2.6$    **b)** $21.68 \div 3.4$    **c)** $92.8 \div 8.2$

**6.** Divide. Round to the nearest tenth where necessary.
   **a)** $7.3 \div 0.4$    **b)** $1.98 \div 1.3$    **c)** $426.8 \div 3.7$

**7.** The quotient of 2 decimals is 0.12. What might the decimals be? Write as many different possible decimal pairs as you can.

**8.** (**Assessment Focus**)    Alex finds a remnant of landscaping fabric at a garden store.
   The fabric is the standard width, with length 9.7 m.
   Alex needs twelve 0.85-m pieces for a garden patio.
   **a)** Will Alex have more fabric than she needs?
       If so, how much more?
   **b)** Will Alex need more fabric? If so, how much more?

**9.** The area of a rectangular lawn is 120.4 m². The width is 5.6 m. What is the length?

**10.** The question $237 \div 7$ does not have an exact quotient.
   The first five digits of the quotient are 33857. The decimal point has been omitted. Use only this information and estimation.
   Write an approximate quotient for each question.
   Justify each answer.
   **a)** $237 \div 0.7$    **b)** $2.37 \div 7$    **c)** $23.7 \div 7$    **d)** $2370 \div 70$

BREAD

0.25 g yeast    3.75 L milk
5 g salt    15 g butter
4 kg flour    0.8 kg sugar
170 g cardamom

**11.** Here is a recipe for bread.
   Sam wants to make one-half the amount.
   Find how much of each ingredient Sam needs.

**12.** Jack has 2.5 L of juice.
   Each day, he drinks 0.4 L.
   How many days will it take Jack to drink the juice?
   Justify your answer.

**Reflect**

Explain how you decide where to place the decimal point when you divide 2 decimals. Use an example in your explanation.

Magazines and newspapers make money by selling advertising space.

The advertising sales representative contacts companies whose products might be of interest to readers. She offers to sell them various sizes of advertisement space at different rates. When talking about ads smaller than a full page, the sales rep uses fractions to describe them. It's much simpler to talk about a $\frac{2}{3}$-page ad instead of a 0.666 667 page ad!

The sales rep tries to sell combinations of ads that can fill pages, with no space left over. A sales rep has sold two $\frac{1}{4}$-page ads and one $\frac{1}{6}$-page ad. She wants to know the possible combinations of ad sizes she can sell to fill the page. What might they be?

# 4.9  Order of Operations with Decimals

**Focus**  Use the order of operations to evaluate expressions.

We use a base ten, or decimal, number system.
Every whole number is also a decimal.
So, we use the same order of operations for decimals as for whole numbers.

## Explore

Work on your own.
Evaluate this expression: $6 \times (15.9 + 36.4) \div 4$
Explain each step.

### Reflect & Share

Compare your solution and answer with that of a classmate.
If your answers are different, who has the correct answer?

## Connect

Here is the order of operations.
- Do the operations in brackets first.
- Then divide and multiply, in order, from left to right.
- Then add and subtract, in order, from left to right.

### Example

Evaluate. $12.4 - (4.7 + 1) + 2.4 \times 3 - 4.8 \div 2$

### Solution

$12.4 - (4.7 + 1) + 2.4 \times 3 - 4.8 \div 2$   **Calculate in brackets.**

$= 12.4 - 5.7 + 2.4 \times 3 - 4.8 \div 2$   **Multiply and divide from left to right.**

$= 12.4 - 5.7 + 7.2 - 2.4$   **Add and subtract from left to right.**

$= 6.7 + 7.2 - 2.4$

$= 13.9 - 2.4$

$= 11.5$

1. Evaluate.
   a) $3.4 + 4 \times 7$    b) $14 - 2.2 \times 5$    c) $8 - 3.6 \div 2$

2. Evaluate.
   a) $7.4 - 3 + 2.3 \times 4$    b) $4.6 + 5.1 - 3.2 \div 2$
   c) $16.4 - (10.8 - 3.1)$    d) $23 \times 6.2 + 4$
   e) $81.2 - (35.8 + 2.1)$    f) $85.7 \div 0.4 \times 7$

3. Evaluate.
   a) $46.78 - 6.1 \times 2.3$    b) $75.06 \times (3.45 - 1.2)$
   c) $(98.5 + 7) \div 2.5$    d) $9.0023 \times 5.1 - 4.32 \times 6$
   e) $8.3 + 46.2 \div 1.4$    f) $70.56 - 32.8 \div 4.1$

**Number Sense**

A number cube has faces labelled 1 to 6.

The cube is rolled 75 times.

About how many times will the number 3 show?

4. Evaluate.
   a) $3.2 + 5.6 \times 7.2 \div 2.4 - 9.3$
   b) $8.5 \times 7 - 6.3 \div 9 + 10.6$
   c) $1.35 + (5 \times 4.9 \div 0.7) - 2.7 \times 2.1$
   d) $(4.7 - 3.1) \times 5 - 7.5 \div 2.5$

5. Evaluate.
   a) $164.5 \div 7 \times 10 + 7.2$    b) $73.8 \times (3.2 + 6.8) - 14.1 \div 0.2$

6. The cross-country team members ran timed circuits. Here are their times: 15.8 min, 12.5 min, 18.0 min, 14.2 min, 13.9 min, 16.0 min, 16.2 min, 17.5 min, 16.3 min, 15.6 min Find the mean time.

**The mean time is the sum of the times divided by the number of times.**

7. **Assessment Focus**
   Evaluate. Show all steps.
   $0.38 + 16.2 \times (2.1 + 4) + 21 \div 3.5$

**Reflect**

Explain why the brackets are unnecessary in this expression:
$(4.2 \times 3.8) - (15.25 \div 6.1)$
Find the answer. Show each step.

# Writing a Math Journal Entry

## 1 THINK about what you did in math.

- Which materials did you use?
- Which problem did you solve?
  How did you solve it?
- What did you learn?
- What are you confused about?
- What vocabulary did you use?
- What was challenging? What was easy?

## 2 TALK about what you did in math.

- Work with a partner or in a group.
- Share your ideas. Listen to the ideas of others.
- What information did your partner or group share that was new?
- Ask your partner or group members about any issue that was confusing … what did they say?

## 3 BRAINSTORM all your ideas.

- Make dot jots of the things you discussed and thought about.
  Don't leave anything out … you can edit it later.
- Think about how you can support your written work. Use graphs, tables, numbers, symbols, diagrams, and so on.

## Reading and Writing in **Math**

**4**

## WRITE your ideas.

- Put your thoughts into words.
  Be sure you follow a logical order.
- Think about what you write. Are you using math language? Underline this language.

**5**

## READ your ideas out loud.

- Listen for missing words.
- Be sure your thoughts are in a logical order.
- Add anything that is missing.
- What is unclear? Why? What would help?
- Add graphs, tables, and so on, that will help explain your written work.

**6**

## READ your work to your partner or group.

- Listen to your partner's or group members' ideas.
- Discuss: What was done well?
  What part was not clear?
  What would help improve the journal entry?

**7**

## REVISE and REWRITE.

- Make the changes that are necessary.
- Rewrite on a new piece of paper if necessary.

## What Do I Need to Know?

### Adding and Subtracting Fractions

There are 4 types of fraction questions. Look at the denominators.

✓ **Same denominators**

For example, $\frac{5}{6}$ and $\frac{2}{6}$

$\frac{5}{6} + \frac{2}{6} = \frac{7}{6}$        $\frac{5}{6} - \frac{2}{6} = \frac{3}{6}$

✓ **Related denominators**

For example, $\frac{1}{6}$ and $\frac{1}{12}$

12 is a multiple of 6, so the lowest common denominator is 12.

$\frac{1}{6} = \frac{2}{12}$

$\frac{1}{6} + \frac{1}{12} = \frac{2}{12} + \frac{1}{12} = \frac{3}{12}$        $\frac{1}{6} - \frac{1}{12} = \frac{2}{12} - \frac{1}{12} = \frac{1}{12}$

✓ **Partially related denominators**

For example, $\frac{1}{6}$ and $\frac{1}{9}$

6 and 9 have the common factor, 3.

So, list multiples to find the lowest common denominator.

Multiples of 6: 6, 12, **18**, 24, 30, …

Multiples of 9: 9, **18**, 27, 36, …

The lowest common denominator is 18.

$\frac{1}{6} = \frac{3}{18}$; $\frac{1}{9} = \frac{2}{18}$; $\frac{1}{6} + \frac{1}{9} = \frac{3}{18} + \frac{2}{18} = \frac{5}{18}$; $\frac{1}{6} - \frac{1}{9} = \frac{3}{18} - \frac{2}{18} = \frac{1}{18}$

✓ **Unrelated denominators**

For example, $\frac{1}{5}$ and $\frac{1}{6}$

5 and 6 have no common factors, so the lowest common denominator is their product: $5 \times 6 = 30$

$\frac{1}{5} = \frac{6}{30}$; $\frac{1}{6} = \frac{5}{30}$; $\frac{1}{5} + \frac{1}{6} = \frac{6}{30} + \frac{5}{30} = \frac{11}{30}$; $\frac{1}{5} - \frac{1}{6} = \frac{6}{30} - \frac{5}{30} = \frac{1}{30}$

### Multiplying a Fraction by a Whole Number

✓ This is the same as repeatedly adding the same fraction.

$4 \times \frac{3}{5} = \frac{3}{5} + \frac{3}{5} + \frac{3}{5} + \frac{3}{5} = \frac{12}{5}$

LESSON

**4.1** **1.** Which fraction is greater? How do you know?

a) $\frac{2}{5}, \frac{2}{6}$      b) $\frac{3}{10}, \frac{1}{2}$

c) $\frac{4}{8}, \frac{3}{6}$      d) $\frac{7}{2}, \frac{7}{3}$

**2.** Add.

a) $\frac{2}{3} + \frac{1}{6}$      b) $\frac{3}{4} + \frac{2}{8}$

c) $\frac{1}{4} + \frac{3}{6}$      d) $\frac{1}{10} + \frac{3}{5}$

**3.** Find 2 fractions that add to $\frac{5}{8}$. Find as many pairs of fractions as you can.

**4.2** **4.** Add.

a) $\frac{2}{3} + \frac{5}{6}$      b) $\frac{1}{2} + \frac{3}{4}$

c) $\frac{1}{2} + \frac{9}{10}$      d) $\frac{8}{8} + \frac{1}{4}$

**5.** Adam eats $\frac{3}{10}$ of a pizza. Julie eats $\frac{2}{5}$ of the pizza.

a) How much of the pizza is eaten?

b) How much is left?

**4.3** **6.** Add. Draw a picture to show each sum.

a) $\frac{1}{3} + \frac{2}{5}$      b) $\frac{1}{2} + \frac{3}{8}$

c) $\frac{2}{3} + \frac{3}{10}$      d) $\frac{3}{5} + \frac{1}{4}$

**7.** Add.

a) $\frac{2}{5} + \frac{5}{6}$      b) $\frac{1}{4} + \frac{2}{5}$

c) $\frac{3}{10} + \frac{5}{6}$      d) $\frac{3}{8} + \frac{2}{3}$

**8.** Add.

a) $6\frac{1}{3} + 2\frac{1}{3}$      b) $1\frac{5}{12} + 2\frac{1}{6}$

c) $2\frac{3}{10} + 3\frac{1}{5}$      d) $5\frac{1}{4} + 2\frac{2}{5}$

**9.** Add.

a) $\frac{2}{3} + \frac{3}{4} + \frac{3}{8}$

b) $\frac{5}{2} + \frac{1}{3} + \frac{2}{5}$

c) $\frac{7}{10} + \frac{3}{4} + \frac{5}{8}$

**4.4** **10.** Subtract.

a) $\frac{1}{2} - \frac{1}{3}$      b) $\frac{7}{10} - \frac{2}{5}$

c) $\frac{3}{4} - \frac{1}{8}$      d) $\frac{5}{6} - \frac{1}{3}$

**11.** Find 2 fractions with a difference of $\frac{1}{4}$. Find as many pairs of fractions as you can. Remember to use fractions with different denominators.

**4.5** **12.** Ali drank $\frac{3}{4}$ cup of water. Brad drank $\frac{2}{3}$ cup of water.

a) Who drank more water?

b) How much more water did he drink?

**13.** Subtract.

a) $\frac{9}{10} - \frac{2}{5}$  b) $\frac{7}{3} - \frac{5}{6}$

c) $\frac{8}{5} - \frac{1}{4}$  d) $\frac{9}{4} - \frac{2}{3}$

**14.** Subtract.

a) $3\frac{3}{4} - 2\frac{1}{8}$  b) $4\frac{4}{5} - 2\frac{2}{3}$

c) $9\frac{1}{2} - 3\frac{1}{3}$  d) $6\frac{3}{4} - 6\frac{1}{5}$

**4.6** **15.** Multiply. Draw a picture to show each answer.

a) $\frac{1}{4} \times 7$  b) $8 \times \frac{3}{8}$

c) $6 \times \frac{7}{10}$  d) $\frac{4}{5} \times 5$

**16.** Sasha had 16 tomatoes in his vegetable garden. He gave: Samira $\frac{1}{8}$ of the tomatoes; Sielen $\frac{1}{8}$ of the tomatoes; and Amina $\frac{1}{4}$ of the tomatoes.

a) What fraction of the tomatoes did Sasha have left?

b) How many tomatoes did Sasha have left?

**17.** Orit spends $\frac{1}{4}$ of her day at school, $\frac{1}{12}$ of her day playing soccer, and $\frac{1}{3}$ of her day sleeping. How many hours are left in Orit's day?

**4.7** **18.** A rectangular park has dimensions 2.8 km by 1.9 km. What is the area of the park?

**4.8** **19.** Nuri has 10.8 L of water. He pours 1.5 L into each of several plastic bottles.

a) How many bottles can Nuri fill?

b) How much water is left over?

**20.** Delia works at the library after school. She earns $7.50/h. She usually works 15 h a week.

a) What does Delia earn in a week? Use estimation to check your answer.

b) One week Delia only works $\frac{1}{2}$ the hours she usually works. What are her earnings that week?

**4.9** **21.** Mr. Statler took his class to the local library 4 times last year. One student had a pedometer. She measured the trip as 1.7 km each way. How far did the students walk back and forth to the library during the year?

**22.** Evaluate.

a) $5.3 + 5.1 \div 3$

b) $12.6 \times (1.5 + 2.5)$

c) $68.9 - 32.7 \times 2$

**23.** Evaluate.

a) $5.9 + 3.7 \times 2.8 - 1.5 \div 0.5$

b) $3.4 \times 1.9 \div 1.7 + 7.2 \div 1.2$

# Practice Test

1. Add or subtract.

   a) $\frac{5}{4} + \frac{3}{8}$    b) $\frac{3}{2} - \frac{3}{5}$    c) $\frac{11}{12} - \frac{2}{3}$    d) $\frac{4}{9} + \frac{7}{6}$

2. a) Find three pairs of fractions that have a sum of $\frac{3}{5}$.

   b) Find three pairs of fractions that have a difference of $\frac{1}{5}$.

3. Add or subtract.

   a) $6\frac{3}{8} - 2\frac{1}{5}$                    b) $4\frac{1}{4} + 2\frac{2}{3}$

4. Lana does yard work. The table shows the approximate time for each job.

   | Job | Time |
   |-----|------|
   | Mow small lawn | $\frac{1}{2}$ h |
   | Mow large lawn | $\frac{3}{4}$ h |
   | Mow lawn/tidy yard | $1\frac{1}{2}$ h |
   | Plant annuals | $2\frac{1}{2}$ h |

   For one Saturday, Lana has these jobs:
   – mow 3 small lawns
   – mow 1 large lawn
   – mow lawn/tidy yard in 2 places
   – plant annuals in 1 place

   Lana needs travel time between jobs, and a break for lunch. Do you think she will be able to do all the jobs? Justify your answer.

5. a) Evaluate.

   i) $\frac{3}{4} + \frac{3}{4} + \frac{3}{4} + \frac{3}{4} + \frac{3}{4} + \frac{3}{4}$    ii) $7 \times \frac{2}{3}$    iii) $\frac{7}{8} \times 8$

   b) Convert each answer in part a to a decimal.

   c) Order the decimals from least to greatest.

6. A 6-kg bag of fertilizer covers a rectangular area of 2.5 m by 5.0 m.

   a) How many bags of fertilizer are needed for a rectangular lawn measuring 7.5 m by 10.2 m?

   b) A 6-kg bag of fertilizer costs $15.50. How much does it cost to fertilize the lawn?

7. Evaluate. Explain each step.
   $12.4 \times (2.9 + 4.6) + 23.7 \div 2.4$

The students at Garden Avenue School are preparing a special book for the school's 100th anniversary. They finance the book by selling advertising space to sponsors.

The students sold the following space:

| Full page | $\frac{1}{2}$ page | $\frac{1}{3}$ page | $\frac{1}{4}$ page | $\frac{1}{6}$ page | $\frac{1}{8}$ page |
|:---:|:---:|:---:|:---:|:---:|:---:|
| 1 | 1 | 1 | 3 | 4 | 5 |

All the advertisements are to fit at the back of the book.

Sam asks: "How many pages do we need for the advertisements?"
Mara asks: "Will the advertisements fill the pages?"
Kathleen asks: "Is there more than one way to arrange these advertisements?"
Can you think of other questions students might ask?

**1.** Find the total advertising space needed.

**2.** Sketch the pages to find how the advertisements can be placed. Use grid paper if it helps.

**3.** Compare your group's sketch with those of other groups. When you made your sketch, what decisions did you make about the shape of each advertisement? Did other groups make the same decisions? Explain.

**4.** What are the fewest pages needed to display the advertisements? Will there be room for any other advertisements? Explain.

**5.** What else might students need to consider as they prepare the layout for the book?

Here are the fees for the advertisements.

| Size | Full page | $\frac{1}{2}$ page | $\frac{1}{3}$ page | $\frac{1}{4}$ page | $\frac{1}{6}$ page | $\frac{1}{8}$ page |
|------|-----------|-----------|-----------|-----------|-----------|-----------|
| Cost ($) | 500 | 360 | 250 | 200 | 150 | 100 |

**Check List**

Your work
should show:

✓ all calculations
  in detail

✓ diagrams of the
  layout for the
  advertisements

✓ a clear explanation
  of how you prepared
  the layout

✓ a clear explanation
  of how students do
  not incur losses

**6.** How much money will students get from the advertisers?

**7.** Students will do the layout on computer.
The cost to copy and bind 500 books is $4750. Use the income from question 6.
**a)** What do the students have to charge per book so they do not incur a loss? Justify your answer.
**b)** The students cannot print fewer than 500 books.
What if they can sell only 350 books?
What do the students have to charge per book so they do not incur a loss? Justify your answer.
**c)** What if the students decide to charge $5 per book?
How many books do the students need to sell so they do not incur a loss? Justify your answer.

## Reflect on the Unit

Choose one operation with fractions and a different operation with decimals.
Write an example that illustrates how to carry out each operation.

**UNIT**

**1**   **1.** Find the number that is:
- a factor of 1000
- not a factor of 100
- a multiple of 5
- has fewer than 3 digits

Explain how you found the number.

**2.** A rectangular pen is built with 60 m of fencing.
The length of each side of the pen is a whole number of metres.
**a)** Which dimensions are possible? Make an organized list of your answers.
**b)** What are the dimensions of the pen with the greatest area? Explain.

**3.** The number 49 is a perfect square. It can be written as $7^2$.
Some numbers that are not perfect squares can be written as the sum of a perfect square and a prime number.
For example: $21 = 4^2 + 5$
**a)** Find all the numbers between 40 and 50 that can be written this way.
**b)** Which numbers in part a can be written more than one way? Show each new way.

**4.** Write the next 3 terms in each pattern. Describe each pattern.
**a)** 49, 36, 25, 16, . . .
**b)** 3, 7, 15, 31, . . .
**c)** 6, 36, 216, 1296, . . .

**2**   **5.** Write each ratio in simplest form.

**a)** saxophones to trumpets
**b)** drums to flutes
**c)** saxophones to total number of instruments

**6.** The ratio of the number of hits to the times at bat for three baseball players is:
Irina, 3:5; Juana, 2:3; Carla, 3:4
**a)** Who has the best record?
**b)** Who had the least success?
Explain your answers.

**7.** The ratio of boys to girls in the sailing club is 4:5.
**a)** There are 15 girls in the club. How many boys are in the club?
**b)** What if 3 boys leave the club? What is the new ratio of girls to boys?

**8.** Identify the view (front, back, side, or top) and the object on each sign. Then draw a different view of that object.

**a)** Post office

**b)** Picnic area

**c)** Microwave oven

**9.** Find the surface area of each rectangular prism.

**a)**

4 cm
1 cm
2 cm

**b)**

5.5 cm
4.5 cm
3.5 cm

**c)**

0.3 m
0.3 m
0.3 m

**10.** Use a large copy of this net.

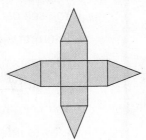

**a)** Fold the net to make an object.

**b)** Sketch the front, back, side, and top view of the object.

**11.** Use fraction strips, number lines, or another model to add or subtract.

**a)** $\frac{3}{8} + \frac{3}{2}$　　**b)** $\frac{2}{3} + \frac{1}{4}$

**c)** $\frac{7}{5} - \frac{1}{2}$　　**d)** $\frac{11}{6} - \frac{4}{3}$

**12.** Skylar and Riley work together on a project. Skylar does $\frac{3}{10}$ of the work. Riley does $\frac{2}{5}$ of the work.

**a)** Who does more work? How much more does this person do?

**b)** What fraction of the project has yet to be done?

**13.** Multiply. Draw a picture to show each answer.

**a)** $4 \times \frac{5}{8}$　　**b)** $\frac{3}{5} \times 5$

**c)** $3 \times \frac{3}{10}$　　**d)** $5 \times \frac{5}{4}$

**14.** Multiply. Record your work on grid paper.

**a)** $3.5 \times 2.1$　　**b)** $0.8 \times 1.2$

**15.** The area of a rectangle is 7.35 m². The width is 2.1 m. What is the length?

**16.** Evaluate.

**a)** $1.25 + 3.6 \times 2.4 \div 1.2$

**b)** $10.5 \div 1.5 - 2.8 \times 0.3$

**c)** $10.1 - 4.5 \div 0.5 + 7.5$

**d)** $(10.1 - 4.5) \div (0.5 + 7.5)$

Why are the answers to parts c and d different?

# UNIT
# 5
# Data Management

David and his friend surveyed their classmates. They wanted to find out which outdoor winter activities the students participated in. They recorded the results in a tally chart.

| Outdoor Winter Activities | |
|---|---|
| **Activity** | **Tally** |
| Skating | ### ### ### ### //// |
| Skiing | ### ### ### |
| Snowboarding | ### ### // |
| Tobogganing | ### ### ### ### ### ### |

- What survey question might the students have asked to get the data in the chart?
- How could you graph the data?
- Which graph is most suitable for the data?

## What You'll Learn

- Collect and organize data on tally charts and stem-and-leaf plots.
- Display data on frequency tables, bar graphs, pictographs, line graphs, and circle graphs.
- Describe and evaluate data presented on charts, tables, and graphs, and solve related problems.
- Use databases and spreadsheets.
- Calculate and use mean, median, and mode.
- Identify and describe trends in graphs.
- Use technology to draw graphs.

## Why It's Important

- You see data and their interpretations in newspapers, magazines, and on TV.
  You need to understand how to interpret these data.

## Key Words

- mean
- median
- mode
- primary data
- secondary data
- biased
- database
- fields
- Statistics Canada
  (Stats Can)
- frequency table
- stem-and-leaf plot
- cluster
- trend
- line graph
- spreadsheet

# Skills You'll Need

## Calculating Mean, Median, and Mode

For any set of numbers:
- The **mean** is the sum of all the numbers divided by the number of numbers.
- The **median** is the middle number when the numbers are arranged in order. When there is an even number of numbers, the median is the mean of the two middle numbers. Half the numbers are above the median and half are below.
- The **mode** is the number that occurs most often. There may be more than one mode. There may be no mode.

### Example

Calculate the mean, median, and mode of these numbers:
7, 13, 10, 12, 14, 8, 9, 7, 11, 6

### Solution

There are 10 numbers in the set.

- For the mean, add the numbers, then divide by 10.
  Mean: $\dfrac{7 + 13 + 10 + 12 + 14 + 8 + 9 + 7 + 11 + 6}{10} = \dfrac{97}{10}$
  $= 9.7$

- For the median, arrange the numbers in order, beginning with the least number. The median is the middle number. Since there are 10 numbers, the median is the mean of the two middle numbers. For 10 numbers in order, the first middle number is $\frac{10}{2} = 5$, or the 5th number. The next middle number is the 6th number.

  6, 7, 7, 8, 9, 10, 11, 12, 13, 14
  Median: $\dfrac{9 + 10}{2} = \dfrac{19}{2}$, or 9.5

- The mode is the number that occurs most often. The mode is 7.

### ✓ Check

**1.** Calculate the mean, median, and mode for the numbers in each set.
   a) 3, 9, 5, 8, 2, 0, 9, 5
   b) 25, 24, 55, 30, 44, 21, 17, 19, 21
   c) 14, 18, 16, 12, 11, 16
   d) 76, 81, 50, 64, 67, 69, 72, 94, 81, 76

**Focus** Analyse data collection and possible bias.

Electronic games are popular among Grade 7 students. Which electronic game do you think Grade 7 students in your class like to play? How could you find out?

## Explore

Work in a group.
Which electronic game is most popular in your class?
Conduct a survey to find out.
What survey question will you ask? Record your results.

### Reflect & Share

Compare your results with those of another group.
How did the survey question affect the results?

## Connect

Mia wanted to find out the favourite singer of her classmates.
She conducted a survey. She asked this question:

"Who is your favourite singer: Bryan Adams _____, Susan Aglukark _____, Celine Dion _____, Sam Roberts _____, Shania Twain _____, or Other _____?"
Mia recorded the results in a tally chart.

| Singer | Number of Students |
|---|---|
| Bryan Adams | ##// |
| Susan Aglukark | #### |
| Celine Dion | #### // |
| Sam Roberts | /// |
| Shania Twain | // |
| Other | #### #### / |

Mia concluded that Celine Dion was the most popular singer of those named.
However, if all the votes in the "Other" category were for the same person, then that person would be the most popular.

The word "data" is plural. So, we say "The data are …" A single piece of information is called "datum."

Since Mia collected the data herself, they are called **primary data**.
Data that are found from the library or using the Internet are called **secondary data**.

It is important that a survey is conducted and data are collected in a fair way. Sometimes, the way a question is asked or written might persuade a person to answer a certain way. This type of question is **biased**. A survey question must be unbiased. That is, the question must not lead a person toward a particular answer.

## Example

How is each survey question biased?
Rewrite the question so it is unbiased.

**a)** "Many students are bored at the end of August.
Should the school year be longer?
Yes _____          No _____ "

**b)** "Some people get sick after visiting patients in a hospital.
Do you think patients in a hospital should have visitors?
Yes _____          No _____          No Opinion _____ "

## Solution

**a)** The question includes a statement about how some students feel.
This may encourage more people to answer "Yes."
An unbiased survey question is:
"The school year is 10 months long. Should it be longer?
Yes _____          No _____ "

**b)** The question includes a statement that may encourage people to answer "No."
An unbiased survey question is:
"Should patients in a hospital have visitors?
Yes _____          No _____          No Opinion _____ "

## Practice

**1.** Are primary data or secondary data collected in each situation?
How do you know?
   **a)** Elly used an encyclopedia to find the area of each continent.
   **b)** Jason read the thermometer to find the outside temperature.
   **c)** Jane looked in the newspaper to see which NHL team won the game.

**2.** Would you use primary or secondary data in each case? Explain.
  **a)** To find the favourite car model in Canada
  **b)** To find the favourite juice of Grade 7 students in your school
  **c)** To find the favourite song of Grade 7 students in Ontario
  **d)** To find the most popular type of transport used by students in your school

**3.** Biased data are unreliable. Yet, sometimes people use biased data. Why do people use biased data?

**4.** Think of a survey you could conduct in your school.
  **a)** Write a biased survey question.
  **b)** Write an unbiased survey question.

**5.** Comment on each survey question.
  If it is biased, write an unbiased question.
  **a)** "Sugar is bad for your teeth. Should children eat candy?
      Yes _____      No _____      No Opinion _____"

  **b)** "Children prefer snowboarding to skiing.
      Which do you think is more fun?
      Snowboarding _____          Skiing _____"

**Number Strategies**

How are these two patterns related?
• 0.75, 1.5, 3, 6, . . .
• 96, 192, 384, 768, . . .

**6.** **Assessment Focus**   Suppose a person intends to open a shoe store in the local mall.
The person is unsure of the style or make of shoes to stock.
What questions should the person ask to make the best decision?
Explain what role a survey might play in the decision.

**7. a)** Predict the favourite hobby or pastime of your classmates.
  **b)** Write a survey question you could ask to find out.
      Explain how you know your question is unbiased.
  **c)** Conduct the survey. Tally the results.
  **d)** How did your prediction compare with your results?

**Reflect**

Why is it important that a survey question is unbiased?

# Using Databases to Find Data

A **database** is an organized collection of data. Examples of databases include a telephone book, a dictionary, an encyclopedia, or a library catalogue.

A database is organized into **fields**. Each field contains specific information. In a library database, a book may be stored with information in each of these fields: title, author, publisher, subject, ISBN (international standard book number), or Dewey decimal number.

**Statistics Canada** (Stats Can) is the federal government department that collects, analyses, and stores data about Canada and Canadians. Two of its Internet databases are **CANSIM** (**Can**adian **S**ocio-economic **I**nformation **M**anagement System) and **E-STAT**.

Stats Can charges a fee for some of its data on CANSIM, but all data are transferred to E-STAT once a year in the summer.

E-STAT is a free database for teachers and students. Your teacher will give you the website addresses for these databases.

To use E-STAT to find data on school attendance for 15- to 24-year-olds, follow these steps:

**1.** Open the E-STAT Website.
You may be asked for your username and password. Ask your teacher for these.

**2.** Click the "Data" tab. Click "Education," as shown above left.

**3.** Under Census databases, click "Enrolment," as shown below left.

**4.** Under 2001 Census of Population (Provinces, Census Divisions, Municipalities), click "2001 School Attendance, Education, Field of Study, Highest Level of Schooling and Earnings," as shown below left.

**5.** Click "Attending school, full time, population 15 to 24 years," as shown above right.

**6.** Choose an output format. For data in a table arranged in rows, click "Table Areas as Rows," as shown below left. The data are displayed as shown below right.

**1.** Use E-STAT or another database.
Research one of the topics below. Print your data.
Be sure to state your source.

- The number of Canadians who had a particular type of occupation at the time of the 1911 Census
- The top 10 movies of the year
- The top 10 music CDs of the year
- A topic of your choice

Write 3 things you know from looking at the data.

## Explore

Work on your own.
Use a novel you are currently reading.
Open it to any page.

➢ Count the number of letters in each of the first 50 words.
Record your data in a tally chart.

| Number of Letters | Tally of Number of Words |
|---|---|
| 1 | |
| 2 | |
| 3 | |
| 4 | |

➢ Graph your data. Justify your choice of graph.
➢ Which is the most common length of word?
➢ Who might be interested in these data?

### Reflect & Share

Compare your most common length of word with that of a
classmate. Should the lengths be the same? Explain.

## Connect

Data can be organized in a tally chart or **frequency table**.
A frequency table is a tally chart with an extra column.

Andrew recorded the different birds that visited his feeder
one morning.

| Birds at the Feeder | | |
|---|---|---|
| **Bird** | **Tally** | **Frequency** |
| Blue jay | //// | 5 |
| Cardinal | //// | 4 |
| Sparrow | //// //// //// // | 17 |
| Robin | //// //// / | 11 |
| Chickadee | //// // | 7 |

To fill in the *Frequency* column, Andrew counted the tallies
for each bird.
He graphed the data using a pictograph.
Andrew chose a key of 1 symbol represents 2 birds.

**Birds at the Feeder**

Key: represents 2 birds

## Example

a) Construct a bar graph of Andrew's data.

b) Compare the graph and tally chart.
How are they alike?

**Solution**

a) Construct a bar graph, below left.
One square represents 2 birds.

**Birds at the Feeder**

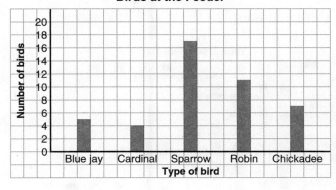

b) The longest bar on the bar graph represents the same bird as the
longest row on the tally chart.
When we rotate the *Tally* column $\frac{1}{4}$ turn counterclockwise,
above right, its shape matches that of the bar graph, above left.

| Favourite Canadian Hockey Team | | |
|---|---|---|
| **Hockey Team** | **Tally** | **Frequency** |
| Calgary Flames | ### /// | |
| Edmonton Oilers | ### / | |
| Montreal Canadiens | ### | |
| Ottawa Senators | ### | |
| Toronto Maple Leafs | ### ### | |
| Vancouver Canucks | ### / | |

| Rolling a Number Cube | | |
|---|---|---|
| **Number** | **Tally** | **Frequency** |
| 1 | | |
| 2 | | |
| 3 | | |

**1.** The table shows the favourite Canadian hockey teams of some Grade 7 students at Hamilton Junior High School.
   a) Write the frequency of each team.
   b) How many students were surveyed?
   c) Which team is the most popular among the sample? The least popular? Give some possible reasons for these results.

**2.** Work with a partner. You will need a number cube labelled 1 to 6.
   a) Roll the number cube 50 times. Make a table. Record the frequency of each number.
   b) Predict the results if you were to roll the number cube 50 more times. Justify your answer.
   c) Compare your results with those of another pair of students. If they are different, explain why.
   d) Graph your data. Justify your choice of graph.

**3.** This pictograph displays the results of a survey.

**Main Use of Internet**

Key: 💻 represents 10 people

   a) What do you think the survey question was? Explain.
   b) How many people were surveyed?
   c) How would the pictograph change if 💻 represented 1 person? 50 people?
   d) Draw a bar graph to display these data.

e) Is a bar graph better than a pictograph to display the data? Explain.

f) Write a question you could answer using the pictograph or bar graph. Answer the question.

**Number Strategies**

Add.

- $\frac{1}{2} + \frac{2}{3}$
- $\frac{3}{4} + \frac{4}{5}$
- $\frac{5}{6} + \frac{6}{7}$

4. This is a double-bar graph.

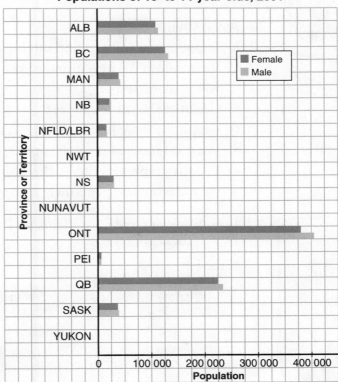

**Populations of 10- to 14-year-olds, 2001**

a) How is this bar graph different from the others in this lesson?

b) How does the female population compare with the male population?

c) Which province(s) have approximately the same number of 10- to 14-year-old females as males?

d) Here are the data for the 3 territories.

|  | Nunavut | Northwest Territories | Yukon |
|---|---|---|---|
| Females | 1550 | 1725 | 1090 |
| Males | 1685 | 1785 | 1225 |

Why are there no bars on the graph for Nunavut and Yukon?

e) Could you use a pictograph to display the data in the double-bar graph? Explain.

**5.** Use an atlas or an almanac.
   **a)** Choose 5 cities in Canada.
   **b)** Choose a recent year.
       Find the population of each city in that year.
   **c)** Record the data in a table.
   **d)** Graph the data. Justify your choice of graph.
   **e)** What do you know from looking at the data?

**6.** **Assessment Focus**
   **a)** Suppose you want to find out how your classmates spend their money. Write a question you could use to survey your classmates.
   **b)** Conduct the survey. Record the data in a frequency table.
   **c)** Graph the data. Justify your choice of graph.
   **d)** What do most of your classmates spend their money on?
   **e)** Use the graph to write 3 other things you know about how your classmates spend their money.

**7.** Two classes of Grade 7 students took a spelling test. The number of words each student misspelled is recorded at the left.

**Spelling Mistakes**

4 7 9 2 1 0 6 5 8 10 7
3 2 12 8 11 3 4 8 4 5
8 15 9 6 2 1 0 17 19
16 3 11 5 10 7 3 7 1 9
10 3 5 8 6 13 8 2 4 6
18 19 5 20 0 1 8 10 3

The interval is 3 because the numbers of mistakes are counted in groups of 3.

| Number of Mistakes | Tally | Frequency |
|---|---|---|
| 0 – 2 | | |
| 3 – 5 | | |

**a)** Copy the frequency table. Continue the pattern of the intervals in the 1st column to 18–20.
   Complete the 2nd and 3rd columns in the frequency table.
**b)** Graph the data.

**Reflect**

When is a pictograph more appropriate than a bar graph?
When is a bar graph more appropriate than a pictograph?
Give examples.

The data, and **stem-and-leaf plot**,
show science test scores for a Grade 7 class.
How are the two displays related?
What can you see in the stem-and-leaf plot that you cannot see in the chart?

**Science Test Scores**

| | | | | | | |
|---|---|---|---|---|---|---|
| 64 | 75 | 89 | 99 | 58 | 53 | 69 |
| 66 | 72 | 81 | 88 | 67 | 75 | 86 |
| 52 | 97 | 77 | 75 | 57 | 61 | 85 |
| 94 | 72 | 81 | 65 | 78 | 81 | 93 |

**Science Test Scores**

| Stem | Leaf |
|---|---|
| 5 | 2 3 7 8 |
| 6 | 1 4 5 6 7 9 |
| 7 | 2 2 5 5 5 7 8 |
| 8 | 1 1 1 5 6 8 9 |
| 9 | 3 4 7 9 |

**This is a stem-and-leaf plot.**

## Explore

Work with a partner.
You will need a metre stick or a tape measure.
Measure each other's height in centimetres.
Write it on the board.
Use the data for the whole class.
Draw a stem-and-leaf plot to show the heights, in centimetres, of
your classmates.

➤ Are any students the same height?
➤ Which is the shortest height? The tallest?
➤ What is the median height?
➤ What is the mode height?
➤ What else do you know from looking at the stem-and-leaf plot?

### Reflect & Share

Compare your stem-and-leaf plot with that of another pair of
classmates. Do your plots match?
If you answer no, how are they different?

Here are the numbers of books students in one Grade 7 class read in one year.
Each number is the number of books one student read.

**Books Read in One Year**

| | | | | | | | |
|---|---|---|---|---|---|---|---|
| 23 | 19 | 43 | 12 | 16 | 18 | 31 | 17 |
| 15 | 23 | 27 | 18 | 13 | 16 | 24 | 10 |
| 16 | 15 | 29 | 25 | 33 | 42 | 20 | 24 |
| 17 | 38 | 36 | 11 | 26 | 31 | 32 | 19 |

We can make a stem-and-leaf plot from these data.

- The least number of books is 10. The greatest number is 43. Students read between 10 and 43 books. Write the tens digits 1 to 4 in a column. These are the **stems**.

**Books Read in One Year**

| Stem | Leaf |
|---|---|
| 1 | 0 1 2 3 5 5 6 6 6 7 7 8 8 9 9 |
| 2 | 0 3 3 4 4 5 6 7 9 |
| 3 | 1 1 2 3 6 8 |
| 4 | 2 3 |

**In a stem-and-leaf plot, the leaves are always numbers from 0 to 9.**

- Start with the least number, 10.
Write 0 as the **leaf** next to the stem, 1.
Continue with the next greatest number, 11.
Write 1 as the next leaf.
Continue in this way.
Record all the leaves in order from the least number to the greatest number.

- Write a title for the plot.

**Example**

Here are the heights, in centimetres, of the members of St. Mark's junior football team.
a) What is the range of the heights of the football players?
b) Draw a stem-and-leaf plot for the data.
c) What is the median height?
d) What is the mode height?

**Heights of Football Players in Centimetres**

| | | | | | | | | |
|---|---|---|---|---|---|---|---|---|
| 147 | 153 | 162 | 171 | 159 | 168 | 145 | 183 | 164 |
| 187 | 153 | 164 | 148 | 164 | 167 | 187 | 179 | |
| 148 | 190 | 188 | 173 | 155 | 177 | 176 | 189 | 192 |

**Solution**

**a)** The least height is 145 cm.
The greatest height is 192 cm.
The range is 192 cm − 145 cm = 47 cm.

**b)** Each number has 3 digits, so the stem will be the hundreds and tens digits. The leaf will be the ones digit. The stems are from 14 to 19. Start with the least number, 145. Write the leaf, 5, next to the stem, 14. Continue to write the leaves, from the least number to the greatest number.

| Heights of Football Players in Centimetres | |
|---|---|
| **Stem** | **Leaf** |
| 14 | 5 7 8 8 |
| 15 | 3 3 5 9 |
| 16 | 2 4 4 4 7 8 |
| 17 | 1 3 6 7 9 |
| 18 | 3 7 7 8 9 |
| 19 | 0 2 |

**c)** There are 26 numbers. This is an even number. The median is the mean of the two middle numbers when the numbers are arranged in order. For 26 numbers in order, the first middle number is $\frac{26}{2} = 13$, or the 13th number. The next middle number is the 14th number. Count the leaves, beginning at 5. The 13th and 14th numbers are 167 and 168.

The median is: $\frac{167 + 168}{2} = 167.5$
The median height is 167.5 cm.

| Heights of Football Players in Centimetres | |
|---|---|
| **Stem** | **Leaf** |
| 14 | 5 7 8 8 |
| 15 | 3 3 5 9 |
| 16 | 2 4 4 4 7 8 |
| 17 | 1 3 6 7 9 |
| 18 | 3 7 7 8 9 |
| 19 | 0 2 |

**d)** The mode is the number that occurs most often. Leaf 4 occurs three times next to stem 16. The mode is 164 cm.

The *Example* shows that, when the data are displayed in a stem-and-leaf plot, the range, the median, and the mode can be found from the plot.
When you organize data in a stem-and-leaf plot, the original data are visible. A frequency table only shows how many numbers are in each group, and not what the numbers are.

**Hours Worked by Part-Time Staff at a Video Store in One Month**

| Stem | Leaf |
|------|------|
| 9 | 1 6 9 |
| 10 | 2 5 6 8 |
| 11 | 0 3 4 4 4 7 |
| 12 | 0 1 2 2 5 6 6 8 9 |
| 13 | 2 3 5 6 7 7 7 7 8 9 9 |

**1. a)** What does this stem-and-leaf plot show?
   **b)** How many part-time employees work at the video store?
   **c)** What is the least number of hours worked? The greatest number of hours worked?
   **d)** What is the range of hours worked?
   **e)** What is the median number of hours worked?
   **f)** What is the mode number of hours worked?

**2.** The masses of parcels, in kilograms, are given.
   **a)** Display the data in a stem-and-leaf plot.
   **b)** Find the greatest mass. The least mass.
   **c)** What is the range of masses?
   **d)** What is the median mass?
   **e)** What is the mode mass?

**Masses in Kilograms**

| | | | | |
|---|---|---|---|---|
| 28 | 32 | 40 | 36 | 31 |
| 40 | 48 | 35 | 38 | 34 |
| 43 | 35 | 41 | 36 | 52 |
| 37 | 47 | 29 | 42 | 35 |
| 33 | 39 | 32 | 48 | 37 |
| 38 | 30 | 35 | 44 | 54 |

**3.** Which type of data cannot be shown in a stem-and-leaf plot? Explain.

**4.** Work with a partner. Use a metre stick to measure each other's stride, to the nearest centimetre. Record the measures on the board. Use the measures for the whole class.
   **a)** Make a stem-and-leaf plot.
   **b)** What did you find out about the strides of your classmates? Write down as much as you can.

**Calculator Skills**

Find two numbers with a difference of 2.75 and a product of 60.125.

**5.** A food manufacturer claims:
   "We guarantee an average of 50 g of peanuts per bag."
   In 6 months, Devon found the masses of peanuts, in grams, in 24 bags. Look at the data.
   **a)** Is the food manufacturer's claim true?
   **b)** How could you use a stem-and-leaf plot to justify your answer?

**Masses of Peanuts in Grams**

50.1, 49.9, 49.0, 48.9,
50.8, 50.3, 51.3, 49.8,
48.8, 49.0, 50.3, 51.2,
49.4, 49.0, 48.1, 49.6,
49.8, 51.3, 50.5, 50.7,
48.7, 51.0, 49.3, 52.5

**6. Assessment Focus**

    **a)** Collect data on the points scored by a basketball team in its last 15 games. The points could be from games played by your school team or a professional team.

    **b)** Make a stem-and-leaf plot.

    **c)** Write 3 things you know from looking at the plot.

## Reflect

Explain why it is easier to read data in a stem-and-leaf plot than data in a table.

## The World of Work

# Meteorologist

A meteorologist is often a specialist. She uses data collection tools suitable for the weather condition being studied. The data collected are pooled nationally and internationally, and studied by a variety of meteorologists and others in related fields. The information and analysis produce severe weather alerts, which can save thousands of lives.

We may not experience surviving a tornado or a hurricane. But there are other weather conditions that are just as destructive. On January 6, 1998, a severe ice-storm hit Quebec, eastern Ontario, and northeastern U.S. Many people called it the largest ecological disaster in the history of Quebec. On February 6, 1998, Quebec was restored to some normalcy.

When was the last time you heard a "severe weather warning"?
Was the prediction correct?
What kinds of data management tools might have been used to predict this event?

# Mid-Unit Review

LESSON

**5.1** **1.** A survey was conducted to decide if a new hockey arena should be built. The question was, "We have one hockey arena that is always in use. Do we need a new hockey arena?

Yes _____ No _____"

a) Is the question biased? Explain.

b) If your answer to part a is yes, rewrite the question so it is not biased.

**5.2** **2.** The pictograph shows the types of movies rented from a video store in one day.

**Movie Rentals in One Day**

Key: represents 4 movies

a) Record the data in a frequency table.

b) Construct a bar graph.

c) Write a question you could answer from the bar graph or pictograph.
Answer the question.

d) What else do you know from the graphs?

**3.** Use an atlas or other database.

a) Choose 5 countries other than Canada.

b) Find the area of each country and Canada.

c) Record the data in a table.

d) Graph the data.

e) How does each country's area compare with Canada's area?

f) What else do you know from the table or graph?

**5.3** **4.** Here are the history test scores for students in Ms. Epstein's class.

**History Test Scores**

| | | | | | | |
|---|---|---|---|---|---|---|
| 56 | 87 | 98 | 34 | 66 | 75 | 50 |
| 69 | 70 | 83 | 99 | 55 | 83 | 56 |
| 62 | 90 | 47 | 92 | 75 | 85 | 68 |
| 98 | 78 | 62 | 51 | 59 | 75 | 81 |
| 58 | 79 | 80 | 94 | 92 | 63 | 71 |

a) Draw a stem-and-leaf plot to represent the data.

b) What is the range of the scores?

c) The pass mark is 50. How many students did not pass the test?

d) Students who scored below 60 had to rewrite the test. How many students rewrote the test?

e) Find the median score.

f) Find the mode score.

# Using *Fathom* to Investigate Scatter Plots

This table lists the Academy Award winners for Best Actress from 1973–2002, and the age of each actress in that year.

| Academy Award Winners for Best Actress | | | | | |
|---|---|---|---|---|---|
| **Actress** | **Year** | **Age** | **Actress** | **Year** | **Age** |
| Glenda Jackson | 1973 | 37 | Jodie Foster | 1988 | 26 |
| Ellen Burstyn | 1974 | 42 | Jessica Tandy | 1989 | 80 |
| Louise Fletcher | 1975 | 41 | Kathy Bates | 1990 | 42 |
| Faye Dunaway | 1976 | 35 | Jodie Foster | 1991 | 29 |
| Diane Keaton | 1977 | 31 | Emma Thompson | 1992 | 33 |
| Jane Fonda | 1978 | 41 | Holly Hunter | 1993 | 35 |
| Sally Field | 1979 | 33 | Jessica Lange | 1994 | 45 |
| Sissy Spacek | 1980 | 30 | Susan Sarandon | 1995 | 44 |
| Katharine Hepburn | 1981 | 74 | Frances McDormand | 1996 | 39 |
| Meryl Streep | 1982 | 33 | Helen Hunt | 1997 | 34 |
| Shirley MacLaine | 1983 | 49 | Gwyneth Paltrow | 1998 | 26 |
| Sally Field | 1984 | 38 | Hilary Swank | 1999 | 25 |
| Geraldine Page | 1985 | 61 | Julia Roberts | 2000 | 33 |
| Marlee Matlin | 1986 | 21 | Halle Berry | 2001 | 33 |
| Cher | 1987 | 41 | Nicole Kidman | 2002 | 35 |

To use *Fathom* to draw a scatter plot for these data, follow these steps:

1. Open *Fathom*. From the File menu, select New.

2. To enter the title:
   Click on the New Collection icon ![icon],
   then click on the screen. Double click Collection 1.
   Type **Academy Award Winners for Best Actress**
   and click OK, as shown at the right.

   | Rename Collection |
   |---|
   | Academy Award Winners for Best Actress |
   | Cancel    OK |

3. To enter the data:
   Click on the New Case Table icon ![icon],
   then click on the screen.

Click on <new>; type **Year**, then press Enter. A new column appears to the right with the heading <new>. Click on the word <new>, type **Age**, then press Enter. Under the headings *Year* and *Age*, input the data from the table on page 185.

**4.** To graph the data:
Click on the New Graph icon  ,
then click on the screen. Two axes appear.
Click on the column heading,
*Year*, and drag it to the horizontal axis.
Click on the column heading,
*Age*, and drag it to the vertical axis.
*Fathom* creates a scatter plot,
as shown at the right.

The range of the data is: 80 – 21, or 59 years.
However, most of the data are located between 31 and 42 years.
The data form a **cluster** between these ages.
This means that, from 1973 to 2002, most winners were between 31 and 42 years old.
There are two large sections without points — between 49 and 61 years, and between 61 and 74 years. These represent gaps in the data. From 1973 to 2002, none of the winners were between 49 and 61 years old, or between 61 and 74 years old.
From the scatter plot, we can see that there is no pattern or **trend** in the data.

Here is another example of data in a scatter plot:
Emidio works part-time as a waiter in a restaurant. The table and scatter plot on page 187 show the hours he worked each week for 12 weeks, and his earnings, in dollars, for each week.

From the scatter plot, the points show an **upward trend** from left to right. Emidio's earnings increase as time increases.
That is, the more hours per week Emidio works, the more he earns.

Here is a third example of data in a scatter plot:
Water is draining out of a swimming pool. The table and
scatter plot show the volume of water, in litres, remaining
in the pool at one-hour intervals.

| Pool Water Draining | | |
|---|---|---|
| | Time_in_hours | Volume_in_litres |
| 1 | 0 | 5200 |
| 2 | 1 | 4700 |
| 3 | 2 | 3900 |
| 4 | 3 | 3300 |
| 5 | 4 | 2600 |
| 6 | 5 | 2100 |
| 7 | 6 | 1100 |

From the scatter plot, the points show a **downward trend**
from left to right.
The volume of water in the pool decreases as time increases.
That is, the more hours the pool drains, the less water there is in it.

✓ **Check**

| Time | Speed (km/h) |
|---|---|
| 12 noon | 0 |
| 12:30 | 70 |
| 1:00 | 85 |
| 1:30 | 100 |
| 2:00 | 100 |
| 2:30 | 100 |
| 3:00 | 0 |
| 3:30 | 0 |
| 4:00 | 100 |
| 4:30 | 65 |
| 5:00 | 0 |

**1.** Emily drove from Toronto to Cornwall.
She left Toronto at 12 noon and arrived in Cornwall at 5 p.m.
The table at the left shows the speed of the car recorded at
different times during her trip.
Use *Fathom* to draw a scatter plot to represent the data.
Describe any trends.
What do you know from looking at the graph?

**Reflect**

Describe 3 different types of scatter plots.
Provide an example for each type.

## 5.4  Line Graphs

**Focus** Display data using line graphs and describe trends.

### Explore

Work with a partner.
Madhu measured the mass of her pet guinea pig
every 5 months, until it was 25 months old.
The data are shown at the left.

➤ One person draws a bar graph.
 The other person draws a line graph.
➤ During which period did the guinea pig
 gain the most mass?
➤ What happened to the mass of the guinea pig after
 15 months? Does this make sense?
➤ Predict the mass of the guinea pig at 30 months.

| Age (months) | Mass (g) |
|---|---|
| 5 | 200 |
| 10 | 350 |
| 15 | 480 |
| 20 | 510 |
| 25 | 520 |

### Reflect & Share

Discuss with your partner which graph is better for displaying the
data. Justify your answer.
Estimate the mass of the guinea pig at 18 months.
Which graph is better to make this estimate? Explain.

### Connect

A **line graph** displays data that change over time.
The line graph on page 189 shows how Leah's height changes as she
gets older.
From 2 to 13 years, each line segment goes up to the right.
This shows that Leah's height increases.
From 13 to 16 years, the line segments still go up to the right,
but they are not as steep.
This shows that Leah's height increases, but at a slower rate
than before.
From 16 years on, the line segments are horizontal.
This shows that Leah's height has stopped increasing.
She has stopped growing taller.

This symbol ⸎ on the vertical axis means that the numbers from 0 to 60 are not shown.

**Leah's Height**

We can use this line graph to find values between data points. At $11\frac{1}{2}$ years, Leah was about 148 cm tall.

## Example

a) Draw a line graph to display these data.

b) Use the graph. Describe any trends in Canada's population.

c) Use the graph. During which period did Canada's population increase the most? The least? How can you tell?

d) Estimate Canada's population in 2011. Explain how you used the graph to do this. What assumption did you make?

| Canada's Population (to the nearest million) | |
|---|---|
| **Years** | **Number (millions)** |
| 1901 | 5 |
| 1911 | 7 |
| 1921 | 9 |
| 1931 | 10 |
| 1941 | 12 |
| 1951 | 14 |
| 1961 | 18 |
| 1971 | 22 |
| 1981 | 25 |
| 1991 | 28 |
| 2001 | 31 |

**Solution**

a) **Step 1.** Draw axes on grid paper. The horizontal axis represents time, in years. Use 1 square for each 10-year interval, starting in 1901. The vertical axis represents population, in millions. The greatest population to be graphed is 31 million. Make 35 the greatest number on the vertical scale. Use 1 square for every 5 million, starting at 0.

**Step 2.** Plot a point on the grid for each pair of entries in the table. Use a ruler to join adjacent points.

**Step 3.** Label the axes. Give the graph a title.

**Canada's Population**

**b)** The graph goes up to the right.
This means that Canada's population increased from 1901 to 2001. In general, the line segments from 1951 to 2001 are steeper than the segments from 1901 to 1951.
This means that the population was increasing at a faster rate in the 2nd half of the century.

**c)** The period in which the line segment is the steepest represents the greatest increase in population. This happened from 1951 to 1971. From 1921 to 1931, the line segment is the least steep. This is when Canada's population had the least increase.

**d)** To predict Canada's population in 2011, extend the last line segment to 2011. From 2011 on the horizontal axis, draw a vertical line to the graph. From the graph, draw a horizontal line to the vertical axis. This line meets the axis at about 34 million. The population of Canada in 2011 will be approximately 34 million.
We assume that Canada's population will continue to grow at the same rate as it did from 1991 to 2001.

**Canada's Population**

# Practice

## Calculator Skills

Three consecutive
2-digit numbers
have a product
of 551 286.

What is the sum of
the three numbers?

**1. a)** What does this line graph show?

   **b)** About how tall was Nathan at each age?

     **i)** 8 years

     **ii)** 12 years

     **iii)** 15 years

   **c)** During which year did
Nathan grow the most?
The least?
How does the graph
show this?

   **d)** Predict Nathan's height at
18 years.
Explain your reasoning.

   **e)** Predict Nathan's height at
50 years. Explain.

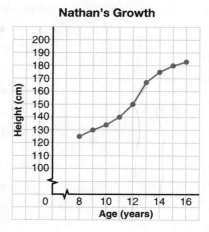

**Nathan's Growth**

**2. a)** What does this table show?

   **b)** Draw a line graph for each city on the same grid.

   **c)** Describe the trends in rainfall for the two cities.
How do the line graphs illustrate these trends?

   **d)** In which month(s) do the line graphs cross?
What does this mean?

   **e)** What is the average annual rainfall for each city?

| Average Monthly Rainfall (cm) | | |
|---|---|---|
| **Month** | **Vancouver** | **Ottawa** |
| January | 14.0 | 1.5 |
| February | 12.0 | 1.6 |
| March | 9.6 | 3.2 |
| April | 5.8 | 5.8 |
| May | 4.9 | 7.5 |
| June | 4.7 | 7.7 |
| July | 2.6 | 8.8 |
| August | 3.5 | 9.2 |
| September | 5.4 | 8.3 |
| October | 11.7 | 7.0 |
| November | 13.8 | 6.3 |
| December | 16.4 | 3.3 |

**3. a)** Research your region on one of these topics:

     **i)** the average precipitation for each month

     **ii)** the maximum temperature for the first day
of each month

     **iii)** the average temperature for each month

   **b)** Organize the data in a table. Draw a line graph.

   **c)** Repeat part a for a city or region in a different part
of Canada.

   **d)** Draw a line graph to display these data on the same grid
as in part b.

   **e)** How are the line graphs alike? How are they different?

   **f)** Write all that you know from looking at the graphs.

| Stopping Distance for a Car | | |
|---|---|---|
| Speed (km/h) | Dry Pavement (m) | Wet Pavement (m) |
| 0 | 0 | 0 |
| 10 | 3 | 6 |
| 20 | 7 | 11 |
| 30 | 12 | 17 |
| 40 | 16 | 26 |
| 50 | 23 | 38 |
| 60 | 30 | 50 |
| 70 | 38 | 64 |
| 80 | 49 | 78 |
| 90 | 60 | 97 |
| 100 | 72 | 120 |

**4. a)** What does stopping distance depend on?

**b)** On the same grid, draw a line graph for dry pavement and for wet pavement.

**c)** Why are line graphs suitable for these data?

**d)** Describe the trends in the graphs.

**e)** A car travels at 75 km/h on dry pavement. What is its stopping distance?

**f)** A car takes 30 m to stop on wet pavement. How fast was it travelling?

**g)** Write a question you could answer using the graph but not the table. Explain why you need the graph instead of the table.

**5. Assessment Focus** Nina owns a shoe store. These tables show data about the shoe store.

i)

| Yearly Sales | |
|---|---|
| Year | Sales ($) |
| 1997 | 579 000 |
| 1998 | 621 000 |
| 1999 | 598 000 |
| 2000 | 634 000 |
| 2001 | 657 000 |
| 2002 | 642 000 |
| 2003 | 675 000 |

ii)

| Sizes of Shoes Sold in May | |
|---|---|
| Size | Number of Pairs Sold |
| 6 | 60 |
| 7 | 239 |
| 8 | 217 |
| 9 | 156 |
| 10 | 61 |
| 11 | 43 |
| 12 | 36 |

**a)** Which data would be best represented with a line graph? Explain.

**b)** Draw a line graph for the table you chose in part a.

**c)** Describe the trends in the data.

**d)** Which type of graph would be suitable for the other table? Explain. Graph the data from the other table.

**e)** What do you know from looking at each graph?

**Reflect**

Why is a line graph the best type of graph to use to make predictions?

# Using Spreadsheets to Record and Graph Data

**Focus** | Display data on graphs using spreadsheets.

**Spreadsheet** software, such as *AppleWorks*, can be used to record, then graph, data.

This table shows the favourite sports of Grade 7 students in Mona's school.

To graph these data using *AppleWorks*, follow these steps:

Open *AppleWorks*. Choose Spreadsheet. Enter the data into rows and columns in the spreadsheet.

| Favourite Sports | |
|---|---|
| **Sport** | **Number of Students** |
| Baseball | 20 |
| Soccer | 15 |
| Hockey | 18 |
| Football | 10 |
| Basketball | 12 |

## To create a bar graph

1. Highlight the data. Include the column heads, but do not include the table title.

2. Click the graph icon 📊 on the tool bar. A Chart Options dialogue box appears. Choose Bar, then click OK, as shown below left.

3. The software creates a legend, which is not needed for a bar graph. To remove the legend, right-click the graph. Choose Chart Options, as shown above right. Select the Labels tab. Click the box next to Show Legend to remove the check mark.

**4.** In the Title box, type **Favourite Sports**, as shown below left.
To insert labels, click the Axes tab. Select X axis. Type **Sport**.
Select Y axis. Type **Number of Students**, as shown below right.
Then click OK.

Your graph should look like the one below.

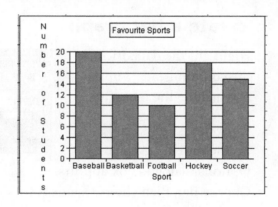

## To create a circle graph

**1.** Use the data on page 193.
Highlight the data as shown below left.
Do not include the column heads or title.

A spreadsheet program uses the term "pie" for a circle graph.

2. Click the graph icon 📊 on the tool bar.
   A Chart Options dialogue box appears.
   Choose Pie, then click OK, as shown bottom right, page 194.
   The circle graph shows a legend at the right.
   The legend shows what sport each sector represents.

3. To add a title, right-click the graph. Choose Chart Options.
   Select the Labels tab. In the Title box, type **Favourite Sports**, as shown below left. Then click OK.
   Your graph should look like the one below right.

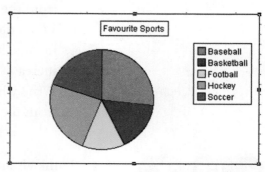

## To create a line graph

These data came from the Statistics Canada website.

| Average Annual Income of Canadian Women | |
|---|---|
| Year | Income ($) |
| 1989 | 28 219 |
| 1990 | 29 050 |
| 1991 | 29 654 |
| 1992 | 30 903 |
| 1993 | 30 466 |
| 1994 | 30 274 |
| 1995 | 30 959 |
| 1996 | 30 606 |
| 1997 | 30 484 |
| 1998 | 32 553 |
| 1999 | 32 026 |

1. Enter the data into rows and columns in the spreadsheet.

2. Highlight the data.
   Include the column heads, but do not include the table title.

3. Click the graph icon 📊 on the tool bar.
   A Chart Options dialogue box appears.
   Choose X-Y Line, then click OK, as shown below.

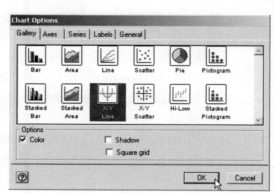

**4.** The software creates a legend, which is not needed for a line graph. To remove the legend, right-click the graph. Choose Chart Options. Select the Labels tab.
Click the box next to Show Legend to remove the check mark.
In the Title box, type **Average Annual Income of Canadian Women**. Then click OK.
Your graph should look like the one below.

- What trend does the graph show? Explain.
- How often did the average income increase? Decrease? How can you tell this from the graph?
- When did the average annual income have the greatest increase? Greatest decrease?
- Write what else you know from the graph.

---

✓ **Check**

**1.** Think about where you met your best friend.
The table at the right lists the places where some Canadians met their best friends.

a) Use a spreadsheet to draw a bar graph and a circle graph.

b) Which graph represents the data better? Explain.

| Place | Number |
|---|---|
| School | 5700 |
| Work | 4100 |
| Club or organization | 1400 |
| Religious organization | 700 |
| Home/neighbourhood | 4300 |
| Through family | 1200 |
| Through friend | 1100 |
| Other | 600 |

**2.** Use a spreadsheet to draw a line graph for the data in the table at the left.

a) What trend does the graph show?

b) Predict the average value, in Canadian dollars, of $1U.S. in 2002 and in 2003. What assumptions did you make?

c) Research to find the average value, in Canadian dollars, of $1U.S. in 2002 and 2003. Where could you get this information? How accurate was your prediction?

| Average Value of $1U.S. | |
|---|---|
| Year | Value in Canadian Dollars |
| 1997 | 1.385 |
| 1998 | 1.484 |
| 1999 | 1.486 |
| 2000 | 1.485 |

**3.** The data below are from the Statistics Canada website.
   **a)** Use a spreadsheet.
   Create a graph to display the data.
   **b)** Which type of graph best represents the data? Explain.
   **c)** Which type of graph could not be used to represent the data? Explain.

| Average Hours of Television Viewing per Week, Fall 2001 | |
| --- | --- |
| **Province** | **Adolescents 12–17 years** |
| Newfoundland/Labrador | 15.8 |
| Prince Edward Island | 12.4 |
| Nova Scotia | 14.1 |
| New Brunswick | 14.1 |
| Quebec | 14.5 |
| Ontario | 12.8 |
| Manitoba | 12.8 |
| Saskatchewan | 12.5 |
| Alberta | 13.3 |
| British Columbia | 10.9 |

**Math Link**

**Your World**

Newspapers often publish survey results. The headlines may be misleading.

Try to find headlines like these. Cut them out. Explain why they are misleading.

Why would newspapers do this?

**Focus** Understand which measure of central tendency best describes a set of data.

## Explore

Work on your own.
Record on the board how many siblings you have.
Use the class data.
Find the mean, the median, and the mode.
Find the range.

*The mean, median, and mode are measures of central tendency. Each measure is an average.*

### Reflect & Share

With a classmate, discuss which measure of central tendency best describes the average number of siblings.

## Connect

A clothing store sold jeans in these sizes in one day:
28  30  28  26  30  32  28  32  26  28  34  38  36  30  34  32  30

To calculate the mean jeans size sold, add the sizes, then divide by the number of jeans sold.

$$\text{Mean} = \frac{28 + 30 + 28 + 26 + 30 + 32 + 28 + 32 + 26 + 28 + 34 + 38 + 36 + 30 + 34 + 32 + 30}{17}$$
$$= \frac{522}{17}$$
$$\doteq 30.7$$

The mean size is approximately 30.7.

**When there is an odd number of data, to find the middle number: Add 1 to the number of data, then divide by 2. This gives the position of the middle number.**

**For example:**

$$\frac{17 + 1}{2} = \frac{18}{2} = 9;$$

**the middle number is 9th.**

To calculate the median, order the jeans sold from least size to greatest size. The middle number is the median.
There are 17 numbers. The middle number is 9th.
26, 26, 28, 28, 28, 28, 30, 30, 30 , 30, 32, 32, 32, 34, 34, 36, 38
The median size is 30.

The mode is the number that occurs most often.
There are two numbers that occur most often.
They are 28 and 30. So, the mode sizes are 28 and 30.

In this situation, the mean, 30.7, is of little use.
The mean does not represent a size.

The median, 30, shows about one-half of the customers bought jeans of size 30 or smaller, and about one-half of the customers bought jeans of size 30 or larger.

The modes, 28 and 30, tell which sizes are purchased more often. The mode is most useful to the storeowner.
He may use the mode to order extra stock of the most popular sizes.

## Example

A bookstore has 15 books in its young adult section. There are 5 different prices. This table shows the number of books at each price.

a) Find the mean, median, and mode prices.
b) Which measure best represents the average price of a young adult book?
c) What is the range of the prices?

| Young Adult Books | |
| --- | --- |
| Price ($) | Number of Books |
| 8.99 | 3 |
| 9.99 | 5 |
| 13.99 | 5 |
| 32.99 | 1 |
| 37.99 | 1 |

**Solution**

a) Mean price:
• Multiply each price by the total number of books at that price, then add the prices.
$(8.99 \times 3) + (9.99 \times 5) + (13.99 \times 5) + 32.99 + 37.99 = 217.85$
• Divide the total price by the total number of books: 15
$\frac{217.85}{15} \doteq 14.52$

The mean price per book is approximately $14.52.

Median price:
There are 15 books.
The table shows the books in order from least price to greatest price.
The median price is the 8th price. The 8th price is $9.99.
The median price is $9.99.

Mode price:
There are two mode prices. They are $9.99 and $13.99.

b) The mean price is not charged for any of the books.
Only two books cost more than the mean of $14.52.

There are two mode prices.
One mode, $9.99, is the same as the median price.

One-half the books cost less than the median price.
One-half cost more.
So, the median price, $9.99, best represents the average cost of a young adult book at the store.

c) For the range, subtract the lowest price from the highest:
$37.99 - 8.99 = 29.00$
The range of prices is $29.00.

## Practice

1. Here are Ira's practice times, in seconds, for the 100-m backstroke: 122, 118, 123, 119, 118, 120, 118, 121, 119
   a) Find the mean, median, and mode of these data.
   b) Of the mean, median, and mode, which do you think best describes Ira's race time? Explain.
   c) What is the range of these data?

2. Caitlin received these test marks in each subject.
   a) Find the mean, median, and mode for each subject.
   b) Explain what information each measure of central tendency gives.
   c) Which subject is Caitlin best at? Worst at? Explain your reasoning.

| Caitlin's Marks | |
|---|---|
| Math | 85 69 92 55 68 75 78 |
| Spelling | 72 81 50 69 81 96 92 |
| History | 68 74 82 80 76 67 74 |

3. The table shows the tips earned by five waiters and waitresses during two weeks in December.
   a) Calculate the mean, median, and mode tips for each week.
   b) Calculate the mean, median, and mode tips for the two-week period.
   c) Compare your answers in parts a and b. Which are the same? Which are different? Explain why.
   d) Which measure of central tendency best represents the tips earned during the two weeks? Explain.

| Weekly Tips Earned ($) | | |
|---|---|---|
| Waiter | Week 1 | Week 2 |
| James | 1150 | 600 |
| Kyrra | 700 | 725 |
| Tamara | 800 | 775 |
| Jacob | 875 | 860 |
| George | 600 | 1165 |

4. Jamal was training for a 400-m race.
   His times, in seconds, for the first five races were:
   120, 118, 138, 124, 118
   a) Find the median and mode times.
   b) Jamal wants his median time after 6 races to be 121 s.
      What time must he get in his 6th race? Explain.

5. Find 5 numbers that have a mean of 24 and a median of 25.
   Justify your answer.
   How many different sets of 5 numbers can you find?
   Show that each set has the mean and median stated.

6. A quality control inspector randomly selects boxes of crackers
   from the production line. She measures their masses. On one day
   she selects 30 boxes. The inspector records these data:
   - 12 boxes: 405 g each          • 4 boxes: 385 g each
   - 4 boxes: 395 g each           • 2 boxes: 380 g each
   - 8 boxes: 390 g each
   a) Which expression can be used to calculate the mean mass?
      Use it to find the mean mass.
      i) $\dfrac{(405 \times 12 + 395 \times 4 + 390 \times 8 + 385 \times 4 + 380 \times 2)}{30}$

      ii) $405 \times 12 + 395 \times 4 + 390 \times 8 + 385 \times 4 + 380 \times 2 \div 30$
   b) For the shipment of crackers to be acceptable, the mean mass
      must be at least 395 g. Is this shipment acceptable? Explain.

7. **Assessment Focus**
   Use these data: 28, 30, 30, 31, 32, 33, 34, 35, 37, 38, 39, 41
   a) Find the mean, median, and mode.
   b) What happens to the mean, median, and mode in each case?
      i) Each number is increased by 10.
      ii) Each number is doubled.
      Explain the results.

**Number Strategies**

Use only the digits 0, 2, 3, and a decimal point. Use each digit only once each time.

Make as many numbers with 2 digits as possible.

Find the sum of the numbers.

**Reflect**

Use your answers from *Practice*. Describe a situation for each case.
a) The mean is the best measure of central tendency.
b) The median is the best measure of central tendency.
c) The mode is the best measure of central tendency.

# 5.6 Evaluating Data Analysis

## Explore

Work on your own.
What do the two graphs below show?
How are the graphs similar? How are they different?
Explain.

Average New House Prices

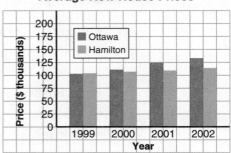

Average New House Prices

### Reflect & Share

Discuss with a classmate:
What impression does each graph give? Explain.
Who may want to use each type of graph?

## Connect

Sometimes, graphs are used to distort information and to mislead.
Look at these graphs.

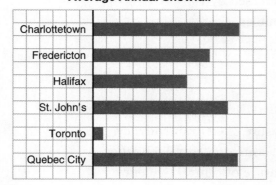

Average Annual Snowfall

This bar graph is misleading.
It suggests that Quebec City has more than
10 times as much snow as Toronto.
This graph has no measurements of the depth
of snow.

**Average Annual Snowfall**

Visually, this graph suggests the same information as the first graph. However, the horizontal scale is labelled with the snowfall.

The scale shows that Toronto has about 135 cm of snow and Quebec City has about 335 cm.

**Average Annual Snowfall**

This graph accurately shows the data. The horizontal scale starts at 0.
The lengths of the bars are shown in the correct ratio. Quebec City has between 2 and 3 times as much snow as Toronto.

## Example

This line graph is used to suggest that salaries have doubled in 6 years.
a) Why is this graph misleading?
b) Redraw the graph to show accurately how salaries have changed in 6 years.

**Salaries Up!**

## Solution

a) Use the vertical scale.
The salary in year 1 is about $34 500.
The salary in year 6 is about $35 750.
The increase in salary is: $35 750 − $34 500 = $1250
The salaries have increased by only $1250 in 6 years.

b) Make a table from the line graph.
Estimate each salary.

| Year | Salary ($) |
|------|-----------|
| 1 | 34 500 |
| 2 | 34 600 |
| 3 | 35 250 |
| 4 | 35 000 |
| 5 | 35 300 |
| 6 | 35 750 |

Draw a graph.
Start the vertical
scale at $0.
Use a scale of 1 square
to represent $5000.

**Salary Increases**

## Practice

1. Which graph is misleading? Explain why it is misleading.

**Food Drive Results**

**Food Drive Results**

2. The two graphs display the Read Books Company's profits for a
   four-month period.

**Read Books Co. Profits**

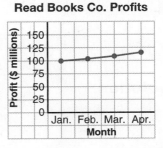

**Read Books Co. Profits**

a) Which graph might the president of the company choose to
   report profits to the shareholders? Why?

b) Which graph might the rival company use to compare
   profits? Why?

c) Predict the company's profit for May.
   What assumptions do you make?

**3.** Why do some graphs display data in a misleading way? Describe how a graph might be drawn to misrepresent data.

**4.** A graph similar to this is part of an advertisement for a truck manufacturer.
With the graph, Manufacturer A says that more than 98 out of 100 of its trucks sold in the last 10 years are still on the road.

**Number of Trucks Still on the Road**

a) What impression does this graph give?

b) How many trucks, out of 100, are still on the road for Manufacturer B? C? D?

c) Do you think Manufacturer A's trucks are more dependable than the other manufacturers' trucks? Explain.

d) Redraw the graph to give an accurate representation of the data.

| Board of Directors' Expenses | |
|---|---|
| Quarter | Amount ($) |
| 1st | 85 000 |
| 2nd | 104 000 |
| 3rd | 125 000 |
| 4th | 155 000 |

**5.** Draw a graph to display the data at the left in each way:
a) The directors want the expenses to look low.
b) The shareholders want to show the expenses are too high.
c) Draw an accurate representation of the data.
For each graph you draw, explain how it shows what you intended.

**6.** **Assessment Focus**
Use newspapers, magazines, or the Internet.
Find a graph that creates a false impression.
a) Describe how the graph creates a false impression.
b) Why might the misleading graph be used?
c) How could the graph be changed to present the data more accurately?
d) Use your suggestions in part c to draw an accurate graph.

**Reflect**

Describe two ways in which a graph may be misleading.

# Making a Study Sheet

**1** Be sure that you know exactly what will be covered on the test or quiz. Ask your teacher if you are not sure. Highlight these areas in your notebook.

**2** List the math vocabulary you will need. Write definitions and provide examples if you need to.

*Congruent figures have exactly the same size and shape. Corresponding angles have the same measure. Corresponding sides have the same length.*

**3** Colour code any formulas you will need.

*Area of rectangle = Length × Width*
*Area of triangle = $\frac{1}{2}$ × Base × Height*

**4** Use pictures to help you remember.

*Polygon: A closed figure formed by three or more line segments*

YES:           NO:

**5**

Copy out a sample problem. Include all necessary examples and discussion.

*Sample Problem:* You have a choice of recess times:
- You may have 30 min a day for the next two weeks, OR
- You may have 1 min of recess the 1st day, 2 min the 2nd day, 4 min the 3rd day, 8 min the 4th day, and so on, for the next two weeks. Which choice would give you more recess time in the 2 weeks? Explain your answer.

*Solution*

This problem is about finding out which recess choice is better. The strategy I will use is to make a table.

| Day | 1 | 2 | 3 |
|---|---|---|---|
| Choice 1 (min) | 30 | 30 | 30 |
| Total time (min) | 30 | 60 | 90 |
| Choice 2 (min) | 1 | 2 | 4 |
| Total time (min) | 1 | 3 | 7 |

**6**

Use word association and patterns to help you remember.

A hexagon has six sides. (Both have an X.)
Octagon -- Octapus (Both have 8 sides/arms.)

# Unit Review

Review any lesson with

online tutorial

## What Do I Need to Know?

☑ **Primary data** are data you collect.

☑ **Secondary data** are found from databases on the Internet, or a library, or other sources.

☑ In a set of data:

The **mean** is the sum of numbers divided by the number of numbers in the set.

The **median** is the middle number, when there is an odd number of data in the set. When there is an even number of data, the median is the mean of the two middle numbers.

The **mode** is the number that occurs most often. A set of data can have no mode, one mode, or more than one mode.

## What Should I Be Able to Do?

For extra practice, go to page 442.

**LESSON**

**5.1**

**1.** A recreation group wants to find out the favourite summer activity of teenagers in the town.
   a) Write an unbiased survey question.
   b) Write a biased survey question. Explain how it is biased.

**5.2**
**5.5**

**2.** The data in this table are from Statistics Canada.

| Average Weekly Earnings in 2001 | |
|---|---|
| **Job** | **Earnings ($)** |
| Forestry | 831 |
| Mining | 1153 |
| Utilities | 1000 |
| Construction | 800 |
| Real Estate | 612 |
| Education | 696 |
| Health Care | 584 |
| Transportation | 742 |

a) What do the data show?

b) Draw a graph to display the data.

c) Explain your choice of graph. Could another type of graph have been used? Why?

d) Which job has the highest weekly earnings? The lowest weekly earnings? How is this shown in your graph?

e) How can the data be used to find the average annual earnings? The average monthly earnings? How might the graph be used to find these?

f) Which average: mean, median, or mode, do you think is shown in the table? Explain your answer.

**5.5** **3.** Jacob collected the data in the table below. The table lists 5 TV shows that air on Sunday evenings. The survey question was "Which of these shows is your favourite?

Everyone Loves Jordan___, Girl Meets World___, Lost in Time___, Metro PD___, Reality Shock___"

| TV Show | Tally | Frequency |
|---|---|---|
| Everyone Loves Jordan | ### ### ### // | |
| Girl Meets World | ### ### | |
| Lost in Time | ### //// | |
| Metro PD | //// | |
| Reality Shock | ### ### ### ### | |

a) Write the frequency of each response.

b) How many people did Jacob survey?

c) Suppose you were a TV producer and had to take one show off the air. Which show would it be? Explain.

d) Suppose you were an advertiser. Which show would you advertise with? Why?

e) Display the data using:
   i) a pictograph
   ii) a bar graph

**5.3** **4.** A quality control inspector
**5.5** measures the masses of boxes of raisins. He wants to know if the average mass of a box of raisins is 100 g.
He randomly chooses boxes from the production department.
The masses, in grams, are recorded below.

**Masses of Boxes of Raisins in Grams**
99.1, 101.7, 99.8, 98.9, 100.8, 100.3, 98.3, 100.0, 97.8, 97.6, 98.5, 101.7, 100.2, 100.2, 99.4, 100.3, 98.8, 102.0, 100.3, 98.0, 99.4, 99.0, 98.1, 101.8, 99.8, 101.3, 100.5, 100.7, 98.7, 100.3, 99.3, 102.5

a) Draw a stem-and-leaf plot.

b) What can you tell from the plot that you could not easily see from the data?

c) Will this shipment be approved? Explain.

d) What is the median?

e) What is the mode?

f) Would the shipment be approved if the mode was used? If the median was used? Explain.

5.4
5.5
**5.** The mean monthly rainfalls for Calgary and Charlottetown are given.

| Mean Monthly Rainfall (cm) | | |
|---|---|---|
| Month | Calgary | Charlottetown |
| January | 1.2 | 9.8 |
| February | 1.0 | 8.2 |
| March | 1.5 | 7.6 |
| April | 2.5 | 7.5 |
| May | 5.3 | 8.0 |
| June | 7.7 | 7.9 |
| July | 7.0 | 7.4 |
| August | 4.9 | 9.0 |
| September | 4.8 | 9.2 |
| October | 1.6 | 9.9 |
| November | 1.2 | 11.5 |
| December | 1.3 | 10.0 |

a) Draw a line graph for each city on the same grid.
b) Describe each graph. Are there any trends? Explain.
c) Do the line graphs cross? What does this mean?
d) Determine the mean annual rainfall for each city. Explain your steps.
e) Determine the median monthly rainfall for each city.
f) What else do you know from the table or the graph?

5.5
**6.** In each case, which is most useful: the mean, median, or mode? Justify your answer.
a) A storeowner wants to know which sweater sizes he should order. Last week he sold 5 small, 15 medium, 6 large, and 2 X-large sweaters.
b) Five of Robbie's friends said their weekly allowances are: $5, $8, $10, $6, and $5. Robbie wants to convince his parents to increase his allowance.
c) Tina wants to know if her math mark was in the top half or bottom half of the class.

5.5
5.6
**7.** A small engineering company has an owner and 5 employees. This table shows their salaries.

| Company Salaries | |
|---|---|
| Position | Annual Salary ($) |
| Owner | 130 000 |
| Manager | 90 000 |
| 2 Engineers | 50 000 |
| Receptionist | 28 000 |
| Secretary | 28 000 |

Which measure of central tendency would you use to describe the average annual salary in each case?
a) You want to attract a new employee.
b) You want to suggest the company does not pay its employees well.

# Practice Test

**1. a)** Explain the difference between primary and secondary data.

**b)** State if primary data or secondary data are used in each case. Justify your answers.

**i)** Anna searched the Internet to find the top ten movies of the year.

**ii)** Rory phoned his friends to ask if they were coming to his party.

**2.** Here are the times, in minutes and seconds, of 28 people who competed in an 800-m race.

**a)** Display the data in a stem-and-leaf plot.

**b)** What is the range of times for the race?

**c)** Find the median time.

**d)** Is there a mode time? If so, what is it? If not, explain how you know.

| 800-m Race Times |
|---|
| 3:25, 3:07, 1:55, 3:11 |
| 2:41, 2:47, 3:04, 1:58 |
| 2:35, 3:25, 3:08, 2:53 |
| 2:29, 3:15, 2:55, 2:28 |
| 3:14, 2:47, 3:07, 2:39 |
| 2:39, 2:43, 3:19, 2:54 |
| 3:11, 2:59, 2:42, 2:57 |

**3.** Parham received these marks on 7 math tests:
91, 75, 95, 80, 83, 86, 68
What mark will he need on his next test in each case?
Justify each answer.

**a)** The mean of his 8 tests is 84.

**b)** The mode of his 8 tests is 86.

**c)** The median of his 8 tests is 84.

| Country of Origin for Visitors to Canada ||
|---|---|
| **Country** | **Number of Visitors** |
| Japan | 500 000 |
| France | 400 000 |
| Germany | 400 000 |
| Australia | 175 000 |
| United Kingdom | 850 000 |
| Mexico | 150 000 |
| Hong Kong | 125 000 |

**4. a)** Graph the data at the left. Explain your choice of graph.

**b)** In the year 2000, approximately 15 000 000 people visited Canada from the U.S.
Suppose you want to add these data to your graph in part a. How would your graph change?

**c)** Redraw the graph in part a.
Include the data from part b.

**d)** Compare the two graphs.
Which graph gives you more information?
Justify your answer.

Your help is needed to organize a school Winter Carnival Day. Think about:
- the classes or grades that should participate
- which activities students would enjoy
- which snacks and drinks should be offered

You will collect, display, and analyse data.

## Part 1

Brainstorm with your classmates. Keep a record of the ideas. Here are some topics you may want to discuss:
- Who will participate in Winter Carnival Day?
  Is it possible for all students in every grade in your school to participate?

Are there special considerations for different age groups?
- What type of indoor and outdoor sports, games, and crafts do you think students in your school would enjoy?
- What types of snacks and drinks should be offered? How much will this cost?

After brainstorming, break into five groups. Each group will be responsible for collecting data and reporting on one of the following topics:
- Indoor sports
- Outdoor sports
- Games
- Crafts
- Snacks and drinks

## Part 2

Your group will collect, display, and analyse data related to your task.

- Write a survey question or questions related to your task.
  Explain how bias can be avoided when writing the question.
- Conduct the survey.
- Display the collected data in different ways.
  Justify your displays.
- Analyse the data.
  What decisions can be made about Winter Carnival Day from your results?
- Prepare a report of your findings.

## Part 3

Present the results of your group work to the rest of the class.

**Check List**

Your work should include:

✓ your survey question and data collection plan

✓ at least two displays of your data

✓ justification for the procedures and displays you chose

✓ your analysis and recommendations

## Reflect on the Unit

Describe the different types of graphs you drew.
What can you tell about the data from each type of graph?
Use examples to explain.

# Measuring Perimeter and Area

You see geometric figures all around you.

Look at these pictures.
Identify a figure.
What would you need to know to find the area of that figure?
What would you need to know to find the perimeter of the figure?

## What You'll Learn

- Use formulas to find the areas of a parallelogram, a triangle, and a trapezoid.
- Find the area and perimeter of an irregular figure.

## Why It's Important

- The ability to measure is a life skill. You measure to find how much paint you need for a wall; how much fencing you need for a garden; how much material you need for drapes; and so on.

## Key Words

- perimeter
- area
- parallelogram
- triangle
- trapezoid

# Skills You'll Need

## Perimeter and Area of a Rectangle

**Perimeter** is the distance around a figure.
**Area** is the amount of surface a figure covers.

### Example 1

**a)** Find the perimeter of each figure.

**i)**

**ii)**

**b)** Find the area of each figure in part a.

### Solution

**a) i)** The figure is a square.
The perimeter of a square is: $P = 4s$
Substitute $s = 5$.
$P = 4 \times 5$
$\quad = 20$
The perimeter is 20 cm.

**ii)** The figure is a rectangle.
The perimeter of a rectangle is: $P = 2(b + h)$
Substitute $b = 7$ and $h = 4$.
$P = 2(7 + 4)$
$\quad = 2 \times 11$
$\quad = 22$
The perimeter is 22 m.

**b) i)** The area of a square is: $A = s^2$
Substitute $s = 5$.
$A = 5^2$
$\quad = 5 \times 5$
$\quad = 25$
The area is 25 cm².

**ii)** The area of a rectangle is: $A = bh$
Substitute $b = 7$ and $h = 4$.
$A = 7 \times 4$
$\quad = 28$
The area is 28 m².

## ✓ Check

**1.** Find the perimeter and area of each figure.

**a)**

**b)**

**c)**

**d)**

**Focus** Use a formula to find the area of a parallelogram.

This is a **parallelogram**.
How would you describe it?

Here is the same parallelogram.
Any side of the parallelogram is a base.
The height is perpendicular to the base.

## Explore

Work with a partner.

You will need a tangram and grid paper.

➤ One tan is a parallelogram. Find its area.

➤ Make another parallelogram by combining tans. Find the area of the parallelogram.

➤ Continue to combine tans to make different parallelograms. Find the area of each parallelogram you make.

➤ Record your work. Draw each parallelogram on grid paper.

➤ Use variables. Write a formula to find the area of a parallelogram.

### Reflect & Share

How did you find the area of each parallelogram?
Which different strategies did you use?
Which strategy helped you write the formula for the area?

**Recall that both a rectangle and a square are parallelograms.**

Any parallelogram that is not a rectangle can be "cut" and rearranged to form a rectangle.

The parallelogram and the rectangle have the same area.
The area of a parallelogram is equal to the area of a rectangle with the same height and base.
To find the area of a parallelogram, multiply the base by the height.

$b$ represents the base.

$h$ represents the height.

Area of rectangle:      Area of parallelogram:
$A = bh$                $A = bh$

## Example

Calculate the area of each parallelogram.

a)

b) The height can be drawn outside the parallelogram.

**Solution**

a) $A = bh$
Substitute $b = 7$ and $h = 5$.
$A = 7 \times 5$
$\quad = 35$
The area of the parallelogram is 35 cm².

b) $A = bh$
Substitute $b = 2.5$ and $h = 7.5$.
$A = 2.5 \times 7.5$
$\quad = 18.75$
The area of the parallelogram is 18.75 m².

**1.** Identify one base and height of each parallelogram.

Recall that you can use a protractor to draw the height perpendicular to the base.

a)

b)

The base of a parallelogram is not always horizontal.

c)

d)

**2.** Find the area of each parallelogram in question 1.

**3. a)** On 1-cm grid paper, draw 3 different parallelograms with each base and height.
  **i)** base: 3 cm; height: 5 cm   **ii)** base: 3.5 cm; height: 7.0 cm
 **b)** Find the area of each parallelogram you drew in part a. What do you notice?

**4.** On 1-cm grid paper, draw as many different parallelograms as you can with each area.
 **a)** 10 cm$^2$   **b)** 18 cm$^2$   **c)** 28 cm$^2$

**5. Assessment Focus** Use 1-cm grid paper.
 Draw a parallelogram, which is not a rectangle, with base 6 cm and height 4 cm.
 **a)** What is the area of the parallelogram?
 **b)** Change the base to draw a parallelogram with twice the area. What is the base?
 **c)** Change the height to draw a parallelogram with twice the area. What is the height?
 **d)** Change the base and height to draw a parallelogram with twice the area.
   How many different pairs of base and height can you find?
 Show your work.

It is Wednesday, January 14.
Kim and Sun-Yi are
working together.

Kim works every Wednesday.
Sun-Yi works every 5th day.

When will Kim and Sun-Yi
next work together?

**6.** The area of each parallelogram is given.
Find each unknown measure.

a) the height    b) the base    c) the height

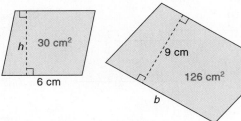

**7.** Use 1-cm grid paper.
Draw a rectangle with the same area as
each parallelogram in question 6.
How many different ways can you do this?

**8.** Sasha is buying paint for
a design on a wall.
Here is part of the design.
Sasha says figure B will need
more paint than figure A.
Do you agree? Explain.

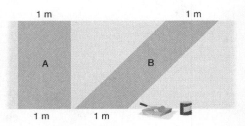

**9.** You will need 1-cm grid paper, ruler, and tracing paper.
Draw a parallelogram with base 10 cm and height 6 cm.
Draw a diagonal to make two triangles.
a) What do you notice about the two triangles?
How can you check your observation?
b) What is the area of the parallelogram?
c) What is the area of each triangle? How do you know?

**Take It Further**

**10.** A restaurant owner built a patio in front of his store to attract
more customers.
a) What is the area of the patio?
b) What is the total area of the patio and gardens?
c) How can you find the area of the gardens?
Show your work.

**Reflect**

What do you need to know to find the area of a parallelogram?
Use an example to explain.

## Explore

Work with a partner.
You will need a ruler and 1-cm grid paper.
Draw each triangle below on 1-cm grid paper.

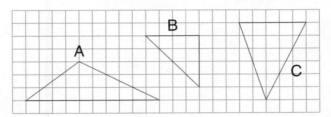

➤ How many different ways can you find the area of each triangle?
  What strategies did you use?
➤ Use what you know about parallelograms.
  Find the area of each triangle.
➤ Use variables. Write a formula to find the area of a triangle.

### Reflect & Share

How did you use a parallelogram to find the area of a triangle?
Compare your formula with that of another pair of classmates.
If the formulas are different, can both of them be used to find the
area of a triangle? Explain.

## Connect

When we draw a diagonal in a parallelogram,
we make 2 congruent triangles.
Congruent triangles have the same area.
So, the area of one triangle is
$\frac{1}{2}$ the area of the parallelogram.
To find the area of this triangle:

Complete a parallelogram on one side of the triangle.

The area of the parallelogram is:

$A = $ base $\times$ height, or $A = bh$

So, $A = 6 \times 5$

$= 30$

The area of the parallelogram is 30 cm².

So, the area of the triangle is: $\frac{1}{2}$ of 30 cm² = 15 cm²

We can write a formula for the area of a triangle.

$A = \frac{1}{2}$ base $\times$ height

$A = \frac{1}{2} bh$

or $A = bh \div 2$

or $A = \frac{bh}{2}$

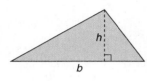

## Example

Find the area of each triangle.

For an obtuse triangle, the height might be drawn outside the triangle.

a)

b)

**Solution**

a) $A = \frac{bh}{2}$

Substitute $b = 3.1$ and $h = 4.2$.

$A = \frac{3.1 \times 4.2}{2}$

$A = 6.51$

The area is 6.51 m².

b) $A = \frac{bh}{2}$

Substitute $b = 17$ and $h = 9$.

$A = \frac{17 \times 9}{2}$

$A = \frac{153}{2}$

$= 76.5$

The area is 76.5 cm².

## Practice

**1.** Identify one base and height of each triangle.

a)

b)

In a right triangle, one base and height are two sides of the triangle.

**c)**

6 m  8 m
10 m

**d)**

7 cm
10 cm
4 cm

**2.** Find the area of each triangle in question 1.

**3. a)** On 1-cm grid paper, draw 3 different triangles with each base and height.
   **i)** base: 4 cm; height: 3 cm      **ii)** base: 7.5 cm; height: 6.5 cm
   **b)** Find the area of each triangle you drew in part a.
   What do you notice?

**4.** On 1-cm grid paper, draw two different triangles with each area.
   **a)** 16 cm²                **b)** 8 cm²                **c)** 10 cm²

**5.** Use 1-cm grid paper.
   **a)** Draw a triangle with area 12 cm².
   **b)** Investigate the different ways you can draw
   a triangle that has:
   **i)** double the area          **ii)** one-half the area
   Write a report of your findings.

**6.** Use 1-cm grid paper.
   **a)** Draw different triangles with base 4 cm and height 6 cm.
   **b)** Find the area of each triangle you draw.
   **c)** Measure the side lengths of each triangle you draw.
   How do you know all the triangles are different?

**7.** The area of each triangle is given. Find each unknown measure.
   **a)** the base                          **b)** the height

20 cm²  4 cm
b

6 cm  h
24 cm²
10 cm

   **c)** the base                          **d)** the height

7.5 cm²  5 cm
b

13 cm
60 cm²
13 cm  h
24 cm

**8.** When you know the area of a triangle, and its base, how can you find its height? Use an example to explain.

**9.** **Assessment Focus**  The owner of a house paints this attic wall. There is a small rectangular window in the wall.
One litre of paint covers 6.5 m².
  a) What is the area that is to be painted?
  b) The paint comes in 1-L cans.
     How many cans does the
     owner need?
     Explain your answer.

**Take It Further**

**10.** A local park has a pavilion to provide shelter.
The pavilion has a roof the shape of a rectangular pyramid.
  a) What is the total area of all four parts of the roof?
  b) One sheet of plywood is
     240 cm by 120 cm.
     It costs $24.95.
     What is the least number
     of sheets of plywood
     needed to cover the roof?
     What is the cost?
     Explain how you got your answer.

**Reflect**

A triangle and a parallelogram have the same base and height.
How are the areas of the triangle and parallelogram related?
Use an example to explain.

# Mid-Unit Review

LESSON

**6.1** **1.** Find the perimeter and area of each figure.

a)

2.5 m

5.0 m

b)

3.4 m

**2.** Find the area of each parallelogram.

a)

2.4 cm 2.0 cm

3.5 cm

b)

2.3 cm

4.0 cm

2.5 cm

c)

3.0 cm

2.0 cm

1.5 cm

**3.** A parallelogram has height 45 cm and base 60 cm.

a) Find its area.

b) What is the base and height of a parallelogram with twice the area?

c) What is the base and height of a parallelogram with one-half the area?

**6.2** **4.** Find the area of each triangle.

a)

6 cm

4 cm

b)

3.5 cm

2.0 cm

3.2 cm 2.3 cm

c)

4.4 m

2.2 m

2.0 m

**5.** Po Ling is planning to pour a concrete patio beside her house. It has the shape of a triangle. The contractor charges $125.00 for each square metre of concrete poured.

4.5 m

4.5 m

What will the contractor charge for the concrete?

**Focus** | Use a formula to find the area of a trapezoid.

This is a **trapezoid**.
How would you describe it?

Recall that a rectangle, a square, and a parallelogram are trapezoids, too.

## Explore

Work with a partner.
You will need scissors.
Your teacher will give you a copy of the figures below.

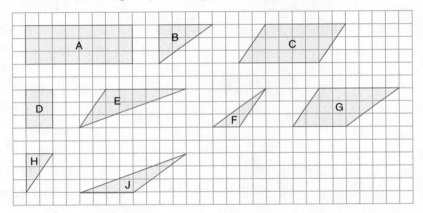

➤ Find the area of each figure.

➤ Cut out the figures.

➤ Identify the trapezoid that is not a parallelogram.

➤ How many different ways can you use the figures to find the area of the trapezoid?

➤ For each way you find, write a formula in words for the area of a trapezoid.

➤ Find the perimeter of the trapezoid.

### Reflect & Share

How did you use what you know about the areas of a triangle, a rectangle, and a parallelogram to find the area of a trapezoid?

We can find the area of a trapezoid by dividing it into other figures. Here are 3 ways to find the area of this trapezoid.

- Make 2 triangles and a rectangle.

Area of trapezoid = area of triangle A + area of rectangle B
+ area of triangle C

- Make 1 triangle and a parallelogram.

Area of trapezoid = area of parallelogram D + area of triangle E

- Make 2 triangles.

Area of trapezoid = area of triangle F + area of triangle G

**Example**

a) Estimate the area of this trapezoid.
b) Calculate the area to check your estimate.

12 cm

4 cm

9 cm

**Solution**

a) Sketch a rectangle with width 4 cm and length between 9 cm and 12 cm, maybe 10 cm. The area of the rectangle is an estimate of the area of the trapezoid.

Area of rectangle = 10 × 4
$$= 40$$

The area of the trapezoid is about 40 cm².

b) Divide the trapezoid into 2 triangles.

Area of triangle A = $\frac{bh}{2}$

Substitute $b = 12$ and $h = 4$.

So, area = $\frac{12 \times 4}{2}$
$$= 24$$

Area of triangle B = $\frac{bh}{2}$

Substitute $b = 9$ and $h = 4$.

So, area = $\frac{9 \times 4}{2}$
$$= 18$$

Area of trapezoid = area of triangle A + area of triangle B
$$= 24 + 18$$
$$= 42$$

The area of the trapezoid is 42 cm².

## Practice

1. Find the area of each trapezoid by dividing it into 2 triangles.

a)

b)

c)

2. Find the area of each trapezoid by dividing it into 1 or 2 triangles and a rectangle.

a)

b)

**Calculator Skills**

Predict each product.
Check your prediction.

What patterns do you see
in the answers?

- $9 \times 9$
- $99 \times 99$
- $999 \times 999$
- $9999 \times 9999$

Use the pattern to
predict the product of
$99\,999 \times 99\,999$.

**3.** Find the area of each trapezoid.

a)

b)

**4.** Find the area and perimeter of each trapezoid.

a)

b)

**5. a)** Estimate the area of each trapezoid.
Check your answer by calculating the area.

i)

ii)

**b)** Can you find the perimeter of each trapezoid in part a?
Explain.

**6. a)** What is the area of each part of this garden?
**b)** Find the area of the whole garden two different ways.

**7.** Suppose you have a piece of string, 4 pushpins,
a ruler, and grid paper.
**a)** Describe how to make a trapezoid with
perimeter 20 cm.
Use your strategy to make the trapezoid.
**b)** Draw the trapezoid on grid paper.
**c)** Find the approximate area of the trapezoid.

**8. Assessment Focus**   Two congruent trapezoids join
to form a parallelogram.

a) How can you use the area of the parallelogram
   to find the area of each trapezoid?
b) Use grid paper. Draw a trapezoid. Use the area of a
   parallelogram to find the area of your trapezoid.
Show your work.

**Take It Further**

**9.** A patio is made with congruent brick tiles.

Each tile is a trapezoid.
a) What is the area of the top face of each tile?
b) Use red Pattern Blocks on triangular grid paper.
   Sketch a patio that uses these trapezoid tiles.
   How many tiles are in your patio?
c) What is the area of your patio?
d) When a patio is built, there is a 3-mm space between tiles for
   the grout.
   Would your completed patio be larger or smaller than the
   area you calculated in part c? Explain.
   How much larger or smaller would it be?

**10.** Use any of the methods you know to find the area of a
trapezoid. Use variables. Write a formula for the area of
a trapezoid.

**Reflect**

How can you use the strategies for finding the area of a trapezoid to
find the areas of a square, rectangle, and parallelogram?
Use examples to explain.

Before construction begins on a shopping mall, the site is precisely measured in different ways for different reasons. Measuring does not stop once construction begins. Initial measurements are checked and rechecked because estimates and plans sometimes change as the project continues.

The first "measurers" on the site are members of a survey team. The first thing they do is to verify the perimeter and area with an older, existing plan. In some cases, the last survey for the site might have been carried out 200 years before.

Most surveyors today have new, technology-based surveying tools. However, the team might use a transit (an angle-measuring device based on a telescope) and stadia (a graduated measuring rod). These measuring devices have been in use since the early 19th century. The survey team may have aerial or satellite photographs, EDM (Electronic Distance Measuring) equipment based on microwaves or lasers, or GPS (Global Positioning System) equipment.

A construction project requires the services of many different suppliers and contractors. One company provides security fencing around the site. Another company lays asphalt for the roads and parking lots. A third company installs the flooring and carpets inside the mall. Some people work from the architect's blueprints to calculate how much to charge for their materials and labour. Other people will send an estimator to do her own measuring. Estimators use a variety of measuring tools: tape measure, trundle wheel, hand-held EDM, and so on. The estimators have to know how to use the measurements they collect.

Recently, a company introduced a digital measuring device. This device is wheeled around the perimeter of the region to calculate the area of the region. Why might this seem to be an impossible calculation? Can you explain how it might work?

## Interpreting a Problem

### Problem

How many different trapezoids can you draw with area 24 cm²?

### Interpret the problem

A trapezoid has at least 1 pair of parallel sides.
A trapezoid could have 2 pairs of parallel sides.
It would then be a rectangle or a parallelogram.

### Solve the problem

*Solution 1*

To draw a rectangle with area 24 cm², find two factors of 24.
The factors in each pair are the base and the height of the rectangle:
$1 \times 24, 2 \times 12, 3 \times 8, 4 \times 6$
Each of these rectangles has area 24 cm².

*Solution 2*

To draw a parallelogram with area 24 cm²,
use the factors in *Solution 1*.
The factors in each pair are the base and the height
of the parallelogram.
Each of these parallelograms has area 24 cm².

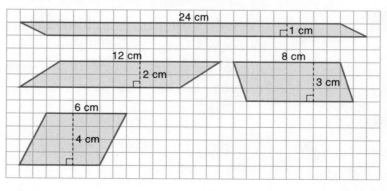

*Solution 3*

To draw a trapezoid (that is not a parallelogram) with area 24 cm²:

Two congruent trapezoids join to form a parallelogram. If each trapezoid has area 24 cm², then the parallelogram has area 48 cm².

Work backward.
Draw a parallelogram with area 48 cm².
Divide it into 2 congruent trapezoids.
A parallelogram with area 48 cm²
can have base 12 cm and height 4 cm.
Choose a length for one base of the
trapezoid, less than 12 cm.
Choose 10 cm. Mark a point
on the top side of the parallelogram
10 cm from the left vertex.
Mark a point on the bottom side of
the parallelogram 10 cm from the right vertex.
Join these points to form two congruent trapezoids.
So, one trapezoid with area 24 cm² looks like this:

## Look back

- What if we had chosen a parallelogram with base 8 cm and height 4 cm?
  What could the trapezoid look like?
- What if we had chosen 5 cm for one base of the trapezoid?
  What would the trapezoid look like?

## Problems

**1.** Draw 3 different trapezoids with area 30 cm².

**2.** Think of other methods to find the area of a trapezoid.
Use a different method to draw a trapezoid with area 20 cm².

## Reflect

Choose an area for a trapezoid. Explain how to draw a trapezoid with that area. Include a diagram.

**Focus** | Find the area and perimeter of an irregular figure.

In *Section 6.3*, you calculated the area of a trapezoid by dividing it into other figures.

You can use a similar strategy to find the areas of other irregular figures.

## Explore

Work with a partner.
A garden in a backyard
has this plan.

How many different ways
can you find the area of
the garden?
What is its perimeter?

### Reflect & Share

Compare your strategies with
those of another pair of students.
What other strategies could you have used?

## Connect

Here are two ways to find
the area of this irregular figure.

➤ Divide the figure into smaller figures whose areas you can find.
Rectangle A has length 9 cm and width 2 cm.
Area of rectangle A: 9 cm × 2 cm = 18 cm²
Since the width of rectangle A is 2 cm,
the length of rectangle B is: 7 cm − 2 cm = 5 cm
Area of rectangle B: 3 cm × 5 cm = 15 cm²
So, the area of the figure is: 18 cm² + 15 cm² = 33 cm²

➤ Draw a rectangle around the figure.
The area of the large rectangle is: 9 cm × 7 cm = 63 cm²
Figure C is a rectangle.
Its width is: 7 cm − 2 cm = 5 cm
Its length is: 9 cm − 3 cm = 6 cm
Area of rectangle C: 5 cm × 6 cm = 30 cm²
So, the area of the figure is: 63 cm² − 30 cm² = 33 cm²

➤ To find the perimeter of the figure, add the side lengths.
Perimeter
= 2 cm + 6 cm + 5 cm + 3 cm + 7 cm + 9 cm
= 32 cm
The perimeter is 32 cm.

**Example**

Here is a plan of the back wall of a barn.
a)  What is the area of
the wall?
b)  One can of paint
covers 40 m².
How many cans are
needed to paint
this wall?

**Solution**

The wall is a rectangle with an isosceles triangle above it.

a) For the triangle:

The base, $b$, is 8 m.

The height, $h$, is 8 m − 5 m = 3 m.

Area = $\frac{bh}{2}$

Substitute $b = 8$ and $h = 3$.

Area = $\frac{8 \times 3}{2}$

= 12

For the rectangle:

Area = $bh$

Substitute $b = 8$ and $h = 5$.

Area = $8 \times 5$

= 40

Area of wall = 40 m² + 12 m²

= 52 m²

The area of the wall is 52 m².

b) The area of the wall is 52 m².

One can of paint covers 40 m².

One can is not enough.

Two cans of paint are needed.

## Practice

1. A living room in a home has the shape, below left.
What is the area of the living room?

2. The rear and front walls of a shed are shown,
above middle and right.
a) Find the area of the rear wall.
b) Find the area of the front wall, excluding
the windows and door.

**Number Strategies**

Which is the next number
in each pattern?
Write each pattern rule.

3, 9, 27, 81, ____

12, 14, 18, 26, ____

52, 28, 16, 10, ____

5, 14, 41, 122, ____

**3.** The diagram shows the basement floor of a home.
   a) Estimate the area and perimeter of the floor.

7.8 m

6.4 m

1.6 m   4.6 m

1.6 m

   b) Calculate the area and perimeter of the floor.
   c) Compare your estimates with your calculations.
      Was your estimate reasonable? Explain.

**4.** This diagram shows a plan of a parking lot.
   a) Estimate the area and
      perimeter of the lot.
   b) Calculate the area and
      perimeter of the lot.
   c) How could you use the grid
      to verify your answers?

Scale: 1 unit = 10 m

**5.** A backyard is a rectangle 15 m long by 10 m wide.
   In one corner, there is a rectangular garden 5 m by 3 m.
   a) Use grid paper. Draw a diagram of the backyard.
   b) Calculate the area of the backyard, excluding the garden.
   c) What if the garden was in a different place in the yard?
      Would the answer to part b be different? Explain.

**6.** **Assessment Focus**   An L-shaped swimming pool has area
   30 m². Each rectangular arm has width 3 m.
   a) Use grid paper. Draw 3 different pools.
   b) Find the perimeter of each pool you drew.
      What do you notice about the perimeters?
   c) What if the width of each arm was 5 m?
      What effect does this have? Explain.

**Reflect**

There are different ways to find the area of an irregular figure.
Which way do you prefer to use?
Use an example to explain your reasoning.

# Trapezoid Challenge

## HOW TO PLAY THE GAME:

**1.** Roll 3 number cubes to get the height and lengths of the 2 parallel sides of a trapezoid.

**2.** Use the geoboard to make a trapezoid with those dimensions.
Choose which number represents which dimension.

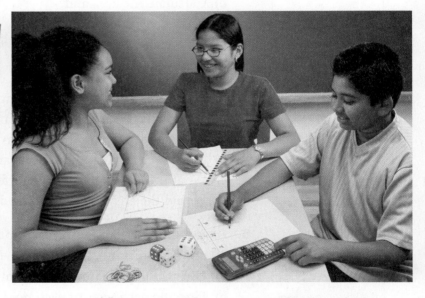

**3.** The area of the trapezoid is your score for the round.

**4.** Take turns.
The winner is the first person to reach 50 points.

**Variation:** Record each trapezoid on grid paper.
No two trapezoids can be the same. If you cannot create a different trapezoid, you forfeit your turn.

## YOU WILL NEED

11 by 11 geoboard; geobands; 3 number cubes labelled 1 to 6; dot paper

## NUMBER OF PLAYERS

3 or 4

## GOAL OF THE GAME

To get 50 points

What strategies did you use to try to win?
Does it matter which of the 3 numbers you use for the height? Explain.

# Unit Review

## What Do I Need to Know?

☑ The *perimeter* of a figure is found by adding the lengths of its sides.

☑ **Area of a Parallelogram**
$A = bh$

☑ **Area of a Triangle**
$A = \frac{bh}{2}$

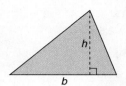

☑ **Area of a Trapezoid**
Divide the trapezoid into:

- Two triangles
- A parallelogram and a triangle
- A rectangle and 2 triangles

☑ **Area of an Irregular Figure**
- Divide the figure into figures whose area you can find, then add the areas.
- Or, draw a rectangle around the figure; subtract the areas of the newly formed figures from the area of the rectangle.

**LESSON**

**6.1**
**6.2**

**1.** Find the area of each figure. Explain your strategy.

a)

b)

c)

d)

**6.3**

**2.** Estimate the area of each trapezoid.
Then, calculate the area to check if your estimate was reasonable.

a)

b)

**3.** Estimate the perimeter of each trapezoid in question 2. Then, calculate the perimeter to check.

**4.** The area of this trapezoid is approximately 150 cm².

Estimate its height.
Show your work.

**6.4** **5.** Find the perimeter and area of each figure.

a)

b)

**6.** A school playground has a paved surface and a grass surface.

a) What is the area of the paved surface?

b) Fencing costs $35.50/m. How much would it cost to fence the grass area?

# Practice Test

1. Find the area and perimeter of each figure.
   Explain your strategies.

   a)

   b)

   c)

   d)

2. How does the area of a triangle change in each case?
   a) Its height is doubled.
   b) Its base is halved.
   c) Its height is doubled and its base is halved.
   Explain how you know.

3. Use 1-cm grid paper.
   Draw an irregular figure with area 64 cm².
   Label all the dimensions of the figure.
   Find the perimeter of the figure.

4. A design has a series of trapezoids.
   For each trapezoid, one parallel
   side is always 1.5 m shorter
   than the other parallel side.
   The height of each trapezoid
   is 6.0 m.
   a) What is the area of the
      6th trapezoid in the design?
   b) How long is the design with
      6 trapezoids?

The owners of a large shopping centre want to build a patio in front of the main entrance to attract more customers. Your task is to design the tiled surface of the patio.
You must use tiles with these shapes: triangle, parallelogram, rectangle, trapezoid

The patio has the shape shown at the right. Each square on this plan has side length 10 cm.

- You must include at least:
  - 3 triangles with different areas
  - 3 parallelograms with different areas
  - 3 rectangles with different areas
  - 3 trapezoids (that are not parallelograms) with different areas

- Use a formula to find the area of each tile.

Your teacher will give you a grid to draw your design.
Complete the design.
Colour the design if it helps to show the different figures.

## Check List

Your work
should show:

✓ the area of each
different figure
you used

✓ the formulas you
used to calculate
the areas

✓ a diagram of
your design on
grid paper

✓ an explanation of
how you created
the design

## Reflect on the Unit

What do you need to know to find the area of a parallelogram, a triangle,
and a trapezoid? Explain.
Include a diagram and an example to show how you found each area.

# UNIT
# 7
# Geometry

Patterns are pleasing to the eye.
They are used by designers,
architects, and engineers to make
their products more attractive.
Look at the quilt pattern.
Which figures are used as
quilt blocks?
Which other figures have
you seen in quilts?

## What You'll Learn

- Identify, describe, compare, and classify figures.
- Identify the conditions that make two figures congruent.
- Construct and analyse tiling patterns.
- Recognize the image of a figure after a transformation.
- Create and analyse designs using transformations.

## Why It's Important

- Geometry is used daily by scientists, architects, engineers, and land developers.
- Geometric attributes, such as congruence and symmetry, enable you to see the world around you in a different way.

## Key Words

- convex polygon
- concave polygon
- tiling the plane
- tessellations

# Skills You'll Need

## Classifying Triangles

Here are two ways to classify triangles.

- By side length
  An equilateral triangle has all sides equal.

An isosceles triangle has 2 sides equal.

A scalene triangle has all sides different.

- By angle measure
  An acute triangle has all angles less than 90°.

A right triangle has one 90° angle.

An obtuse triangle has one angle greater than 90°.

### ✓ Check

Use square dot paper or isometric dot paper.

**1.** Draw an isosceles triangle.
Is it acute, obtuse, or right? How do you know?

**2.** Draw an obtuse triangle.
Is it equilateral, scalene, or isosceles? How do you know?

**3.** Can you draw an obtuse isosceles triangle?
If you can, draw it.
If you cannot draw the triangle, say why it cannot be drawn.

**4.** Can you draw a right equilateral triangle?
If you can, draw it.
If you cannot draw the triangle, say why it cannot be drawn.

# Constructing a Triangle

Here are two ways to construct a triangle, using a ruler, compass, and protractor.

## Example 1

Construct △ABC with AB = 4 cm, BC = 6 cm, and CA = 7 cm.

### Solution

You will need a ruler and compass.

*Step 1* Sketch the triangle.

*Step 2* Construct the triangle:
Use a ruler to draw side BC = 6 cm.
With the compass point and pencil 7 cm apart,
put the compass point on C and draw an arc.
All points on this arc are 7 cm from C.
With the compass point and pencil 4 cm apart,
put the compass point on B and draw an arc.
All points on this arc are 4 cm from B.
Make sure the arc intersects the first arc you drew.
Mark a point where the arcs intersect.
This point is 7 cm from C and 4 cm from B.
Label the point A. Join AB and AC. Label each side with its length.

### Example 2

Construct △BCD with BC = 6 cm, ∠B = 110°, and ∠C = 30°.

### Solution

You will need a ruler and protractor.

*Step 1* Sketch the triangle.

*Step 2* Construct the triangle:

Use a ruler to draw side BC = 6 cm.

Use a protractor to make an angle of 110° at B.

Use a protractor to make an angle of 30° at C.

Label point D where the arms of the angles intersect.

Label the known side and angles.

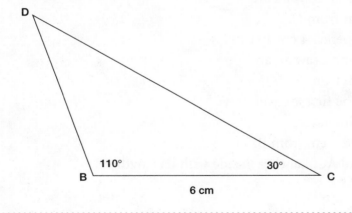

## ✓ Check

**5.** Construct each triangle.

    **a)** △CDE with CD = 4 cm, DE = 7 cm, CE = 9 cm

    **b)** △DEF with DE = 7 cm, ∠D = 80°, ∠E = 30°

# Plotting Points on a Coordinate Grid

When we draw a horizontal axis and a vertical axis on grid paper,
we have a coordinate grid.
The axes intersect at the origin, O.

We label each axis with numbers, beginning with 0 at the origin.

A point on a grid is described by its coordinates.

Point A has coordinates (4, 6).
To plot point A, start at 4 on the horizontal axis, then move up 6 spaces.
Mark a point. This is point A.

Point B has coordinates (0, 3).
To plot point B, start at 0, then move up 3 spaces. Point B is on the vertical axis.

Point C has coordinates (6, 0).
To plot point C, mark a point at 6 on the horizontal axis.

## ✓ Check

6. On grid paper, draw a coordinate grid.
   Plot each point on the grid.
   A(5, 7), B(3, 8), C(10, 4), D(9, 1), E(0, 8), F(5, 0)

7. a) Where are all the points with horizontal coordinate 0?
   b) Where are all the points with vertical coordinate 0?

Look around the classroom.
Name the different figures you see.
Which figure is most common?

## Explore

Work with a group.
You will need a ruler and a protractor.
Your teacher will give you a large copy of these figures.

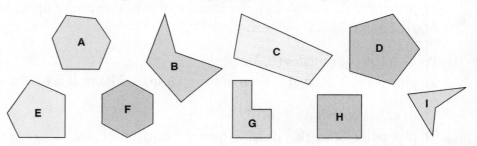

➤ Identify each figure.
   Describe it.
➤ Choose two figures.
   How many different ways can you compare them?
➤ Choose three figures. How are they the same?
   How are they different?

### Reflect & Share

Share your results with another group of classmates.
Work together to classify the figures in different ways.

A polygon is a closed figure with sides that are line segments.
Exactly 2 sides meet at a vertex.
The sides intersect only at the vertices.

This figure is a polygon.

These figures are *not* polygons.

**A regular polygon has line symmetry and rotational symmetry.**

**Recall that matching arcs or symbols in angles show that the angles are equal.**

A regular polygon has all sides equal and all angles equal.
These polygons are regular.

A **convex polygon** has all angles less than 180°.
These polygons are convex.

A **concave polygon** has at least one angle greater than 180°.
These polygons are concave.

**An angle that is greater than 180° is a reflex angle.**

## Example

Here is a regular hexagon.
a) How many lines of symmetry does it have?
b) What is the rotational symmetry?

a) Trace the hexagon.
Fold the tracing paper so that one part of the hexagon coincides with the other.
The fold line is a line of symmetry.
Repeat the folding as many times as possible.

A regular hexagon has 6 lines of symmetry: 3 lines join opposite vertices, and 3 lines join the midpoints of opposite sides.

**Label two corresponding vertices. Then you know when the tracing is back at the starting position.**

b) Trace the hexagon. Place the tracing to coincide with the hexagon.
Rotate the tracing about its centre until the tracing coincides with the hexagon again.
Count how many times you can do this.

The tracing coincides with the hexagon 6 times.
So, a regular hexagon has rotational symmetry of order 6.

# Practice

**1.** Explain why each figure is not a polygon.

a)

b)

**2. a)** Is each polygon regular? How do you know?

i)

ii)

iii)

**b)** Which polygons in part a have:
**i)** line symmetry?
**ii)** rotational symmetry?
How do you know?

3. Identify the figures in each flag.
   Describe each figure as many ways as you can.
   **a)** Congo   **b)** Bosnia-Herzegovina   **c)** Guyana   **d)** Seychelles

4. Describe each figure. How are the figures the same? Different?
   **a)**

   **b)**

   **c)**

5. Match each polygon with its description below.

   **a)** an isosceles triangle with an angle of 40°
   **b)** a rhombus with a right angle
   **c)** a pentagon with an angle of 120°
   **d)** a parallelogram with an angle of 60°
   **e)** an obtuse triangle with an angle of 110°

6. Use square dot paper or isometric dot paper.
   Draw each polygon.
   **a)** an isosceles triangle with a height of 4 units
   **b)** a parallelogram with an angle of 45°
   **c)** a trapezoid with a 90° angle and a 45° angle
   **d)** a kite with exactly one right angle
   **e)** a parallelogram with a 90° angle
   **f)** a scalene obtuse triangle
   **g)** an isosceles right triangle
   **h)** a hexagon with exactly 3 right angles

7. Identify each polygon.
   Describe it as many ways as you can.

**A quadrilateral is a polygon with 4 sides.**

**8.** Use dot paper.

   **a)** Draw a quadrilateral. Label it A.

   **b)** Draw another quadrilateral that differs from quadrilateral A in only one way. Label it B.

   **c)** Continue to draw quadrilaterals that differ in only one way. Label each one you draw. Change one side or angle each time. How many different quadrilaterals can you draw?

**Number Strategies**

Find the next 3 numbers in each pattern.

What is each pattern rule?

• 23, 28, 26, 31, 29,…

• 6, 9, 15, 27, 51,…

• 1, 3, 9, 27,…

**9. Assessment Focus**

The 3 points A, B, C are vertices of a polygon.
Copy the points on dot paper.

   **a)** Find other vertices and sketch each figure.

   **i)**   a trapezoid with line symmetry

   **ii)**  a kite

   **iii)** a parallelogram

   **iv)**  a pentagon

   **b)** How many other figures can you make that have these points as 3 vertices? Identify each figure. Describe it as many ways as you can.

**10.** The lengths of three sides of a quadrilateral are 5 cm, 5 cm, and 8 cm.

   **a)** Sketch and name the different quadrilaterals possible.

   **b)** Suppose one angle is 90°. Which quadrilaterals are possible now? Justify your answer.

**Math Link**

**Your World**

The Department of Highways uses different figures for road signs. Which road signs use each of these figures: pentagon, octagon, square, circle, rectangle, triangle?

**Reflect**

Choose 3 different polygons. Sketch each polygon as many different ways as you can. Describe each polygon.

**Focus** Identify the conditions for congruence.

## Explore

Work on your own.

You will need a ruler, protractor, and compass.

For each set of measurements given, how many different triangles can you draw?

➤ Construct a triangle with sides of length 5 cm, 7 cm, and 9 cm.

➤ Construct a triangle with two sides of length 9 cm and 5 cm, and one angle of 30°.

➤ Construct a triangle with one side of length 5 cm and two angles of 40° and 60°.

### Reflect & Share

Compare your triangles with those of several classmates.

➤ How many different triangles can you draw in each case?
 - when you know 3 sides
 - when you know 2 sides and 1 angle
 - when you know 1 side and 2 angles

➤ What measurements do you need to know to be able to draw exactly one triangle?

## Connect

➤ When 3 sides of a triangle are given, only one triangle can be drawn. So, if we know that two triangles have the same 3 sides, those triangles must be congruent.

**Congruent figures have the same size and shape. These triangles are drawn to scale.**

We say: Triangle ABC is congruent to triangle EDF.

We write: △ABC ≅ △EDF

△ABC and △EDF have:

corresponding sides equal     and     corresponding angles equal

**We list the corresponding vertices of the triangles in the same order.**

AB = ED                              ∠A = ∠E

BC = DF                              ∠B = ∠D

AC = EF                              ∠C = ∠F

➤ When 2 sides and 1 angle of a triangle are given, there are two cases to consider.

- The given angle is between the 2 sides. Only one triangle can be drawn.

**You may have to flip or rotate one triangle so both triangles face the same way.**

So, triangle GHJ is congruent to triangle LKM or △GHJ ≅ △LKM

- The given angle is *not* between the 2 sides. Sometimes more than one triangle can be drawn.

△PQR and △STU are *not* congruent.

➤ When 2 angles and the side between them are given, only one triangle can be drawn.

△BCD ≅ △FGE

---

## Example

Are the figures in each pair congruent? How do you know?

**a)**

**b)**

**a)** △ABC and △FED have 2 pairs of corresponding angles equal and 1 pair of corresponding sides equal:

$\angle A = \angle F = 30°$

$\angle B = \angle E = 70°$

$AB = FE = 10$ cm

So, △ABC and △FED are congruent: △ABC ≅ △FED

**b)** Quadrilateral ABCD and quadrilateral EFGH have 4 pairs of corresponding sides equal. But the quadrilaterals have different shapes. So, the quadrilaterals are not congruent.

Part b of the *Example* shows that for two quadrilaterals to be congruent, it is not sufficient that 4 pairs of corresponding sides are equal. We need to know that the corresponding angles are equal, too.

# Practice

**1.** Look at the triangles below.
Find pairs of congruent triangles.
Explain why they are congruent.

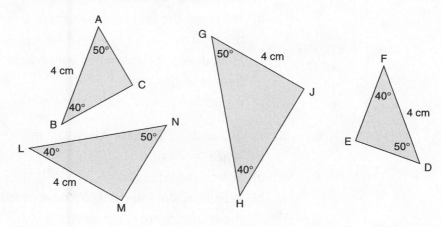

**2.** Are quadrilaterals ABCD and KLMN congruent?
How do you know?

When you name congruent
triangles, remember to list
corresponding vertices in
the same order.

**3.** In each figure below, name pairs of congruent triangles.
Explain how you know they are congruent.
Try to find more than one way to show
the triangles are congruent.

**a)** ABCD is a kite.

**b)** PQRS is a parallelogram.

**c)** EFGH is a rhombus.

**d)** JKLM is a rectangle.

**4.** For each figure below:
**a)** Sketch the figure.
**b)** What are the fewest measurements you need to know to draw
the figure?
**c)** How does your answer to part b help you identify congruent
figures of this type?
**i)** parallelogram       **ii)** rectangle       **iii)** square

**5.** △ABC and △DEF have AB = DE = 6 cm and
BC = EF = 7 cm.
**a)** Sketch the triangles.
**b)** What else do you need to know to tell if
the triangles are congruent?

**Mental Math**

Which three
factors of 24 have
a sum of 20?

6. **Assessment Focus**   Use dot paper.
   a) Draw two quadrilaterals with equal sides, but the
      quadrilaterals are not congruent.
      Explain why the quadrilaterals are not congruent.
   b) Use the 4 side lengths in part a. Draw two congruent
      quadrilaterals with these side lengths.
      Explain how you know the quadrilaterals are congruent.
   c) Explain how the quadrilaterals in parts a and b are different.

7. Alex called a carpet store.
   He wanted a piece of
   carpet to repair a
   damaged rug.
   Alex asked for a piece
   measuring 3 m by 4 m
   by 5 m by 6 m.
   Explain why the
   salesperson could not
   help Alex.

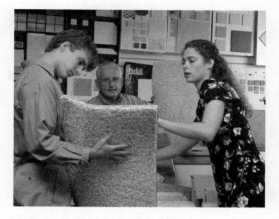

8. a) Are all isosceles triangles with two 50° angles congruent?
      Explain.
   b) Are all isosceles triangles with two 50° angles and exactly one
      side of length 10 cm congruent? Explain.

**Take It Further**

9. Construct a right triangle with one side 5 cm and
   the longest side 8 cm.
   a) Can you draw two different triangles with those
      measurements?
   b) If your answer to part a is yes, draw the triangles.
   c) If your answer to part a is no, explain how you know that only
      one triangle can be drawn with these measurements.

**Reflect**

Describe the different ways you can tell if
two triangles are congruent.

# Mid-Unit Review

LESSON

**7.1** **1.** Identify each figure.

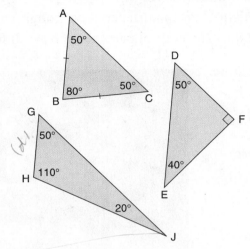

a) a scalene triangle with
   an angle of 50°
b) an isosceles triangle with
   an angle of 50°
c) a right triangle with
   an angle of 50°
d) an obtuse triangle with
   an angle of 50°
e) an acute triangle with
   an angle of 50°

**7.1** **2.** Use dot paper.
**7.2**
   a) Draw 2 congruent concave
      hexagons. How do you know the
      hexagons are congruent? How do
      you know they are concave?
   b) Draw 2 congruent convex
      hexagons. How do you know the
      hexagons are convex? How do
      you know they are congruent?

**7.2** **3.** Segment AB is one side of △ABC.
      Use dot paper.
   a) Draw △ABC.

   b) Draw a triangle congruent
      to △ABC. How do you know
      the triangles are congruent?
   c) Draw a triangle that is *not*
      congruent to △ABC.
      How do you know the triangles
      are *not* congruent?

**4.** Use these figures.

   a) Identify 2 figures that are *not*
      congruent. How do you know
      they are not congruent?
   b) Identify 2 congruent figures. How
      do you know they are congruent?

**Focus** Recognize transformation images.

## Explore

Work with a partner.

Your teacher will give you a large copy of these figures.

Use tracing paper and a
Mira if they help.

The shaded figure has been translated, rotated, and reflected.
Each labelled figure is the image after a transformation.
Identify the transformation that produced each image.
Explain how you know.

### Reflect & Share

Discuss your strategies for identifying each transformation.
What is special about a reflection image? A translation image?
A rotation image?

We can show transformations on a grid.

## Translation

**The translation image and the shaded figure are congruent.**

The shaded figure is translated 5 units right and 3 units up. Its translation image is figure A. The translation arrow shows the movement in a straight line.

## Reflection

**The reflection image and the shaded figure are congruent.**

The shaded figure is reflected in a horizontal line 1 unit below the figure. Its reflection image is figure B.

The figures have different orientations. That is, you flip one figure to make it coincide with the other figure.

## Rotation

**The rotation image and the shaded figure are congruent.**

The shaded figure is rotated a $\frac{1}{4}$ turn clockwise. The turn centre is the vertex indicated. The rotation image is figure C.

We get the same image if the shaded figure is rotated a $\frac{3}{4}$ turn counterclockwise about the turn centre.

Here are the three images and the shaded figure on the same grid.

We can show transformations on a coordinate grid.

## Example

Look at these rectangles.

Is one rectangle a transformation image of the other? Explain.

**Solution**

Let the blue rectangle be the original figure.
And let the red rectangle be the image.

*Solution 1*

The red rectangle is the image after a translation of 3 units right. The translation arrow shows the movement.

*Solution 2*

**Use a Mira to verify the image.**

The red rectangle is the image after a reflection in a vertical line through (3, 0) on the horizontal axis.

*Solution 3*

**Use tracing paper to verify the image.**

The red rectangle is the image after a rotation of a $\frac{1}{2}$ turn about the point with coordinates (3, 3).

The *Example* shows that an image may be the result of any one of the 3 transformations.
It also shows a rotation about a turn centre that is not on the figure.

# Practice

**1.** Use the figures below.

Identify the transformation for which:
**a)** Figure B is the image of Figure A.
**b)** Figure C is the image of Figure A.
**c)** Figure E is the image of Figure B.
**d)** Figure A is the image of Figure D.
**e)** Figure C is the image of Figure D.

**2.** Identify each transformation.

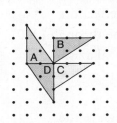

**a)** Figure A is the image of Figure B.
**b)** Figure B is the image of Figure C.
**c)** Figure C is the image of Figure D.
**d)** Figure D is the image of Figure A.

**3.** Draw this flag on a coordinate grid. The coordinates are A(11, 11), B(11, 13), C(11, 15), and D(12, 14).
Draw the image of the flag after each transformation.
**a)** a translation 3 units right
**b)** a translation 5 units down
**c)** a reflection in a vertical line through (9, 0)
**d)** a reflection in a horizontal line through (0, 8)
**e)** a rotation of a $\frac{1}{2}$ turn about point A
**f)** a rotation of a $\frac{1}{4}$ turn clockwise about point C

## Number Strategies

Add or subtract, as indicated.
- $\frac{5}{8} + \frac{7}{6}$
- $\frac{17}{10} - \frac{3}{4}$
- $\frac{11}{12} - \frac{2}{3}$
- $\frac{4}{5} + \frac{5}{6}$

**4.** How many different ways can each figure be described as a transformation of another figure? Explain.

**5. a)** Which pairs of congruent figures do *not* represent a figure and its transformation image? How do you know?

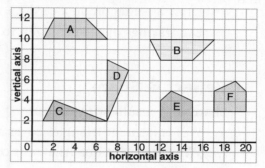

**b)** For each pair of congruent figures that do show a transformation, identify the transformation.

**6.** **Assessment Focus**   Use grid paper.
In each case, describe the figure you drew.
**a)** Draw a figure for which a translation image is also a reflection image and a rotation image. Draw the translation image.
**b)** Draw a figure for which a translation image is also a reflection image, but *not* a rotation image. Draw the translation image.
**c)** Draw a figure for which a translation image is *not* a reflection image *nor* a rotation image. Draw the translation image.

**Take It Further**

**7.** Describe Figure A as a transformation image of Figure B as many different ways as possible.

**Reflect**

When you see a figure and its transformation image on a grid, how do you identify the transformation?
Use diagrams in your explanation.

## Explore

Work on your own.

You will need index cards, a ruler, and scissors.

➤ Draw a triangle on a card. Cut it out.
   Use tracings of the triangle to cover a piece of paper.

**You can rotate or flip the figure to try to make it fit.**

➤ Draw a quadrilateral on a card. Cut it out.
   Use tracings of the quadrilateral to cover a piece of paper.

➤ Draw a pentagon on a card. Cut it out.
   Use tracings of the pentagon to cover a piece of paper.

### Reflect & Share

Share your results with the class.

•  Will congruent triangles cover a page and leave no gaps? Explain.

•  Will congruent quadrilaterals cover a page and leave no gaps?
   Explain.

•  Will congruent pentagons cover a page and leave no gaps?
   Explain.

How can you tell if congruent figures will cover a page
and leave no gaps?

## Connect

When congruent copies of a figure cover a page and leave no gaps,
we say the figure **tiles the plane**.

➤ A triangle always tiles the plane.

**At any point where vertices meet, the angles add to 360°.**

➤ A quadrilateral always tiles the plane.

At any point where vertices meet, the angles add to 360°.

## Example

Will a pentagon always tile the plane? Explain.

## Solution

If we can find a pentagon that does *not* tile the plane,
we can say that a pentagon does not always tile the plane.
Draw a regular pentagon.
Use tracing paper to repeat the pentagon to try to cover the page.

This pentagon does not cover the page.
It leaves gaps that are rhombuses.
Five vertices do not meet.
There are points where 3 vertices meet and
the sum of the angles is less than 360°.
There are points where 2 vertices meet and
the sum of the angles is less than 360°.
So, a pentagon does not always tile the plane.

In the *Practice* questions, you will investigate to find which other figures *do* tile the plane.

1. Use dot paper.
   Draw a convex hexagon that is not regular.
   Try to cover the dot paper with copies of this hexagon.
   Does the hexagon tile the plane? Explain.

2. Use dot paper.
   Draw a concave hexagon.
   Try to cover the dot paper with copies of this hexagon.
   Does the hexagon tile the plane? Explain.

3. Here is a regular octagon.

   Trace this octagon.
   Try to tile the plane.
   What do you notice?

4. Look at the picture called *Reptiles,* drawn by M.C. Escher.

   Which figure do you think Escher started with?
   Explain how Escher's reptiles tile the plane.

**5.** A floor tile is a regular hexagon.
What happens when you try to tile a rectangular floor with a regular hexagon?
Use isometric dot paper to find out.

**6.** Why do most tiling patterns in floors and patios use squares or rectangles?

**7.** **Assessment Focus**

Not all pentagons tile the plane. Use grid paper.

a) Find a pentagon that will tile the plane.
Describe the pentagon.
Explain how it tiles the plane.

b) How many different pentagons can you find that will tile the plane? Draw each pentagon and show how it tiles the plane.

c) Explain why some pentagons tile the plane, while others do not.

**8.** In question 3, you discovered that a regular octagon will not tile the plane.
Use grid paper. Find an octagon that will tile the plane.
Explain how it tiles the plane.

**Take It Further**

**9.** Think about "tiling" in nature. Which figures are used?

**Reflect**

How can you tell if a polygon will tile the plane?
Use examples in your explanation.

**Focus**   Create and analyse designs using transformations.

## Explore

Work on your own.

You will need isometric dot paper.

Choose two or more of these Pattern Blocks.

Make a design to cover a page.

Copy your design on dot paper.

Label each figure in your design.

Explain your design in terms of transformation images.

That is, how do you rotate, translate, or reflect each Pattern Block to generate the design? Write your instructions carefully.

### Reflect & Share

Trade instructions with a classmate.

Generate your classmate's pattern.

Check your version of the pattern with your classmate's.

How do they compare?

## Connect

In *Section 7.4*, you investigated tiling patterns.

You used congruent copies of one figure.

You discovered that not all octagons tile the plane.

But an octagon and a square can tile the plane,

as shown in the *Example* that follows.

## Example

Use transformations to describe how to construct this design.

## Solution

Label the figures in the design, as shown.

Start with the shaded octagon.

*Step 1*   To get octagon A, rotate the shaded octagon a $\frac{1}{2}$ turn about a turn centre that is at the midpoint of the right side.

Repeat a similar rotation to get figure B from figure A.

*Step 2*   To get octagon D, rotate the shaded octagon a $\frac{1}{2}$ turn about a turn centre that is at the midpoint of the bottom side.

Repeat a similar rotation to get octagon E from octagon A.

Look at the shaded square.

*Step 3*   To get square J, rotate the shaded square a $\frac{1}{2}$ turn about the midpoint of the top side of octagon A.

Repeat a similar rotation to get square K from square J.

*Step 4*    To get square L, rotate the
shaded square a $\frac{1}{2}$ turn about the
midpoint of the left side of
octagon A.

Repeat a similar rotation to get square M from square J.

## Practice

**1.** Here is the design from the *Example*.

a) Use translations to describe how to construct this design.

b) Use reflections to describe how to construct this design.

**2.** Use this figure and transformations to create a design
on grid paper.

Describe the design in terms of transformations.

**3.** Use isometric paper. Use a parallelogram and an equilateral
triangle to make a design.
Use transformations to describe the design.

**4.** Draw a figure. Use transformations of the figure to make a
border design for a photo frame.
Draw the design. Describe how you made it.

### Number Strategies

Which number is
the least?

• the sum of all the
factors of 30

• the sum of all the
factors of 46

• the product of all
the factors of 67

**5.** The Alhambra is a walled city and fortress in Granada, Spain. It was built in the 14th century. Here is part of one of its many tiling patterns.

Copy this pattern on dot paper.
Continue the pattern to cover the page.
Use transformations to describe the pattern.

**6.** **Assessment Focus**
Use dot paper or grid paper.
Create a design that uses 2 or more figures
that together tile the plane.
Colour your design.
Use transformations to describe your design.
Try to describe your design as many ways as you can.

**7.** Here is a flooring pattern.

Use a copy of this pattern.
Use transformations to describe the patterns in one square.

**Reflect**

When you use transformations to describe a design,
how do you decide which transformation to use?
Include a design in your explanation.

# Using a Computer to Transform Figures

Software, such as *The Geometer's Sketchpad*, can be used to transform figures.
Follow these steps:

1. Open *The Geometer's Sketchpad*.
   From the File menu, choose **New Sketch**.

To make a "grid paper" screen:

2. From the **Edit** menu, click on **Preferences**.
   Select the **Units** tab.
   Check that the Distance Units are cm.
   Click **OK**.

3. From the **Graph** menu, choose **Define Coordinate System**.
   The screen has grid lines and two numbered axes.

4. Click on each axis and the two red dots.
   The axes and the dots are highlighted.
   From the **Display** menu, choose **Hide Objects**.
   The axes and dots disappear.
   The screen appears like a piece of grid paper.

5. From the **Graph** menu, choose **Snap Points**.

## Translating a Figure

6. To create a quadrilateral:
   From the **Toolbox**, choose ![diagonal line tool].
   Click and drag to construct
   a quadrilateral.

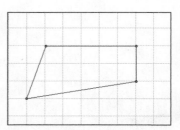

7. To translate the quadrilateral:
   From the **Toolbox**, choose ![arrow tool].
   Click each side of the
   quadrilateral to select it.
   The quadrilateral is highlighted.

8. From the **Transform** menu, choose **Translate**.
   Under **Translation Vector:**, choose **Rectangular**.
   Under **Horizontal:**, choose **Fixed Distance**.
   Enter 2.0 cm for the Horizontal distance.
   Under **Vertical:**, choose **Fixed Distance**.
   Enter 2.0 cm for the Vertical distance (below left).
   Click **Translate** to get the quadrilateral and its image
   after a translation 2 right, 2 up (below right).

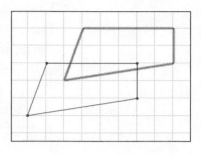

9. Drag any vertex or side of the original figure.
   See what happens to the translation image.

10. From the **Edit** menu, choose **Undo Translate Point**.
    The screen shows the original quadrilateral and translation
    image.
    To print the quadrilateral and its translation image,
    from the **File** menu, choose **Print**.

11. Repeat *Steps 7* to *10* using different horizontal
    and vertical distances.

## Rotating a Figure

12. From the **File** menu, choose **New Sketch**.
    Follow *Steps 2* to *5* to make a "grid paper" screen.

13. To create a triangle:
    From the **Toolbox**, choose 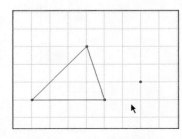.
    Click and drag to construct a triangle.

14. To rotate the triangle:
    From the **Toolbox**, choose ⬚.
    Click to place a point near the triangle.

**15.** Click to select the point.
From the **Transform** menu, choose **Mark Center**.
This is the turn centre for your rotation.

**16.** From the **Toolbox**, choose .
Click to select each side of the triangle.
The triangle is highlighted.

**17.** From the **Transform** menu, choose **Rotate**.
Under **Rotate By:**, choose **Fixed Angle**.
Enter 90 degrees. Click **Rotate** to show the triangle and its
image after a rotation of 90° counterclockwise.

**18.** Drag any vertex or side of the original figure.
See what happens to the rotation image.

**19.** From the **Edit** menu, choose **Undo Translate Point**.
The screen shows the original triangle and rotation image.

**20.** Repeat *Steps 16* to *19* using a different number of degrees
of rotation. Print the figure and its rotation image.

## Reflecting a Figure

**21.** Repeat *Step 12*.

**22.** To create a polygon:
From the **Toolbox**, choose .
Click and drag to construct a polygon.

**23.** To reflect the polygon:
With the Straightedge Tool still selected, draw a vertical
line near your polygon. The line is highlighted.

**24.** From the **Transform** menu, choose **Mark Mirror.**
The line is a mirror line.

**25.** From the **Toolbox,** choose .
Click to select each side of the polygon.
The polygon is highlighted.

**26.** From the **Transform** menu, choose **Reflect.**
The polygon and its reflection image are shown.

**27.** Drag any vertex or side of the original figure.
See what happens to the reflection image.

**28.** Drag either end point from the mirror line.
See what happens.

**29.** From the **Edit** menu, choose **Undo Translate Point.**
Do this two times. The screen shows the original polygon
and its reflection image.

**30.** Repeat *Steps 23* to *28* using a horizontal mirror line.
Print the figure and its reflection image.

✓ **Check**

Use any or all of the transformations above to make a design that
covers the screen.
Print your design.

## Choosing a Strategy

**Remember to count squares of different sizes.**

1. A train is travelling at a rate of 1 km every 45 s. At this rate, how far will the train travel in 1 h?

2. How many squares are in this rectangle?

3. Use grid paper. Try to draw a quadrilateral with each number of lines of symmetry.
   **a)** 0          **b)** 1          **c)** 2
   **d)** 3          **e)** 4          **f)** 5
   Which quadrilaterals could you not draw? Explain.

## Strategies

- **Make a table.**
- **Use a model.**
- **Draw a diagram.**
- **Solve a simpler problem.**
- **Work backward.**
- **Guess and check.**
- **Make an organized list.**
- **Use a pattern.**
- **Draw a graph.**
- **Use logical reasoning.**

4. Use grid paper. Draw this figure:
   It has at least 1 line of symmetry.
   It has perimeter 24 units.
   It has area 23 square units.

5. Copy the diagram below.
   Write these numbers in the boxes: $\frac{1}{6}, \frac{1}{3}, \frac{1}{2}, \frac{2}{3}, \frac{5}{6}, 1$;
   so the sum of the fractions along each side is :
   **a)** $1\frac{1}{2}$                      **b)** 2

6. What fraction of the area of a tangram is triangles?

7. Write the next five terms in each pattern. Describe each pattern rule.
   **a)** $\frac{A \qquad E\ F}{B\ C\ D}$
   **b)** 1, 5, 10, 25, …
   **c)** O, T, T, F, F, S, S, …

**8.** This rectangular prism is made with 12 different coloured cubes. The colours are black, white, red, orange, light green, dark green, light blue, dark blue, brown, yellow, pink, and purple.

**Using linking cubes to build the prism.**

**a)** The colours on the left face are light green, orange, brown, and red.

Draw and colour the back face of the prism.

Another congruent prism is made from the coloured cubes. The colours on the front face are: red, orange, dark green, light blue, black, and white.

The colours on the top face are: red, black, white, pink, purple, and yellow.

The colours on the right face side are: light blue, white, yellow, and brown.

The colours on the left face side are: red, dark green, pink, and dark blue.

**b)** Build the prism. Sketch the prism.

**c)** What colours are on the bottom face of the prism? How do you know?

**9.** In her fitness program Jessie runs on Mondays, Wednesdays, and Saturdays, and swims on Tuesdays and Fridays. Malcolm runs every third day and swims on the day after each run.

Jessie and Malcolm run together on Saturday July 6.

On what days and dates in July will they:

**a)** run together again?

**b)** swim together?

# Office Space Planner

An office space planner plans the best use of the office space. He ensures that employees have a workplace that is functional and attractive. Systems furniture is a series of connected partitions, work surfaces, and cabinets. It is frequently used in offices. The planner uses a computer to design multiple 'standard' work areas. Each work area is designed to meet the needs of a group of employees with similar jobs. The work areas are also designed to 'fit' with other work areas of the same size and shape, and with work areas that have different sizes and shapes. It's all a bit of a puzzle! The space planner must solve the puzzle using geometry and an understanding of how people work and interact (ergonomics).

A workplace, where every work area or 'cubicle' is identical, is often seen as 'cell-like' or dehumanizing. Suppose you are an office planner. What might you do to make groups of work areas more appealing, and still make the best use of the available floor area?

# Unit Review

## What Do I Need to Know?

☑ **Conditions for Congruent Triangles**

Two triangles are congruent if:

- three pairs of corresponding sides are equal

- two pairs of corresponding sides are equal and the corresponding angles between these sides are equal

- two pairs of corresponding angles are equal and the corresponding sides between these angles are equal

☑ **Conditions for Congruent Figures**

For figures that are not triangles, two figures are congruent if corresponding sides are equal *and* corresponding angles are equal.

LESSON

**7.1**

1. Use grid paper or dot paper. Draw each figure.
   a) a concave hexagon
   b) a convex pentagon
   c) a concave quadrilateral
   d) a figure that is not a polygon
   e) a regular triangle

   Describe the attributes of each figure. Include angle measures.

2. Use grid paper or dot paper. Draw each figure.
   a) a hexagon with exactly 2 lines of symmetry
   b) a triangle with rotational symmetry of order 3
   c) a pentagon with exactly 3 acute angles
   d) a pentagon with exactly 3 obtuse angles

   Describe the attributes of each figure. Include angle measures.

**7.2**

3. Are the figures in each pair congruent? How do you know?

   a)

   b)
   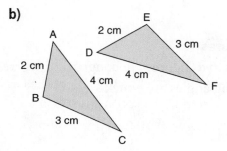

**7.3**

4. Plot these points on a coordinate grid:
   A(4, 6), B(4, 7), C(7, 9), and D(6, 6).
   Join the points to form a quadrilateral.
   The coordinates of the vertices of 3 images are given.
   Identify the transformation that produced each image.
   a) C(7, 9), E(5, 12), F(4, 12), G(4, 10)
   b) I(4, 16), J(6, 16), K(7, 13), L(4, 15)
   c) M(9, 4), N(8, 1), P(6, 1), Q(6, 2)

**7.4**

5. Copy this figure on grid paper.

   How many different ways can you use the figure to tile the plane? Show each way you find.

**7.5**

6. Draw 2 different figures on grid paper that will together tile the plane.
   Use the figures to make a design.
   Colour one of each figure.
   Use transformations to explain how to create the design beginning with each coloured figure.

# Practice Test

1. Use the figures below.

Identify:
   **a)** two congruent figures, and explain how you know they are congruent
   **b)** two figures that are *not* congruent, and explain how you know they are not congruent
   **c)** a scalene triangle with a 60° angle
   **d)** a quadrilateral with a 60° angle

2. Two triangles are congruent if they have 3 matching sides. Suppose two triangles have 3 matching angles. Are the triangles congruent? Justify your answer.

3. Three students looked at a figure and its transformation image.
   Igal said the picture showed a translation.
   Shaian said the picture showed a rotation.
   Cherie said the picture showed a reflection.
   All three students were correct. What might the picture be?
   Draw a diagram to show your thinking.

4. Julie will use both of these tiles to cover her floor.

   Use isometric paper.
   Draw 2 different designs Julie could use.
   For each design, use transformations to explain how to create the design.

When we tile the plane with congruent copies of one figure, we make a **tessellation.**

M.C. Escher was a famous Dutch artist.
He designed many different tessellations.

You will create two designs in the Escher style.
The first design is in the style of *Reptiles*, on page 268.

## Part 1

Use square dot paper or grid paper.
Tile the plane with a figure of your choice.
Sketch a design on one figure.
Repeat the sketch until every figure in the plane has the design.
Use transformations to describe how to generate the design beginning with one tile.

## Part 2

You could start with a rectangle, parallelogram, or regular hexagon, instead.

Start with a square. Draw congruent curves on 2 sides.
A curve that goes "in" on one side must go "out" on the other side.
Draw different congruent curves on the other 2 sides.

Trace the new figure on cardboard.
Cut out the figure.
Use it to tile the plane.

Add details to your tile
so it represents an
animal or an object
of your choice.

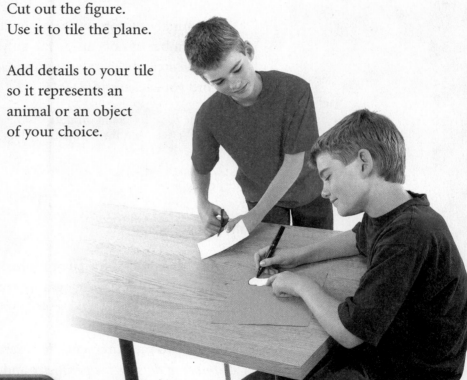

### Check List

Your work
should show:

✓ the initial tile you
created for each
design

✓ the designs
you created

✓ how you used
transformations to
create the designs

✓ the correct use of
mathematical
language

## Reflect on the Unit

How are transformations related to congruent figures?
Include diagrams in your explanation.

# Pick's Theorem

**Materials:**
- 11 pin by 11 pin geoboard
- geobands
- square dot paper
- 0.5-cm grid paper

Work with a partner.

When a polygon is drawn on square dot paper, there are dots on the perimeter and dots inside.
Is there a relationship between the numbers of these dots?

As you complete this *Investigation*, include all your work in a report that you will hand in.

➤ Make a convex polygon on the geoboard.
Draw the polygon on square dot paper.
Count:
- the number of dots on the perimeter of the polygon
- the number of dots inside the polygon
Find the area of the polygon in square units.
Record your results in a table.

| Polygon | Number of dots on the perimeter | Number of dots inside | Area in square units |
|---------|-------------------------------|----------------------|----------------------|
|         |                               |                      |                      |
|         |                               |                      |                      |
|         |                               |                      |                      |

➤ Repeat this process for 10 or more different polygons.
Include triangles, parallelograms, trapezoids, pentagons, hexagons, and so on.

➤ Choose two measurements: for example,
*Number of dots on the perimeter* and *Number of dots inside*.
Draw a scatter plot of the data.
What trends do you see in the graph? Explain.

➤ What patterns do you see in the table?
How can you use the patterns to write an expression for the area of a polygon in terms of the number of dots inside the polygon and the number of dots on the perimeter?

➤ Use variables.
Let the number of dots on the perimeter be $p$.
Let the number of dots inside be $i$.
Write a formula for the area, $A$, of a polygon in terms of $p$ and $i$.
This relationship is called **Pick's Theorem**.

## Take It Further

➤ What happens to the area when the number of dots on the perimeter increases while the number of dots inside the polygon stays the same?
➤ What happens to the area when the number of dots inside the polygon increases while the number of dots on the perimeter stays the same?

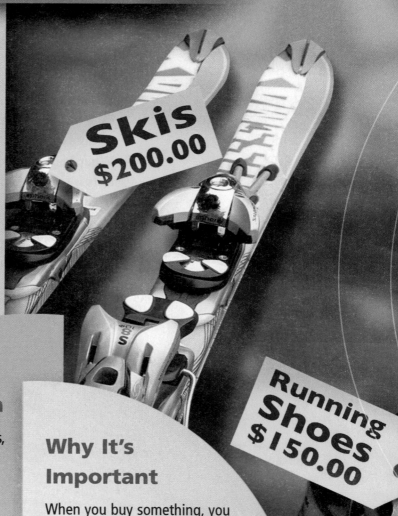

# UNIT 8

# Working with Percents

Stores offer goods on sale to encourage you to spend your money.

What is the sale price of each item in the picture?
How did you calculate the sale price?
What do you need to add to find the price you pay?

Ice Skates
$50.00

Skis
$200.00

Running
Shoes
$150.00

## What You'll Learn

- Relate decimals, fractions, and percents.
- Solve problems that involve fractions, decimals, and percents.
- Multiply decimals.
- Divide decimals.
- Draw circle graphs by hand.

## Why It's Important

When you buy something, you pay sales tax. To be able to calculate the sales tax is useful. Then you know if you have enough money to buy the item.

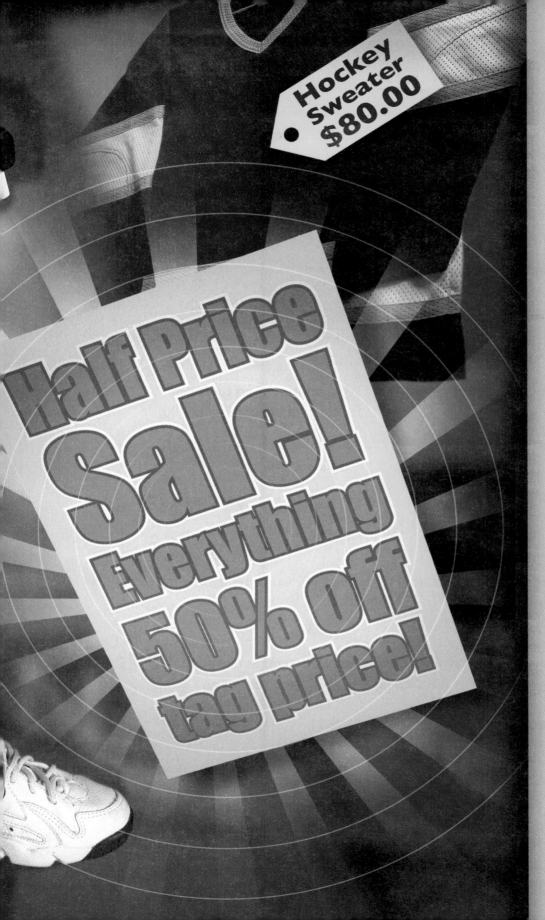

**Key Words**

- percent
- percent circle

**UNIT 8**

# Skills You'll Need

## Writing a Fraction As a Decimal

To write a fraction as a decimal, try to write an equivalent fraction with denominator 100.

When we cannot write an equivalent fraction, we use a calculator to divide.

 **Example 1**

Convert each fraction to a decimal.

**a)** $\frac{3}{5}$　　　　　　　　　　　**b)** $\frac{7}{8}$

**Solution**

**a)** $\frac{3}{5}$

Write an equivalent fraction.

$$\frac{3}{5} \overset{\times 20}{\underset{\times 20}{=}} \frac{60}{100}$$

$\frac{60}{100} = 0.60$

So, $\frac{3}{5} = 0.60$

**b)** $\frac{7}{8}$

We cannot write an equivalent fraction with denominator 100.

Use a calculator.

$\frac{7}{8}$ means $7 \div 8$.

Key in: 7 $\boxed{\div}$ 8 $\boxed{=}$ to display 0.875

$\frac{7}{8} = 0.875$

Some conversions from fractions to decimals are worth remembering.
Try to remember these:

$\frac{1}{2} = 0.5$　　$\frac{1}{4} = 0.25$　　$\frac{1}{5} = 0.2$　　$\frac{1}{8} = 0.125$　　$\frac{1}{10} = 0.1$　　$\frac{1}{100} = 0.01$

You can use these conversions to write other fractions as decimals.
For example, since $\frac{1}{10} = 0.1$, then $\frac{2}{10} = 0.2$, $\frac{3}{10} = 0.3$, and so on.

## ✓ Check

**1.** Write each fraction as a decimal. Use mental math.

　**a)** $\frac{3}{4}$　　　　　**b)** $\frac{2}{5}$　　　　　**c)** $\frac{6}{10}$　　　　　**d)** $\frac{68}{100}$

**2.** Write each fraction as a decimal.

　**a)** $\frac{5}{8}$　　　　　**b)** $\frac{3}{16}$　　　　　**c)** $\frac{3}{8}$　　　　　**d)** $\frac{7}{16}$

# Percent

**Percent** means per hundred. One whole, or 1, is 100%.
So, 70% means $\frac{70}{100}$, 4% means $\frac{4}{100}$, and 100% means $\frac{100}{100}$, or 1.

## Example 2

What percent of this hundredths chart is shaded each colour?

**a)** Red **b)** Blue **c)** Yellow

## Solution

**a)** There are 11 red squares out of 100 squares.
That is: $\frac{11}{100} = 11\%$

**b)** There are 55 blue squares out of 100 squares.
That is: $\frac{55}{100} = 55\%$

**c)** There are 34 yellow squares out of 100 squares.
That is: $\frac{34}{100} = 34\%$

## ✓ Check

Use a hundred chart.

**3.** Shade:

    **a)** 15% red     **b)** 26% yellow     **c)** 43% green     **d)** 10% blue

**4.** What percent of the hundred chart in question 3 is not shaded?

We see uses of percent everywhere.

What do you know from looking at each picture?

## Explore

Work with a partner.
Your teacher will give you a large copy of this puzzle.
Describe each puzzle piece as a fraction, a decimal, and a percent of the whole puzzle.

### Reflect & Share

Compare your answers with those of another pair of classmates.
If the answers are different, how do you know which are correct?

## Connect

➤ Since a percent can be written as a fraction, a percent can also be written as a decimal.
  We can use number lines to illustrate the relationships.
  For example:

$$25\% = \frac{25}{100} = 0.25 \qquad 125\% = \frac{125}{100} = 1.25$$

0      $\frac{25}{100}$, or $\frac{1}{4}$      $\frac{100}{100}$      $\frac{125}{100}$, or $\frac{5}{4}$

0      0.25      1.0      1.25

0      25%      100%      125%

➤ Conversely, a decimal can be written as a percent:

$$0.15 = \frac{15}{100} = 15\% \qquad\qquad 1.15 = \frac{115}{100} = 115\%$$

➤ To write a fraction as a percent, first write the fraction with denominator 100.

For example:

When a decimal has 3 digits after the decimal point, we can write it as a fraction with denominator 1000.

➤ Some fractions cannot be written with denominator 100. Use a calculator to divide.

$$\frac{5}{8} = 0.625$$
$$= \frac{625}{1000} \qquad \text{Divide numerator and denominator by 10.}$$
$$= \frac{62.5}{100}$$
$$= 62.5\%$$

## Example

a) Write each percent as a fraction and as a decimal.
   i) 75%         ii) 9%         iii) 130%

b) Write each fraction as a percent and as a decimal.
   i) $\frac{2}{5}$         ii) $\frac{5}{2}$

Draw number lines to show how the numbers are related.

**Solution**

a)  i)  $75\% = \frac{75}{100} = 0.75$

 ii)  $9\% = \frac{9}{100} = 0.09$

 iii)  $130\% = \frac{130}{100} = 1.30$

b)  i)  $\frac{2}{5}$ $\;=\;$ $\frac{40}{100} = 40\%$    ii)  $\frac{5}{2}$ $\;=\;$ $\frac{250}{100} = 250\%$

$\frac{40}{100} = 0.40$    $\frac{250}{100} = 2.50$

## Practice

**1.** What percent of each hundred chart is shaded?
Write each percent as a fraction and a decimal.

a)      b)      c)

**2.** Write each fraction as a percent.
Sketch number lines to show how the numbers are related.

a) $\frac{1}{4}$     b) $\frac{3}{10}$     c) $\frac{7}{5}$     d) $\frac{3}{4}$

**3.** Write each fraction as a decimal and a percent.

a) $\frac{2}{10}$   b) $\frac{3}{50}$   c) $\frac{4}{25}$   d) $\frac{23}{20}$   e) $\frac{14}{10}$

**4.** Fred had 8 out of 10 on a test. Janet had 82% on the test.
Who did better? How do you know?

**5.** This equilateral triangle is 20% of a larger figure.
Use triangular grid paper.
Draw a figure that shows 100%.
Is there more than one answer? Explain.

**6.** This orange square represents 25% of a larger figure.
Use 2-cm grid paper.
  **a)** Draw 50% of the larger figure.
  **b)** Draw 75% of the larger figure.
  **c)** Draw the larger figure.
  **d)** Draw 125% of the larger figure.

**7.** **Assessment Focus**   You will need a sheet of paper and
coloured pencils.
Divide the paper into these 4 sections.
  • 1 blue section that is $\frac{1}{2}$ the page
  • 1 red section that is 10% of the page
  • 1 yellow section that is 25% of the page
  • 1 green section to fill the remaining space
Explain how you did this.
What percent of the page is the green section?
How do you know?

**8.** What does it mean when someone states, "She gave it 110%"?
How can this comment be explained using math?

**Take It Further**

**9.** Suppose each pattern is continued on a hundred chart.
The numbers in each pattern are coloured red. For each pattern,
what percent of the numbers on the chart are red?
Explain your strategy for each pattern.
  **a)** 4, 8, 12, 16, 20, …       **b)** 1, 3, 5, 7, …
  **c)** 2, 4, 8, 16, …             **d)** 1, 3, 7, 13, …

**Number Strategies**

How many:
• centimetres in 1 m?
• square centimetres in 1 m²?
• cubic centimetres in 1 m³?

Sketch a picture to show each relationship.

**Reflect**

Suppose you know your mark out of 20 for an English test.
How could you write the mark as a percent?

# Showdown

## HOW TO PLAY THE GAME:

1. Cut out the cards, then shuffle them. Deal all the cards. Each player stacks his cards face down in a pile.

2. Players turn over the first card in their piles, then compare the numbers. The player whose card shows the greater number wins and takes both cards.
   Both cards are placed in a "captured pile" next to the winner's original pile. See *Step 6* when there is a tie.

3. Play continues until all cards are turned up.

4. Each player then shuffles his captured pile of cards and play continues.

5. The game ends when one player has no cards.

6. **Showdown**   If there is a tie between two cards, a showdown occurs. Each player takes the next two cards from his pile and places them face down on top of the original card. A third card is then turned over by each player, and these cards are compared.
   The player whose card shows the greater number takes all cards involved in the showdown. If there is a tie, another showdown occurs until the tie is broken.

**YOU WILL NEED**

2 sheets of SHOWDOWN playing cards (48 cards); scissors; a calculator

**NUMBER OF PLAYERS**

2

**GOAL OF THE GAME**

To have all the cards when the game ends

What strategies did you use to find which number was greater?

Note: If a player is unable to place cards in a showdown because the player has only one card, the player's last card is the turnover card.

**Focus** Use mental math and estimation.

## Explore

Work with a partner.
Look at the surface of your desk.

There is probably a textbook on it, and maybe a pencil case, an eraser, or a ruler.

How much of the surface is covered?
How much of the surface is not covered?

Use a calculator and a ruler.
Estimate the percent of your desk's surface that is covered and the percent that is not. Show your work.

### Reflect & Share

Compare your results with those of another pair of classmates. Discuss the strategies you used to find the percent of surface not covered.

## Connect

Here is a sketch of a yard.

Round 245 to 250 to get a "friendly" number. Both 250 and 750 have 250 as a common factor.

➤ To find the percent of the yard that is covered by the house, garage, and drive, calculate the area covered by
- the house: 15 m × 10 m = 150 m²
- the garage and the drive: 19 m × 5 m = 95 m²

Total area covered is: 150 m² + 95 m² = 245 m²
The area of the yard is: 30 m × 25 m = 750 m²
The fraction of the yard that is covered is: $\frac{245}{750}$
For an estimate of the fraction, round 245 to 250.
The fraction of the yard that is covered is about $\frac{250}{750} = \frac{1}{3}$.
$\frac{1}{3}$ is about 30%.
So, about 30% of the yard is covered by the house, garage, and drive.

➤ To find the percent of the yard made up of garden and grass:
The yard is 100%.
Subtract: 100% − 30% = 70%
So, about 70% of the yard is made up of garden and grass.
We can show these percents on a number line.

We can use mental math to estimate and calculate percent.

## Example 1

There are 27 students in the Grade 7 class.
Five students are left-handed.
a)  What is the fraction of students who are left-handed?
b)  Estimate the percent of students who are left-handed.

**Solution**

a)  The fraction of students who are left-handed is $\frac{5}{27}$.
b)  *Method 1*
One whole or 100% is 27 students.
50% of 27 students is about 14 students.
25% of 27 students is about 7 students.
So, the percent of students who are left-handed is less than 25%.

*Method 2*
Approximate $\frac{5}{27}$ to a "friendly" fraction: $\frac{5}{27} \doteq \frac{5}{25}$

$$\frac{5}{25} \overset{\times 4}{\underset{\times 4}{=}} \frac{20}{100} = 20\%$$

Approximately 20% of the students are left-handed.

A "friendly" fraction has a denominator such as 5, 10, 20, 25, 50. A fraction with one of these denominators can be more easily converted to a percent.

## Example 2

A pair of pants costs $39.99.
The sales tax is 15%.
Estimate the cost of the pants.

### Solution

**Mental math strategy:
A quick way to find
10% is to move the
decimal point
1 place to the left:
10% of 40. = 4.0**

Round $39.99 to $40.
To find 15%, find 10% and 5%.
10% of $40 = 0.1 × $40 = $4
5% is $\frac{1}{2}$ of 10%.
So, 5% of $40 = $\frac{1}{2}$ of $4 = $2
So, the sales tax is $4 + $2 = $6.
The cost of the pants is about $40 + $6 = $46.
We can show these percents on a number line.

## Practice

**1.** Estimate the percent of each figure that is shaded.

a)

b)

c)

d)

**2.** Find 10% of each number.
   **a)** 50      **b)** 40      **c)** 90      **d)** 300
   **e)** 75      **f)** 33      **g)** 45      **h)** 18

**3.** Use your answers to question 2.
   Find 5% of each number in question 2.

**4.** Use your answers to questions 2 and 3.
Find 15% of each number in question 2.

**5.** This strip is 12 cm long.

Find the length of:
**a)** 25% of the strip          **b)** 10% of the strip
**c)** 20% of the strip          **d)** 150% of the strip
Sketch number lines to illustrate your answers.

**6.** A pair of shoes costs $65. The sales tax is 15%. Explain how
to find the cost of the shoes using two different methods.

**7.** Estimate.
 **a)** 49% of 150          **b)** 31% of 40
 **c)** 149% of 60          **d)** 98% of 54
 **e)** 90% of 44           **f)** 61% of 88
 **g)** 2% of 200           **h)** 5% of 81

**8.** Scott estimated that 22% of 160 is approximately 30.
Do you agree with his estimate? Explain.
Sketch number lines to support your answer.

**9.** There were 341 pine trees and spruce trees in a woodlot.
One hundred twenty-two trees were pine.
 **a)** What fraction of the trees were spruce?
 **b)** Estimate the percent of spruce trees.

**10.** In a parking lot, there are 45 North American cars and
21 foreign cars.
 **a)** What fraction of the cars are foreign?
 **b)** Estimate the percent of cars that are foreign.
 **c)** Estimate the percent of cars that are not foreign.

**11.** **Assessment Focus**   Look at the front and back cover of this
textbook, including the spine. Explain how you might estimate
the percent of the book cover that is illustrated.
Show all your steps. Provide numbers to support your answer.

---

**Mental Math**

How many squares are
there on an 8 by 8
checkerboard?

Remember to count
squares of all sizes.

**12.** About 8% of Canada is covered by fresh water.
The area of Canada is approximately 9 970 000 km².
  **a)** Estimate the area of Canada covered by fresh water.
  **b)** About how much of Canada is not covered by fresh water?

**13.** About 23% of Canada is covered by tundra.
Use the data in question 12.
Estimate the area of tundra in Canada.

**14.** Raji's bedroom floor has an area of 12 m². She estimates that her bed, desk, and bookshelf cover approximately 7.5 m² of floor space.
  **a)** What fraction of the floor space is not covered?
  **b)** What percent of the floor space is not covered?
Sketch number lines to illustrate your answers.

**Take It Further**    **15.** Edward estimates he has travelled approximately 80 km.
The total length of Edward's trip is 430 km.
About what percent does Edward still have left to go?

**Reflect**

Which percents can you find by using mental math or estimation?
Give an example of how to find each percent you name.

**Math Link**

**Your World**

Percents are printed on the side of a cereal box to indicate the nutritional value of the contents. The percents relate to every 30-g serving (about 1 cup). Suppose there is a 10% sugar content. Then, in a 30-g serving, there are 3 g of sugar per cup of cereal. Next time you look for a box of your favourite cereal, check out the percents of sugar and fat. Compare them to another brand of cereal. Would your family doctor or dentist approve of your choice? Explain.

**Focus**   Multiply decimals with hundredths.

## Explore

Work with a partner.

How could you find how much you save on an item that originally cost $48.00?
Find several ways to solve this problem.

### Reflect & Share

Compare strategies with another pair of classmates.
Which strategy would you use if the sale was 45% off? Explain.

## Connect

A paperback novel originally cost $7.99.
It is on sale at 15% off.
To find how much you save, calculate 15% of $7.99.
$15\% = \frac{15}{100} = 0.15$
So, 15% of $7.99 $= \frac{15}{100}$ of 7.99
$= 0.15 \times 7.99$

Recall, from Unit 4, how we multiply two decimals with tenths.
We use the same method to multiply two decimals with hundredths.
To multiply: $0.15 \times 7.99$, multiply without the decimal points.
Then insert the decimal point in the answer by estimation or by counting decimal places.

$$
\begin{array}{r}
799 \\
\times\ 15 \\
\hline
3995 \\
7990 \\
\hline
11985
\end{array}
$$

There is a total of 4 decimal places in the question; so, there will be 4 decimal places in the answer.

Estimate:
15% is about 20%, which is $\frac{1}{5}$.
$7.99 is about $10.00.

So, $0.15 \times 7.99$ is about $\frac{1}{5}$ of 10, which is 2.

So, $0.15 \times 7.99 = 1.1985$

Round to 2 decimal places.

1.1985 is 1.20, to 2 decimal places.

You save $1.20 by buying the book on sale.

We can show this on a number line.

## Example

A park has an area of 52.6 km².

Sixty-five percent of the park is forest.

The rest of the park is lakes.

What is the area of the lakes?

## Solution

65% of the park is forest.

So, $100\% - 65\%$, or 35% of the park is lakes.

The area of the lakes is: 35% of 52.6

$35\% = \frac{35}{100} = 0.35$

So, 35% of $52.6 = 0.35 \times 52.6$

Multiply: $526 \times 35$

$$
\begin{array}{r}
526 \\
\times\ 35 \\
\hline
2630 \\
15780 \\
\hline
18410
\end{array}
$$

**Since the area of the park is given to 1 decimal place, we round the answer to 1 decimal place.**

Estimate:

35% of 52.60 is about 50% of 50, which is 25.

So, $0.35 \times 52.6 = 18.41$

35% of 52.6 km² is 18.41 km².

The area of the lakes is about 18.4 km².

**1.** Calculate.
   **a)** 10% of 27.3  **b)** 20% of 48.4  **c)** 1% of 30.6  **d)** 120% of 81.2

**2.** Find.
   **a)** 18% of 36  **b)** 24% of 67  **c)** 98% of 28  **d)** 67% of 112

**3.** Find each percent of $59.99.
   **a)** 25%  **b)** 75%  **c)** 30%  **d)** 70%  **e)** 80%  **f)** 90%

**4.** The regular price of a radio is $60.00. Find the sale price when the radio is on sale for:
   **a)** 25% off  **b)** 30% off  **c)** 40% off

**5.** Find the cost of each item on sale.
   Each item has a 15% sales tax added to the sale price.
   **a)** coat: 55% off $90  **b)** shoes: 45% off $40

**6.** (Assessment Focus)
   **a)** Calculate each percent of 52.3.
      How can you do this by completing only one multiplication?
      **i)** 2%  **ii)** 20%  **iii)** 200%
   **b)** Make up a similar example. Choose a number and 3 related percents. Show how you only need to multiply once to find all the percents of the number.

**7.** How is calculating 25% of $15.00 the same as calculating 15% of $25.00? How are the calculations different? Sketch number lines to illustrate your answer.

**8.** A garage floor is rectangular.
   Its length is 9.0 m and its width is 5.1 m.
   The length and width of a Toyota Corolla are 4.5 m and 1.7 m.
   What percent of the garage floor is occupied by the car?

**Number Strategies**

Use Pattern Blocks.

Suppose the red block represents 1 whole.

What does each block represent?
- the blue block
- the green block
- the yellow block

**Reflect**

Choose a percent. Choose an amount of money.
Calculate the percent of the money. Show your work.

# Mid-Unit Review

**8.1** **1.** Write each fraction as a decimal and as a percent. Sketch number lines to illustrate.

a) $\frac{4}{5}$   b) $\frac{3}{25}$   c) $\frac{118}{50}$   d) $\frac{7}{20}$

**2.** Write each fraction as a decimal and as a percent. Sketch number lines to illustrate.

a) $\frac{27}{20}$   b) $\frac{14}{25}$   c) $\frac{15}{8}$   d) $\frac{7}{16}$

**3.** This right isosceles triangle is 20% of a larger figure.

Draw a figure that represents 100%.

**8.2** **4.** Estimate the percent of each figure that is shaded.

a)    b)

**5.** In a piggy bank, there were 21 pennies, 32 nickels, and 13 dimes.

a) What fraction of the coins were nickels?

b) Estimate the percent of coins that were nickels.

c) How much money was in the piggy bank?

d) Estimate the percent of money that was in dimes.

**6.** Find 10% of each number.

a) 28   b) 66   c) 35   d) 180

**7.** Use the results of question 6. Find 60% of each number in question 6.

**8.** Use estimation. Find an approximate percent for each fraction.

a) $\frac{14}{17}$   b) $\frac{21}{30}$   c) $\frac{118}{60}$   d) $\frac{172}{80}$   e) $\frac{2}{21}$

**9.** Estimate.

a) 14% of 98   b) 61% of 52
c) 76% of 202   d) 98% of 134

**8.3** **10.** a) Find:

i) 5% of $1.00

ii) 30% of $1.00

iii) 130% of $1.00

iv) 20% of $1.00

b) Sketch a number line to illustrate your answers to part a.

**11.** Toni wants to buy a shirt. The original price is $85.00, but it is on sale for 30% off.
Toni will pay 15% sales tax. How much will the shirt cost?

**12.** How is calculating 85% of $40.00 the same as calculating 40% of $85.00? How are the calculations different? Sketch number lines to illustrate your answers.

# 8.4

# Drawing Circle Graphs

**Focus** Use circle graphs to display data and solve problems.

You have drawn a circle graph using a computer.
Now that you can calculate percents,
you can draw a circle graph by hand.
This is a **percent circle**.
The circle is divided into
100 congruent sectors.
Each sector is 1% of
the whole circle.
You can draw a circle graph
on a percent circle.

## Explore

Work with a partner.
Your teacher will give you a percent circle.
Everyone in the class writes on the board the number of siblings
he or she has.
Copy this table.
Record the data.

| 0 Siblings | 1 Sibling | 2 Siblings | More than 2 Siblings |
|---|---|---|---|
|  |  |  |  |

Use the percent circle.
Draw a circle graph to display the data.
Write 2 questions you can answer by looking at the graph.

### Reflect & Share

Trade questions with another pair of classmates.
Use your graph to answer your classmates' questions.
Compare graphs. If they are different, try to find out why.
How did you use fractions and percents to draw a circle graph?

## Connect

Sector angle

360° = 100%

Recall that a circle graph shows how parts of a set of data compare
with the whole set.
Each sector of a circle graph represents a percent of the whole circle.
The whole circle represents 100% and has a central angle of 360°.

This table shows the 2003 top 10 Ladies' Professional Golf Association (LPGA) money winners' place of birth.

| Asia | Australia | Europe | North America |
|------|-----------|--------|---------------|
| Kung | Teske | Sorenstam | Daniel |
| Pak | | | Inkster |
| Park | | | Jones |
| Han | | | Ochoa |

To draw a circle graph to show what percent of the top 10 were born in each place, follow these steps.

*Step 1*
Write the number of players born in each place as a fraction of 10, then as a percent.

Asia: $\frac{4}{10} = 0.4 = \frac{40}{100} = 40\%$      Australia: $\frac{1}{10} = 0.1 = \frac{10}{100} = 10\%$

Europe: $\frac{1}{10} = 0.1 = \frac{10}{100} = 10\%$      North America: $\frac{4}{10} = 0.4 = \frac{40}{100} = 40\%$

The area of the circle represents all the golfers.
All the sector angles add to 360°.

*Step 2*

**To check, add the angles. The sum should be 360°.**

$$\begin{array}{r} 144° \\ 36° \\ 36° \\ + 144° \\ \hline 360° \end{array}$$

To find the sector angle for each place of birth, multiply each decimal by 360°.
Round to the nearest degree, when necessary.
Asia 40%: 0.40 × 360° = 144°
Australia 10%: 0.10 × 360° = 36°
Europe 10%: same as Australia, so 36°
North America 40%: same as Asia, so 144°

*Step 3*
Construct a circle.
Use a protractor to construct each sector angle.
Start with the smallest angle. Draw a radius.
Measure 36°.

Start the next sector where the previous sector finished.
Label each sector with its name and percent.
Write a title for the graph.

**Top 10 LPGA Winners' Place of Birth**

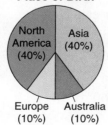

## Example 1

This circle graph shows the world's gold production.

**World's Gold Production**

In 2002, the world's gold production was approximately 2300 t. About how much gold would have been produced in each country?

a)  Canada

b)  South Africa

**Solution**

a)  7% is produced in Canada.
Mass of gold = 7% × 2300
= 0.07 × 2300
= 161
About 161 t would have been produced in Canada.

b)  35% is produced in South Africa.
Mass of gold = 35% × 2300
= 0.35 × 2300
= 805
About 805 t would have been produced in South Africa.

## Example 2

These four oceans have an area of approximately 337 million km². 

a)  Draw a circle graph to represent the data in the table.

b)  Find the area of the largest ocean.

| Ocean | Percent of Total Area |
|---|---|
| Atlantic | 25 |
| Arctic | 3 |
| Indian | 22 |
| Pacific | 50 |

**Solution**

a)  Each area is written as a percent of the total area of the oceans.
The area of the circle represents the total area of the oceans.
To find the sector angle for each ocean, multiply each percent by 360°.

Atlantic: 25% of 360° = 0.25 × 360°
= 90°

**Round each angle to the nearest degree, when necessary.**

Arctic: 3% of 360° = 0.03 × 360°
= 10.8°
≐ 11°

Indian: 22% of 360° $= 0.22 \times 360°$
$= 79.2°$
$\doteq 79°$
Pacific: 50% of 360° $= 0.50 \times 360°$
$= 180°$

Areas of Oceans

Construct a circle.
Use a protractor to construct each sector angle.
Label each sector with its name and percent.
Write a title for the graph.

**b)** The largest ocean is the Pacific Ocean.
Its area is:
50% of 337 000 000 km² $= 0.50 \times 337\ 000\ 000$ km²
$= 168\ 500\ 000$ km²
The largest ocean has an area about 168 500 000 km².

## Practice

**1.** This circle graph shows the ages of viewers of a TV show.
One week, approximately 250 000 viewers tuned in.
How many viewers were in each age group?
**a)** 13 to 19    **b)** 20 to 29    **c)** 40 and over

**2. a)** Can the data in each table below be displayed in a circle
graph? Explain.

**i)**

| Canadians, Educational Attainment, 2001 | |
|---|---|
| 0 to 8 years of elementary school | 10% |
| Some secondary school | 17% |
| Graduated from high school | 20% |
| Some post secondary education | 9% |
| Post-secondary certificate or diploma | 28% |
| University degree | 16% |

**ii)**

| Canadian Households with These Appliances, 2000 | |
|---|---|
| Automobiles | 64% |
| Cell phone | 42% |
| Dishwasher | 51% |
| Internet | 42% |

**b)** For the data that could not be displayed in a circle graph,
state what type of graph you would use to display it.

**3.** The table shows the number of Grade 7 students with each eye colour at Northern Public School.

| Eye Colour | Number of Students |
|------------|--------------------|
| Blue       | 11                 |
| Brown      | 24                 |
| Green      | 9                  |
| Grey       | 6                  |

a) Calculate the percent of students with each eye colour.
b) Draw a circle graph to represent the data.

**4.** In a telephone survey, 400 people voted for their favourite radio station.

| Radio Station | Votes |
|---------------|-------|
| MAJIC99       | 88    |
| EASY2         | ?     |
| ROCK1         | 120   |
| HITS2         | 100   |

a) How many people chose EASY2?
b) Write the number of people who voted for each station as a percent of the total number surveyed.
c) Draw a circle graph to display the results of the survey.

**Calculator Skills**

How many times can you multiply 2 by itself until the product gets too great for your calculator display? Write the greatest product as a power of 2.

**5.** **Assessment Focus**  Choose some labels from canned food, cereal boxes, or other foods.
a) List the nutritional information on each label.
b) Calculate the mass of each nutrient as a percent of the total mass.
c) Draw a circle graph to display the percent of each nutrient. Show your work.

**Take It Further**

**6.** This circle graph shows the percent of Earth's land occupied by each continent. The area of North America is approximately 220 million $km^2$. Use the percents in the circle graph. Find the approximate area of each of the other continents.

**Area of Earth's Land**
Australia (5%)
Europe (7%)
Antarctica (8%)
S. America (12%)
N. America (18%)
Asia (30%)
Africa (20%)

**Reflect**

What do you need to know about percents to be able to draw a circle graph? Include an example in your answer.

# Dividing to Find Percents

## Explore

Work with a partner.

Suppose you pay
$15.00 for a shirt.
How could you find
out what the original
price was?
Draw a diagram to model this problem.
Show several strategies for solving the problem.

### Reflect & Share

Compare your strategies with those of another pair of classmates.
Which strategies can you use to find the original price if you paid
35% of the original price? Explain.

## Connect

Jenny wanted to know her brother Alan's mass.
Alan told Jenny that 15% of his mass is 6.75 kg.

```
       6.75 kg                              ? kg
   |------|------------------------------------|
   0     15%                                 100%
```

Jenny knows what 15% is.
She wants to find 100%.

15% is 6.75.
So, 1% is: $\frac{6.75}{15}$
Use long division: $6.75 \div 15$
1% is 0.45.
So, 100% is: $0.45 \times 100 = 45$
Alan's mass is 45 kg.

$$
\begin{array}{r}
0.45 \\
15\overline{)6.75} \\
\underline{6\ 0}\phantom{0} \\
75 \\
\underline{75} \\
0
\end{array}
$$

```
       6.75 kg                             45 kg
   |------|------------------------------------|
   0     15%                                 100%
```

## Example

This sign appeared in a shop window.

Eric pays $58.50 for a jacket.
What is the list price of the jacket?

SALE | YOU PAY 65% | OF THE LIST PRICE!

### Solution

**Use a calculator or long division to find $\frac{\$58.50}{65}$.**

65% of the list price is $58.50.
So, 1% of the list price is: $\frac{\$58.50}{65} = \$0.90$

And, 100% is: $\$0.90 \times 100 = \$90.00$
The list price of the jacket is $90.00.

$58.50   $90.00

0         65%    100%

## Practice

1. 25% is 1.25 m.
   a) What is 50%?           b) What is 100%?
   Sketch a number line to show your answer.

2. 35% is 4.2 kg.
   a) What is 1%?            b) What is 100%?
   Sketch a number line to show your answer.

3. 45% is 13.5 cm.
   a) What is 1%?            b) What is 100%?
   Sketch a number line to show your answer.

4. The principal reported that 75% of the total number of families attended the school's Fun Fair. Three hundred sixty families went to the fair. How many families have children at the school?

5. A hockey team played 30 games. It won 60% of the games. How many games did the team lose?

6. Grace has read 30% of a book. She has read 72 pages. How many pages are in the book?

**Number Strategies**

Add or subtract.
- $\frac{3}{5} + \frac{3}{6}$
- $\frac{4}{5} - \frac{1}{2}$
- $\frac{3}{4} + \frac{4}{3}$
- $\frac{5}{6} - \frac{1}{4}$

**7.** Paco ate 25% of a 16-slice pizza and placed the rest in the fridge. Santos ate 25% of the leftovers.
   **a)** How many pieces were left?
   **b)** What percent of the original pizza remained?

**8.** This year, 40 more children joined the local soccer club than last year. This is a 10% increase. How many students played in the club last year?

**9.** (Assessment Focus)   Anika wants to buy a blouse.
   The original price is $75.00. It is on sale for 30% off.
   Anika will pay 15% sales tax.
   **a)** How much will the blouse cost?
   **b)** Does it make any difference to the cost in each situation?
      **i)** The 30% is taken off before the 15% tax is added.
      **ii)** The 15% tax is added before the 30% is taken off.
      Explain. Draw number lines to show your thinking.

**10.** Write your own problem that involves working with percents. Solve your problem. Show your work.

**Take It Further**

**11.** A pair of shoes in a clearance store went through a series of reductions.
   The regular price was $125. The shoes were reduced by 20%.
   Three weeks later, the shoes were reduced by a further 20%.
   Later in the year, the shoes were advertised for sale at $\frac{3}{4}$ off the ticket price.
   Sean wants to buy the shoes. He has to pay 15% sales tax.
   **a)** Sean has $40.00. Can Sean buy the shoes? Explain.
   **b)** If your answer to part a is yes, how much change does Sean get?
   Sketch number lines to illustrate your work.

**12.** A box was $\frac{3}{4}$ full. The box fell on the floor.
   Thirty marbles fell out. This was 20% of the marbles that were in the box. How many marbles were in a full box?

**Reflect**

How does a good understanding of percents help you outside the classroom? Give an example.

## Strategies

- Make a table.
- Use a model.
- Draw a diagram.
- Solve a simpler problem.
- Work backward.
- Guess and check.
- Make an organized list.
- Use a pattern.
- Draw a graph.
- Use logical reasoning.

Use a calculator when you need to.

**1.** Write 720 as the product of consecutive whole numbers. Find all the possible ways.

**2.** A digital clock shows this time.
Seven minutes past 7 is a palindromic time.

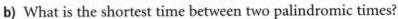

   **a)** List all the palindromic times between noon and midnight.

   **b)** What is the shortest time between two palindromic times?

**3.** I am a perfect square less than 400.
The sum of my digits is also a perfect square.
Which number could I be? Find all possible numbers.

**4.** The trail around Lake Pender is 20 km long.
How long do you think it would take you to walk around the lake? Explain.

**5.** Jack's heart rate is 72 beats/min.
How long will it take for Jack's heart to beat one million times?

**6.** A 4-cm cube is painted red on the top and bottom faces, blue on the front and back faces, and green on the side faces.
The cube is cut into 1-cm cubes.
How many of the small cubes will have:

   4 cm

   4 cm

   **a)** 3 colours of paint?

   **b)** 2 colours?

   **c)** 1 colour?

   **d)** no paint?

**7.** Use dot paper.
Draw a quadrilateral with at least two sides equal.
How many different quadrilaterals can you draw?

8. The decimals 0.1, 0.2, 0.3, up to 1.0, are
   written on ten cards.
   How many sets of three cards have
   a sum of 2?

9. Use 1-cm grid paper.
   Draw a 6 cm by 4 cm rectangle.
   Shade $\frac{1}{4}$ red.
   Shade $\frac{1}{3}$ of the remainder blue.
   Shade $\frac{1}{2}$ of the unshaded area green.
   What fraction is unshaded?

10. A small company consists of the owner and 3 employees.
    The owner earns $10 000 a month. The employees earn
    $4000, $4000, and $6000 per month.
    a) The employees ask the owner for a pay raise.
       Should they use the mean, median or mode salary when they
       present their case? Explain.
    b) Should the owner use the mean, median or mode when she
       explains she cannot give the employees a raise? Explain.

11. The area of a rectangular field is 3496 m².
    Its perimeter is 260 m.
    What are the dimensions of the field?

12. This figure comprises a square and two halves of a
    congruent square.

    Arrange the parts of the figure to produce each new figure.
    a) a rectangle  b) a parallelogram  c) a trapezoid  d) a triangle
    Sketch your answers.

The World of Work

# Sports Trainer

Sports trainers use scientific research and scientific techniques to maximize an athlete's performance. An athlete may be measured for percent body fat, or percent of either fast- or slow-twitch muscle fibre.

A trainer may recommend the athlete eat pre-event meals that contain a certain percent of carbohydrate, or choose a "sports drink" that contains a high percent of certain minerals. The trainer creates and monitors exercise routines. These enable the athlete to attain a certain percent of maximum heart rate, speed, or power.

Most sports drinks contain minerals. Research shows that the most effective sports drink has a magnesium to calcium ratio of 1:2. The body absorbs about 87% of magnesium in a drink, and about 44% of calcium in a drink. One sports drink lists 100 mg of calcium per scoop. About how much magnesium is there in 1 scoop?

# Unit Review

## What Do I Need to Know?

✓ Here are some fractions, decimals, and percents you should know.

$1 = 1.0 = 100\%$          $\frac{1}{5} = 0.2 = 20\%$

$\frac{1}{2} = 0.5 = 50\%$          $\frac{1}{10} = 0.1 = 10\%$

$\frac{1}{4} = 0.25 = 25\%$          $\frac{1}{100} = 0.01 = 1\%$

## What Should I Be Able to Do?

For extra practice, go to page 445.

**LESSON**

**8.1** **1.** Write each fraction as a decimal and as a percent.

a) $\frac{8}{20}$     b) $\frac{14}{5}$     c) $\frac{14}{25}$

d) $\frac{7}{10}$     e) $\frac{9}{8}$     f) $\frac{17}{10}$

**2.** Write each number two other ways.

a) 0.18     b) 0.3

c) 80%     d) $\frac{3}{8}$

**3.** This rectangle is 40% of a larger figure.

Use grid paper.
a) Draw a figure that shows 100%.

b) Draw a figure that shows 120%.

**8.2** **4.** Estimate.

a) 39% of 250     b) 41% of 89

c) 19% of 60     d) 91% of 46

e) 97% of 64     f) 59% of 98

g) 3% of 300     h) 4% of 92

**5.** A DVD costs $29.99. The sales tax is 15%. Estimate the cost of the DVD.

**8.3** **6.** There are 35 students in a Grade 7 class. On one day, 20% of the students were at a sports meet. How many students were in class?

**7.** The regular price of a DVD player is $120.00. What is the sale price in each case?

a) 25% off     b) 30% off

c) 40% off     d) 50% off

e) 60% off     f) 45% off

**8.** The regular price for a mountain bike is $640.00. It is on sale for 30% off. The sales tax is 15%.

a) Jamie bought the bike at the regular price. What did it cost her?

b) Sam bought the bike on sale. How much did Sam save?

**9.** This circle graph shows the surface area of the Great Lakes.

**Areas of the Great Lakes**

Michigan (23%)   Superior (34%)
Huron (24%)
Ontario (8%)
Erie (11%)

a) Which lake has a surface area about $\frac{1}{4}$ of the total area?

b) Explain why Lake Superior has that name.

c) The total area of the Great Lakes is about 244 000 km². Find the surface area of Lake Erie.

**10.** These tables show energy resources and electricity generation in Canada.

| Primary Energy Resources in Canada, 2001 | |
|---|---|
| Coal | 11% |
| Hydro-electric | 27% |
| Natural gas | 24% |
| Nuclear | 6% |
| Oil | 32% |

| Electricity Generation by Fuel Type, 2001 | |
|---|---|
| Coal | 18% |
| Hydro-electric | 61% |
| Natural gas | 4% |
| Nuclear | 13% |
| Oil | 4% |

a) Draw a circle graph to display the data in each table.

b) What do you know from looking at the two graphs?

**11.** Here are 25 players on the Toronto Maple Leafs roster for the 2003/2004 season. The table shows each player's place of birth.

| USSR | Canada | Europe | U.S. |
|---|---|---|---|
| Antropov | Belak | Berg | Fitzgerald |
| Mogilny | Belfour | Kaberle | Johnson |
| | Berehowsky | Nolan | Kidd |
| | Domi | Pilar | Klee |
| | Marchment | Ponikarovsky | |
| | McCabe | Reichel | |
| | Nieuwendyk | Renberg | |
| | Perrott | Sundin | |
| | Roberts | | |
| | Stajan | | |
| | Tucker | | |

a) Draw a circle graph to show what percent of the team was born in each place.

b) What if a U.S.-born player was traded for a USSR-born player? How would the graph change?

**12.** Eighty percent of Areyana's height is 140 cm. How tall is Areyana? Draw a number line to illustrate your answer.

**13.** At Lakehead Elementary School, 280 students participate in a walk for charity. That is 70% of the students in the school. How many students attend the school?

# Practice Test

1. How can 25% of one item be different from 25% of another? Explain.

2. The strip below is 25% of a longer strip.
   a) What is the length of a strip that is 80% of the longer strip?
   b) Draw the longer strip.

3. Find.
   a) 600% of 40
   b) 60% of 40
   c) 6% of 40
   What patterns do you see in the answers?

4. The regular price of a pair of shoes is $75.00.
   The shoes are on sale for 25% off.
   The sales tax is 15%.
   a) What is the sale price of the pair of shoes?
   b) What do the shoes cost, with sales tax?

| Type of Land Cover in Canada | |
|---|---|
| Type | Percent of Total Area |
| Forest and taiga | 45 |
| Tundra | 23 |
| Wetlands | 12 |
| Fresh water | 8 |
| Cropland and rangeland | 8 |
| Ice and snow | 3 |
| Human use | 1 |

5. The table shows the type of land cover in Canada, as a percent of the total area.
   a) Draw a circle graph to display these data.
   b) Did you need to know the area of Canada to draw the circle graph? Explain.

6. This spring, 26 dogs were adopted from the local animal shelter.
   This is 130% of the number of dogs that were adopted last spring.
   How many dogs were adopted last spring?
   Draw a number line to illustrate your answer.

**BASKETBALL BACKBOARD, RIM, POLE REGULAR $299.99** 15% OFF

Suppose you won a competition at a shopping mall.

You won $500.00 to spend at any store in the mall.

You wait to spend your money until the mall has a sidewalk sale.

Look at the items for sale.

How would you spend your money?

Don't forget to add 15% sales tax for each item.

How much do you save by buying the items on sale?

Show your work.

Use number lines to illustrate your work.

SALE

RUNNING SHOES REGULAR $89.99 40% OFF

INLINE SKATES REGULAR $69.99 10% OFF

BIKE HELMETS REGULAR $39.99 25% OFF

BICYCLE REGULAR $249.99 20% OFF

ALL BLOUSES/ SHIRTS REGULAR $49.99 25% OFF

**SPORTS RADIO**
REGULAR $39.99
20% OFF

**PORTABLE CD PLAYER** REGULAR $139.99
35% OFF

**BLANK CDS PACKAGE OF 10**
REGULAR $9.99
15% OFF

**DVD PLAYER**
REGULAR $129.99
30% OFF

**ALL PAPERBACK BOOKS**
REGULAR $8.99
15% OFF

ALL **HARDCOVER BOOKS** REGULAR $34.99
20% OFF

## Check List

Your work
should show:

✓ a list of the items
you bought and
what you paid for
each one

✓ a number line to
illustrate each
calculation

✓ how much you
saved by buying the
items on sale

✓ how you calculated
the sales tax

## Reflect on the Unit

What have you learned about percents and how they are used?

UNIT

**1**  **1.** Use grid paper.
Draw a picture that shows a square
root of each number.
**a)** 49    **b)** 16    **c)** 144

**2**  **2.** To make a pot of tea for 4 people,
you need 3 tea bags.
**a)** How many tea bags are needed
for each number of people?
**i)** 8    **ii)** 12    **iii)** 16    **iv)** 20
**b)** How many tea bags are needed
for 6 people? Explain.

**3**  **3.** Students in a Grade 7 class are filling
shoe boxes with toys for children in
other countries. A shoe box
measures 30 cm by 18 cm by 16 cm.
**a)** Find the volume of a shoe box.
The students fill 24 shoe boxes.
Eight shoe boxes are packed into
a larger box.
**b)** What could the dimensions of
this larger box be?
**c)** What are the most likely
dimensions of the larger box?
Justify your choice.

**4**  **4. a)** Multiply: 3.6 × 2.4
**b)** Which other pair of factors has
the same product as the product
in part a?
How many different pairs of
factors can you find?
Explain your work.

**5**  **5.** To celebrate his birthday, Justin and
his friends played miniature golf.
Here are their scores: 29, 33, 37, 24,
41, 38, 48, 26, 36, 33, 40, 29, 36, 22,
31, 38, 42, 35, 33
**a)** Draw a stem-and-leaf plot.
It was a par 36 course. This
means that a good golfer takes 36
strokes to complete the course.
**b)** How many scores were under
par? At par? Over par?
**c)** What was the range of the scores?
**d)** Calculate the mean, median, and
mode scores.

**6.** Some Grade 7 students were
surveyed about the average number
of hours they spend reading each
week, and their overall English mark
out of 100. Here are the data:

| Time (h) | Mark | Time (h) | Mark |
|----------|------|----------|------|
| 0 | 55 | 0 | 60 |
| 0.5 | 65 | 0.5 | 62 |
| 1 | 70 | 1 | 84 |
| 1 | 68 | 1.5 | 75 |
| 1.5 | 78 | 2 | 83 |
| 2 | 85 | 2 | 77 |
| 2 | 88 | 2 | 81 |
| 2.5 | 91 | 2.5 | 79 |
| 2.5 | 80 | 3 | 90 |

**a)** Draw a scatter plot. What trends
do you see?
**b)** Do you think a student will get a
better English mark if he reads
more? Explain.

6

**7.** A parallelogram has base 2.4 cm
and height 3.9 cm.
   **a)** What is the area of the
   parallelogram?
   **b)** What is the area of a triangle
   with the same base and
   height as the parallelogram?

**8.** Find the area and perimeter of this
trapezoid.

**9.** Find the area and perimeter of this
figure.

7    **10.** Use dot paper.
Draw two congruent figures.
Trade figures with a classmate.
Explain how you know your
classmate's figures are congruent.

**11.** These quadrilaterals are congruent.

   **a)** What is the length of EH?
   **b)** What is the measure of ∠BCD?
   Justify your answers.

**12.** Use grid paper.
   **a)** Choose a figure that tiles
   the plane.
   Create a design with your figure.
   **b)** Choose one figure as Figure A.
   Describe the position of another
   figure as a transformation image
   of Figure A.
   Do this for 5 different figures.

8    **13.** The regular price of a scooter is
$89.99. The scooter is on sale for
20% off.
   **a)** What is the sale price of
   the scooter?
   **b)** There is 15% sales tax. What
   would a person pay for the
   scooter?

**14.** How is calculating 30% of $70 the
same as calculating 70% of $30?
Sketch number lines to illustrate
your answer.

# UNIT
# 9
# Integers

**Pacific**    **Mount**

Northwest
Territories

Victo
Isla.

Yukon
Territory

British
Columbia

Alberta

Saskatchewan

Canada has 6 time zones.
- What time is it where you are now?
- You want to call a friend
  in Newfoundland.
  What time is it there?
- In the province or territory farthest
  from you, what might students be
  doing now?

What other questions can you ask
about this map?

## What You'll Learn

- Use integers to describe
  real-life situations.
- Model integers with
  coloured tiles.
- Compare and order integers.
- Add integers.
- Subtract integers.

## Why It's Important

- We use integers to compare
  temperatures with the
  temperature at which water freezes.
- Integers extend the whole number
  work from earlier grades.

**ntral**    **Eastern**    **Atlantic**    **Newfoundland**

Baffin
Island

Labrador

Quebec

Newfoundland

Ontario

New
Brunswick

P.E.I.

Nova
Scotia

## Key Words

- positive number
- negative number
- integer
- positive integer
- negative integer
- opposite integers
- zero pair

# Skills You'll Need

## Mental Math Strategies for Addition and Subtraction

**Example**

Add or subtract.
Use mental math.

a) $38 + 17$        b) $111 - 64$

**Solution**

a) $38 + 17$

Make a friendly number. Subtract from one number and add to the other.

So, $38 + 17 = 38 + 2 + 17 - 2$     **Subtract 2 from 17.**
                        **Add 2 to 38.**
          $= 40 + 15$
          $= 55$

b) $111 - 64$

Subtract the ones, then subtract the tens.

Subtract 4: $111 - 4 = 107$     **Count back by 1s**
Then subtract 60: $107 - 60 = 47$    **to subtract 4.**
So, $111 - 64 = 47$

## ✓ Check

Use mental math.

1. Add or subtract. What strategy did you use?
   a) $22 + 88$    b) $69 - 29$    c) $93 + 38$    d) $132 - 85$

2. In a magic square every row, column, and diagonal has the same sum.
   Copy and complete each magic square. Explain how you did it.

a)

|   | 1 | 6 |
|---|---|---|
|   | 5 | 7 |
| 4 |   | 2 |

b)

| 17 | 10 |    |
|----|----|----|
|    | 14 |    |
| 13 | 18 |    |

We measure temperature in degrees Celsius. The highest temperature in Prince George, BC, on April 27, 2004, was 12°C.
12 is a **positive number**.
12°C is the difference between the temperature of the air and the temperature at which water freezes, 0°C.

We may not be able to use a positive number to express a difference.
For example, the temperature inside a freezer is 4°C less than the freezing point of water. We represent this difference as −4°C.

−4 is a **negative number**.
We say "negative 4."

**When we talk about temperatures below zero, we say "minus 4," rather than "negative 4."**

## Explore

Work with a partner.
Use a positive or a negative number to represent each situation.
• eight degrees above zero
• ten degrees below zero
• parking three levels below ground level
• two points ahead in a soccer game
• a loss of sixteen dollars
• taking four steps backward

### Reflect & Share

Compare your answers with those of another pair of classmates.
For each situation, how did you decide whether to use a positive number or a negative number?

Positive and negative whole numbers are called **integers**.
We put + in front of a number to indicate it is a **positive integer**.

We can show integers on a number line.
The number line may be vertical, like a thermometer.

The positive integer, +20, is 20 units above 0.

The **negative integer**, −30, is 30 units below 0.

A number line may be horizontal.

Use any math operation. Use the numbers around the circle. Write as many ways as you can to make the number in the circle.

2    1

**100**

5    10

**Opposite integers** are the same distance from 0 but are on opposite sides of 0.
For example, +2 and −2 are opposite integers.
They are the same distance from 0 and are on opposite sides of 0.

2 units    2 units

−2    0    +2

+4 and −4 are also opposite integers, as are +21 and −21.

**1.** Mark each integer on a number line.
   **a)** +1        **b)** −5        **c)** −2        **d)** +9

**2.** Write the opposite of each integer.
   **a)** +3        **b)** −1        **c)** −8000        **d)** +10

**3.** Use a positive or negative integer to represent each situation.
   **a)** thirty-five degrees Celsius below zero in Yellowknife
   **b)** a weather balloon 28 000 m above Earth's surface
   **c)** diving 35 m below the ocean's surface
   **d)** earning $500

Use question 3 as a model.

**4.** Use each integer below to describe a situation.
   **a)** +4        **b)** −5        **c)** +120        **d)** −8500

**5.** Describe two situations in which you might use negative and positive integers. Write integers for your situations.

**6. Assessment Focus** Statistics Canada reported these data about Canada's population.

| Years | Births | Deaths | Immigrants | Emigrants |
|---|---|---|---|---|
| 1961-66 | 2 249 000 | 731 000 | 539 000 | 280 000 |
| 1996-2001 | 1 704 000 | 1 095 000 | 1 051 000 | 270 000 |

a) Which numbers can be represented by positive integers? Negative integers? Explain.

b) For each column of data in the table, find the difference in the numbers. Write the difference as a positive or negative integer. Explain your choice of integer.

c) Choose one time period. Use a number line and integers to explain the relationship between births and deaths.

d) Choose one time period. Use integers to explain the relationships between immigrants and emigrants.

**Take It Further**

**7.** Changes in stock prices on the Stock Exchange are written as positive or negative integers.

a) Express each change as an integer.
  i) The value of Apple Computers increased $2.
  ii) Palm Tech dropped from $25 to $22.
  iii) MDS started the day at $13 and ended the day at $12.
  iv) Steve bought Global stock at $10 and sold it for $15.

b) Look at the two stock prices in part a, ii. How are the prices related?

c) Look at the two stock prices in part a, iv. How are the prices related?

d) How can an integer be used to show the relationship between two prices of a stock? Explain.

Find the price of a stock in the financial section of a newspaper. Follow the price every day for one month. How are integers used to show how the stock price changes?

**Reflect**

Suppose you read a situation that can be described with integers. What clues do you look for to help you decide whether to use a positive or negative integer? Use examples in your explanation.

Elevation is the height above or below sea level. Elevation influences climate and how people live. For example, crops will not grow at elevations above 5300 m.

### Explore

Work with a partner.

You will need an atlas or Internet access.

Here are some examples of extreme elevations around the world:

| | |
|---|---|
| Vinson Massif, Antarctica | 4897 m above sea level |
| Dead Sea, Israel/Jordan | 411 m below sea level |
| Bottom of Great Slave Lake | 458 m below sea level |
| Mt. Nowshak, Afghanistan | 7485 m above sea level |
| Challenger Deep, Pacific Ocean | 10 924 m below sea level |

Research to find at least 4 more extreme elevations in Canada. Two should be above sea level, and two should be below sea level. Order *all* the elevations from least to greatest.

### Reflect & Share

What strategies did you use to order the elevations? What other ways could you display these data to show the different elevations?

### Connect

We use the symbols > and < to show order. The symbol points to the lesser number.

+5 is to the right of +3 on a number line.

+5 is greater than +3, so we write: +5 > +3

+3 is less than +5, so we write: +3 < +5

+3 is to the right of −4 on a number line.
+3 is greater than −4, so we write: +3 > −4
−4 is less than +3, so we write: −4 < +3

−3 is to the left of −1 on a number line.
−3 is less than −1, so we write: −3 < −1
−1 is greater than −3, so we write: −1 > −3

## Example

For the integers 0, +1, −2, +3, −5:

a) Use a number line to order the integers from least to greatest.
b) Write the opposite of each integer.
   Show the opposites on a number line.
c) Order the opposites from least to greatest.

## Solution

a) Mark each integer on a number line.

The integers increase from left to right.
So, the integers from least to greatest: −5, −2, 0, +1, +3

b) The opposite of an integer is its mirror image reflected in a vertical line drawn through 0 on a number line.
   The opposite of −5 is +5. The opposite of −2 is +2.
   Since 0 is the reference point, 0 is its own opposite.
   The opposite of +1 is −1. The opposite of +3 is −3.

c) So, the opposite integers from least to greatest: −3, −1, 0, +2, +5

1. Copy each number line. Fill in the missing integers.

a)

-4        -2        0   +1   +2        +4

b)

        -7        -5        -3        -1        +1

2. Order the integers in each set from least to greatest.
   a) +5, +13, +1     b) −3, −5, −4     c) +4, −2, +3

3. Order the integers in each set from greatest to least.
   a) +4, +1, +8     b) −7, −5, −3     c) 0, +4, −4

4. Order the integers in each set from least to greatest.
   a) +5, −5, +4, +2, −2          b) −8, −12, +10, 0, −10
   c) +41, −39, −41, −15, −25     d) +1, −1, +2, −2, +3

5. Order the integers in each set from greatest to least.
   a) +14, −25, −30, +3, −10     b) 0, +1, +2, −1, −2
   c) −29, +27, −11, −4, +6      d) −7, +8, −9, +10, −11

6. This table shows the coldest temperatures ever recorded in 6 provinces and territories.
   a) Draw a thermometer like the one shown. Mark each temperature on it.

| Province or Territory | Coldest Temperature °C |
|---|---|
| Alberta | − 61 |
| Manitoba | − 53 |
| Nova Scotia | − 47 |
| Nunavut | − 64 |
| Ontario | − 58 |
| Quebec | − 54 |

   b) Order the temperatures in part a from least to greatest. How can you use your thermometer to do this?

7. Copy and complete by placing < or > between the integers. Use a number line if it helps.
   a) +5 ☐ +10     b) −5 ☐ −10     c) −6 ☐ 0
   d) −5 ☐ −4      e) +100 ☐ −101  f) −80 ☐ −40

8. **Assessment Focus**

   Look at the integers in the box.

   | | +4 | |
   |---|---|---|
   | −8 | | −5 |
   | | +9 | |
   | 0 | | +8 |

   a) Which integers are:
      i)   greater than 0?
      ii)  between −3 and +3?
      iii) greater than −10 and less than −5?
      iv)  less than +1?
   b) What other questions can you ask about these integers? Write down your questions and answer them.

9. On January 18, 2002, the temperature in Charlottetown, Prince Edward Island, was −21°C; in Sydney, Nova Scotia, it was −23°C; in Point Lepreau, New Brunswick, it was −22°C. Which place was the warmest? Coldest? How do you know?

**Take It Further**

10. a) Draw a number line from −6 to +6. Find the integer that is:
       i)   halfway between −6 and +6
       ii)  halfway between −5 and +1
       iii) halfway between −5 and −1
       iv)  1 less than +3
       v)   3 more than −4
       vi)  4 less than −1
    b) Explain why the answer for part a, ii is different from the answer for part a, iii.
    c) −3 is halfway between two integers on a number line. Draw a number line and mark the two integers on it.

11. One day, the temperature in Wabash Lake, Newfoundland, was −41°C; in Pelly Bay, Nunavut, it was −51°C. The temperature in Churchill, Manitoba, was halfway between these temperatures. What was the temperature in Churchill?

12. Copy each pattern. Extend the pattern for 3 more terms. Describe each pattern in words.
    a) −5, −3, −1, +1, ...        b) +7, +4, +1, −2, ...
    c) −20, −18, −16, −14, ...    d) −5, −10, −15, −20, ...

### Reflect

When two integers have different signs, how can you tell which is greater? When two integers have the same sign, how can you tell which is greater?

**Focus**   Use coloured tiles to represent integers.

We can use coloured tiles to represent integers.

One yellow tile ▢ can represent $+1$.

One red tile ◼ can represent $-1$.

A red tile and a yellow tile combine to model 0:  We call this a **zero pair**.

## Explore

Work with a partner.
You will need coloured tiles.
How many different ways can you use coloured tiles
to model each number?

➤ $0, +1, +2, +3, +4$
➤ $-1, -3, -5, -6$

Draw a picture to show the tiles you used for each way you found.

### Reflect & Share

Compare your models with those of another pair of classmates.
Look at all the models that represent one integer.
How do you know that all the models represent that integer?

## Connect

We can model any integer in many ways.

Each set of tiles below models $+5$.

**Each pair of 1 yellow tile and 1 red tile makes a zero pair. The pair models 0.**

## Example

Use coloured tiles to model −4 three different ways.

**Solution**

Start with 4 red tiles to model −4.
Add different numbers of zero pairs.
Each set of tiles below models −4.

Adding 4 zero pairs does not change the value.

Adding 2 zero pairs does not change the value.

Adding 7 zero pairs does not change the value.

## Practice

1. Write the integer modelled by each set of tiles.

a)        b)        c)

d)        e)        f)

2. Use yellow and red tiles to model each integer. Draw the tiles.

   a) −6        b) +7        c) +6        d) −2
   e) +9        f) −4        g) 0         h) +10

3. Work with a partner. Place 10 yellow and 10 red tiles in a bag.

   a) Pull out a handful of tiles.
      Tell the integer that the
      tiles model.

   b) Have your partner tell what
      other set of tiles could
      model this integer.

**Mental Math**

Sarah ran a marathon in 3 h and 41 min. The race started at 7:45 a.m. At what time did Sarah finish?

**4. Assessment Focus**

a) Choose an integer between −9 and +6. Use coloured tiles to model the integer.

b) How many more ways can you find to model the integer? Create a table to order your work.

c) What patterns can you find in your table?

d) Explain how the patterns in your table can help you model an integer between −90 and +60.

**5. a)** Suppose you have 10 yellow tiles. How many red tiles would you need to model +2? How do you know?

b) Suppose you have 100 yellow tiles. How many red tiles would you need to model +2? How do you know?

**Math Link**

**Sports**

In golf, a hole is given a value called **par**.
Par is the number of strokes a good golfer takes to reach the hole.
A score of +2 means a golfer took 2 strokes more than par, or 2 strokes over par.
A score of −1 means a golfer took 1 stroke fewer than par, or 1 stroke under par.
Some scores have special names.
A score of +1 is a bogey.
A score of −1 is a birdie.
A score of −2 is an eagle.

In a golf tournament, the golfer with the fewest strokes wins the game.

**Reflect**

Explain how it is possible to use different sets of red and yellow tiles to model the same integer.

Recall that when you add two numbers,
such as 5 + 3,
you combine 5 counters with
3 counters to obtain 8 counters.

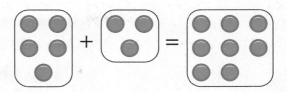

You can add two integers in a similar way.
You know that +1 and −1 combine to make a zero pair.
We can combine coloured tiles to add integers.

## Explore

Work with a partner.
You will need coloured tiles.
➤ Choose two different positive integers.
   Add the integers.
   Draw a picture of the tiles you used.
   Write the addition equation.
➤ Repeat the activity for a positive integer and a negative integer.
➤ Repeat the activity for two different negative integers.

### Reflect & Share

Share your equations with another pair of classmates.
How did you use the tiles to find a sum of integers?
How can you predict the sign of the sum?

## Connect

➤ To add two positive integers: (+5) + (+4)
   Model each integer with tiles.

   +5: ▢ ▢ ▢ ▢ ▢

   +4: ▢ ▢ ▢ ▢

Combine the tiles. There are 9 yellow tiles.
They model +9.

This is an addition equation. ——→ So, $(+5) + (+4) = +9$

➤ To add a negative integer and a positive integer: $(-6) + (+9)$
Model each integer with tiles. Circle zero pairs.

−6:
+9:

There are 6 zero pairs.
There are 3 yellow tiles left.
They model +3.
So, $(-6) + (+9) = +3$

➤ To add two negative integers: $(-3) + (-7)$
Model each integer with tiles.

−3: ■ ■ ■
−7: ■ ■ ■ ■ ■ ■ ■

Combine the tiles. There are 10 red tiles.
They model −10.
So, $(-3) + (-7) = -10$

## Example

Add. $(+6) + (-5) + (-4)$

**Solution**

$(+6) + (-5) + (-4)$
Model each integer with tiles.
Circle zero pairs.

+6:
−5:
−4:

There are 3 red tiles left.
They model −3.
So, $(+6) + (-5) + (-4) = -3$

Use coloured tiles.

**1.** What sum does each set of tiles model?
Write the addition equation.

a)

b)

c)

d)

e)

f)

**2.** What sum does each set of tiles model?
How do you know you are correct?
a) 3 yellow tiles and 2 red tiles
b) 3 yellow tiles and 4 red tiles
c) 2 red tiles and 2 yellow tiles

**3.** Use coloured tiles to represent each sum. Find each sum.
Sketch the tiles you used.
a) $(+2) + (-2)$    b) $(-4) + (+4)$    c) $(+5) + (-5)$

**4.** Add. Sketch coloured tiles to show how you did it.
a) $(+2) + (+3)$    b) $(-3) + (+4)$    c) $(-4) + (-1)$
d) $(+1) + (-1)$    e) $(-3) + (-4)$    f) $(+5) + (-2)$

**5.** Add.
a) $(+4) + (+3)$    b) $(-7) + (+5)$    c) $(-4) + (-5)$
d) $(+8) + (-1)$    e) $(-10) + (-6)$    f) $(+4) + (-13)$

**6.** Represent each sentence with integers, then find each sum.
a) The temperature is $-3°C$ and rises 4 degrees Celsius.
b) Ravinder earned $5 and spent $3.

**7.** Write 3 integer addition problems.
Trade problems with a classmate.
Solve your classmate's problems with coloured tiles.

About what fraction of
the large square is
shaded in each
diagram?

a)

b)

c)

8. Add. Sketch coloured tiles to show how you did it.
   a) $(+1) + (+2) + (+3)$     b) $(+2) + (-1) + (+3)$
   c) $(-3) + (-1) + (-1)$     d) $(+4) + (-3) + (+1)$
   e) $(-4) + (+1) + (-2)$     f) $(-5) + (-3) + (-2)$

9. Copy and complete.
   a) $(+5) + \square = +8$     b) $\square + (-3) = -4$   c) $(+3) + \square = +1$
   d) $(-5) + \square = -3$     e) $(+2) + \square = +1$   f) $\square + (-6) = 0$

10. **Assessment Focus**
    a) Add: $(+3) + (-7)$
    b) Suppose you add the integers in the opposite order:
       $(-7) + (+3)$. Does the sum change?
       Use coloured tile drawings and words to explain the result.
    c) How is $(-3) + (+7)$ different from $(+3) + (-7)$? Explain.

11. In a magic square every row, column, and diagonal has the same
    sum. Copy and complete each magic square. How did you do it?

a)

b)

**Take It Further**

12. Add.
    a) $(+4) + (+1) + (+1) + (+1)$
    b) $(-3) + (+2) + (-1) + (+1)$
    c) $(+3) + (-2) + (-1) + (-1)$

13. Copy the triangle at the left.
    Place the numbers $-6, -5, -4, -3, -2, -1$ in the triangle
    so the sums of the sides are the same.
    Explain how you solved the problem.

**Reflect**

Explain how to add two integers when the integers have:
• the same signs
• opposite signs

# Adding Integers

We can show the addition of whole numbers on a number line.

$4 + 2 = 6$

We can also show the addition of integers on a number line.

## Explore

Work with a partner.
You will need copies of this number line.

➤ Choose two different positive integers.
Use a number line to add them.
Write the addition equation.
➤ Repeat the activity for a positive integer and a negative integer.
➤ Repeat the activity for two different negative integers.

### Reflect & Share

Trade your addition problems with another pair of classmates.
Answer your classmates' problems.
Compare answers.
If the answers do not agree, decide who is correct. Explain.

## Connect

➤ To add a positive integer, move right (in the positive direction).

**Start at −2.**
**Move 3 units right.**

$(-2) + (+3)$
$(-2) + (+3) = +1$

> To add a negative integer, move left (in the negative direction).

**Start at −2.**
**Move 3 units left.**

$$(-2) + (-3)$$
$$(-2) + (-3) = -5$$

We can use patterning to add integers.

## Example 1

Add. $(+5) + (-2)$

**Solution**

$(+5) + (-2)$
Think of a pattern. Start with facts you know.
Continue the pattern until you reach the fact you want.
$(+5) + (+2) = +7$
$(+5) + (+1) = +6$
$(+5) + (0) = +5$
$(+5) + (-1) = +4$
$(+5) + (-2) = +3$

## Example 2

Sandra and Joe buy and sell CDs at a flea market.
In August, they bought 14 CDs for $5 each.
They sold 6 CDs for $9 each.
**a)** Did Sandra and Joe make money or lose money in August?
**b)** How much money did they make or lose?

**Solution**

Expenses: $14 \times \$5 = \$70$      Income: $6 \times \$9 = \$54$
**a)** Since the expenses are greater than the income,
Sandra and Joe lost money in August.
**b)** Draw a number line.

$$(-70) + (+54) = -16$$

In August, Sandra and Joe lost $16.

Use a number line when it helps.

**1.** Add.

    **a)** $(+1) + (+3)$         **b)** $(-1) + (+3)$

    **c)** $(-3) + (+1)$         **d)** $(-1) + (-3)$

**2.** Find each sum. Use a pattern when you can.

    **a)** $(+4) + (+2)$         **b)** $(+5) + (-3)$

    **c)** $(-4) + (-2)$         **d)** $(-8) + (+2)$

**3. a)** Reverse the order of the integers in question 2, then add.

    **b)** Compare your answers to the answers in question 2. What do you notice?

    **c)** Make a general statement about your observations.

**4.** Look at these thermometers. Find each temperature after:

    **a)** it falls 4°C         **b)** it falls 7°C         **c)** it rises 6°C

**5. a)** The temperature rises 7°C, then drops 2°C. What is the overall change in temperature?

    **b)** Adrian loses $4, then earns $8. Did Adrian gain or lose overall?

    **c)** The value of a stock went up $3, then down $2. What was the final change in the value of the stock?

**6.** Add.

    **a)** $(+12) + (+3)$         **b)** $(+13) + (-7)$

    **c)** $(-5) + (-10)$         **d)** $(-5) + (+8)$

    **e)** $(-8) + (-7)$         **f)** $(+4) + (-10)$

**Mental Math**

Which expression does
not belong? Why?

$12 \times 4 \times 50$

$25 \times 10 \times 10$

$24 \times 100$

$99 \times 20 + 420$

$80 \times 30$

$90 \times 30 - 300$

**7.** Add.

  **a)** $(+30) + (+10)$      **b)** $(+20) + (-10)$

  **c)** $(-35) + (-5)$       **d)** $(-15) + (+18)$

  **e)** $(-82) + (+79)$     **f)** $(-58) + (-22)$

**8.** **Assessment Focus**   Use an example to explain why each
statement is true.

Use a number line to support your explanations.

  **a)** The sum of two opposite integers is 0.

  **b)** The sum of two positive integers is always positive.

  **c)** The sum of two negative integers is always negative.

  **d)** The sum of a negative integer and a positive integer is
sometimes negative and sometimes positive.

**9.** Add.

  **a)** $(+4) + (+3) + (-6)$     **b)** $(-2) + (-4) + (+1)$

  **c)** $(-5) + (+3) + (-4)$     **d)** $(+6) + (-8) + (+2)$

  **e)** $(+12) + (-3) + (-2)$    **f)** $(-5) + (-8) + (-10)$

**10.** The temperature in North Bay is 23°C.
The temperature falls 7°C, then rises 12°C.
What is the final temperature?
How did you find out?
Which model did you use?

**11.** Susanna earned $24, spent $7, earned $12 more, and spent $10
more. Express her earnings and spendings using integers.
How much money does Susanna have left over from her
earnings and spendings?

**Take It Further**

**12.** Copy and complete.

  **a)** $(+10) + \square = +25$     **b)** $(-10) + \square = -25$

  **c)** $(+20) + \square = +15$     **d)** $(-20) + \square = -15$

  **e)** $(+35) + \square = +17$     **f)** $(-35) + \square = -17$

**Reflect**

You have used three models to add integers.
Which model do you prefer? Why?

# Mid-Unit Review

LESSON

**9.1** **1.** Draw a number line. Show each integer on the number line: +3, −2, −5, 0

**2.** Use an integer to represent each situation.
a) 12°C below zero
b) a golf score of 3 strokes above par
c) 10 m above sea level
d) a drop of $2 in the price of a stock
e) $25 earned
f) a mountain elevation of 1500 m

**9.2** **3.** Order these integers from least to greatest.
a) +4, −3, −2, +1, −4
b) +18, +50, 0, −50, −17

**9.3** **4.** Use red and yellow tiles to model each integer two different ways. Draw the tiles.
a) −5  b) 0
c) +8  d) −1
e) +3  f) −7

**9.4** **5.** Use coloured tiles to add. Draw pictures of the tiles you used.
a) (+4) + (−1)
b) (−3) + (−2)
c) (−5) + (+1)
d) (+6) + (+3)
e) (−4) + (−8)
f) (+4) + (+8)

**9.5** **6.** Use a number line to add.
a) (+3) + (+2)  b) (−5) + (−1)
c) (−10) + (+8)  d) (+6) + (−5)
e) (−8) + (+8)  f) (−5) + (+12)

**7.** Use patterns to add.
a) (+6) + (−3)  b) (−2) + (+8)
c) (+5) + (−9)  d) (−4) + (+9)

**8.** Add.
a) (+4) + (+1) + (−2)
b) (−3) + (−1) + (−4)
c) (−5) + (+1) + (+3)
d) (+6) + (−5) + (−8)

**9.** a) Puja earned $50, was given $10, and spent $20.
How much did Puja then have?

b) The temperature starts at +5°C, goes up 2°C, then drops 10°C. What is the final temperature?
c) The population of a city was 124 000, then it dropped by 4000 people. What was the population then?

**10.** a) Add. (+4) + (−5)
b) Find another pair of integers that has the same sum as part a. Do this 3 times.

# Subtracting Integers with Tiles

To add integers, we combine groups of tiles.
To subtract integers, we do the reverse:
we "take away" tiles from a group.

Recall that equal numbers of
red and yellow tiles model 0.
For example, $(-5) + (+5) = 0$

Adding 0 to a set of tiles does
not change its value.
For example, $(-3) + 0 = -3$

## Explore

Work with a partner.
You will need coloured tiles.
Use tiles to subtract. Sketch the tiles you used in each case.

- $(+5) - (+3)$
- $(+5) - (-3)$
- $(-3) - (+5)$
- $(-3) - (-5)$

### Reflect & Share

Compare your results with those of another pair of classmates.
Did they draw the same sets of tiles? Explain.
When you subtracted, how did you know how many tiles to use
to model each integer?

## Connect

To use tiles to subtract integers, we model the first integer, then take
away the number of tiles indicated by the second integer.

We can use tiles to subtract: $(+5) - (+9)$

Model $+5$.

There are not enough tiles to take away +9.
To take away +9, we need 4 more yellow tiles.

We add zero pairs without changing the value.
Add 4 yellow tiles and 4 red tiles. They represent 0.

By adding 0, the integer the tiles represent has not changed.
Now take away the 9 yellow tiles.

Since 4 red tiles remain, we write: $(+5) - (+9) = -4$

**Example**

Use tiles to subtract.

**a)** $(-2) - (-6)$      **b)** $(-6) - (+2)$      **c)** $(+2) - (-6)$

**Solution**

**a)** $(-2) - (-6)$

Model $-2$.

There are not enough tiles to take away $-6$.
To take away $-6$, we need 4 more red tiles.

We add zero pairs without changing the value.
Add 4 red tiles and 4 yellow tiles.

Now take away 6 red tiles.

Since 4 yellow tiles remain, we write: $(-2) - (-6) = +4$

**b)** $(-6) - (+2)$

Model $-6$.

There are no yellow tiles to take.
We need 2 yellow tiles to take away.

We add zero pairs.
Add 2 yellow tiles and 2 red tiles.

Now take away 2 yellow tiles.

Since 8 red tiles remain, we write: $(-6) - (+2) = -8$

**c)** $(+2) - (-6)$

Model $+2$.

There are no red tiles to take.
We need 6 red tiles to take away.

We add zero pairs.
Add 6 red tiles and 6 yellow tiles.

Now take away 6 red tiles.

Since 8 yellow tiles remain, we write: $(+2) - (-6) = +8$

Notice the results in the *Example*, parts b and c.
When we reverse the order in which we subtract two integers,
the answer is the opposite integer.
$(-6) - (+2) = -8$
$(+2) - (-6) = +8$

**1.** Use tiles to subtract. Draw pictures of the tiles you used.
   **a)** $(+7) - (+4)$    **b)** $(-2) - (-2)$    **c)** $(-9) - (-6)$
   **d)** $(+4) - (+2)$    **e)** $(-8) - (-1)$    **f)** $(+3) - (+3)$

**2.** Use tiles to subtract.
   **a)** $(-1) - (-4)$    **b)** $(+3) - (+8)$    **c)** $(-4) - (-11)$
   **d)** $(+7) - (+8)$    **e)** $(-4) - (-6)$    **f)** $(+1) - (+10)$

**3.** Subtract.
   **a)** $(-4) - (-1)$    **b)** $(+8) - (+3)$    **c)** $(-11) - (-4)$
   **d)** $(+8) - (+7)$    **e)** $(-6) - (-4)$    **f)** $(+10) - (+1)$

**4.** Subtract.
   **a)** $(+4) - (-7)$    **b)** $(-2) - (+8)$    **c)** $(-9) - (+5)$
   **d)** $(+6) - (-8)$    **e)** $(-3) - (+6)$    **f)** $(-5) - (+7)$

**5.** Subtract.
   **a)** $(+4) - (+5)$    **b)** $(-3) - (+5)$    **c)** $(-4) - (+3)$
   **d)** $(-1) - (-8)$    **e)** $(+8) - (-2)$    **f)** $(+4) - (-7)$

**6.** Write 3 integer subtraction problems.
   Trade problems with a classmate.
   Solve your classmate's problems.

**7. a)** Use coloured tiles to subtract each pair of integers.
   **i)** $(+3) - (+1)$ and $(+1) - (+3)$
   **ii)** $(-3) - (-2)$ and $(-2) - (-3)$
   **b)** What do you notice about each pair of problems in part a?

**8.** $(+5) - (-2) = +7$
   Predict the value of $(-2) - (+5)$.
   Explain the reasoning for your choice.

**9.** **Assessment Focus**  Use integers.
   Write a subtraction problem that would give each answer.
   How many problems can you write each time?
   **a)** $+2$        **b)** $-3$        **c)** $+5$        **d)** $-6$

**Calculator Skills**

Assume the $\div$ key on your calculator does not work.

Find two ways to use your calculator to divide:
888 $\div$ 24

**10.** Here is a magic square:

| 0 | +5 | −2 |
|---|---|---|
| −1 | +1 | +3 |
| +4 | −3 | +2 |

a) Subtract +4 from each entry.
   Is it still a magic square? Why?
b) Subtract −1 from each entry.
   Is it still a magic square? Why?
c) Make up your own magic square.

**Take It Further**

**11. a)** Find two integers with a sum of −1 and a difference of +5.
   **b)** Create and solve a similar integer problem.

**12.** Evaluate.
   a) $(+4) + (+1) - (+3)$        b) $(+1) - (+2) - (-1)$
   c) $(-3) - (+1) + (+4)$        d) $(-2) - (-4) + (-1)$
   e) $(+2) - (+1) - (+4)$        f) $(+1) - (+2) + (+1)$

**13.** Copy and complete.
   a) $(+4) - \square = +3$
   b) $(+3) - \square = -1$
   c) $\square - (+1) = +4$

**14.** Which expression in each pair has the greater value?
   Explain your reasoning.
   a) i) $(+3) - (-1)$        ii) $(-3) - (+1)$
   b) i) $(-4) - (-5)$        ii) $(+4) - (+5)$

**Reflect**

Here are 4 types of subtraction problems:
• (negative integer) – (negative integer)
• (negative integer) – (positive integer)
• (positive integer) – (positive integer)
• (positive integer) – (negative integer)
Write a problem for each type of subtraction.
Show how you use tiles to solve each problem.

# Subtracting Integers

**Focus** Subtract integers using number lines and patterns.

Just as we can show addition of whole numbers on a number line, we can show subtraction of whole numbers on a number line.

$7 - 5 = 2$

## Explore

Work with a partner.
You will need copies of this number line.

➤ Use the number line to subtract.

| | |
|---|---|
| $(+6) - (-4)$ | $(-3) - (+5)$ |
| $(-5) - (-4)$ | $(+7) - (+10)$ |

Check your answers using coloured tiles.

➤ Subtract.       Add.

| Subtract. | Add. |
|---|---|
| $(+7) - (+2)$ | $(+7) + (-2)$ |
| $(-7) - (-2)$ | $(-7) + (+2)$ |
| $(+7) - (-2)$ | $(+7) + (+2)$ |
| $(-7) - (+2)$ | $(-7) + (-2)$ |

What do you notice about the answers in each row?
What patterns do you see in each subtraction and addition?
Check your pattern using other integers.

### Reflect & Share

Compare your answers with those of another pair of classmates.
How can you use addition to subtract two integers?

➤ To subtract two whole numbers, such as 5 − 2, we think, "What do we add to 2 to get 5?"
We add 3 to 2 to get 5; so, 5 − 2 = 3

We can do the same to subtract two integers.
For example, to subtract: $(+5) - (-2)$
Think: "What do we add to −2 to get +5?"

We add +7 to −2 to get +5; so, $(+5) - (-2) = +7$
We also know that $(+5) + (+2) = +7$.
We can look at other subtraction equations and related addition equations.

| | |
|---|---|
| $(+9) - (+4) = +5$ | $(+9) + (-4) = +5$ |
| $(-9) - (-4) = -5$ | $(-9) + (+4) = -5$ |
| $(-9) - (+4) = -13$ | $(-9) + (-4) = -13$ |
| $(+9) - (-4) = +13$ | $(+9) + (+4) = +13$ |

In each case, the result of subtracting an integer is the same as adding the opposite integer.
For example,

$(-9) - (+4) = -13$            $(-9) + (-4) = -13$

Subtract +4.            Add −4.

➤ To subtract an integer, we add the opposite integer.
For example, to subtract: $(+3) - (-6)$

**The opposite of −6 is +6.**

Add the opposite: $(+3) + (+6)$

So, $(+3) - (-6) = +9$

## Example 1

Use a number line to subtract.

**a)** $(+2) - (+9)$           **b)** $(+2) - (-9)$

**Solution**

**a)** To subtract: $(+2) - (+9)$
Add the opposite: $(+2) + (-9)$
Use a number line.
$(+2) + (-9) = -7$

**b)** To subtract: $(+2) - (-9)$
Add the opposite: $(+2) + (+9)$
Use a number line.
$(+2) + (+9) = +11$

## Example 2

On April 27, 2004, the highest temperature in Windsor was +5°C and the highest temperature in Yellowknife was −2°C.
What is the difference in temperature? Interpret the answer.

**Solution**

The difference between +5 and −2 can be written in two ways:

$(+5) - (-2)$                          $(-2) - (+5)$
Add the opposite: $(+5) + (+2)$       Add the opposite: $(-2) + (-5)$
$(+5) + (+2) = +7$               $(-2) + (-5) = -7$
The difference in temperature       The difference in temperature
is +7°C.                              is −7°C.
The temperature in Windsor is       The temperature in Yellowknife
7°C greater than the temperature    is 7°C less than the temperature
in Yellowknife.                       in Windsor.

**1.** Rewrite using addition.
   **a)** $(+6) - (+4)$    **b)** $(-5) - (+4)$    **c)** $(-2) - (-3)$
   **d)** $(+4) - (-2)$    **e)** $(+1) - (+1)$    **f)** $(+1) - (-1)$

**2.** Use a number line to subtract.
   Use coloured tiles to check your answers.
   **a)** $(+2) - (+1)$    **b)** $(+4) - (-3)$    **c)** $(-4) - (-1)$
   **d)** $(-5) - (+2)$    **e)** $(-2) - (-6)$    **f)** $(-3) - (-7)$

**3.** **a)** Reverse the order of the integers in question 2, then subtract.
   **b)** How are the answers different from those in question 2?
   Explain.

**4.** Use a number line to subtract.
   **a)** $(+10) - (+5)$    **b)** $(+7) - (-3)$    **c)** $(-8) - (+6)$
   **d)** $(-10) - (+5)$    **e)** $(-4) - (+4)$    **f)** $(-4) - (-4)$

**5.** Find the difference between:
   **a)** a temperature of $+3°C$ and $-5°C$
   **b)** a temperature of $-15°C$ and $-10°C$
   **c)** an elevation of 5 m above sea level and
   one of 2 m below sea level
   **d)** a golf score of 1 below par and one of 3 below par

**6.** The table shows the average afternoon temperatures
   in January and April for four Canadian cities.
   Find the difference between the temperatures in April and
   January for each city. Show your work.

|     | City | January Temperature | April Temperature |
|-----|------|---------------------|-------------------|
| a)  | Calgary | −4°C | +13°C |
| b)  | Iqaluit | −22°C | −10°C |
| c)  | Toronto | −3°C | +12°C |
| d)  | Victoria | +7°C | +13°C |

**Calculator Skills**

Find each answer.
- $15 \times (32 + 41)$
- $198 - 104 \div 13$
- $14 \times 15 - 16 \times 9$

**7.** Use patterns to subtract.
   a) Subtract: $(+2) - (+5)$
      Start the pattern with $(+6) - (+5) = +1$.
   b) Subtract: $(+7) - (-3)$
      Start the pattern with $(+7) - (+4) = +3$.
   c) Subtract: $(-3) - (+7)$
      Start the pattern with $(+8) - (+7) = +1$.

**8.** **Assessment Focus**
   a) Subtract: $(-6) - (+11)$
   b) Suppose we subtract the integers in the opposite order:
      $(+11) - (-6)$
      How does the answer compare with the answer in part a?
      Use number lines or patterns to explain.
   c) How is $(+6) - (-11)$ different from $(-6) - (+11)$?
      Explain.

**9.** This table shows the mean daily maximum temperatures in degrees Celsius for Rankin Inlet for each month.

| Jan. | Feb. | Mar. | Apr. | May | June | July | Aug. | Sept. | Oct. | Nov. | Dec. |
|------|------|------|------|-----|------|------|------|-------|------|------|------|
| −28 | −28 | −23 | −12 | −2 | +8 | +16 | +14 | +6 | −3 | −16 | −24 |

   a) What is the median?
   b) What is the range?
   c) What is the mode?

**10.** Evaluate.
   a) $(+4) - (+2) - (+1)$       b) $(-2) - (+1) - (-4)$
   c) $(-1) + (-2) - (+1)$       d) $(+5) - (+1) + (-2)$
   e) $(+10) - (+3) - (-5)$      f) $(-7) - (+1) + (-3)$

**11.** Show three ways that $+4$ can be written as the difference of two integers.

**Reflect**

Choose two integers: one positive, one negative.
Add the integers. Subtract the integers.
Explain how the subtraction of two integers is related to addition.

# Choosing a Strategy

## Strategies

- Make a table.
- Use a model.
- Draw a diagram.
- Solve a simpler problem.
- Work backward.
- Guess and check.
- Make an organized list.
- Use a pattern.
- Draw a graph.
- Use logical reasoning.

1. A textbook is opened at random. The product of the page numbers is 23 256. What is the number on the left hand page?

2. Ms. Pantuso has a bag of candies that she wants to share equally among the students in her class.
   On Monday, all 20 students were present. If she had shared the candies, she would have had 7 candies left over.
   On Tuesday, two boys were absent. If she had shared the candies, she would again have had 7 left over.
   On Wednesday, the two boys were still absent and one girl was absent. Ms. Pantuso shared all the candies among the students with none left over.
   a) What was the least number of candies Ms. Pantuso could have had?
   b) How many candies did each student receive?

3. Briony wants to print copies of her new brochure.
   The local print shop charges 15¢ a copy for the first 25 copies, 12¢ a copy for the next 50 copies, and 8¢ a copy for any additional copies.
   How much would Briony pay for each number of copies?
   a) 60 copies          b) 240 copies

4. What is the greatest number of 5 cm by 3 cm rectangles that can be cut from a 20 cm by 10 cm sheet of cardboard?

5. Mr. Anders estimates it will take him 4 h to build a wall.
   His assistant would take 6 h to build the wall.
   a) What fraction of the wall could each person build in one hour?
   b) Suppose they worked together. What fraction could they build in one hour?
   c) How long would it take them to build the wall?

6. The mean of five numbers is 13.
   The mode is 16.
   The median is 14.
   Write two sets of numbers that satisfy these conditions.

**7.** A rectangular prism has a square base, and a volume of 36 cm³. What are the possible whole number dimensions of the prism?

**8.** Copy this figure on grid paper. Add one square to make the figure symmetrical. How many solutions can you find?

**9.** Eight students wrote a math test. Their mean mark was 54%. Another student wrote the test and scored 99%. What is the mean mark for the nine students?

**10.** Write 45 as the sum of consecutive integers. How many solutions can you find?

**11. a)** The product of two whole numbers is 1000. No number contains a zero. What are the numbers? How many different answers can you find?

**b)** The product of three whole numbers is 1000. No number contains a zero. What are the numbers? How many different answers can you find?

**12.** A book contains 124 pages numbered from 1 to 124. How many times does the digit 7 appear?

The modern historian does a lot of 'detective' work, especially when reading old documents or journals that describe timelines. Adding or subtracting days, months, or years from a known date is a regular part of the work. The historian must deal with modern timekeeping conventions, such as Common Era (CE) and Before Common Era (BCE). But he must also know that, throughout history, different societies had different ways of describing time. Often it was simply recorded as a period of time before or after another significant date or event.

Suppose you read this entry in an 18th century explorer's journal dated May 21:

**A fortnight is 2 weeks.**

*"We have been following this river for a fortnight. Three days into our journey we came upon a great waterfall blocking our path and had to portage around it. But the river has been calm since."*

How would you be able to calculate what date the waterfall was discovered?

Suppose you knew that Augustus Caesar died in 14 CE at the age of 77. Can you calculate the year of his birth? Explain.

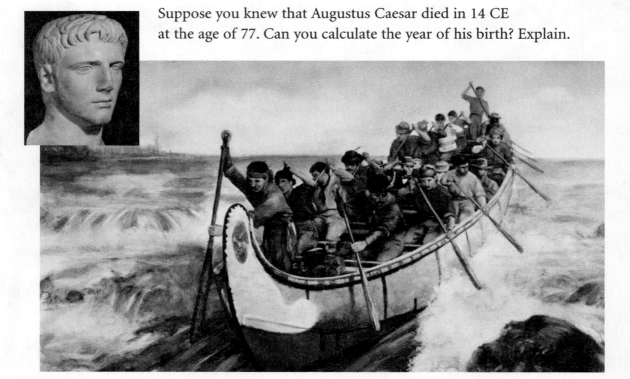

## What Do I Need to Know?

### ☑ Integer Models

- You can use a number line to show integers.

Negative numbers are to the left of 0. Positive numbers are to the right of 0.

- Coloured tiles model integers.

$-1$      $+1$

### ☑ Adding Integers

- You can use tiles to add integers.

$(-7) + (+2) = -5$

- You can use a number line to add integers.

$(+6) + (-3) = +3$

### ☑ Subtracting Integers

- You can use tiles to subtract integers: $(+3) - (-7)$
  We need enough red tiles to take away 7 of them.
  Model +3:

Since there are not enough tiles to take away $-7$, add 7 yellow tiles and 7 red tiles. Now take away 7 red tiles. There are 10 yellow tiles left.

$(+3) - (-7) = +10$

- You can also subtract by adding the opposite:

$(-5) - (-8) = -5 + (+8)$
$$= +3$$

LESSON

**9.1**

1. Draw a number line. Mark each integer on the number line: $+3, -5, +1, -2$

2. Use an integer to represent each situation.
   a) a golf score of 2 strokes under par
   b) 250 m below sea level
   c) 32°C
   d) a loss of $125
   e) an increase of $3 in the monthly cost of cable television

**9.2**

3. Order these integers from least to greatest: $+200, -55, +150, -3, -54$

**9.4**
**9.6**

4. Use tiles to add or subtract.
   a) $(-1) + (+3)$
   b) $(+3) + (-4)$
   c) $(-2) - (+3)$
   d) $(-1) - (-3)$

**9.5**
**9.7**

5. Use a number line to add or subtract.
   a) $(-1) + (+3)$
   b) $(+6) + (-4)$
   c) $(-4) - (+6)$
   d) $(-5) - (-3)$

6. When you add two positive integers, their sum is always a positive integer. When you subtract two positive integers, is their difference always a positive integer? Explain.

7. At midnight in North Bay, the temperature was $-5$°C. During the next 24 h, the temperature rose 12°C, then dropped 9°C. What was the final temperature? Show your work.

**9.6**
**9.7**

8. Use tiles or a number line to subtract.
   a) $(+4) - (+1)$
   b) $(+5) - (-1)$
   c) $(+2) - (-2)$
   d) $(-4) - (+1)$
   e) $(-6) - (-2)$
   f) $(-10) - (-5)$
   g) $(-4) - (-2)$

9. Use tiles or a number line. Find the difference between:
   a) a temperature of $+5$°C and $-7$°C
   b) an elevation of $-100$ m and $+50$ m
   c) a golf score of 1 over par and 2 under par

10. Subtract.
    a) $(+3) - (+1)$
    b) $(-5) - (-2)$
    c) $(+100) - (+60)$
    d) $(-100) - (+60)$

11. a) Find 5 pairs of integers with a sum of $-6$.
    b) Find 5 pairs of integers with a difference of $-3$.

# Practice Test

1. We measure time in hours.
   Suppose 12 noon is represented by the integer 0.
   a) Which integer represents 1 p.m. the same day?
   b) Which integer represents 10 a.m. the same day?
   c) Which integer represents 12 midnight the same day?
   d) Which integer represents 10 p.m. the previous day?

2. Order all the integers in question 1 from least to greatest.

3. Evaluate.
   a) $(+5) + (-8)$     b) $(-3) - (+7)$     c) $(-9) + (-1)$
   d) $(-4) + (+10)$    e) $(-6) - (-2)$     f) $(+12) - (-11)$

4. Without calculating the sum, how can you tell if the sum of two integers will be:
   a) zero?              b) negative?              c) positive?
   Include examples in your explanations.

5. Here is a different type of dartboard.

   A player throws 3 darts at the board. His score is the sum of the integers in the areas his darts land. Assume all 3 darts hit the board.
   a) How many different scores are possible?
   b) Find each score.

6. The lowest temperature possible is approximately −273°C.
   The temperature at which water boils is 100°C.
   What is the difference in these temperatures?

**TIME ZONES**

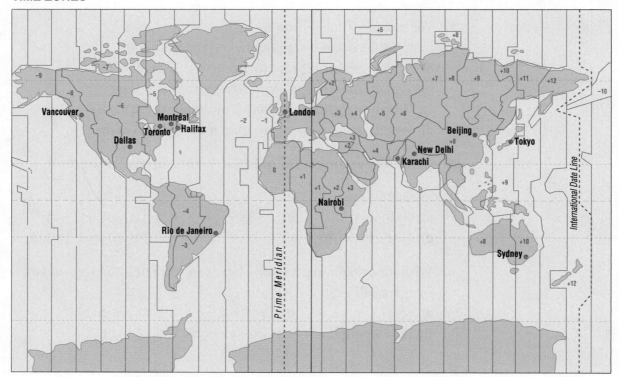

The map shows the world's time zones. Greenwich, in London, England, is the reference point, or the zero for the time zones. Its time is called UTC, or Coordinated Universal Time. London, England, is also in this time zone. The positive and negative integers on the map show the changes in time from UTC.

The 2008 Summer Olympics will be held in Beijing, China.

1. The local start times of some Olympic events are given. If family members want to watch these events live, in Sudbury (the same time zone as Toronto), what time should they "tune in"?
   a) 200-m backstroke at 2:00 p.m.
   b) 100-m dash at 7:00 p.m.
   c) gymnastics at 11:00 p.m.
   d) middleweight boxing at 8:00 a.m.

**2.** An event is broadcast live in Montreal at 9:00 p.m.
What time is it taking place in Beijing?

**3.** Two pen pals plan to meet in Beijing for the Olympics.
Atsuko lives in Tokyo, Japan.
She can get a direct flight to Beijing that takes 4 h.
Paula lives in Sydney, Australia, and her direct flight takes 13 h.
What time does each girl leave her country to arrive in Beijing
at 6 p.m., Beijing time?

**Check List**

Your work
should show:

✓ how you used
integers to solve
each problem

✓ the strategies you
used to add and
subtract integers

✓ correct calculations

✓ a clear explanation
of how integers
relate to time zones

**4.** Olympic funding depends on money from North American
television networks. What problems will the organizers of
the Beijing Olympics encounter when they plan the times
for events?

**5.** Make up your own problem about the time zone map.
Solve your problem.

Show your work. Show how you can use integers to
solve each problem.

## Reflect on the Unit

Choose a positive integer and a negative integer.
How many different ways can you add them? Subtract them?
Show your work.
If you used number lines, patterns, or coloured tiles, draw pictures to show
how you used them.

# Patterning and Algebra

Students in a grade 7 class were raising money for charity.
Some students had a "bowl-a-thon."

This table shows the money that one student raised for different bowling times.

| Time (h) | Money Raised ($) |
|:---:|:---:|
| 1 | 8 |
| 2 | 16 |
| 3 | 24 |
| 4 | 32 |
| 5 | 40 |
| 6 | 48 |

- What patterns do you see in the table?
- Suppose you drew a graph of the data. What might the graph look like?

## What You'll Learn

- Describe, extend, and explain patterns.
- Use patterns to make predictions.
- Show patterns as graphs.
- Write and evaluate algebraic expressions.
- Read and write equations.
- Solve equations.

## Why It's Important

- Extending a pattern is a useful problem-solving strategy.
- Using algebra is an efficient way to describe a pattern.

## Key Words

- ordered pairs
- algebraic expression
- evaluate
- equation
- solve an equation

# Skills You'll Need

## Order of Operations

Recall this order of operations.

**Brackets**                    Perform operations inside the brackets.

**Divide and multiply**         Do in order from left to right.

**Add and subtract**            Do in order from left to right.

### Example

Simplify.

**a)** $6 + 3 \times 4$      **b)** $(5 + 3) \div 2$      **c)** $18 \div 3 \times 2$

### Solution

**a)** $6 + 3 \times 4 = 6 + 12$      Multiply first.

   $\qquad\qquad\quad = 18$      Then add.

**b)** $(5 + 3) \div 2 = 8 \div 2$      Add in brackets first.

   $\qquad\qquad\quad = 4$      Then divide.

**c)** $18 \div 3 \times 2 = 6 \times 2$      Divide first.

   $\qquad\qquad\quad = 12$      Then multiply.

## ✓ Check

**1.** Simplify.

   **a)** $5 \times 7 + 2$      **b)** $5 \times (7 + 2)$      **c)** $13 + 2 \times 8$

   **d)** $13 + 2 - 8$      **e)** $13 + 8 \div 2$      **f)** $13 - 8 \div 2$

   **g)** $12 \div 4 + 2$      **h)** $12 \div (4 + 2)$      **i)** $12 + 4 \div 2$

**2. a)** Simplify.

   **i)** $3 + 4 \times 2 + 5$      **ii)** $3 \times 4 + 2 \times 5$      **iii)** $3 \times (4 + 2) \times 5$

   **iv)** $3 \times (4 + 2) + 5$      **v)** $3 \times 4 \times 2 + 5$      **vi)** $3 + 4 + 2 \times 5$

   **b)** All the expressions in part a have the same numbers and the same operations. Why are the answers different?

# Graphing on a Coordinate Grid

(3, 2) is an **ordered pair**. It tells the position of a point on a grid.

In an ordered pair, the first number is the horizontal distance from the origin, O.

The second number is the vertical distance from the origin.

We use a letter to label a point.

To plot point A(3, 2), start at 3 on the horizontal axis, then move up 2.

To plot point B(1, 4), start at 1 on the horizontal axis, then move up 4.

The numbers in an ordered pair are also called the coordinates of a point.

✓ **Check**

**3.** Write the ordered pair for each point on the grid.

**4.** On graph paper, draw a grid.
Plot and label these points:
A(2, 9), B(5, 3), C(8, 8), D(0, 10)

**5.** The graph shows the money earned for the time worked.
  **a)** How much money was earned in 4 h?
  **b)** How long will it take to earn $12.00?
  **c)** What is the hourly rate of pay?

## Explore

Work with a partner.

➤ Suppose this pattern continues.

Describe the pattern.
What is the next figure in the pattern?
What is the 17th figure?
How can you find out without drawing 17 figures?

➤ Suppose this pattern continues.

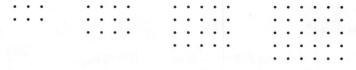

| Figure 1 | Figure 2 | Figure 3 | Figure 4 |

Describe the pattern.
What is the next figure in the pattern?
How many dots will there be in the 15th figure?
How can you find out without drawing 15 figures?

### Reflect & Share

How are the two patterns the same?
How are they different?
Compare your answers with those of another pair of classmates.
Did you use the same strategies to answer the questions? Explain.

## Connect

Here is a pattern of triangles.

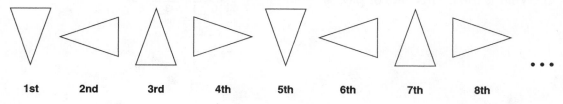

| 1st | 2nd | 3rd | 4th | 5th | 6th | 7th | 8th |

The pattern is made up of different positions of an isosceles triangle. To get the next term each time, rotate the triangle a $\frac{1}{4}$ turn clockwise about its centre.

The core of the pattern is 4 triangles.

The 5th term is the same as the 1st term.

The 6th term is the same as the 2nd term, and so on.

To find any term in the pattern, we find which of the first 4 terms it matches.

Think of multiples of 4: 4, 8, 12, 16, 20, 24, 28, …

All the 4th, 8th, 12th, 16th, 20th, 24th, 28th, … terms have the triangle pointing to the right.

To find the 99th term, we find the closest multiple of 4.

100 is a multiple of 4, so the 100th term is the same as the 4th term.

The 99th term will be the same as the 3rd term:

The 99th term is the triangle pointing up.

We can use the same ideas to make predictions with number patterns.

**Example**

Each pattern continues.
  i)  Describe each pattern.
  ii)  Write the next 3 terms.
  iii) Find the 50th term.
  a)  4, 7, 10, 13, …                    b)  1, 4, 9, 16, …

**Solution**

a)  4, 7, 10, 13, …
  i)  The pattern begins with 4.
      To get the next term, add 3 each time.
  ii)  The next 3 terms are: $13 + 3 = 16$
                               $16 + 3 = 19$
                               $19 + 3 = 22$
      The next 3 terms are 16, 19, 22.

**iii)** Since the terms increase by 3 each time, compare the pattern
with multiples of 3.

Pattern:        4, 7, 10, 13, 16, 19, 22, ...

Multiples of 3: 3, 6,  9, 12, 15, 18, 21, ...

Each term in the pattern is 1 more than a multiple of 3.

So, the terms in the pattern are multiples of 3, plus 1.

The 1st term: $1 \times 3 + 1 = 4$

The 2nd term: $2 \times 3 + 1 = 7$

The 3rd term: $3 \times 3 + 1 = 10$

The 4th term: $4 \times 3 + 1 = 13$, and so on

The 50th term: $50 \times 3 + 1 = 151$

The 50th term is 151.

**b)** 1, 4, 9, 16, ...

**i)** The pattern begins with 1.

To get the 2nd term, add 3.

To get the 3rd term, add 5.

To get the 4th term, add 7.

To get each successive term, increase the number
you add by 2 each time.

**ii)** The next 3 terms are: $16 + 9 = 25$

$$25 + 11 = 36$$
$$36 + 13 = 49$$

The next 3 terms are 25, 36, 49.

**Recall that a perfect
square is the product of
a number and itself.**

**iii)** To use the same method to get the 50th term, we would need
to know the 49th term and what to add.

So, we look at the pattern a different way.

The pattern is: 1, 4, 9, 16, 25, 36, 49, ...

These are the perfect squares: $1^2, 2^2, 3^2, 4^2, 5^2, 6^2, 7^2, ...$

So, the 50th term is: $50^2 = 2500$

The 50th term is 2500.

**1.** This pattern continues.

   ...

   **a)** Describe the pattern.
   **b)** Sketch the next 3 terms.
   **c)** Sketch the 29th term and the 49th term.

**2.** This pattern continues.

   **a)** Describe the pattern.
   **b)** Sketch the next 3 terms.
   **c)** Describe the 18th term and the 38th term.
      Sketch them if you can.

**3.** For each pattern:
   **i)** Describe the pattern.
   **ii)** Write the next 3 terms.
   **iii)** Find the 40th term. Explain how you found it.
   **a)** 6, 9, 12, 15, …      **b)** 6, 10, 14, 18, …   **c)** 6, 11, 16, 21, …

**4.** There is a pattern in the patterns in question 3.
   Write the first 5 terms of the next pattern. Justify your answer.

**5.** For each pattern:
   **i)** Describe the pattern.
   **ii)** Write the next 3 terms.
   **iii)** Find the 20th term.
   **a)** 2, 4, 8, 16, …        **b)** 3, 6, 12, 24, …

**6.** Look at the patterns below.
   How are they the same? How are they different?
   **i)** Write the next 3 terms for each pattern.
   **ii)** Write the 20th term in each pattern.
   **a)** 2, 5, 10, 17, 26, …    **b)** 0, 3, 8, 15, 24, …

Estimate each product.
Order the products from
least to greatest.

• 24.8 × 3.2

• 35.23 × 2.89

• 13.21 × 5.78

• 5.5 × 15.5

What strategies did
you use?

**7.** This pattern continues.

a) Describe the pattern.

b) Sketch the next 3 terms.

c) Describe the 17th term and the 37th term.
Sketch them if you can.

**8.** **Assessment Focus**   Create two different number patterns.
Each pattern must contain the numbers 12 and 32.
Describe each pattern in words.
Write the next 4 terms in each pattern.

**Take It Further**

**9.** a) Describe this pattern. The pattern continues.

b) How many squares would be in the 10th figure?

c) What are the perimeters of the 4th figure and 5th figure?

d) What is the perimeter of the 10th figure?

e) How many squares are there in the figure with perimeter 72?

f) Could you make one of the figures using exactly 27 small
squares? Explain.

Use a geoboard and
geoband if they help.

**10.** Create two different number patterns that contain the numbers
16, 20, and 25. Write the first 5 terms in each pattern.

**Reflect**

Describe how you identify a number pattern.
Use two different examples from this lesson.

# 10.2 Graphing Patterns

## Explore

Work with a partner.
You will need grid paper.
One CD costs $10.

➤ Copy and complete this table.
  Find the cost for up to 10 CDs.

➤ Graph the data in the table.

| Number of CDs | Cost ($) |
|---------------|----------|
| 0 | |
| 2 | |
| 4 | |
| 6 | |
| 8 | |
| 10 | |

### Reflect & Share

Describe the patterns in the table.
How are these patterns shown in the graph?

## Connect

We can use a table and a graph to illustrate number patterns.
Recall this pattern from *Section 10.1, Example, page 369*.

Term 1: 4
Term 2: 7
Term 3: 10
Term 4: 13
Term 5: 16
Term 6: 19

We write these terms in a table.

| Term Number | Term Value |
|-------------|------------|
| 1 | 4 |
| 2 | 7 |
| 3 | 10 |
| 4 | 13 |
| 5 | 16 |
| 6 | 19 |

We plot these data on a graph.
The *Term number* is plotted on the horizontal axis.
The *Term value* is plotted on the vertical axis.

The graph is a set of points that lie on a straight line.
To get from one point to the next, move 1 unit right and 3 units up.
Moving 1 unit right is the same as adding 1 in the first column
to get the next term number.
Moving 3 units up is the same as adding 3 in the second column
to get the next term value.

We can use a table related to an Input/Output machine to make a pattern.

## Example 1

a) Complete the table for this pattern:
   Multiply each number by 2, then add 3.

b) Graph the pattern.
   Explain how the graph shows the pattern.

| Input | Output |
|-------|--------|
| 1 | |
| 2 | |
| 3 | |
| 4 | |
| 5 | |

**Solution**

a) Multiply each Input number by 2, then add 3.

$1 \times 2 + 3 = 5$
$2 \times 2 + 3 = 7$
$3 \times 2 + 3 = 9$
$4 \times 2 + 3 = 11$
$5 \times 2 + 3 = 13$

| Input | Output |
|-------|--------|
| 1 | 5 |
| 2 | 7 |
| 3 | 9 |
| 4 | 11 |
| 5 | 13 |

b) The points lie on a straight line.
   To get from one point to the next,
   move 1 unit right and 2 units up.
   Moving 1 unit right is the same as
   adding 1 to an Input number to get
   the next Input number.
   Moving 2 units up is the same as
   adding 2 to an Output number to get
   the next Output number.

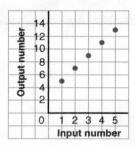

## Example 2

a) Describe the patterns in this table.

b) Use the patterns to extend the table
   3 more rows.

c) Graph the table in part b. Explain how the
   graph shows the patterns.

| Input | Output |
|-------|--------|
| 1 | 10 |
| 2 | 9 |
| 3 | 8 |
| 4 | 7 |
| 5 | 6 |

**a)** The numbers in the Input column start at 1
and increase by 1 each time.
The numbers in the Output column start at 10
and decrease by 1 each time.
The sum of matching Input and Output numbers is 11.

**b)** The next 3 Input numbers are 6, 7, 8.
The next 3 Output numbers are 5, 4, 3.

| Input | Output |
|-------|--------|
| 1 | 10 |
| 2 | 9 |
| 3 | 8 |
| 4 | 7 |
| 5 | 6 |
| 6 | 5 |
| 7 | 4 |
| 8 | 3 |

**c)** The graph is
a set of points
that lie on a
straight line.

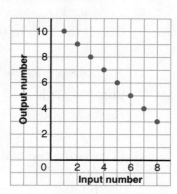

The line goes down to the right.
As the Input numbers increase from 1 to 8,
the Output numbers decrease from 10 to 3.

# Practice

| Input | Output |
|-------|--------|
| 1 | |
| 2 | |
| 3 | |
| 4 | |
| 5 | |

**1.** Copy and complete this table for each pattern.
   **a)** Multiply each Input number by 3.
   **b)** Add 2 to each Input number.
   **c)** Multiply each Input number by 3, then add 2.
   **d)** Add 2 to each Input number, then multiply by 3.

**2.** Copy and complete this table for each pattern.
   **a)** Divide each Input number by 10.
   **b)** Subtract 3 from each Input number.
   **c)** Divide each Input number by 10,
      then subtract 3.

| Input | Output |
|-------|--------|
| 100 | |
| 80 | |
| 60 | |
| 40 | |
| 20 | |

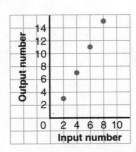

**3.** Look at this graph.
  a) Make an Input/Output table for the graph.
  b) What patterns do you see in the table?
  c) Extend the table 3 more rows. Explain how you did this.

**4.** The students at a school sell pins at a school fair to raise money for charity.
  The students charge $1.50 per pin.
  a) Copy and complete this table.
  b) Graph the data in the table in part a.
  c) Suppose you know how many pins were sold.
     How can you find how much money was collected:
     **i)** by using the table?     **ii)** by using the graph?

| Number of Pins | Money Collected |
|---|---|
| 10 | |
| 20 | |
| 30 | |
| 40 | |
| 50 | |
| 60 | |

**5.** For each table:
  **i)** Describe the pattern in the Output column.
  **ii)** How can you find an Output number when you know an Input number?
  **iii)** Write the next 3 rows in each table.

**a)**

| Input | Output |
|---|---|
| 2 | 6 |
| 4 | 8 |
| 6 | 10 |
| 8 | 12 |
| 10 | 14 |

**b)**

| Input | Output |
|---|---|
| 2 | 6 |
| 4 | 12 |
| 6 | 18 |
| 8 | 24 |
| 10 | 30 |

**c)**

| Input | Output |
|---|---|
| 2 | 6 |
| 4 | 10 |
| 6 | 14 |
| 8 | 18 |
| 10 | 22 |

**6.** **Assessment Focus**  Mr. Francis is planning a school picnic.
  a) Mr. Francis estimates he needs 2 sandwiches for each student, plus 3 extras. Make a table for the number of sandwiches needed for 5, 10, 15, 20, 25, 30 students.
  b) Mr. Francis estimates he needs 1 drink for each student, plus 5 extras. Make a table for the number of drinks needed for up to 30 students.
  c) Draw graphs for the tables in parts a and b.
     Explain how each graph shows the patterns in the tables.

**Take It Further**

**7. a)** Copy this pattern on grid paper.
Extend the pattern to show the next 2 figures.

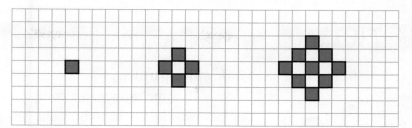

**Calculator Skills**

Three numbers have
a product of 24.5.
One number is 0.25.
What might the other
two numbers be?

**b)** Copy and complete this table for the first 5 figures.

| Figure Number | Number of Blue Squares |
| --- | --- |
| | |

**c)** Draw a graph to show the data in the table.

**d)** How is this graph different from other graphs you have drawn?

**e)** How could you use the graph or the table to find the number
of blue squares in the 9th figure?

**Reflect**

Explain how a pattern in words can be represented by a table
and a graph.
Use an example in your explanation.

**Math Link**

**History**
The word "algebra" comes from the Arabic
word "al-jabr." This word appeared in the
title of one of the earliest algebra texts,
written around the year 825 by
al-Khwarizmi. He lived in what is
now Uzbekistan.

**Focus**   Use a variable to represent a set of numbers.

## Explore

Work with a partner.
Tehya won some money in a competition.
She has two choices as to how she gets paid.
Choice 1: $20 per week for one year
Choice 2: $400 cash now plus $12 per week for one year

Which method would pay Tehya more money? Explain.
For what reason might Tehya choose the method that pays less?

### Reflect & Share

Work with another pair of classmates.
For each choice, write a rule you can use to calculate the total money
Tehya has received at any time during the year.

## Connect

Recall how we used variables in the formulas for the area and
perimeter of a rectangle.

Area: $A = bh$
Perimeter: $P = 2(b + h)$

In these formulas, $b$ represents the length of the base
and $h$ represents the height.

We can also use a variable to represent a number in an expression.
For example, we know there are 100 cm in 1 m.
There are $2 \times 100$ cm in 2 m.
There are $3 \times 100$ cm in 3 m.
To write an expression for the number of centimetres in any number
of metres, we say there are $n \times 100$ cm in $n$ metres.
$n$ is a variable.
$n$ represents any number we choose.

We can choose any letter as a variable.
The letters $n$ and $x$ are frequently used.
The expression $n \times 100$ is written $100n$.
$100n$ is an **algebraic expression**.

Variables are written in italics so they are not confused with units of measurement.

Here are some other algebraic expressions, and their meanings.
In each case, $n$ represents the number.
- Three more than a number: $3 + n$ or $n + 3$
- Seven times a number: $7n$
- 8 less than a number: $n - 8$
- Twenty divided by a number: $\frac{20}{n}$

## Example 1

A car travels at an average speed of 50 km/h.
How far will the car travel in: **a)** 3 h?          **b)** $t$ hours?

### Solution

$t \times 50$ is equal to $50 \times t$, which is written $50t$.

In 1 h, the car travels 50 km.
**a)** In 3 h, the car travels: $3 \times 50$ km $= 150$ km
**b)** In $t$ hours, the car travels: $t \times 50$ km $= 50t$ kilometres

## Example 2

Write an algebraic expression for each statement.
**a)** the amount of money earned at $5/h
**b)** the perimeter of a square
**c)** eight more than three times a number
**d)** double a number and subtract 5

### Solution

We often choose a letter to remind us what the variable represents.
$t$ for time
$s$ for side length
$n$ for number

For each statement, choose a variable to represent the number.
**a)** Let $t$ hours represent the time worked.
   Then, the amount earned is $5 \times t$, or $5t$ dollars.
**b)** Let $s$ centimetres represent the side length of the square.
   Then, the perimeter in centimetres is $4 \times s$, or $4s$ centimetres.
**c)** Let $n$ represent the number.
   Three times the number: $3n$
   Then add 8: $3n + 8$
**d)** Let $x$ represent the number.
   Double the number means 2 times the number: $2x$
   Then subtract 5: $2x - 5$

# Practice

**If you use $x$ as a variable, write it so it is not confused with a multiplication sign, ×.**

**1.** Write an algebraic expression for each statement.
   **a)** six more than a number
   **b)** a number multiplied by eight
   **c)** a number decreased by six
   **d)** a number divided by four

**2.** A person earns $4/h baby-sitting.
   Find the money earned for each time.
   **a)** 5 h          **b)** 8 h          **c)** $t$ hours

**3.** Find the area of a rectangle for each length and width.
   **a)** length: 8 cm; width: 6 cm
   **b)** length: 10 cm; width: 5 cm
   **c)** length: $l$ centimetres; width: $w$ centimetres

**4.** A person walks at an average speed of 5 km/h.
   Find the distance walked in each time.
   **a)** 2 h          **b)** 5 h          **c)** $t$ hours

**Remember that the fraction bar indicates division.**

**5.** Write each algebraic expression in words.
   Use the words "a number" in place of the variable.
   **a)** $n + 8$          **b)** $6a$          **c)** $\frac{p}{5}$
   **d)** $k - 11$          **e)** $27 - n$          **f)** $x^2$

**6.** Write an algebraic expression for each statement.
   **a)** Double a number and add three.
   **b)** Subtract five from a number, then multiply by two.
   **c)** Subtract one-half of a number from 17.
   **d)** Divide a number by seven, then add six.
   **e)** A number is subtracted from twenty-eight.
   **f)** Twenty-eight is subtracted from a number.

**7. a)** Write each expression in words.
      **i)** $(40 - 3)r$               **ii)** $40 - 3r$
   **b)** How are the expressions and statements in part a similar?
      Different?

**380**   UNIT 10: Patterning and Algebra

**Number Strategies**

The regular price of a pair of running shoes is $74.99. What is the sale price in each case?

• 50% off

• 25% off

• 30% off

• 70% off

**8. a)** Write an algebraic expression for each statement.

    **i)** three more than a number

    **ii)** a number added to three

    **iii)** three less than a number

    **iv)** a number subtracted from three

  **b)** How are the expressions in part a alike? How are they different? Explain.

**9.** Write each expression in words.

  **a)** $6h + 5$     **b)** $\frac{(n-3)}{4}$     **c)** $\frac{t}{4} + 12$

  **d)** $3(x - 3)$     **e)** $32 - \frac{w}{5}$     **f)** $\frac{w}{5} - 32$

**10.** **Assessment Focus**

  **a)** Use the cards below to make an algebraic expression for each statement. Write the expression.

    **i)** nine times a number subtract 4

    **ii)** the sum of four times a number and nine

    **iii)** a number plus five

    **iv)** nine more than one-quarter of a number

  **b)** Create two more expressions using the cards. Write each expression in words.

  Show your work.

**11.** A pizza with cheese and tomato toppings costs $8.00. There is a cost of $1 for each extra topping. Write an algebraic expression for the cost of a pizza with $e$ extra toppings.

**Reflect**

Why do we write algebraic expressions? How are they useful?

# Mid-Unit Review

**10.1** **1.** For each pattern:

    **i)** Describe the pattern.

    **ii)** Write the next 3 terms.

    **iii)** Find the 10th term.

    **a)** 5, 8, 11, 14, …

    **b)** 14, 25, 36, 47, …

    **c)** 1, 8, 27, 64, …

    **d)** 1, 3, 7, 15, 31, …

**2. a)** Describe this pattern.

The pattern continues.

    **b)** Write the dimensions of the next 2 rectangles.

    **c)** Write the areas of the first 5 rectangles.

    **d)** What are the dimensions and area of the 19th rectangle?

    **e)** Which rectangle has area 110 square units?

**10.2** **3. a)** Complete the table in the next column for this pattern: Multiply each term by 4, then subtract 1.

    **b)** Graph the pattern. Explain how the graph shows the pattern.

| Input | Output |
|-------|--------|
| 1 | |
| 2 | |
| 3 | |
| 4 | |
| 5 | |
| 6 | |

**4. a)** Describe the pattern in the Output column.

    **b)** How can you find an output number when you know an input number?

| Input | Output |
|-------|--------|
| 1 | 8 |
| 2 | 11 |
| 3 | 14 |
| 4 | 17 |
| 5 | 20 |
| 6 | 23 |

    **c)** Write the next 3 rows in the table.

    **d)** Graph the table. Explain how the graph shows the pattern.

**10.3** **5.** Write an algebraic expression for each statement.

    **a)** eleven more than a number

    **b)** four less than a number

    **c)** a number divided by three

    **d)** a number multiplied by nine

    **e)** the sum of five times a number, and 2

    **f)** seventeen more than two times a number

**6.** Write each expression in words. Use the words "a number" in place of each variable.

    **a)** $n + 3$   **b)** $21 - h$   **c)** $9n$   **d)** $\frac{a}{4}$

**Focus** Substitute a number for a variable in an algebraic expression.

Work with a partner.
Ms. Prasad plans to hold a party for a group of her friends.
The cost of renting a room is $25.
The cost of food is $3 per person.
Which algebraic expression gives the total cost, in dollars,
of the party for *n* people?

$3 + 25n$        $28n$        $28 + n$        $25 + 3n$

Check your answer by finding the cost for 10 people.

### Reflect & Share

Compare your answer with that of another pair of classmates.
How did you decide which expression was correct?
How does the expression change in each of the following cases?

- The cost of food doubles.
- The rent of the room doubles.

**When we replace a variable with a number, we substitute a number for the variable.**

When we replace a variable with a number in an algebraic
expression, we **evaluate** the expression. That is, we find the value of
the expression for a particular value of the variable.

Recall the work you did in *Unit 6 Measuring Perimeter and Area*.
You substituted numbers for variables in the formulas for area
and perimeter.
We use the same method to evaluate algebraic expressions.

### Example

Write each algebraic expression in words.
Then evaluate for the value of the variable given.

a)  $5k + 2$ for $k = 3$        b)  $\frac{(x - 3)}{5}$ for $x = 13$

**Solution**

a) $5k + 2$ means 5 times a number, then add 2.
Replace $k$ with 3 in the expression $5k + 2$.
Use the order of operations.

*5k means 5 × k.*

$$5k + 2 = 5 \times 3 + 2 \qquad \text{Multiply first.}$$
$$= 15 + 2 \qquad \text{Add.}$$
$$= 17$$

b) $\frac{(x - 3)}{5}$ means subtract 3 from a number, then divide by 5.
Replace $x$ with 13.

$$\frac{(x - 3)}{5} = \frac{(13 - 3)}{5} \qquad \text{Do the operation in brackets first.}$$
$$= \frac{10}{5} \qquad \text{Divide.}$$
$$= 2$$

Recall that a variable is a symbol that can represent a set of numbers.
If we substitute consecutive numbers in an algebraic expression,
we get a pattern.
Use the algebraic expression $3n + 2$.
Substitute $n = 1, 2, 3, 4,$ and 5.

When $n = 1, 3n + 2 = 3(1) + 2$
$$= 3 + 2$$
$$= 5$$

When $n = 2, 3n + 2 = 3(2) + 2$
$$= 6 + 2$$
$$= 8$$

When $n = 3, 3n + 2 = 3(3) + 2$
$$= 9 + 2$$
$$= 11$$

When $n = 4, 3n + 2 = 3(4) + 2$
$$= 12 + 2$$
$$= 14$$

When $n = 5, 3n + 2 = 3(5) + 2$
$$= 15 + 2$$
$$= 17$$

Use the values of $n$ as the Input.
Use the values of $3n + 2$ as the Output.
Then, write the patterns in a table.
To get each Output number, multiply the
Input number by 3, then add 2.

| Input $n$ | Output $3n + 2$ |
|---|---|
| 1 | 5 |
| 2 | 8 |
| 3 | 11 |
| 4 | 14 |
| 5 | 17 |

**1.** Evaluate each expression by replacing $x$ with 4.

a) $x + 5$  b) $3x$  c) $2x - 1$

d) $\frac{x}{2}$  e) $3x + 1$  f) $20 - 2x$

**Mental Math**

Find each sum.

- $(-2) + (+10)$
- $(-6) + (-9)$
- $(+8) + (-7)$
- $(+11) + (+7)$

**2.** Evaluate each expression by replacing $z$ with 7.

a) $z + 12$  b) $10 - z$  c) $\frac{(z+5)}{2}$

d) $3(z - 1)$  e) $35 - 2z$  f) $3 + \frac{z}{7}$

**3.** Write each algebraic expression in words.
Then, evaluate the expression for $n = 3$.

a) $n - 1$  b) $5n + 2$  c) $\frac{n}{3} + 5$

d) $n + 1$  e) $2(n + 9)$  f) $\frac{(n + 7)}{2}$

**4.** Copy and complete each table. Explain how to get an Output number when you know the Input number.

a)

| Input $x$ | Output $2x$ |
|---|---|
| 1 | |
| 2 | |
| 3 | |
| 4 | |
| 5 | |

b)

| Input $m$ | Output $10 - m$ |
|---|---|
| 1 | |
| 2 | |
| 3 | |
| 4 | |
| 5 | |

c)

| Input $p$ | Output $3p + 4$ |
|---|---|
| 1 | |
| 2 | |
| 3 | |
| 4 | |
| 5 | |

**5.** Jason works at a local fish and chips restaurant.
He earns $7/h during the week, and $9/h on the weekend.

a) Jason works 8 h during the week and 12 h on the weekend.
Write an expression for his earnings.

b) Jason works $x$ hours during the week, and 5 h on the weekend. Write an algebraic expression for his earnings.

c) Jason needs $115 to buy sports equipment.
He worked 5 h on the weekend.
How many hours does Jason need to work during the week to have the money he needs?

**6. Assessment Focus**   Kouroche is organising an overnight camping trip. The cost of renting a cabin is $20. The cost of food is $9 per person.

a) How much will the trip cost if 5 people go? 10 people go?

b) Write an algebraic expression for the cost of the trip if $p$ people go.

c) Suppose the cost of food doubles.
   Write an expression for the total cost of the trip for $p$ people.

d) Suppose the cost of the cabin doubles.
   Write an expression for the total cost of the trip for $p$ people.

e) Explain why using the variable $p$ is helpful.

**7.** A value of $n$ is substituted in each expression to get the number in the box. Find each value of $n$.

a) $5n$      30      b) $3n - 1$      11

c) $4n + 7$      15      d) $5n - 4$      11

e) $4 + 6n$      40      f) $\frac{n}{8} + 1$      5

**Take It Further**

**8.** Each table shows patterns. Write an algebraic expression to describe how each Output relates to the Input.

a)

| Input $x$ | Output |
|---|---|
| 1 | 3 |
| 2 | 6 |
| 3 | 9 |
| 4 | 12 |

b)

| Input $x$ | Output |
|---|---|
| 1 | 1 |
| 2 | 4 |
| 3 | 7 |
| 4 | 10 |

c)

| Input $x$ | Output |
|---|---|
| 5 | 2 |
| 10 | 7 |
| 15 | 12 |
| 20 | 17 |

**9.** Find a value for $p$ and a value for $q$ so that $p - 3q$ has a value of 1. How many different ways can you do this? Explain.

**Reflect**

Explain why it is important to use the order of operations when evaluating an algebraic expression. Use an example to explain.

**Focus**   Translate statements into equations.

## Explore

Work with a partner.

- Write an algebraic expression for these statements:
  Think of a number.
  Multiply it by 3.
  Add 4.
- The answer is 13. What is the original number?

### Reflect & Share

Compare your answer with that of another pair of classmates.
If you found different values for the original number, who is correct?
Can both of you be correct?
How can you check?

## Connect

When we write an algebraic expression as being equal to a number,
we have an **equation**.
For example, we have an algebraic expression $3x + 2$.
When we write $3x + 2 = 11$, we have an equation.
An equation is a statement that two expressions are equal.

Here is another example.
Zena bought 3 CDs.
All 3 CDs had the same price.
The total cost was $36.
What was the cost of 1 CD?

We can write an equation for this situation.
Let $p$ dollars represent the cost of 1 CD.
Then $3p = 36$ is an equation that represents this situation.

## Example 1

Mark thinks of a number.
He multiplies the number by 2, then adds 15.
The answer is 35. Write an equation for the problem.

**Solution**

Let $n$ represent the number Mark thinks of.
Multiply the number by 2: $2n$
Then add 15: $2n + 15$
The equation is: $2n + 15 = 35$

## Example 2

Write an equation for each sentence.
a) Three more than a number is 15.
b) Five less than a number is 7.
c) A number subtracted from 5 is 1.
d) A number divided by 3 is 10.

**Solution**

a) Three more than a number is 15.
Let $x$ represent the number.
Three more than $x$: $x + 3$
The equation is: $x + 3 = 15$

b) Five less than a number is 7.
Let $x$ represent the number.
Five less than $x$: $x - 5$
The equation is: $x - 5 = 7$

c) A number subtracted from 5 is 1.
Let $x$ represent the number.
$x$ subtracted from 5: $5 - x$
The equation is: $5 - x = 1$

d) A number divided by 3 is 10.
Let $x$ represent the number.
$x$ divided by 3: $\frac{x}{3}$
The equation is: $\frac{x}{3} = 10$

**1.** Write an equation for each sentence.
   **a)** Eight more than a number is 12.
   **b)** Three times a number is 12.
   **c)** Eight less than a number is 12.

**2.** Write a sentence for each equation.
   **a)** $12 + n = 19$   **b)** $3n = 18$   **c)** $12 - n = 5$   **d)** $\frac{n}{2} = 6$

**3.** Write an equation for each sentence.
   **a)** Five added to two times a number is 35.
   **b)** Eight plus one-half a number is 24.
   **c)** Six subtracted from three times a number is 11.

**4.** Write each equation in words.
   **a)** $5x - 7 = 37$   **b)** $\frac{x}{3} + 4 = 9$   **c)** $17 - 2x = 3$

**5.** Match each equation with the correct sentence.
   **a)** $n + 4 = 8$   A. Four less than a number is 8.
   **b)** $4n = 8$   B. Four more than four times a number equals 8.
   **c)** $4n - 4 = 8$   C. The sum of four and a number is 8.
   **d)** $n - 4 = 8$   D. Four less than four times a number equals 8.
   **e)** $4 + 4n = 8$   E. The product of four and a number is 8.

**6.** Alona thinks of a number. She divides the number by 4, then adds 10. The answer is 14. Write an equation for the problem.

**7.** **Assessment Focus**   Write an equation for each sentence.
   **a)** Bhavin's age 7 years from now will be 20.
   **b)** Five times the number of students is 295.
   **c)** The perimeter of a rectangle with length 15 cm and width $w$ centimetres is 38 cm.
   **d)** The cost of 2 tickets at $x$ dollars each and 5 tickets at $4 each is $44.

   Which equation was the most difficult to write? Explain.

**Reflect**

Describe the difference between an equation and an expression.
Give an example of each.

**Focus** Solve equations by inspection and by systematic trial.

## Explore

Work with a partner.
On the way home from school, 3 students get off the bus at the first stop. Seven get off at the next stop. Five get off at the next stop. Ten get off at the next stop. There are now 2 students left on the bus. How many students were on the bus when it left the school? How many different ways can you solve the problem?

### Reflect & Share

Discuss your strategies for finding the answer with another pair of classmates.
Did you use an equation? Did you use reasoning?
Did you draw a picture? Explain.

## Connect

Recall the equation about the cost of 1 CD, from *Section 10.5 Reading and Writing Equations*, page 387.
The equation is $3p = 36$, where $p$ is the cost of 1 CD.
When we use the equation to find the value of $p$,
we **solve the equation.**

Here are 2 ways to solve this equation.

*Method 1: By Systematic Trial*
$3p = 36$
We choose a value for $p$ and substitute.
When $p = 10$, $3p = 30$
30 is too small, so choose a greater value of $p$.

When $p = 20$, $3p = 60$
60 is too large, so choose a lesser value of $p$.

When $p = 15$, $3p = 45$
45 is too large, so choose a lesser value of $p$.

When $p = 12$, $3p = 36$
This is correct.
The cost of 1 CD is $12.

*Method 2: By Inspection*
$3p = 36$
We find a number which, when multiplied by 3, has product 36.
We know that $3 \times 12 = 36$; so, $p = 12$.
The cost of 1 CD is $12.

We say that the value $p = 12$ makes the equation $3p = 36$ true.
A value $p = 10$ would not make the equation true because $3 \times 10$ does not equal 36.
The value $p = 12$ is the only solution to the equation.
That is, there is only one value of $p$ that makes the equation true.

**Example 1**

Solve by inspection.
a) $x + 7 = 10$
b) $\frac{24}{n} = 6$
c) $40 - y = 30$
d) $9z + 2 = 38$

**Solution**

a) $x + 7 = 10$
Which number added to 7 gives 10?
We know that $3 + 7 = 10$; so, $x = 3$.

b) $\frac{24}{n} = 6$
This means $24 \div n = 6$.
Which number divided into 24 gives 6?
We know that $24 \div 4 = 6$; so, $n = 4$.

c) $40 - y = 30$
Which number subtracted from 40 gives 30?
We know that $40 - 10 = 30$; so, $y = 10$.

d) $9z + 2 = 38$
9 times which number, plus 2, gives 38?
We know $36 + 2 = 38$
So, 9 times which number is 36?
We know that $9 \times 4 = 36$; so, $z = 4$.

## Example 2

Solve by systematic trial.

**a)** $2a - 28 = 136$

**b)** $\frac{y}{4} = 220$

## Solution

**a)** $2a - 28 = 136$

When the numbers are large, use a calculator.

Try $a = 50$; then, $2 \times 50 - 28 = 72$

72 is too small, so choose a greater value of $a$.

Try $a = 100$; then, $2 \times 100 - 28 = 172$

172 is too big, so choose a lesser value of $a$.

Try $a = 75$; then, $2 \times 75 - 28 = 122$

122 is too small, so choose a greater value of $a$.

Try $a = 80$; then, $2 \times 80 - 28 = 132$

132 is too small, but it is close to the value we want.

Try $a = 82$; then, $2 \times 82 - 28 = 136$

This is correct.

$a = 82$ is the solution.

**b)** $\frac{y}{4} = 220$

Use a calculator. We know the number is much greater than 220, because the number is divided by 4 to get 220.

Try $y = 1000$; then, $\frac{1000}{4} = 250$    This is too big.

Try $y = 900$; then, $\frac{900}{4} = 225$    This is closer, but still too big.

Try $y = 850$; then, $\frac{850}{4} = 212.5$    This is too small.

Try $y = 880$; then, $\frac{880}{4} = 220$    This is correct.

$y = 880$ is the solution.

We can write, then solve, an equation to solve a problem.

## Example 3

Kiera shared 420 hockey cards equally among her friends.
Each friend had 105 cards.

**a)** Write an equation that describes this situation.

**b)** Solve the equation to find how many friends shared the cards.

**Solution**

a) Let $h$ represent the number of friends who shared the cards.
Then, each friend had $\frac{420}{h}$ cards.
Also, each friend had 105 cards.
So, the equation is: $\frac{420}{h} = 105$

b) Solve $\frac{420}{h} = 105$ by inspection.
Think: $420 \div h = 105$
Which number divides into 420 to give the quotient 105?
We know $400 \div 4 = 100$; so, try $h = 4$.
$420 \div 4 = 105$
So, the solution is $h = 4$.
Four friends shared the cards.

## Practice

1. Solve each equation.
   a) $x + 3 = 12$
   b) $y + 9 = 9$
   c) $10 + 2z = 20$
   d) $17 + 3c = 26$

2. Solve each equation.
   a) $x - 4 = 3$
   b) $10 - n = 10$
   c) $2z - 7 = 1$
   d) $13 - 4k = 5$

3. Shenker has 45 CDs.
   He gives 10 CDs to his brother.
   a) Write an equation you can solve to find how many CDs Shenker has left.
   b) Solve the equation.

4. Solve by inspection.
   a) $x + 4 = 15$
   b) $2k - 13 = 3$
   c) $3y = 24$
   d) $\frac{z}{9} = 2$

5. Solve by systematic trial.
   a) $n + 5 = 33$
   b) $8z = 88$
   c) $43 - 3y = 16$
   d) $\frac{x}{7} = 4$

**Mental Math**

Estimate.
- $\frac{1}{4}$ of 22
- $\frac{2}{5}$ of 36
- $\frac{2}{3}$ of 91
- $\frac{3}{8}$ of 79

**6.** The perimeter of a square is 156 cm.
  **a)** Write an equation you can solve to find the side length of the square.
  **b)** Solve the equation.

**7.** The side length of a regular hexagon is 9 cm.
  **a)** Write an equation you can solve to find the perimeter of the hexagon.
  **b)** Solve the equation.

**8.** Use questions 6 and 7 as a guide.
  **a)** Write your own problem about side length and perimeter of a figure.
  **b)** Write an equation you can use to solve the problem.
  **c)** Solve the equation.

**9.** Eli has 130 comic books.
  He gives 10 to his sister, then shares the rest equally among his friends.
  Each friend has 24 comic books.
  **a)** Write an equation you can solve to find how many friends were given comics.
  **b)** Solve the equation.

**10.** Find the value of $n$ that makes each equation true.
  **a)** $3n = 27$
  **b)** $2n + 3 = 27$
  **c)** $2n - 3 = 27$
  **d)** $\frac{n}{3} = 27$
  **e)** $\frac{n}{2} + 3 = 27$
  **f)** $\frac{3n}{2} = 27$

**11.** **Assessment Focus**   Write a problem that can be described by each equation. Solve each equation.
  Which equation was the most difficult to solve? Explain.
  **a)** $2x - 1 = 5$
  **b)** $4y = 24$
  **c)** $\frac{z}{38} = 57$
  **d)** $5x + 5 = 30$
  **e)** $\frac{25}{y} = 5$
  **f)** $52 - 4 = 4x$

**Reflect**

How does knowing your number facts help you solve an equation by inspection? Give examples in your explanation.

# Clothes Buyer

When you buy a pair of jeans, do you ever wonder who bought the jeans for the store to sell to you? The clothes buyer balances all kinds of purchasing variables (purchase price, quantity discounts, foreign exchange, shipping, and taxes) as well as selling variables (profit margin, the effect of price on sales, regional variations) to make the best purchase decision. If he buys too much stock, or at the wrong price, the company could end up selling the clothes at a loss. If the buyer buys too little, he misses out on sales, and customers go elsewhere. The buyer may use a spreadsheet. He can try different "what if" scenarios by changing either the variables or the formulas in the spreadsheet.

A buyer knows that the sales of an item (thousands of units per month) peak a few months after arrival and then slow down over time. However, sales of seasonal or trendy items peak almost immediately, remain steady for a couple of months, and then drop off quickly. What might graphs that show these two sales trends look like?

# Choosing a Strategy

## Strategies

- **Make a table.**
- **Use a model.**
- **Draw a diagram.**
- **Solve a simpler problem.**
- **Work backward.**
- **Guess and check.**
- **Make an organized list.**
- **Use a pattern.**
- **Draw a graph.**
- **Use logical reasoning.**

**1.** There are 2 schools. Each school has 3 buildings. Each building has 4 floors. Each floor has 5 classrooms. Each classroom has 6 rows of desks. Each row has 7 desks.
How many desks are there in the two schools?

**2. a)** Write the next three terms in this pattern: 1, 4, 3, 6, 5, 8, 7, …
**b)** What is the pattern rule?
**c)** Write the 21st and the 50th terms. Explain how you did this.

**3.** Here is a pattern of tiles.

Term 1          Term 2          Term 3

**a)** Make a table to show the numbers of red and blue tiles in each term.
This pattern continues.
**b)** How many red tiles will there be in the 20th term?
**c)** How many blue tiles will there be in the 100th term?
**d)** What will be the total number of tiles in the 30th term?
**e)** How many red tiles will be in the term that has 48 blue tiles? How do you know?

**4.** A can that contains 5 red balls and 3 green balls has a mass of 43 g.
When the can contains 3 red balls and 5 green balls, the mass is 37 g.
When the can contains 1 red ball and 1 green ball, the mass is 19 g.
What is the mass of the can and each ball?

**5.** Marisha and Irfan have money to spend at the carnival.
If Marisha gives Irfan $5, each person will have the same amount of money. If, instead, Irfan gives Marisha $5, Marisha will have twice as much as Irfan.
How much money does each person have?

**Household Waste**

**6.** The graph shows the garbage put out by 21 households in one week.

  a) How does the mass of garbage relate to the number of people in the household?

  b) Give three possible reasons why one household has 13 kg of garbage.

  c) Give three possible reasons why one household has 1 kg of garbage.

**7.** For a school trip, the charge for using the school bus is $50. The cost of food is $10 per student.

  a) Copy and complete this table for up to 10 students.

| Number of students | 1 | 2 | 3 | 4 | 5 |
|---|---|---|---|---|---|
| Total cost of trip ($) | | | | | |

  b) What is the total cost for each number of students?
    **i)** 12  **ii)** 15  **iii)** 20

  c) Each person pays a fair share. What is the cost per person when each number of students goes on the trip?
    **i)** 5  **ii)** 10  **iii)** 15

**Courier Company Costs**

**8.** The graph shows the price charged by a local courier company to collect and deliver packages.

  a) What is the cost to have 6 packages collected and delivered?

  b) Extend the pattern in the graph. What is the cost to have 8 packages collected and delivered?

  c) Why does it cost $15 to collect and deliver one package, but only $17 to collect and deliver 2 packages?

**9.** I am a 3-digit number.
My hundreds digit is the square of my ones digit.
My tens digit is the product of my hundreds digit and my ones digit.

  a) What number, or numbers, could I be?

  b) What do you notice about your answer(s)?

# Unit Review

Review any lesson with

online tutorial

## What Do I Need to Know?

✓ A variable is a letter or symbol that represents a number, or a set of numbers.
A variable can be used to write an expression:
"3 more than a number" is $3 + n$.
A variable can be used to write an equation:
"4 more than a number equals 11" is $4 + n = 11$.

✓ We can solve equations by:
- inspection
- systematic trial

## What Should I Be Able to Do?

For extra practice, go to page 447.

**LESSON**

**10.1**

1. For each pattern:
   i) Describe the pattern.
   ii) Write the next 3 terms.
   iii) Find the 20th term.
      Explain how you did this.
   a) 5, 12, 19, 26, …
   b) 3, 9, 27, 81, …
   c) 96, 93, 90, 87, …
   d) 10, 21, 32, 43, …
   e) 9, 13, 17, 21, …

2. Your favourite aunt gives you 1¢ on April 1, 2¢ on April 2, 4¢ on April 3. She continues doubling the daily amount until April 12.
   a) How much will you get on April 12?
   b) What is the total amount you will receive?

3. a) Describe this pattern:
      2, 5, 11, 23, 47, …
   b) Write the next 3 terms.
   c) Write a similar pattern.
      Use a different start number.

4. This pattern continues.

   a) Describe the pattern.
   b) Sketch the next 3 figures.
   c) Describe the 12th figure and the 22nd figure.
      Sketch them if you can.

**5.** Copy and complete this table for each pattern.

| Input | Output |
|-------|--------|
| 4 | |
| 6 | |
| 8 | |
| 10 | |
| 12 | |

a) Add 3 to each Input number.

b) Multiply each Input number by 2.

c) Subtract 3 from each Input number.

d) Divide each Input number by 2.

e) Divide each Input number by 2, then add 3.

f) Multiply each Input number by 2, then subtract 3.

**6.** Look at this graph.

a) Make an Input/Output table for the graph.

b) What patterns do you see in the table?

c) Extend the table 3 more rows. Explain how you did this.

d) What happens if you try to extend the table further?

**7. a)** Describe the patterns in this table.

b) Use the patterns to extend the table 3 more rows.

| Input | Output |
|-------|--------|
| 5 | 1 |
| 15 | 3 |
| 25 | 5 |
| 35 | 7 |
| 45 | 9 |
| 55 | 11 |

**8.** Write an algebraic expression for each statement.

a) twenty more than a number

b) one less than a number

c) a number increased by ten

d) a number multiplied by thirteen

**9.** Write each algebraic expression in words.

a) $n + 4$      b) $25 - h$

c) $\frac{a}{5}$      d) $5 - 2n$

**10.** Evaluate each expression for $x = 3$.

a) $x + 8$      b) $9x$

c) $2x - 1$      d) $\frac{x}{2}$

e) $10x + 4$      f) $9 - 3x$

**11.** A value of $n$ is substituted in each expression to get the number in the box. Find each value of $n$.

a) $5n$          40

b) $6n - 1$    11

c) $2n + 8$    16

d) $3n - 4$    14

---

**12.** One pair of running shoes costs $70.
   **a)** What is the cost of 3 pairs? 7 pairs?
   **b)** What is the cost of $r$ pairs of running shoes?
   **c)** Write an algebraic expression for the number of pairs of shoes you could buy for $d$ dollars.

**10.5 13.** Write each equation in words.
   **a)** $x + 3 = 17$
   **b)** $3y = 24$
   **c)** $\frac{x}{4} = 5$
   **d)** $3y - 4 = 20$
   **e)** $7 + 4x = 35$

**14.** Write a problem that can be represented by each equation.
   **a)** $x + 5 = 21$
   **b)** $5n - 2 = 28$

**15.** Write an equation for each sentence.
   **a)** Six times the number of people in the room is 258.
   **b)** The area of a rectangle with length 6 cm and width $w$ centimetres is 36 cm².
   **c)** One-half of a number is 6.

**16.** Write a problem that can be represented by each equation.
   **a)** $x + 2 = 23$
   **b)** $4 - x = 12$
   **c)** $5x = 35$
   **d)** $\frac{x}{9} = 5$

**17.** Write an equation to find the length of one side of an equilateral triangle with perimeter 24 cm.

**10.6 18.** Solve each equation.
   **a)** $12 = 3n$
   **b)** $21 - n = 18$
   **c)** $\frac{27}{n} = 9$
   **d)** $\frac{n}{9} = 27$
   **e)** $n - 21 = 30$
   **f)** $3n + 2 = 11$

**19.** Solve each equation.
   **a)** $17 - 3n = 2$
   **b)** $17 + 3n = 47$
   **c)** $3n - 17 = 4$
   **d)** $\frac{n}{17} = 25$

**20.** At Queen Mary School, 98 students walk to school. There are 250 students in the school.
   **a)** Write an equation you can solve to find how many students do not walk to school.
   **b)** Solve the equation.

**21.** At Sir Robert Borden School, twice as many students take the bus as walk to school. Seventy-four students walk to school.
   **a)** Write an equation you can solve to find how many students take the bus.
   **b)** Solve the equation.

# Practice Test

**1.** **a)** Copy and complete the table for this pattern:
Multiply each number by 5, then subtract 3.
**b)** Graph the pattern.
Explain how the graph shows the pattern.
**c)** Extend the table 3 more rows.
Plot the point for each row on the graph.
**d)** How can you find the Output number when the Input number is 47?
**e)** How can you find the Input number when the Output number is 47?
**f)** Can the Input number be 100? Explain.
**g)** Can the Output number be 100? Explain.

| Input | Output |
|-------|--------|
| 1     |        |
| 2     |        |
| 3     |        |
| 4     |        |
| 5     |        |

**2.** Angelina wins money in a competition.
She is given the choice as to how she is paid.
Choice 1: Get $1 the 1st day, $2 the 2nd day, $4 the 3rd day, $8 the 4th day, and so on.
This pattern continues for 3 weeks.
Choice 2: Get $1 000 000 today.
**a)** With which method of payment will Angelina get more money?
**b)** How did you use patterns to solve this problem?
**c)** After how many days will the money Angelina gets from Choice 1 be approximately $1 000 000?

**3.** Here are 5 algebraic expressions: $2 + 3n$, $2n + 3$, $3n - 2$, $\frac{2n}{2}$, $\frac{3n}{2}$
Are there any values of $n$ that will produce the same number when substituted in two or more of the expressions?
Investigate to find out. Show your work.

**4.** Solve each equation by systematic trial or by inspection.
**a)** $3x + 90 = 147$      **b)** $\frac{84}{h} = 12$
**c)** $\frac{26}{y} + 3 = 16$      **d)** $147 - 3x = 90$
Explain your choice of method in each case. Show your work.

Two students raised money for charity in a bike-a-thon. The route was from Timmins to Kapuskasing, a distance of 165 km.

## Part 1

Ingrid cycled at an average speed of 15 km/h.
How far does Ingrid travel in 1 h? 2 h? 3 h? 4 h? 5 h?
Record the results in a table.

| Time (h) | | | | | |
|---|---|---|---|---|---|
| Distance (km) | | | | | |

Graph the data in the table.
Graph *Time* horizontally and *Distance* vertically.

Write an algebraic expression for the distance Ingrid travels in *t* hours.
Use the expression to find how far Ingrid travels in 7 h.
How could you check your answer?

Write an equation to represent Ingrid travelling 135 km in *t* hours.
Solve the equation.
What have you found out?

## Part 2

Liam cycled at an average speed of 20 km/h.
Repeat *Part 1* for Liam.

## Part 3

How are the graphs for Ingrid and Liam alike?
How are they different?

## Part 4

Ingrid's sponsors paid her $25 per kilometre.
Liam's sponsors paid him $20 per kilometre.
Make a table to show how much money each student raised for every 10 km cycled.

| Distance (km) | Money Raised by Ingrid ($) | Money Raised by Liam ($) |
|---|---|---|
| 10 | | |
| 20 | | |
| 30 | | |

How much money did Ingrid raise if she cycled *d* kilometres?
How much money did Liam raise if he cycled *d* kilometres?

Liam and Ingrid raised equal amounts of money.
How far might each person have cycled? Explain.

## Reflect on the Unit

How are number patterns related to algebra?
How are algebraic expressions related to equations?
Give examples in your explanation.

# Probability

Many games involve probability and chance. One game uses this spinner or a number cube labelled 1 to 6.

You can choose to spin the pointer or roll the number cube. You win if the pointer lands on red. You win if you roll a 6. Are you more likely to win if you spin the pointer or roll the number cube? Explain.

## What You'll Learn

- Use the language of probability.
- Conduct simple experiments.
- List the possible outcomes of experiments by using tree diagrams, modelling, and lists.
- Identify possible outcomes and favourable outcomes.
- State the probability of an outcome.
- Understand how probability can relate to sports and games of chance.
- Use probability to solve problems.

## Why It's Important

In the media, you hear and read statements about the probability of everyday events, such as living to be 100 or winning the lottery.
To make sense of these statements, you need to understand probability.

## Key Words

- probability
- outcome
- tree diagram
- relative frequency
- experimental probability
- theoretical probability

## Converting Fractions and Decimals to Percents

Percent (%) means "per hundred" or out of one hundred.

**Example**

Express each fraction as a decimal, then as a percent.

**a)** $\dfrac{9}{50}$ **b)** $\dfrac{1}{4}$ **c)** $\dfrac{5}{8}$ **d)** $\dfrac{7}{16}$

**Solution**

To convert a fraction to a decimal, try to write
an equivalent fraction with denominator 100.

**a)** $\dfrac{9}{50} = \dfrac{18}{100}$ ($\times 2$)

**b)** $\dfrac{1}{4} = \dfrac{25}{100}$ ($\times 25$)

$\dfrac{18}{100} = 0.18$, or 18%

$\dfrac{25}{100} = 0.25$, or 25%

When you cannot write an equivalent fraction, use a calculator to divide.

**c)** $\dfrac{5}{8} = 5 \div 8$
$= 0.625$
$= 62.5\%$

**d)** $\dfrac{7}{16} = 7 \div 16$
$= 0.4375$
$= 43.75\%$

### ✓ Check

**1.** Express each decimal as a percent.
   **a)** 0.1 **b)** 0.01 **c)** 0.24 **d)** 0.05

**2.** Express each fraction as a decimal, then as a percent.
   **a)** $\dfrac{7}{10}$ **b)** $\dfrac{3}{5}$ **c)** $\dfrac{9}{25}$ **d)** $\dfrac{3}{4}$

**3.** Express each fraction as a decimal, then as a percent.
   **a)** $\dfrac{7}{40}$ **b)** $\dfrac{3}{8}$ **c)** $\dfrac{13}{16}$ **d)** $\dfrac{51}{200}$

**Focus** Investigate outcomes of experiments.

When you roll a number cube, the outcomes
are equally likely.
For a spinner with sectors of equal areas,
when the pointer is spun,
the outcomes are equally likely.

## Explore

Work with a partner. You will need a number cube labelled 1 to 6,
and a spinner similar to the one shown below.

List the possible outcomes of rolling the number cube
and spinning the pointer.
How many outcomes include rolling a 4?
How many outcomes include landing on red?
How many outcomes have an even number on the cube and the
pointer landing on blue?

### Reflect & Share

Compare the strategy you used to find the outcomes with that of
another pair of classmates.
Was one strategy more efficient than another? Explain.

## Connect

An outcome is the possible result of an experiment or an action.
When a coin is tossed, the possible outcomes are heads or tails.
To show the possible outcomes for an experiment that has two or
more actions, we can use a **tree diagram**.

When 2 coins are tossed, the outcomes for each coin
are heads (H) or tails (T).
List the outcomes of the first coin toss.
For each outcome, list the outcomes of the second coin toss.
Then list the outcomes for the coins tossed together.

| 1st Coin | 2nd Coin | Outcomes |
|----------|----------|----------|
| H | H | HH |
|   | T | HT |
| T | H | TH |
|   | T | TT |

There are 4 possible outcomes: HH, HT, TH, TT

## Example

Farah tosses a coin and spins the pointer on this spinner.

a) Draw a tree diagram to show
   the possible outcomes.
b) List all the possible outcomes.
c) How many outcomes include the
   pointer landing on pink?
d) How many outcomes include tails?

**Solution**

a) The sectors on the spinner
   have equal areas, so the
   outcomes are equally likely.
   The possible outcomes for
   the spinner are: pink (P),
   yellow (Y), or blue (B).
   For each colour, the possible
   outcomes for tossing the coin
   are: heads (H) or tails (T)

| Spinner | Coin | Outcomes |
|---------|------|----------|
| P | H | PH |
|   | T | PT |
| Y | H | YH |
|   | T | YT |
| B | H | BH |
|   | T | BT |

b) The outcomes are: pink/heads, pink/tails, yellow/heads,
   yellow/tails, blue/heads, blue/tails

c) There are two outcomes with the colour pink:
   pink/heads, pink/tails

d) There are three outcomes with tails:
   pink/tails, yellow/tails, blue/tails

1. List the possible outcomes in each case.
   a) spinning the pointer
   b) rolling a number cube labelled 1 to 6

2. List the possible outcomes in each case.
   a) the colour of a traffic light when you reach it
   b) the gender of a baby who is born
   c) the points scored in a hockey game
   d) the suit of a card pulled from a deck of playing cards

3. The Scenic Railroad sells tickets for trips on Saturdays and Sundays. All-day and half-day trips are available. There are adult, child, and senior fares. Draw a tree diagram to show the possible ticket types.

4. Use a tree diagram to show the possible combinations for breakfast. You must choose one of each:
   • eggs or fruit
   • toast, pancakes, or cereal
   • milk or juice

5. Jim has to choose an outfit. His choices of pants are black, grey, or navy. His sweater choices are red, beige, white, or yellow.
   a) Draw a tree diagram to display all the possible outfits.
   b) How many outfits have either black pants or a white sweater?
   c) How many outfits do not have black pants or do not have a white sweater?
   d) How many outfits have a black sweater?

**Mental Math**

Simplify.
- $(-3) + (+5)$
- $(-3) + (-5)$
- $(+3) + (-5)$
- $(+3) - (+5)$

6. A deli offers 2 soups, 4 salads, 5 sandwiches, and 3 beverages. How many choices are there for a customer who wants each of the following meals?
   a) a salad and a beverage
   b) soup, a sandwich, and a beverage
   c) soup, a salad, and a beverage
   d) a sandwich or salad, and a soup

## 7. Assessment Focus

**a)** Copy and complete this table.
Show the sums when two number cubes are rolled.

*When one cube shows 1 and the other cube shows 4, then the sum is 5.*

| Sum of Numbers on Two Cubes | | | | | | |
|---|---|---|---|---|---|---|
| Number on Cube | 1 | 2 | 3 | 4 | 5 | 6 |
| 1 | 2 | 3 | 4 | 5 | 6 | 7 |
| 2 | | | | | | |
| 3 | | | | | | |
| 4 | | | | | | |
| 5 | | | | | | |
| 6 | | | | | | |

**b)** How many different outcomes are there for the sum of the numbers on the cubes?

**c)** In how many ways can the sum be 6?

**d)** In how many ways can the sum be 9?

**e)** In how many ways can the sum be 2 or 12?

**f)** Why do you think 7 is a lucky number?

**g)** Draw a tree diagram to show these results. Why do you think a table was used instead of a tree diagram?

Show your work.

**Take It Further**

**8.** A lock combination comprises the four digits from 1 to 4 in any order.
How many possible combinations are there in each case?

**a)** The digits cannot repeat within the code.

**b)** The digits can repeat within the code.

### Reflect

Explain why a tree diagram is helpful to list the outcomes of an experiment.

**Focus** Determine probability from experiments.

Work with a partner.
You will need a coin.
When you toss a coin, which outcome do you think is more likely?
Do you think the outcomes are equally likely? Explain.

| Outcome | Tally | Frequency |
|---------|-------|-----------|
| Heads   |       |           |
| Tails   |       |           |

➤ Toss the coin 50 times.
How many times do you think you will get heads?
Record the results in a table.

➤ Write the number of heads as a fraction of the
total number of tosses.
Write the number of tails as a fraction of the
total number of tosses.
Add the fractions. What do you notice?

### Reflect & Share

How do the results compare with your prediction?
Combine your results with those of another pair of classmates.
This is same as tossing the coin 100 times.
Write the new fractions for 100 tosses.
Add the fractions. What do you notice?

The **relative frequency** is the number of times an outcome occurs
divided by the total number of times the experiment is conducted.

$$\text{Relative frequency} = \frac{\text{Number of times an outcome occurs}}{\text{Number of times experiment is conducted}}$$

The relative frequency may be written as a fraction, a decimal, or a
percent. Relative frequency is also called **experimental probability**.

When a thumbtack is dropped, it can land with its point up or on its side.
Here are the results of 100 drops:

| Outcome | Frequency |
|---|---|
| Point up | 46 |
| On its side | 54 |

Relative frequency of Point up $= \dfrac{\text{Number of times Point up}}{\text{Total number of drops}}$

$= \dfrac{46}{100}$, or 0.46

Relative frequency of On its side $= \dfrac{\text{Number of times On its side}}{\text{Total number of drops}}$

$= \dfrac{54}{100}$, or 0.54

| Outcome | Frequency | Relative Frequency |
|---|---|---|
| Point up | 46 | 0.46 |
| On its side | 54 | 0.54 |

The sum of the relative frequencies for an experiment is 1.
That is, $\dfrac{46}{100} + \dfrac{54}{100} = 0.46 + 0.54$
$= 1$

## Example

The number of times a player goes up to bat is referred to as the player's "at bats."
This table shows the number of at bats and hits for some of the greatest players in the Baseball Hall of Fame.

| Players in Baseball Hall of Fame | | |
|---|---|---|
| Player | At Bats | Hits |
| Aaron | 12 364 | 3771 |
| Cobb | 11 429 | 4191 |
| Gehrig | 8 001 | 2721 |
| Jackson | 9 864 | 2584 |
| Mantle | 8 102 | 2415 |
| Mays | 10 881 | 3283 |

**In baseball, a "batting average" is a relative frequency.**

a) Calculate the batting average for each player.

b) Order the players from greatest to least batting average.

## Solution

a) To calculate each player's batting average, divide the number of hits by the number of at bats.
Round each batting average to 3 decimal places.

**Use a calculator to write each fraction as a decimal.**

$\text{Aaron} = \dfrac{3771}{12\ 364}$

$\doteq 0.305$

$\text{Gehrig} = \dfrac{2721}{8001}$

$\doteq 0.340$

$\text{Mantle} = \dfrac{2415}{8102}$

$\doteq 0.298$

$\text{Cobb} = \dfrac{4191}{11\ 429}$

$\doteq 0.367$

$\text{Jackson} = \dfrac{2584}{9864}$

$\doteq 0.262$

$\text{Mays} = \dfrac{3283}{10\ 881}$

$\doteq 0.302$

**b)** The batting averages, from greatest to least, are:
0.367, 0.340, 0.305, 0.302, 0.298, 0.262
The players, from greatest to least batting average, are:
Cobb, Gehrig, Aaron, Mays, Mantle, and Jackson

## Practice

| Name | At Bats | Hits |
|------|---------|------|
| Yang Hsi | 58 | 26 |
| Aki | 41 | 20 |
| David | 54 | 23 |
| Yuk Yee | 36 | 11 |
| Eli | 49 | 18 |
| Aponi | 42 | 15 |
| Leah | 46 | 22 |
| Devadas | 45 | 17 |

**1.** This table shows data for a baseball team.
Find the batting average of each player.
Round each answer to 3 decimal places.

**2.** Write each relative frequency as a decimal to 3 decimal places.
   **a)** A telemarketer made 200 phone calls and 35 new customers signed up. What is the relative frequency of getting a customer? Not getting a customer?
   **b)** A quality controller tested 175 light bulbs and found 5 defective. What is the relative frequency of finding a defective bulb? Finding a good bulb?

**3.** A paper cup is tossed.
The cup lands with the top up 27 times, the top down 32 times, and on its side 41 times.
   **a)** What are the possible outcomes of tossing a paper cup?
   **b)** Are the outcomes equally likely? Explain.
   **c)** State the relative frequency of each outcome.

**4. a)** Conduct the paper cup experiment in question 3.
Decide how to hold the cup to drop it.
Repeat the experiment until you have 100 results.
   **b)** Compare your results with those from question 3.
Are the numbers different? Explain.

**5.** Use 3 red counters and 3 yellow counters.
You may place some or all of the counters in a bag.
You then pick a counter without looking.
How many different ways can you place the counters in the bag so you are more likely to pick a red counter than a yellow counter? Explain.

**6.** Copy and continue the table to show all months of the year.
Have each student write her or his month of birth on the board.
Find the number of students who were born in each month.

**a)** Complete the table.

| Month | Tally | Frequency | Relative Frequency |
|-------|-------|-----------|--------------------|
| January | | | |
| February | | | |
| March | | | |

**b)** What is the relative frequency for birthdays in the same month as yours?

**c)** Find the sum of the relative frequencies. Explain why this sum makes sense.

**Number Strategies**

Find each percent.
- 10% of $325.00
- 15% of $114.00
- 20% of $99.99
- 25% of $500.00

**7.** **Assessment Focus**   A regular octahedron has faces labelled
1 to 8. Two of these octahedra are rolled.
The numbers on the faces the octahedra land on are added.
Work with a partner. Use the regular octahedra you made in
Unit 3. Label the faces of each octahedron from 1 to 8.

Conduct an experiment to find the relative frequency of getting a
sum of 7 when two regular octahedra are rolled.

**a)** Report your results.

**b)** How are the results affected if you conduct the experiment
10 times? 50 times? 100 times? Explain.

**Reflect**

Suppose you know the relative frequency of one outcome
of an experiment.
How can you use that to predict the likelihood of that outcome
occurring if you conduct the experiment again?
Use an example to explain.

# Mid-Unit Review

LESSON

**11.1** **1.** Jenna plays a video game on her computer. Each time she plays, she can choose an easy, intermediate, or challenging level of difficulty. She can also choose 1 or 2 players. Use a tree diagram to show the possible game choices.

**2.** Use a tree diagram to show the possible lunch choices.

LUNCH SPECIAL
1 side dish • 1 main dish • 1 drink

| SIDE DISH | MAIN DISH | DRINK |
|-----------|-----------|-------|
| Egg roll | Sweet and sour chicken | Low-fat milk |
| Soup | Chop suey | Juice |
| Fried rice | Broccoli beef | Pop |

**11.2** **3.** Write each relative frequency as a decimal.

a) An air traffic controller's records show 512 planes landed one day. Seventeen planes were 727s. What is the relative frequency of a 727 landing?

b) A cashier served 58 customers in one shift. Thirty-two customers paid cash. What is the relative frequency of a customer paying cash?

c) Qam spun a pointer on a spinner 95 times. The pointer landed on purple 63 times. What is the relative frequency of landing on purple?

**4.** You will need 4 cubes: 2 of one colour, 2 of another colour; and a bag. Place the cubes in the bag. Pick 2 cubes without looking. Design and conduct an experiment to find the relative frequency of choosing 2 matching cubes.

**5.** A number cube is labelled 1 to 6.
a) What are the possible outcomes when this cube is rolled?
b) Are these outcomes equally likely? Explain.
c) Design and conduct an experiment to find the relative frequency of each outcome.
d) Do the results confirm your prediction in part b? Explain.
e) How does your answer to part d depend on the number of times you roll the number cube? Explain.

**6.** There are 3 blue counters and 3 green counters in a bag. You may add to the bag or remove from the bag, as listed below. You put:
a) 1 red counter in the bag
b) 1 more green counter in the bag
c) 2 blue counters in the bag
You then pick a counter without looking. Which of the actions above would make it more likely that you would pick a green counter? Explain.

# Theoretical Probability

## Explore

Work in a group.
A carnival game has a bucket of different-coloured balls.
Each player is asked to predict the colour of the ball
he or she will select.
The player then selects a ball, without looking.
If the guess is correct, the player wins a prize.
After each draw, the ball is returned to the bucket.

Use linking cubes.
Put 4 red, 3 blue, 2 yellow, and 1 green cube in a bag.
Suppose you take 1 cube without looking.
Predict the probability that you will pick each colour.
Play the game 50 times.
What is the experimental probability for picking each colour?
How does each predicted probability compare with the
experimental probability?

### Reflect & Share

Combine your results with those of another group of students.
How does each experimental probability compare with the
predicted probability now?

## Connect

Recall that when the outcomes of an experiment are equally likely,
the probability of any outcome is:

$$\text{Probability} = \frac{\text{Number of favourable outcomes}}{\text{Number of possible outcomes}}$$

This is called the **theoretical probability**, but we usually say
"probability."
You find the probability by analysing the possible outcomes rather
than by experimenting.

When you pick an object without looking, the object is picked at random.

Twenty counters were put in a bag:
7 green, 6 black, 5 orange, and 2 purple
You take one counter from the bag without looking.
There are 4 outcomes: green, black, orange, and purple
Suppose the favourable outcome is black.
Then, the probability of picking a black counter is: $\frac{6}{20} = 0.3$

Suppose the favourable outcome is green.
Then, the probability of picking a green counter is: $\frac{7}{20} = 0.35$

Note that the outcomes are not equally likely.

We can predict the possible number of times an outcome will occur by multiplying the probability by the number of repetitions.
Suppose we pick a counter at random 54 times.
Then, the predicted number of times a black counter is picked is:
$0.3 \times 54 = 16.2$
We would expect to pick a black counter about 16 times.
However, we may never pick a black counter, or we might always pick a black counter.

### Example

Suppose you roll a number cube 100 times. Predict how many times:
**a)** a 1 will show
**b)** a 5 will show
**c)** a 1 or a 5 will show
**d)** a 1 or a 5 will not show
How are the answers to parts c and d related?

### Solution

When a number cube is rolled, there are six possible outcomes.
The outcomes are equally likely.

**a)** The probability of rolling a 1 is $\frac{1}{6}$.
So, the predicted number of times a 1 will show in 100 rolls is:
$\frac{1}{6} \times 100 = \frac{100}{6} \doteq 17$

**b)** The probability of rolling a 5 is also $\frac{1}{6}$.
So, the predicted number of times a 5 will show is also about 17.

**c)** The probability of rolling a 1 or a 5 is $\frac{2}{6}$, or $\frac{1}{3}$.

So, the predicted number of times a 1 or a 5 will show is:

$\frac{1}{3} \times 100 = \frac{100}{3} \doteq 33$

**d)** For a 1 and a 5 not to show, a 2, 3, 4, or 6 shows.

The probability of rolling a 2, 3, 4, or 6 is $\frac{4}{6}$, or $\frac{2}{3}$.

So, the predicted number of times a 1 or a 5 does not show is:

$\frac{2}{3} \times 100 = \frac{200}{3} \doteq 67$

The predicted number of times a 1 or a 5 shows and the predicted number of times a 1 or a 5 does not show are:

$33 + 67 = 100$

An outcome occurs or it does not occur. So,

| Predicted number of times an outcome occurs | + | Predicted number of times the outcome does not occur | = | Number of times the experiment is conducted |

In the *Example* part c, in 100 rolls, a 1 or a 5 will show about 33 times. This does not mean that a 1 or a 5 will show *exactly* 33 times, but the number of times will likely be close to 33.

The more times an experiment is conducted, the closer the experimental probability is to the theoretical probability.

## Practice

**1.** A bag contains these granola bars: 12 apple, 14 banana, 18 raisin, and 10 regular. You pick one bar at random. Find the probability of choosing:

   **a)** a banana granola bar      **b)** an apple granola bar

When you see the word "probability" in a sentence, it means theoretical probability.

**2.** There are 8 names in a hat. You pick one name without looking. Find each probability.

   **a)** A three-letter name will be picked.

   **b)** A five-letter name will be picked.

   **c)** Laura will be picked.

   **d)** Jorge will not be picked.

**Number Strategies**

Simplify.
- $\frac{5}{8} + \frac{3}{4}$
- $\frac{4}{5} - \frac{2}{3}$
- $1\frac{3}{10} + 2\frac{1}{2}$
- $\frac{2}{3} + \frac{2}{5} + \frac{3}{10}$

**3.** Is each statement true or false? Explain.

   **a)** If you toss a coin 10 times, you will never get 10 heads.

   **b)** If you toss a coin 10 times, you will always get exactly 5 heads.

   **c)** If you toss a coin many times, the number of heads should be approximately $\frac{1}{2}$ the number of tosses.

**4.** The pointer on this spinner is spun 100 times. Is each statement true or false? Justify your answer.

   **a)** The pointer will land on *Win* about 33 times.

   **b)** The pointer will land on *Win*, *Lose*, and *Tie* an equal number of times.

   **c)** The pointer will land on *Lose* exactly 33 times.

**5.** Two hundred fifty tickets for a draw were sold. The first ticket drawn wins the prize.

   **a)** Joe purchased 1 ticket. What is the probability Joe will win?

   **b)** Maria purchased 10 tickets. What is the probability Maria will win?

   **c)** Ivan purchased 25 tickets. What is the probability Ivan will *not* win?

**6.** **Assessment Focus**

   **a)** Construct a spinner with red, yellow, blue, and green sectors, so the following probabilities are true.
   - The probability of landing on red is $\frac{1}{4}$.
   - The probability of landing on yellow is $\frac{1}{2}$.
   - The probability of landing on blue is $\frac{1}{6}$.
   - The probability of landing on green is $\frac{1}{12}$.

   Explain how you drew your spinner.

   **b)** In 200 trials, about how many times would the pointer land on each colour?

   **c)** Suppose the spinner had been constructed so the probability of landing on yellow was $\frac{1}{4}$.
   What effect would this have on the probability of landing on each other colour? Explain.

**Reflect**

How are theoretical probability and experimental probability similar? Different?
Use an example to explain.

### Explore

Work with a partner.
You will play the *Sum and Product* game.
You will need 4 blank cards and a bag.
Write the numbers from 1 to 4 on the cards.
Place the cards in the bag.
Each person picks a card.
Both of you find the sum and the product of the two numbers.
One of you is Player A, the other is Player B.
If the sum is less than or equal to the product, Player A gets a point.
If the sum is greater than the product, Player B gets a point.

➤ Who is likely to win? Explain your reasoning.
➤ Play the game several times; you choose how many times. Who won?
➤ How does your prediction of the winner compare with your result?

### Reflect & Share

Compare your results with those of another pair of classmates.
Work together to come up with an explanation of who is more likely to win.

### Connect

➤ Probability can be expressed as a fraction, a decimal, or a percent. When probability is expressed as a percent, we use the word "chance."
For example, the weather forecast is a 40% chance of rain today. This means that the probability of rain is: $\frac{40}{100} = 0.4$

➤ When an outcome is certain, the probability of it occurring is 1. For example, when we toss a coin, the probability of it landing heads or tails is 1.
When an outcome is impossible, the probability of it occurring is 0. For example, when we roll a number cube labelled 1 to 6, the probability of a 7 showing is 0.

**Example**

Flick This is an Ultimate Frisbee team.
The team plays 3 games against 3 other teams.
All 4 teams have equal chances of winning.

a) What is the chance that Flick This will win all three of its games?

b) What is the chance that Flick This will win exactly one game?

c) What is the chance that Flick This will win at least two games?

**Solution**

For any game, the possible outcomes are win (W) or lose (L).
These outcomes are equally likely. Draw a tree diagram to list the possible results of 3 games for Flick This.

| 1st Game | 2nd Game | 3rd Game | Outcomes |
|----------|----------|----------|----------|
| | | W | WWW |
| | W | L | WWL |
| W | | W | WLW |
| | L | L | WLL |
| | | W | LWW |
| | W | L | LWL |
| L | | W | LLW |
| | L | L | LLL |

There are 8 possible outcomes.

a) There is 1 outcome in which Flick This wins all three games: WWW
So, the probability of 3 wins is: $\frac{1}{8} = 0.125$
So, the chance of winning 3 games is 12.5%.

**The word "exactly" is included because "winning one game" might be interpreted as winning one or more games.**

b) There are 3 outcomes in which Flick This wins exactly one game: WLL, LWL, LLW
So, the probability of winning exactly 1 game is: $\frac{3}{8} = 0.375$
So, the chance of winning exactly 1 game is 37.5%.

c) There are 4 outcomes in which Flick This wins at least two games: WWW, WWL, WLW, LWW
So, the probability of winning at least 2 games is: $\frac{4}{8} = \frac{1}{2} = 0.5$
So, the chance of winning at least 2 games is 50%.

1. The 1st, 2nd, and 3rd place winners of a contest can be female or male. This tree diagram shows the possible outcomes of the contest.

| 1st Place | 2nd Place | 3rd Place | Outcomes |
|---|---|---|---|
| | | F | FFF |
| | F | M | FFM |
| F | | F | FMF |
| | M | M | FMM |
| | | F | MFF |
| | F | M | MFM |
| M | | F | MMF |
| | M | M | MMM |

   a) How many possible outcomes are there?
   b) What is the probability that all the winners are female?
   c) What is the probability that none of the winners is male?
   d) How are the answers to parts b and c related? Explain.

2. On this spinner, the pointer is spun once.
   The colour is recorded.
   The pointer is spun a second time.
   The colour is recorded.

   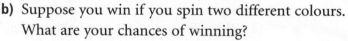

   a) Suppose you win if you spin the
      same colour on both spins.
      What are your chances of winning?
   b) Suppose you win if you spin two different colours.
      What are your chances of winning?

3. a) Three coins are tossed. Find the chance of tossing:
      i) one heads and two tails   ii) exactly two heads
      iii) at least two tails          iv) no heads
   b) Why do we need the words "at least" in part a, iii?
      What if these words were left out?
      How would the answer change?
   c) Why do we need the word "exactly" in part a, ii? What if this
      word was left out? How would the answer change?

4. At a carnival, the game with the least chance of winning often
   has the greatest prize. Explain why this might be.

5. There are four children in a family.
   What is the chance of each event?
   a) There are two boys and two girls.
   b) There is at least one girl.
   c) All four children are of the same gender.

6. **Assessment Focus**   The school cafeteria has this lunch menu.
   A student chooses a sandwich and a vegetable. Assume the
   choice is random.
   a) Find the probability of each
      possible combination.
   b) Suppose 3 desserts were added
      to the menu. Each student
      chooses a sandwich, a
      vegetable, and a dessert.
      How would the probabilities of
      possible combinations change?
      Use examples to explain your thinking.

| Lunch Menu | |
|---|---|
| **Sandwich** | **Vegetable** |
| Grilled Cheese | Broccoli |
| Chicken | Carrots |
| Tuna | |

**Take It Further**

7. At the school carnival, there is a game with two spinners.

Spinner A

Spinner B

You get two spins.
You may spin the pointer on each spinner once, or spin the
pointer on one spinner twice.
If you get pink on one spin and yellow on another spin (the order
does not matter), you win.
To have the greatest chance of winning, what should you do?
Explain.

**Calculator Skills**

Which three
consecutive prime
numbers have a
product of 7429
and a sum of 59?

**Reflect**

How is probability related to chance?
Use an example in your explanation.

# Choosing a Strategy

## Strategies

- Make a table.
- Use a model.
- Draw a diagram.
- Solve a simpler problem.
- Work backward.
- Guess and check.
- Make an organized list.
- Use a pattern.
- Draw a graph.
- Use logical reasoning.

**1.** For her birthday, Janine was given a row of 25 pennies.
Her father replaced every second coin with a nickel.
Her mother replaced every third coin with a dime.
Her brother replaced every fourth coin with a quarter.
Her uncle replaced every fifth coin with a loonie.
How much did Janine get on her birthday?

**2.** Arif has a part-time job.
He was offered $96 per week or $4.50/h.
Which is the better deal? Explain.

**3.** **a)** The perimeter of a rectangle is 36 cm.
What is the maximum possible area of the rectangle?
**b)** The sum of the length, width, and height of a rectangular prism is 18 cm.
What is the maximum possible volume of the prism?

**4.** What fraction of this figure is shaded?

**5.** Divide the square at the left into four congruent figures.
Record each way you find on dot paper.
Find at least ten different ways to do this.

**6.** Running shoes cost $79.99. They are on sale for 20% off.
The sales tax of 15% has to be added.
Which would you choose? Explain.
**a)** Take the 20% off the price, then add the 15% sales tax.
**b)** Add the 15% sales tax, then take off the 20%.

**7.** The Magic Money Box doubles any amount of money placed in it, then adds $1 to it.
Yesterday I placed a sum of money in the box and got a new amount.
Today I put the new amount in the box and got $75 out.
How much did I put in the box yesterday?

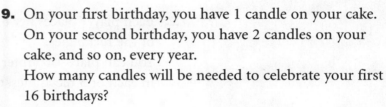
**8.** Play this game with a partner.
Each of you needs an octahedron
and a cube like these:
The faces of a red octahedron are
labelled from +1 to +8.
The faces of a white cube are
labelled from +1 to +6.
Take turns to roll the two solids.
Subtract the red number from
the white number.
The person with the lesser number
scores a point.
The first person to reach 20 points
is the winner.

**9.** On your first birthday, you have 1 candle on your cake.
On your second birthday, you have 2 candles on your
cake, and so on, every year.
How many candles will be needed to celebrate your first
16 birthdays?

**10.** A radio station plays an average of 16 songs every hour.
One-half the songs are pop, one-quarter are jazz,
one-eighth are country, and the rest are classical.
One show is 3 h long. The songs are played at random.
**a)** How many classical songs would be played?
**b)** What is the probability that the first song played
is jazz?

**11.** An octahedron has eight faces labelled 1 to 8.
A cube has six faces labelled 1 to 6.
**a)** Both solids are rolled. What is the probability that the
sum of the numbers is 8?
**b)** Both solids are rolled. What is the probability that the
sum of the numbers is a prime number?

**Game**

## HOW TO PLAY THE GAME:

**1.** Each player draws 6 rectangles on a piece of paper.

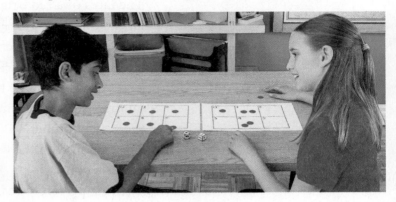

Label each rectangle from 0 to 5.

**2.** Each player places her 6 counters in any or all of the rectangles.
You can place 1 counter in each rectangle, or 2 counters in each of 3 rectangles, or even 6 counters in 1 rectangle.

**3.** Take turns to roll the number cubes.
Find the difference of the numbers.
You remove counters from the rectangle labelled with that number.
For example, if you roll a 6 and a 4, then 6 − 4 = 2; so, remove all counters from rectangle 2.

**4.** The winner is the first person to have no counters left in any rectangle.

### YOU WILL NEED

2 number cubes labelled 1 to 6; 12 counters

### NUMBER OF PLAYERS

2

### GOAL OF THE GAME

To remove all counters from all rectangles

What strategies can you use to improve your chances of winning this game?

### Sports

You know that a batting average of 0.300 means that a player has an average of 3 hits in 10 at bats. Research other examples of relative frequency in sport. Write what you find out.

# Unit Review

## What Do I Need to Know?

☑ Relative frequency $= \dfrac{\text{Number of times an outcome occurs}}{\text{Number of times experiment is conducted}}$

☑ Theoretical probability $= \dfrac{\text{Number of favourable outcomes}}{\text{Number of possible outcomes}}$

## What Should I Be Able to Do?

For extra practice, go to page 448.

**LESSON**

**11.1**

**1. a)** Use a tree diagram to show the possible combinations for a breakfast. You can choose:
- a banana, an orange, or an apple
- carrots, celery, or cucumber, and
- yogurt or cheese

**b)** How many outcomes have a banana and cheese?

**c)** How many outcomes have an orange, celery, or a yogurt?

**d)** How many outcomes do not have an apple?

**2.** Four coins are tossed.
**a)** List all the possible outcomes.
**b)** How many outcomes have exactly 1 head?
**c)** How many outcomes have exactly 2 tails?
**d)** How many outcomes have at least 3 tails?

**11.2**

**3.** A biologist tested a new vaccine. She found that in 500 trials, the test was successful 450 times.
**a)** What is the relative frequency that the vaccine is successful?
**b)** Suppose the vaccine is used on 15 000 people. How many successes can be expected?

**4.** The owner of a shop recorded customer sales for one week.

| Gender | Purchase | No Purchase | Total |
|--------|----------|-------------|-------|
| Male   | 125      | 65          | 190   |
| Female | 154      | 46          | 200   |

Determine the relative frequency of each outcome.
**a)** A customer is male.
**b)** A customer is female.
**c)** A customer makes a purchase.
**d)** A male does not make a purchase.
**e)** A female makes a purchase.

**5.** Is each statement true or false? Explain.
   **a)** When a coin is tossed 100 times, it will never show tails 100 times.
   **b)** When a coin is tossed 100 times, it is unlikely to show heads 100 times.
   **c)** When a coin is tossed 100 times, it will show tails exactly 50 times.
   **d)** The more often a coin is tossed, the more likely that $\frac{1}{2}$ the results will be tails.

**11.3** **6.** In a game show, each contestant spins the wheel once to win the money shown.

   **a)** Are the probabilities of winning the amounts equally likely? Explain.
   **b)** What is the probability of winning $100?
   **c)** What is the probability of winning less than $50?
   **d)** What is the probability of winning from $30 to $70?

**7.** Twenty cards are numbered from 1 to 20. The cards are shuffled. A card is drawn. Find the probability that the card has:

   **a)** an odd number
   **b)** a multiple of 4
   **c)** a number that is not a perfect square
   **d)** a prime number

**11.4** **8.** Each of the numbers 1 to 15 is written on a separate card. The cards are shuffled and placed in a pile face down. A card is picked from the pile. Its number is recorded. The card is returned to the pile. In 99 trials, about how many times would you expect each outcome?
   **a)** a 6
   **b)** a multiple of 3
   **c)** a number less than 10
   **d)** an even number

**9.** What is the chance of each outcome?
   **a)** tossing 2 coins and getting:
      **i)** 2 heads
      **ii)** 1 tail and 2 heads
   **b)** tossing 3 coins and getting:
      **i)** 1 head and 2 tails
      **ii)** at least 1 tail

**10.** An electronic game has three coloured sectors. A colour lights up at random, followed by a colour lighting up at random again. What is the chance the two consecutive colours are the same?

# Practice Test

1. A theatre shows movies on Saturday and Sunday.
   There are matinee and evening shows.
   There are adult, child, and senior rates.
   Draw a tree diagram to show the possible ticket types.

2. A number cube is labelled 1 to 6.
   The cube is rolled 60 times.
   Predict how many times each outcome will occur.
   Explain each answer.
   a) 1 is rolled.
   b) An even number is rolled.
   c) A number greater than 3 is rolled.
   d) 9 is rolled.

3. a) In Sarah's first 30 times at bat, she had 9 hits.
      What is Sarah's batting average?
   b) In Sarah's next game, she had 3 hits in 4 times at bat.
      What is Sarah's new batting average?
   c) How many hits would you expect Sarah to have in 90 times at
      bat? Explain your reasoning.

4. A number cube is labelled 1 to 6.
   Suppose you roll a number cube twice.
   Is it more likely you will get a 3 then a 5, or a 3 then a 3?
   Explain your reasoning.

5. In the game "rock, paper, scissors," 2 players make hand signs.
   Players can make a hand sign for rock, paper, or scissors.
   On the count of 3, players show
   their hand signs.
   Suppose the players choose
   their signs at random.
   In 75 games, how many times
   would you expect to see both
   players showing rock?

**Part 1**

Emma and Jonah created a spinner game called Match/No-Match.
Two people play the game.
A player spins the pointer twice.

If the pointer lands on the same colour (a match), the player scores.
If the pointer lands on different colours (a no-match),
the opponent scores.

Jonah and Emma reasoned that, since there are two matching
combinations (red/red and green/green), a player should score
only 1 point for a match, and the opponent should score
2 points for a no-match.

Play the Match/No-Match game. Take at least 50 turns each.

Use the results to find the relative frequency of a match and of a no-match.

List the possible outcomes of a turn (two spins).
Find the theoretical probability of a match and a no-match.

Do you think the players have equal chances of winning? Explain.

**Part 2**

Design a game using spinners, number cubes, coins, or any other materials.
The game should use two different items.

Play the game.

Do the players have equal chances of winning? Explain.
Calculate some probabilities related to your game.
Show your work.

**Check List**

Your work should show:

✓ all calculations of frequency or probability, in detail

✓ diagrams, tables, or lists to show possible outcomes and results of each game

✓ an explanation of players' chances of winning each game

✓ correct use of the language of probability

## Reflect on the Unit

Give at least two examples of how you use probability in everyday life.

# Cross Strand Investigation

## A Population Simulation

Work with a partner.

An animal population changes from year to year depending on the rates of birth and death, and on the movement of the animals. A **simulation** is a model of a real situation. You will use a simulation to investigate how an animal population might decline.

As you complete this *Investigation*, include your completed table, graph, and written answers to the questions. You will hand these in.

**Materials:**

- a paper cup
- 30 to 40 two-sided counters
- 0.5-cm grid paper

➤ The counters are the animals in your population.
  Count the number of animals.
  Record that number for Year 0 in the *Population* table.
➤ Put the counters in the cup.
  Choose which colour will be "face up."
  Pour the counters from the cup.
  Counters that land face up represent animals that died or moved away during the first year. Set them aside.
  Count the number of animals left.

Record that number as the population for Year 1.
Calculate and record the decrease in population.
Write the decrease as a fraction of the previous year's population.
Write the fraction as a percent.
➤ Place the counters representing live animals back in the cup.
Repeat the experiment for Year 2.
Record the data for Year 2 in the table.
➤ Continue the simulation. Record your data for up to 8 years, or until you run out of animals.
➤ Graph the population data.
Plot *Year* horizontally and *Number of Animals* vertically.
Explain your choice of graph.
What trends do you see in the graph?

| Population | | | | | | | | | |
|---|---|---|---|---|---|---|---|---|---|
| Year | 0 | 1 | 2 | 3 | 4 | 5 | 6 | 7 | 8 |
| Number of animals | | | | | | | | | |
| Decrease in population | | | | | | | | | |
| Change as a fraction | | | | | | | | | |
| Change as a percent | | | | | | | | | |

➤ Describe the patterns you see in the table. Approximately what fraction and percent of the population remain from year to year?
➤ Use the patterns to predict the population for Year 9.
➤ How long does it take the population of animals to decrease to one-half its original size?
➤ What would happen to a population if there were no births to add to the population each year?

## Take It Further

➤ Suppose you repeated this experiment, beginning with more animals. Would you see the same pattern? Explain.
Combine your data with data of other students to find out.
➤ Which environmental factors may cause an animal population to change?

**UNIT**

**1**  **1.** Write the first 5 multiplies of each number.
a) 6          b) 9          c) 12

**2.** Write all the factors of each number.
a) 36          b) 57          c) 75

**2**  **3.** There are two patchwork quilts.
In quilt A, the ratio of red squares to green squares is 5:7.
In quilt B, the ratio of red squares to green squares is 4:5.
The quilts are the same size.
Which quilt has more red squares?
Use grid paper to show your answer.

**3**  **4. a)** Write the formula for the surface area of a cube, with edge length $c$ units.
**b)** Write the formula for the surface area of a rectangular prism with dimensions $l$ units by $w$ units by $h$ units.
**c)** How can you get the formula for the surface area of a cube from the formula for the surface area of a rectangular prism? Use pictures in your explanation.

**4**  **5.** Add or subtract.
a) $2\frac{3}{4} - 1\frac{1}{3}$
b) $3\frac{1}{3} + 2\frac{3}{5}$
c) $3\frac{4}{5} - 2\frac{1}{10}$
d) $\frac{3}{10} + 1\frac{1}{2}$
e) $\frac{3}{8} + \frac{7}{4} + \frac{7}{2}$
f) $\frac{9}{10} + \frac{1}{2} + \frac{6}{5}$

**6.** Divide. Round the quotient to the nearest tenth where necessary.
a) $7.22 \div 1.9$
b) $7.22 \div 2.1$
c) $8.97 \div 2.3$
d) $8.98 \div 2.4$

**5**  **7. a)** The people who run the cafeteria survey students about their favourite foods.
How might the survey results affect the menu?
**b)** A local hair salon collects data on the number of clients who would like hair appointments on Sundays.
How might these data affect the days the salon is open?

**8.** Annette's practice times for a downhill ski run, in seconds, are:
122, 137, 118, 119, 124, 118, 120, 118
**a)** Find the mean time.
**b)** Find the median time.
**c)** Find the mode time.
**d)** Which measure of central tendency best represents the times? Explain.
**e)** What is the range?
**f)** What time must Annette get in her next run so the median is 120 s? Explain.
**g)** What time must Annette get in her next run so the mean is 121 s? Is this possible? Explain.

**9. a)** What does this table show?

| Toronto Blue Jays' Average Game Attendance ||
|---|---|
| Year | Average Attendance |
| 1991 | 47 966 |
| 1992 | 49 402 |
| 1993 | 49 732 |
| 1994 | 50 098 |
| 1995 | 39 257 |
| 1996 | 31 600 |
| 1997 | 31 967 |
| 1998 | 30 300 |
| 1999 | 26 710 |
| 2000 | 21 058 |
| 2001 | 23 690 |
| 2002 | 20 209 |
| 2003 | 22 215 |

**b)** Do you think the average is the mean, the median, or the mode? Explain your choice.

**c)** Draw a line graph to display these data.

**d)** What trends does the graph show?
Find out what happened to change the trend.

**e)** Draw a graph to display the data each way.

  **i)** The marketing department wants attendance to look as great as possible.

  **ii)** The shareholders want to show that the attendance is too low.

**f)** Explain how each graph in part e shows what was intended.

**6** **10.** Find the area of each figure.

**a)**

**b)**

**c)**

**d)**

**11.** If you can, find the perimeter of each figure in question 10. For which figures can you not find the perimeter? Explain.

**7  12. a)** Plot these points on a grid: A(3, 2), B(4, 5), C(7, 5), and D(8, 4).
Join the points to draw figure ABCD.
**b)** Translate the figure in part a.
**c)** Rotate the figure in part a.
**d)** Reflect the figure in part a.
Trade grids with a classmate. Identify each of your classmate's transformations.

**8  13.** A sweater is on sale for 25% off the regular price.
The sale price is $37.50.
What was the regular price?
Sketch a number line to illustrate the answer.

**14.** A theatre has 840 seats. For one performance, the theatre was 75% full.
**a)** How many people were in the theatre?
**b)** By the end of the performance, 30 people had left. How many people were in the theatre then?
**c)** Ninety percent of the remaining audience stood to give the performers a standing ovation. How many people were still sitting?

**9  15.** Order these integers from least to greatest.
$+5, -6, -8, +2, 0, -5, -1$

**16.** Add or subtract. Use coloured tiles or number lines.
**a)** $(+5) + (-9)$
**b)** $(-1) + (-5)$
**c)** $(+2) - (-8)$
**d)** $(-9) - (-3)$

**17.** A rock climber climbed 3 m, was lowered 1 m, then climbed 5 m more.
**a)** How high did she climb?
**b)** The total height of the climb is 10 m. How much farther does she have to climb?
Use coloured tiles if they help.

**18.** The temperature at 6 a.m. is $-10°C$.
During the day, the temperature rises 17°C.
What is the new temperature?

**10  19.** Write each algebraic expression in words.
**a)** $2 - 3x$      **b)** $3x - 2$
**c)** $35 - y$      **d)** $y + 35$
**e)** $2(x + 2)$    **f)** $\frac{z}{5} + 10$

**20.** Write each statement as an algebraic expression.
**a)** a number divided by twelve
**b)** one-twelfth of a number
**c)** eleven added to five times a number

**21.** Students are fund raising by washing cars.
The students charge $6.00 per car.

a) Copy and complete this table.

| Numbers of Cars | Money Collected ($) |
|---|---|
| 5 | |
| 10 | |
| 15 | |
| 20 | |
| 25 | |
| 30 | |

b) Graph the data in the table in part a.

c) What patterns do you see in the table? How could you extend each pattern?

d) Suppose you know how many cars were washed. How can you find how much money was collected in each case?
  i) by using the table
  ii) by using the graph

e) Suppose 27 cars were washed. How much money was collected?
How many different ways can you find the answer? Explain.

**22.** Solve each equation.

a) $2x + 3 = 15$

b) $\frac{x}{3} = 15$

c) $\frac{15}{x} = 3$

d) $2x - 3 = 15$

**23.** Evan had $852.00.
He shared the money equally with his brother and sister.

a) Write an equation you can solve to find out how much money each person got.

b) Solve the equation.

**24.** a) What are the possible outcomes when 3 coins are tossed?

b) What is the probability of each outcome?

c) Design and conduct an experiment to find the relative frequency of each outcome.

d) Write each relative frequency as a decimal.

e) How do the probabilities and relative frequencies compare? Is this what you expect? Explain.

**25.** Each letter of the word PROBABILITY is written on a card. The cards are placed in a box. Suppose you pick a card, at random, record the letter, then replace the card.
In 55 trials, about how many times would you expect each outcome?

a) a P   b) a B   c) a vowel   d) an X

**26.** Anca rolls two number cubes labelled 3 to 8. She adds the numbers that show on the cubes. List the possible outcomes. Use a tree diagram if it helps.

# Extra Practice

**1.** Jean bought DVDs that cost $23, $18, $29, $52, and $24, including tax. How much did he spend?

**2.** Canada has 891 163 km² of water. One hundred fifty-eight thousand three hundred sixty-four square kilometres of this water is in Ontario. How much water is in the rest of Canada?

**3.** An auditorium has 1456 seats. There are 28 seats in each row. How many rows are there?

**4.** One pair of running shoes costs $99. How much would 99 pairs cost? How can you find out using mental math?

**5.** The average Canadian walks and runs about 193 000 km in a lifetime.
   **a)** About how far is this per year? Per week?
   **b)** Do you think the estimates in part a are reasonable? Explain.

**6.** Find the factors of each number.
   **a)** 36         **b)** 56         **c)** 96

**7.** Write the first 10 multiples of each number.
   **a)** 12         **b)** 15         **c)** 20

**8.** Find the greatest common factor of each pair of numbers.
   **a)** 18, 42         **b)** 60, 33
   **c)** 25, 75         **d)** 48, 84

**9.** Find the square of each number.
   **a)** 7         **b)** 17
   **c)** 27         **d)** 37

**10.** Find the lowest common multiple of each pair of numbers.
   **a)** 18, 8         **b)** 24, 10
   **c)** 36, 15         **d)** 42, 24

**11.** Find a square root of each number. Use grid paper. Draw a diagram to show each square root.
   **a)** 81         **b)** 144
   **c)** 225         **d)** 400

**12. a)** Find the area of a square with side length 14 cm.
   **b)** What is the perimeter of the square?

**13. a)** Find the side length of a square with area 900 m².
   **b)** What is the perimeter of the square?

**14.** Find the perimeter of a square with area 169 cm².

**15.** What is the volume of a cube with edge length 15 cm? How can you use exponents to find out?

**16.** Write in exponent form.
   **a)** $4 \times 4 \times 4 \times 4 \times 4$
   **b)** $12 \times 12 \times 12 \times 12$

**17. a)** Evaluate.
   **i)** $5 \times 9 + 5$
   **ii)** $56 \times 9 + 6$
   **iii)** $567 \times 9 + 7$
   **b)** Predict the answer for $5678 \times 9 + 8$. Use a calculator to check.

**1. a)** Draw a diagram to show the ratio 6:7.
   **b)** Draw a diagram to show the ratio 2:7.

**2.** Write each ratio in simplest form.
   **a)** 22:11      **b)** 21:12
   **c)** 25:15      **d)** 14:56

**3.** Write three ratios equivalent to each ratio. Show your work in tables.
   **a)** 5:7      **b)** 36:10
   **c)** 9:4      **d)** 32:44

**4.** Use these diagrams.

Figure A

Figure B

Figure C

Which diagram shows each red to blue ratio?
   **a)** 2:1      **b)** 2:3      **c)** 3:5

**5.** Arlene is 12 years old.
   Her brother is 4 years old.
   **a)** What is the ratio of their ages?
   **b)** What will the ratio be in one year?
   **c)** How old will Arlene and her brother be when the ratio of their ages is 2:1?

**6.** Two buckets contain equal numbers of Pattern Blocks. In Bucket A, the ratio of triangles to squares is 1:3. In Bucket B, the ratio of triangles to squares is 3:4.
   **a)** Which bucket contains more triangles? More squares? How do you know?
   **b)** What is the ratio of the number of triangles in Bucket A to the number of squares in Bucket B?

**7.** In a hockey club storeroom, the ratio of sticks to helmets is 5:3.
   **a)** There are 12 helmets.
      How many sticks are there?
   **b)** One new stick is added. What is the new ratio of sticks to helmets?

**8.** On a school trip, the ratio of boys to girls is 4 to 5.
   The ratio of girls to adults is 7 to 2.
   **a)** What is the ratio of boys and girls to adults?
   **b)** One hundred forty-six people went on the trip. How many were girls?

**9.** Find a pair of numbers between 30 and 50 that have a ratio of 6:5. How many different pairs can you find?

**10.** A spice mixture contains 5 g of coriander, 3 g of cumin, and 2 g of peppercorns.
   **a)** What is the ratio of the mass of each spice to the total mass?
   **b)** How much of each spice is needed to make 1 kg of spice mixture?

**1.** Use 3 linking cubes.
Use square dot paper.
   **a)** Make an object.
   Draw the front, back, side, and top
   views of the object.
   **b)** How many different objects can you
   make with 3 linking cubes?
   Make each additional object.
   Draw its front, back, side, and
   top views.

**2.** Find each object in the classroom.
Sketch its front, back, top, and side views.
   **a)** bookcase   **b)** table   **c)** pencil

**3.** Draw a pictorial diagram of each solid.
   **a)**

   **b)**

   **c)**

   **d)**

**4. a)** Draw the cube in question 3 on
   isometric dot paper.
   **b)** Draw the rectangular prism in
   question 3 on isometric dot paper.

**5.** Use 4 linking cubes.
Make an object that is not a
rectangular prism.
Draw the object on isometric dot paper.

**6.** Use formulas.
   **a)** Find the area and perimeter of a
   rectangle with base 12.5 cm and
   height 3.6 cm.
   **b)** Find the area and perimeter of a
   square with side length 5.6 m.

**7.** Use formulas.
   **a)** Find the surface area of a rectangular
   prism with length 6 cm, height 7 cm,
   and width 4 cm.
   **b)** Find the volume of the prism in part a.
   **c)** Find the surface area of a cube with
   edge length 1.8 cm.
   **d)** Find the volume of the cube in part c.

**8.** Anthony is wrapping a birthday gift in
a box that measures 30 cm by 20 cm
by 8 cm.
   **a)** What is the surface area of the box?
   **b)** How much wrapping paper is
   needed if allowance is made for
   overlap? Sketch a diagram to
   illustrate your answer.

**9.** A shed has the shape of a rectangular
prism. It is 2 m high, 3 m wide, and
4 m long. The walls and doors are to
be painted inside and out. The roof,
ceilings, and floor are to be painted.
The shed has two windows; each
measures 1 m by 1 m. What is the area
that will be painted?

1. Write in simplest form.
   a) $\frac{18}{12}$
   b) $\frac{12}{27}$
   c) $\frac{6}{9}$
   d) $\frac{8}{4}$

2. Draw a diagram to show how to write each improper fraction as a mixed number.
   a) $\frac{5}{3}$
   b) $\frac{7}{5}$
   c) $\frac{14}{4}$
   d) $\frac{22}{6}$

3. Use a calculator.
   Write each fraction as a decimal.
   a) $\frac{17}{18}$
   b) $\frac{13}{4}$
   c) $\frac{3}{5}$
   d) $\frac{7}{3}$

4. Use fraction strips and number lines to add.
   a) $\frac{2}{3} + \frac{3}{2}$
   b) $\frac{1}{4} + \frac{7}{8}$
   c) $\frac{3}{5} + \frac{2}{10}$
   d) $\frac{5}{3} + \frac{1}{12}$

5. The sum: $\frac{2}{3} + \frac{1}{5}$ is $\frac{13}{15}$.
   Use this result to add these fractions.
   a) $1\frac{2}{3} + 1\frac{1}{5}$
   b) $3\frac{2}{3} + \frac{1}{5}$
   c) $\frac{1}{3} + \frac{1}{5} + \frac{1}{3}$
   d) $\frac{1}{5} + 1\frac{2}{3}$

6. Use fraction strips and number lines to subtract.
   a) $\frac{7}{8} - \frac{1}{2}$
   b) $\frac{7}{6} - \frac{2}{4}$
   c) $1 - \frac{5}{8}$
   d) $\frac{11}{6} - \frac{2}{3}$

7. Add.
   a) $\frac{1}{5} + \frac{3}{8}$
   b) $\frac{5}{4} + \frac{1}{6}$
   c) $\frac{4}{3} + \frac{1}{5}$
   d) $\frac{7}{6} + \frac{1}{8}$

8. Subtract.
   a) $\frac{7}{4} - \frac{4}{3}$
   b) $\frac{6}{5} - \frac{5}{6}$
   c) $\frac{3}{5} - \frac{2}{4}$
   d) $\frac{7}{8} - \frac{4}{5}$

9. Add.
   a) $\frac{2}{3} + \frac{1}{2} + \frac{3}{4}$
   b) $\frac{2}{5} + \frac{3}{10} + \frac{5}{2}$
   c) $\frac{4}{9} + \frac{5}{6} + \frac{1}{3}$
   d) $\frac{3}{2} + \frac{1}{6} + \frac{4}{5}$

10. Write each sum as a multiplication question.
    a) $\frac{3}{5} + \frac{3}{5} + \frac{3}{5} + \frac{3}{5} + \frac{3}{5}$
    b) $\frac{7}{4} + \frac{7}{4} + \frac{7}{4}$

11. Find each sum in question 10.

12. Multiply.
    Draw a diagram to show each answer.
    a) $\frac{2}{8} \times 5$
    b) $\frac{11}{6} \times 3$
    c) $4 \times \frac{7}{2}$
    d) $6 \times \frac{1}{8}$

13. Multiply.
    Draw a picture on grid paper to show the product.
    a) $2.3 \times 3.4$
    b) $1.8 \times 2.2$
    c) $4.1 \times 3.7$
    d) $1.7 \times 2.9$

14. Divide.
    a) $3.5 \div 1.4$
    b) $18.2 \div 5.2$
    c) $10.08 \div 3.6$
    d) $6.75 \div 4.5$

15. Find the area of a rectangular vegetable plot with length 10.8 m and width 5.2 m.

16. A rectangular quilt has area 3.15 m². The quilt is 2.1 m long. What is its width?

17. One kilogram of grapes cost $5.89.
    a) How much do 2.4 kg cost?
    b) How much change is there from a $20-bill?

18. Evaluate.
    a) $3.5 + 2.4 \times 1.7 - 3.8$
    b) $15.3 - 8.75 \div 2.5 \times 1.2$

**1.** This graph was produced with a spreadsheet program.

**Mexico City Temperatures**

**a)** What is the approximate high temperature in May? In June?

**b)** Estimate the difference between the average high and the average low temperatures in October.

**c)** During which months does the average high temperature increase? When does the average low temperature increase?

**d)** Write one question for which each following statement is the answer.

   **i)** The highest temperature is about 26°C.

   **ii)** The lowest temperature is about 13°C.

**2.** The table shows the approximate areas of some countries.

| Country | Area (km²) |
|---------|-----------|
| Austria | 84 000 |
| Costa Rica | 51 000 |
| Denmark | 43 000 |
| Greece | 132 000 |
| Japan | 378 000 |
| Italy | 301 000 |
| Spain | 195 000 |

**a)** Draw a bar graph. Explain why a line graph would not be appropriate.

**b)** Use your graph. Estimate the difference between the areas of Greece and Italy.

**c)** Use the table. Estimate the difference between the areas of Greece and Italy.

**d)** Look at a map of Europe. Are your answers for parts b and c reasonable?

**e)** Estimate the sum of the areas of Austria, Denmark, and Spain. Explain how you estimated the sum.

**3.** Here are the heights in centimetres of some 12-year-old students.
125, 152, 134, 141, 153, 127, 168, 154, 139, 147, 132, 137, 163, 133

**a)** Draw a stem-and-leaf plot.

**b)** What is the median height?

**c)** What is the mode? The mean?

**4.** The median shoe size of eight 12-year-old boys is $6\frac{1}{2}$. What might the shoe sizes be? Explain your answer.

**5.** Here are the times, in minutes and seconds, for 28 swimmers who raced in the 200-m backstroke:
2:25, 3:01, 1:45, 3:15, 2:30, 2:54, 3:10, 1:59, 2:25, 3:10, 3:09, 2:43, 2:18, 3:04, 2:53, 2:28, 3:14, 2:37, 3:03, 2:39, 2:27, 2:43, 3:09, 2:54, 3:11, 2:38, 2:42, 2:57

**a)** Draw a stem-and-leaf plot.

**b)** What is the range?

**c)** Which stem has the most leaves? What does this mean?

**d)** What is the median time?

**e)** What is the mode time?

1. **a)** On 0.5-cm grid paper, draw 3 different parallelograms with base 5.5 cm and height 8.5 cm.
   **b)** What is the area of each parallelogram in part a?

2. On 0.5-cm grid paper, draw 3 different parallelograms with area 24 cm². What is the base and height of each parallelogram?

3. Use a formula. Find the area of a parallelogram with base 11.3 cm and height 5.7 cm.

4. The window below consists of 5 pieces of glass. Each piece that is a parallelogram has a base of 1.6 m. What is the area of one parallelogram?

2.4 m

5. The base of each triangle in the window above is 0.8 m.
   **a)** What is the area of one triangle?
   **b)** What is the area of the window? Explain how you found the area.

6. **a)** On 0.5 cm-grid paper, draw 3 different triangles with base 4.5 cm and height 7.5 cm.
   **b)** What is the area of each triangle in part a?

7. On 0.5-cm grid paper, draw 3 different triangles with area 12 cm².
   **a)** What is the base and height of each triangle?
   **b)** How are the triangles in part a related to the parallelograms in question 2?

8. Use a formula. Find the area of a triangle with base 4.3 cm and height 2.6 cm.

9. **a)** Find the area of the shaded region in the square below.

4.8 cm
2.4 cm
1.2 cm

   **b)** How many different ways can you find the area? Explain each way.
   **c)** Estimate the perimeter of the shaded region in part a.
   **d)** Can you calculate the perimeter of the shaded region in part a? Explain.

10. Calculate the perimeter and area of this figure.

3.4 m
3.0 m
1.6 m
0.6 m
4.2 m

Use these figures for questions 1 to 5.

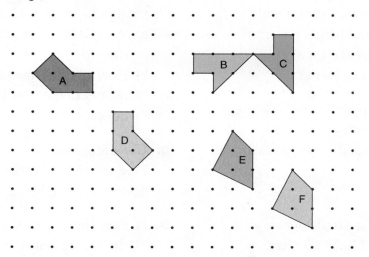

1. Classify each figure. Describe its attributes.

2. Identify pairs of congruent figures. Explain how you know the figures are congruent.

3. Identify the transformation that each pair of congruent figures represents.

4. a) Use one figure from each pair. Try to tile the plane with each figure. Identify the figures that tile the plane.
   b) For each figure that does not tile the plane:
      • Find another figure that combines with the figure to tile the plane.
      • Tile the plane with the two figures combined.

5. Use one tiling pattern from question 4. Use one of each type of figures. Explain how you can use transformations to tile the plane.

6. Use square dot paper or isometric dot paper. Draw each polygon.
   a) an equilateral triangle with side length 3 units
   b) a rhombus with base 4 units and an angle of 60°
   c) an acute isosceles triangle

7. Which figures in question 6 have line symmetry? Draw the lines of symmetry on the figures.

8. Plot these points on a grid: A(10, 8), B(10, 10), C(12, 12), D(13, 9) Join the points to make a quadrilateral. Draw the image of the quadrilateral after each transformation.
   a) a translation 3 units right and 4 units up
   b) a reflection in a vertical line through (7, 0)
   c) a rotation of a $\frac{1}{4}$ turn clockwise about A

**1.** Estimate what percent of each figure is shaded. Explain your strategy.

a)

b)

c)

d)
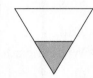

**2.** Write each fraction as a percent, then as a decimal.

a) $\frac{3}{4}$  b) $\frac{3}{2}$  c) $\frac{3}{5}$  d) $\frac{3}{20}$

**3.** Find each percent.
a) 10% of $200  b) 1% of $85
c) 10% of $60  d) 1% of $187
e) 10% of $55  f) 10% of $140
g) 1% of $5  h) 15% of $10

**4.** Find each percent. Explain your strategy.
a) 2% of $100
b) 4% of $300
c) 2% of $700
d) 3% of $800
e) 5% of $3000
f) 9% of $500
g) 4% of $100
h) 5% of $1000

**5.** Leigh drove 1470 km from Smith Falls, ON to Thunder Bay, ON. She stopped 370 km from Smith Falls. About what percent of her trip had she completed when she stopped?

**6.** Calculate the 15% sales tax and the total cost of each item.
a) a bicycle that costs $349.99
b) a CD that costs $17.98

**7.** This year 27 students will graduate from Central School. This is 15% of the school's population. What is the population of the school?

**8.** The depth of deep sea trenches is measured from sea level. The Tonga Trench in the South Pacific is 10 800 m deep. Yap Trench in the West Pacific is 79% of the depth of the Tonga Trench. How deep is the Yap Trench, to the nearest 10 m?

**9.** This graph shows how much time is spent in one day watching different types of TV programs.

**TV Programs**

a) Which type of program is watched for the greatest amount of time?
b) Which two types of programs are watched for approximately the same amount of time?
c) Estimate the fraction of time spent watching sitcoms.
d) Suppose TV is watched for 1000 days. Estimate how much time is spent watching sitcoms.

1. Use an integer to describe each situation.
   a) The water level of Lake Superior rises 5 cm after low tide.
   b) The lowest recorded temperature is 89°C below 0°C recorded at Vostok, Antarctica, in 1983.
   c) A submarine river known as the Cromwell current flows below the surface of the Pacific ocean at depths up to 400 m.
   d) Mount Manaslu in Nepal has a height of 8156 m.

2. Use an integer to describe each situation.
   a) The time is 9 s before take-off.
   b) You earned $25 since yesterday.
   c) The average temperature close to the South Pole is 50°C below 0°C.

3. Sketch a number line. Show the integer that is 3 less than +2.

4. Replace each □ with < or > to make a true statement.
   a) $-3$ □ $+5$     b) $-2$ □ $-4$
   c) $+1$ □ $0$     d) $+8$ □ $-10$

5. Order the integers from least to greatest.
   $0, -2, +4, -15, +1, -1, +5$

6. Write the integer that is out of order.
   a) $-5, -2, +1, +17, +13$
   b) $-34, -7, +3, +7, -12$
   c) $-11, +11, +13, -13, +27$
   d) $-4, -3, +2, -1, 0$

7. Add.
   a) $(+6) + (+9)$     b) $(-4) + (-7)$
   c) $(-8) + (-6)$     d) $(-11) + (+5)$

   e) $(+7) + (-8)$     f) $(-9) + (-12)$
   g) $(+13) + (-3)$     h) $(-5) + (-8)$

8. Subtract.
   a) $(-14) - (+7)$     b) $(+12) - (+9)$
   c) $(+16) - (-4)$     d) $(-11) - (-8)$
   e) $(+22) - (+3)$     f) $(+14) - (-7)$
   g) $(-19) - (-11)$     h) $(+18) - (-3)$

9. Add.
   Write the addition equation.
   a) $(+4) + (+2)$     b) $(-2) + (+3)$
   c) $(-3) + (-2)$     d) $(+5) + (-6)$
   e) $(-23) + (+4)$     f) $(-19) + (-3)$
   g) $(+13) + (-2)$     h) $(+9) + (+13)$

10. Subtract.
    Write the subtraction equation.
    a) $(+5) - (+3)$     b) $(+3) - (-4)$
    c) $(-5) - (+3)$     d) $(-7) - (-4)$
    e) $(+13) - (-12)$  f) $(-22) - (+32)$
    g) $(-23) - (-23)$  h) $(-7) - (+10)$

11. On December 11, the predicted high and low temperatures in Kenora, ON, were $-1$°C and $-9$°C.
    a) Which is the high temperature and which is the low temperature?
    b) What is the difference in temperatures?

12. Add or subtract as indicated.
    a) $(+6) + (+6)$     b) $(+6) + (-6)$
    c) $(-6) + (+6)$     d) $(-6) + (-6)$
    e) $(+6) - (+6)$     f) $(+6) - (-6)$
    g) $(-6) - (+6)$     h) $(-6) - (-6)$

1. Each pattern continues.
   For each pattern:
   i) Describe the pattern.
   ii) Write the next 3 terms.
   iii) Find the 15th term.
      Explain how you found it.
      a) 2, 5, 8, 11, 14, …
      b) 1, 3, 6, 8, 11, …
      c) 1, 3, 6, 10, 15, …
      d) 3, 6, 11, 18, 27, …

2. a) Copy and complete this table for
      this pattern:
      Multiply each Input number by 4,
      then subtract 1.

   | Input | Output |
   |-------|--------|
   | 1     |        |
   | 2     |        |
   | 3     |        |
   | 4     |        |
   | 5     |        |

   b) Extend the table 3 more rows.
   c) What patterns do you see in the table?
   d) Graph the data.
   e) Explain how the graph shows the
      patterns in the table.

3. Write each algebraic expression in words.
   a) $x + 2$   b) $5 - y$   c) $3p$   d) $\frac{z}{2}$

4. Write an algebraic expression for
   each statement.
   a) four more than two times a number
   b) four less than two times a number
   c) a number divided by four
   d) two less than four times a number

5. Evaluate each expression by replacing
   $n$ with 3.
   a) $4 + n$   b) $4 - n$   c) $4 + \frac{3}{n}$
   d) $4 - \frac{6}{n}$   e) $\frac{(n + 5)}{4}$   f) $\frac{(n - 1)}{2}$

6. Write an equation for each sentence.
   a) Three more than a number is 18.
   b) The sum of 6 and a number is 71.
   c) A number divided by 5 is 14.
   d) The product of 4 and a number
      is 64.

7. Write each equation in words.
   a) $3p = 9$   b) $\frac{15}{n} = 3$
   c) $r - 6 = 13$   d) $24n = 552$

8. Write an equation you can solve to
   answer each question.
   a) Ray scored 14 points in the game.
      Tung scored 8 more points than Ray.
      How many points did Tung score?
   b) Nema has 4 times as many hockey
      cards as Tamar.
      Tamar has 156 cards.
      How many cards does Nema have?
   c) Adriel cycled 80 km less than Alona
      cycled. Alona cycled 218 km.
      How far did Adriel cycle?

9. Solve by inspection.
   a) $n + 5 = 30$   b) $n - 5 = 30$
   c) $5n = 30$   d) $\frac{n}{5} = 30$
   e) $\frac{30}{n} = 5$   f) $5n + 10 = 30$

10. Solve by systematic trial.
    a) $3x + 5 = 26$   b) $3x - 5 = 25$
    c) $24 - 3x = 6$   d) $24 + 3x = 66$
    e) $\frac{x}{13} = 19$   f) $\frac{414}{x} = 18$

1. The 12 face cards (J, Q, K) from a deck of cards are placed in a bag. One card is taken from the bag at random. The pointer on this spinner is spun.

   a) List the possible outcome of taking a card and spinning the pointer.
   b) How many outcomes include taking the Jack of spades?
   c) How many outcomes include landing on a green sector?

2. You will need a deck of playing cards.
   a) Make a table with these headings.

| Outcome | Tally | Frequency | Relative Frequency |
|---------|-------|-----------|--------------------|
|         |       |           |                    |

   b) A card is picked at random from the deck. Assume the suit does not matter. List the possible outcomes in the *Outcome* column.
   c) Are the outcomes in part b equally likely? Explain.
   d) Pick a card at random from the deck. Record it in the *Tally* column. Return the card to the deck. Return this experiment until you have 50 results. Complete the *Frequency* column.
   e) Calculate and record the relative frequencies.

   f) Do the results confirm your answer in part c? Explain.

3. A number cube is labelled 1 to 6. The number cube is rolled 150 times. Predict the number of times:
   a) a 1 will show
   b) a multiple of 3 will show
   c) a number less than 4 will show

4. A box contains 3 red, 2 green, and 4 white candies. Carmen picked one candy at random, found it was white, and ate it. She picked a second candy at random, found it was red, and ate it. Carmen picked a third candy at random. Which colour is it most likely to be? Explain.

5. In the game SCRABBLE, there are 100 tiles. Two tiles are blank. Here is the number of tiles for each letter: A, 9; B: 2; C: 2; D: 4; E: 12; F: 2; G: 3; H: 2; I: 9, J: 1; K: 1; L: 4; M: 2; N: 6; O: 8; P: 2; Q: 1; R: 6; S: 4; T: 6; U: 4; V: 2; W: 2; X: 1; Y: 2; Z: 1.
   The 100 tiles are placed in a bag. One tile is picked at random.
   a) Which letter has the greatest probability of being picked?
   b) What is the probability of picking a blank?
   c) Which letter has the least probability of being picked?
   d) Which letters have the same probability of being picked? What are these probabilities?
   e) Does any letter have a 0% chance of being picked? Explain.

1. Find 2 consecutive prime numbers whose product is 899.

2. Use four 6s to make 42.

3. Use 25 coins to make $1.

4. Move one number from one box to another box so the sums of the numbers in the boxes will then be equal.

5. Use the digits 0, 1, 2, 3, 4, 5, 6, 7, 8, 9 to make a true equation.
$$(\square + \square - \square + \square - \square + \square) \times (\square - \square + \square - \square) = 0$$

6. Lloyd gave $\frac{1}{2}$ his hockey cards to Jenny. He then gave $\frac{2}{3}$ of his remaining cards to Jerome. Lloyd ended up with 10 cards. How many cards did he start with?

7. Find 4 consecutive odd numbers that add to 120.

8. Leave the numerals in the order shown below. Place only + and − signs to make a true equation.
1 2 3 4 5 6 7 8 9 0 = 100

9. Use five 5s to make 30.

10. Use 3 five times to make 31.

11. Copy this figure on grid paper. How many rectangles are there in the figure?

12. Use the digits 0, 1, 2, 3, 4, 5, 6, 7, 8, 9 to make a true equation.
$$\square\square + \square\square + \square + \square\square + \square + \square + \square = 99$$

13. Use square dot paper. Outline a square array of 25 dots. Move only up and to the right. How many paths can you take from A to B?

14. Use seven 4s to make 100.

15. Without using a calculator, find the sum of the whole numbers from 1 to 100, inclusive. Try to find a quick way to do this. Explain your thinking.

16. Twenty-four players enter a singles tennis tournament. How many matches must be played to find a winner?

**17.** Copy this diagram. How can you remove 6 line segments from this figure to get 2 triangles?

**18.** Two organisms are placed in a container. Their numbers double every 24 h. At the end of 14 days, the container is full.
When was it half full?

**19.** The number 2 is special because $2 + 2 = 4$ and $2 \times 2 = 4$. Find another pair of numbers whose sum equals their product. Don't use 0. The numbers may be different.

**20.** The sum of the digits of a 2-digit number is 5. When the digits are reversed, the new number is 9 less than the original number.
What was the original number?

**21.** Ali started a job on Monday, June 1. He was paid 1¢ the first day, 2¢ the second day, 4¢ the third day, and so on. His earnings doubled each day. He worked Monday to Friday all through June.
How much did he earn altogether?

**22.** Suppose you have a 5-L container and an 8-L container. You need exactly 2 L of water in one of the containers.
How can you do this?

**23.** Joanne had a bag of potatoes. When she counted them by 2s, she had 1 left over.
When she counted them by 3s, there were 2 left over.
When she counted them by 4s, there were 3 left over.
When she counted them by 5s, there were none left over.
How many potatoes were in the bag?

**24.** Ms. Jones built a fence around her square vegetable garden.
Each side had 10 fence posts.
How many fence posts did she use?

**25.** Choose a digit. Use 3 of these digits to make 30. Try to find more than one way to do this.

**26.** Use counters to make this triangle. How can you move 3 of the counters to make the triangle point down instead of up?

**27.** A kettle leaked 2 drops the first day, 4 drops the second day, and 8 drops the third day. It continues to leak following this pattern.
When will the 500th drop leak?

**28.** The mass of a bag of stone chips is 20 kg plus half a bag of stone chips.
What is the mass of a bag and a half of stone chips?

# Illustrated Glossary

**acute angle:** an angle measuring less than 90°

**acute triangle:** a triangle with three acute angles

**algebraic expression:** a mathematical expression containing a variable: for example, $6x - 4$ is an algebraic expression

**angle:** the figure formed by two rays from the same endpoint

**approximate:** a number close to the exact value of an expression; the symbol $\doteq$ means "is approximately equal to"

**area:** the number of square units needed to cover a region

**array:** an arrangement in rows and columns

**assumption:** something that is accepted as true, but has not been proved

**average:** a single number that represents a set of numbers; see *mean*, *median*, and *mode*

**bar graph:** a graph that displays data by using horizontal or vertical bars (see page 175)

**bar notation:** the use of a horizontal bar over a decimal digit to indicate that it repeats; for example, $1.\overline{3}$ means 1.333 333 …

**base:** the side of a polygon or the face of a solid from which the height is measured; the factor repeated in a power

**bias:** an emphasis on characteristics that are not typical of the entire population

**capacity:** the amount a container can hold

**circle graph:** a diagram that uses parts of a circle to display data (see page 307)

**common denominator:** a number that is a multiple of each of the given denominators; for example, 12 is a common denominator for the fractions $\frac{1}{3}, \frac{5}{4}, \frac{7}{12}$

**common factor:** a number that is a factor of each of the given numbers; for example, 3 is a common factor of 15, 9, and 21

**composite number:** a number with three or more factors; for example, 8 is a composite number because its factors are 1, 2, 4, and 8

**concave polygon:** has at least one angle greater than 180°

**cone:** a solid formed by a region and all line segments joining points on the boundary of the region to a point not in the region

**congruent:** figures that have the same size and shape, but not necessarily the same orientation

**consecutive numbers:** integers that come one after the other without any integers missing; for example, 34, 35, 36 are consecutive numbers, so are $-2, -1, 0,$ and 1

**convex polygon:** has all angles less than 180°

**coordinate axes:** the horizontal and vertical axes on a grid

**coordinate grid:** a two-dimensional surface on which a coordinate system has been set up

**coordinates:** the numbers in an ordered pair that locate a point on the grid

**cube:** a solid with six congruent square faces

**cube number:** a power with exponent 3; for example, 8 is a cube number because $8 = 2^3$

**cubic units:** units that measure volume

**cylinder:** a solid with two parallel, congruent, circular bases

**data:** facts or information

**database:** an organized collection of facts or information, often stored on a computer

**denominator:** the term below the line in a fraction

**diagonal:** a line segment that joins two vertices of a figure, but is not a side

**digit:** any of the symbols used to write numerals; for example, in the base-ten system the digits are 0, 1, 2, 3, 4, 5, 6, 7, 8, and 9

**dimensions:** measurements, such as length, width, and height

**dodecahedron:** a polyhedron with 12 faces

**equation:** a mathematical statement that two expressions are equal

**equilateral triangle:** a triangle with three equal sides

**equivalent:** having the same value; for example, $\frac{2}{3}$ and $\frac{6}{9}$ are equivalent fractions; 2:3 and 6:9 are equivalent ratios

**estimate:** a reasoned guess that is close to the actual value, without calculating it exactly

**evaluate:** to substitute a value for each variable in an expression, then simplify; to find the answer

**even number:** a number that has 2 as a factor; for example, 2, 4, 6

**event:** any set of outcomes of an experiment

**experimental probability:** the probability of an event calculated from experimental results; another name for the *relative frequency* of an outcome

**exponent:** a number, shown in a smaller size and raised, that tells how many times the number before it is used as a factor; for example, 2 is the exponent in $6^2$

**expression:** a mathematical phrase made up of numbers and/or variables connected by operations

**factor:** to factor means to write as a product; for example, $20 = 2 \times 2 \times 5$

**formula:** a rule that is expressed as an equation

**fraction:** an indicated quotient of two quantities

**fraction strips:** strips of paper used to model fractions (see page 121)

**frequency:** the number of times a particular number occurs in a set of data

**frustum:** part of a cone or pyramid that remains when a cut is made parallel to the base, and the top of the cone or pyramid is removed (see page 90)

**greatest common factor (GCF):** the greatest number that divides into each number in a set; for example, 5 is the greatest common factor of 10 and 15

**hectare:** a unit of area that is equal to 10 000 m²

**hexagon:** a six-sided polygon

**horizontal axis:** the horizontal number line on a coordinate grid

**icosahedron:** a polyhedron with 20 faces

**image:** the figure that results from a transformation

**improper fraction:** a fraction with the numerator greater than the denominator; for example, both $\frac{6}{5}$ and $\frac{5}{3}$ are improper fractions

**integers:** the set of numbers ... −3, −2, −1, 0, +1, +2, +3,...

**intersecting lines:** lines that meet or cross; lines that have one point in common

**isometric view:** a representation of an object as it would appear in three dimensions

**isosceles acute triangle:** a triangle with two equal sides and all angles less than 90°

**isosceles obtuse triangle:** a triangle with two equal sides and one angle greater than 90°

**isosceles right triangle:** a triangle with two equal sides and a 90° angle

**isosceles triangle:** a triangle with two equal sides

**kite:** a quadrilateral with two pairs of equal adjacent sides

**line graph:** a graph that displays data by using points joined by line segments (see page 189)

**line segment:** the part of a line between two points on the line

**line symmetry:** a figure has line symmetry when it can be divided into 2 congruent parts, so that one part coincides with the other part when the figure is folded at the line of symmetry; for example, line *l* is the line of symmetry for figure ABCD

**lowest common multiple (LCM):** the lowest multiple that is the same for two numbers; for example, the lowest common multiple of 12 and 21 is 84

**magic square:** an array of numbers in which the sum of the numbers in any row, column, or diagonal is always the same (see page 326)

**magic sum:** the sum of the numbers in a row, column, or diagonal of a magic square

**mass:** the amount of matter in an object

**mean:** the sum of a set of numbers divided by the number of numbers in the set

**median:** the middle number when data are arranged in numerical order; if there is an even number of data, the median is the mean of the two middle numbers

**midpoint:** the point that divides a line segment into two equal parts

**mixed number:** a number consisting of a whole number and a fraction; for example, $1\frac{1}{18}$ is a mixed number

**mode:** the number that occurs most often in a set of numbers

**multiple:** the product of a given number and a natural number; for example, some multiples of 8 are 8, 16, 24,...

**natural numbers:** the set of numbers 1, 2, 3, 4, 5,...

**negative number:** a number less than 0

**numerator:** the term above the line in a fraction

**obtuse angle:** an angle greater than 90° and less than 180°

**obtuse triangle:** a triangle with one angle greater than 90°

**octagon:** an eight-sided polygon

**octahedron:** a polyhedron with 8 faces

**odd number:** a number that does not have 2 as a factor; for example, 1, 3, 7

**operation:** a mathematical process or action such as addition, subtraction, multiplication, or division

**opposite integers:** two integers with a sum of 0; for example, +3 and −3 are opposite integers

**order of operations:** the rules that are followed when simplifying or evaluating an expression

**outcome:** a possible result of an experiment or a possible answer to a survey question

**parallel lines:** lines on the same flat surface that do not intersect

**parallelogram:** a quadrilateral with both pairs of opposite sides parallel

**pentagon:** a five-sided polygon

**per capita:** for each person

**percent:** the number of parts per 100; the numerator of a fraction with denominator 100

**perfect cube:** a number that is the cube of a whole number; for example, 64 is a perfect cube because $64 = 4^3$

**perfect square:** a number that is the square of a whole number; for example, 16 is a perfect square because $16 = 4^2$

**perimeter:** the distance around a closed figure

**perpendicular lines:** intersect at 90°

**pictograph:** a graph that uses a symbol to represent a certain number, and repetitions of the symbol illustrate the data (see page 176)

**pictorial diagram:** shows the shape of an object in two dimensions

**polygon:** a closed figure that consists of line segments; for example, triangles and quadrilaterals are polygons

**polyhedron (*plural,* polyhedra):** a solid with faces that are polygons

**population:** the set of all things or people being considered

**positive number:** a number greater than 0

**power:** an expression of a product of equal factors; for example, $4 \times 4 \times 4$ can be expressed as $4^3$; 4 is the base and 3 is the exponent

**prediction:** a statement of what you think will happen

**primary data:** data collected by oneself; first-hand

**prime number:** a whole number with exactly two factors, itself and 1; for example, 2, 3, 5, 7, 11, 29, 31, and 43

**prism:** a solid that has two congruent and parallel faces (the *bases*), and other faces that are parallelograms

**probability:** the likelihood of a particular outcome; the number of times a particular outcome occurs, written as a fraction of the total number of outcomes

**product:** the result when two or more numbers are multiplied

**pyramid:** a solid that has one face that is a polygon (the *base*), and other faces that are triangles with a common vertex

**quadrilateral:** a four-sided polygon

**quotient:** the result when one number is divided by another

**range:** the difference between the greatest and least numbers in a set of data

**rate:** a certain quantity or amount of one thing considered in relation to a unit of another thing

**ratio:** a comparison of two or more quantities with the same unit

**rectangle:** a quadrilateral that has four right angles

**rectangular prism:** a prism that has rectangular faces

**rectangular pyramid:** a pyramid with a rectangular base

**reflection:** a transformation that is illustrated by a figure and its image in a mirror line

mirror line

**reflex angle:** an angle between 180° and 360°

**regular dodecahedron:** a regular polyhedron with 12 congruent faces; each face is a regular pentagon (see page 90)

**regular hexagon:** a polygon that has six equal sides and six equal angles

**regular icosahedron:** a regular polyhedron with 20 congruent faces; each face is an equilateral triangle (see page 90)

**regular octagon:** a polygon that has eight equal sides and eight equal angles

**regular octahedron:** a regular polyhedron with 8 congruent faces; each face is an equilateral triangle (see page 90)

**regular polygon:** a polygon that has all sides equal and all angles equal

**regular polyhedron:** a solid with faces that are congruent regular polygons, with the same number of edges meeting at each vertex (see page 76)

**related denominators:** two fractions where the denominator of one fraction is a factor of the other; their lowest common denominator is the greater of the two denominators

**relative frequency:** the number of times a particular outcome occurred, written as a fraction of the total number of times the experiment was conducted

**repeating decimal:** a decimal with a repeating pattern in the digits that follow the decimal point; it is written with a bar above the repeating digits; for example, $\frac{1}{11} = 0.\overline{09}$

**rhombus:** a parallelogram with four equal sides

**right angle:** a 90° angle

**right triangle:** a triangle that has one right angle

**rotation:** a transformation in which a figure is turned about a fixed point

**rotational symmetry:** a figure that coincides with itself in less than one full turn is said to have rotational symmetry; for example, a square has rotational symmetry of order 4 about its centre O

**sample/sampling:** a representative portion of a population

**scale:** the ratio of the distance between two points on a map, model, or diagram to the distance between the actual locations; the numbers on the axes of a graph

**scalene triangle:** a triangle with all sides different

**scatter plot:** a graph of data that is a set of points

**secondary data:** data not collected by oneself, but by others; data found from the library, or the Internet

**similar figures:** figures with the same shape, but not necessarily the same size

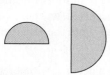

**simplest form:** a ratio with terms that have no common factors, other than 1; a fraction with numerator and denominator that have no common factors, other than 1

**spreadsheet:** a computer-generated arrangement of data in rows and columns, where a change in one value results in appropriate calculated changes in the other values

**square:** a rectangle with four equal sides

**square number:** the product of a number multiplied by itself; for example, 25 is the square of 5

**square root:** a number which, when multiplied by itself, results in a given number; for example, 5 is a square root of 25

**statistics:** the branch of mathematics that deals with the collection, organization, and interpretation of data

**stem-and-leaf plot:** an arrangement of data; for two-digit numbers, the tens digits are shown as the "stems" and the ones digits as the "leaves" (see page 179)

**straight angle:** an angle measuring 180°

**straightedge:** a strip of wood, metal, or plastic with a straight edge, but no markings

**surface area:** the total area of the surface of an object

**symmetrical:** possessing symmetry; see *line symmetry* and *rotational symmetry*

**term:** of a fraction is the numerator or the denominator of the fraction

**terminating decimal:** a decimal with a certain number of digits after the decimal point; for example, $\frac{1}{8} = 0.125$

**tessellation:** a tiling pattern

**tetrahedron:** a solid with four triangular faces; a triangular pyramid

**theoretical probability:** the number of favourable outcomes written as a fraction of the total number of possible outcomes

**three-dimensional:** having length, width, and depth or height

**transformation:** a translation, rotation, or reflection

**translation:** a transformation that moves a point or a figure in a straight line to another position on the same flat surface

**trapezoid:** a quadrilateral that has at least one pair of parallel sides

**tree diagram:** a diagram that resembles the roots or branches of a tree, used to count outcomes (see page 408)

**triangle:** a three-sided polygon

**two-dimensional:** having length and width, but no thickness, height, or depth

**unit fraction:** a fraction that has a numerator of 1

**unit price:** the price of one item, or the price of a particular mass or volume of an item

**unit rate:** the quantity associated with a single unit of another quantity; for example, 6 m in 1 s is a unit rate; it is written as 6 m/s

**unrelated denominators:** two fractions where the denominators have no common factors; their lowest common denominator is the product of the two denominators

**variable:** a letter or symbol representing a quantity that can vary

**vertex** (*plural,* **vertices**)**:** the corner of a figure or a solid

**vertical axis:** the vertical number line on a coordinate grid

**volume:** the amount of space occupied by an object

**whole numbers:** the set of numbers 0, 1, 2, 3,…

**zero pair:** two opposite numbers whose sum is equal to zero

# Index

## A

acute triangle, 246
adding fractions, 128–130
　　using models, 124, 125
adding integers, 341, 342, 359
adding mixed numbers, 131
addition,
　　mental math strategies, 326
algebraic expression, 379
　　evaluating, 383, 384
*AppleWorks*, 193–196
"approximate" symbol, 144
area,
　　of irregular figure, 234–236,
　　　239
　　of parallelogram, 217, 218,
　　　239
　　of rectangle, 94, 106, 216
　　of square, 106, 216
　　of trapezoid, 226–228, 239
　　of triangle, 221, 222, 239
average speed, 64, 69

## B

bar graph, 175, 193
base, 23, 34, 76 *illustration*
Base Ten Blocks, 145, 146
biased, 170
booklets, 2, 3 *Investigation*

## C

CANSIM II, 172
circle graphs, 194, 306–309
circle models, 120, 124
cluster, 186
common denominator, 128–130,
　　136, 137
common factor, 15
common multiples, 16
composite number, 15, 34
concave polygon, 251
congruent figures, 255, 256, 281
conversions,
　　decimals and fractions to
　　　percents, 406
　　fractions to decimals, 290
converting metric units, 44
convex polygon, 251

coordinate grid,
　　graphing on, 367
　　plotting points on, 249
　　transformations on, 263
coordinates of a point (*see*
　　ordered pair)
cube, 76, 77
　　surface area of, 106
　　volume of, 24, 106
cube numbers, 24, 31, 34

## D

data,
　　collection, 169
　　graphing with spreadsheets,
　　　193–196
　　recording, 174, 175
databases, 172, 173
decimals, 118, 119
　　as fractions and percents,
　　　292–294
　　converting to percents, 406
　　dividing, 149–151
　　from fractions, 290
　　multiplying, 145–147
　　order of operations with, 154
dividend, 19
dividing decimals, 149–151
divisibility rules, 9
divisor, 19
dodecahedron, 90
downward trend, 187

## E

edge, 76 *illustration*
elevation, 330
equations, 387, 388, 398
　　solving, 390–393
equilateral triangle, 246
equivalent fractions, 121, 132
equivalent ratios, 50, 51, 69
Escher, M.C., 268, 284, 285
E-STAT, 172, 173
evaluate, 383
expanded form of a number, 24,
　　25, 34
experimental probability,
　　411–413
exponents, 23–25, 34

expressions,
　　variables in, 378, 379

## F

face, 76 *illustration*
factors, 14–16, 34
*Fathom*, 185–187
Fibonacci numbers, 38
fields, 172
figures,
　　classifying, 250, 251
　　congruent, 255–257, 281
fraction strips, 121
fractions,
　　adding, 128–130
　　adding using models, 124, 125
　　adding with Pattern Blocks,
　　　116
　　as decimals and percents,
　　　292–294
　　combining, 120, 121
　　converting to percents, 406
　　"friendly," 298
　　repeated addition, 141, 142
　　subtracting, 136, 137
　　subtracting using models, 132,
　　　133
　　subtracting with Pattern
　　　Blocks, 116
　　writing as a decimal, 290
frequency, 412
frequency table (*also* tally chart),
　　174
"friendly" fraction, 298
frustum, 91

## G

*Geometer's Sketchpad, The*, 82, 83
　　drawing transformations,
　　　274–277
graphing,
　　on coordinate grids, 367
　　patterns, 373–375
graphs,
　　drawing circle, 306–309
　　misleading information in,
　　　202, 203
greatest common factor (GCF),
　　15, 42

**H**

hexagon, 251, 252
hexagonal pyramid, 76
    *illustration*
hypothesis, 72

**I**

icosahedron, 89, 90
inspection,
    solving equations by, 391–393,
      398
integers, 327, 328
    adding, 341, 342, 359
    adding with tiles, 337, 338,
      359
    comparing and ordering, 330,
      331
    modelling/representing, 334,
      335, 359
    subtracting, 351–353, 359
    subtracting with tiles,
      346–348, 359
irregular figures, 234–236, 239
isometric, 77
isometric dot paper, 77
isosceles triangle, 246

**L**

leaf, 180, 181
length,
    unit prefixes of, 152
line graphs, 188–190, 195, 196
line symmetry,
    in a hexagon, 252
    in a polygon, 251
lowest common denominator,
    129, 130, 136, 137, 158
lowest common multiple (LCM),
    16, 43, 129

**M**

*Math Link*
    art, 86
    history, 377
    measurement, 152
    social studies, 61
    sports, 336
    sports, 426
    your world, 27
    your world, 197
    your world, 224
    your world, 254

your world, 301
mean, 168, 198–200, 208
measuring irregular figures,
    234–236
median, 168, 198–200, 208
mental math strategies, 8, 326
metric units,
    converting, 44
mixed numbers,
    adding, 131
    subtracting, 138
mode, 168, 198–200, 208
models,
    for adding fractions, 124, 125
    for subtracting fractions, 132,
      133
multiples, 16
multiplying,
    a fraction by a whole number,
      158
    by 0.1, 0.01, and 0.001, 117
    by 10, 100, 1000, 7
    decimals, 145–147

**N**

negative integer, 328
negative number, 327
nets, 89–91
number patterns, 368–370
numbers,
    expanded form of, 24, 25, 34
    standard form of, 24, 25, 34
    uses of, 10, 11

**O**

objects,
    sketching views of, 78, 79,
      84–86
obtuse triangle, 246
octahedron, 90
operations,
    order of, 154, 366
opposite integers, 328
ordered pair (*also* coordinates of
    a point), 367
outcomes, 407, 408

**P**

parallelogram,
    area of, 217, 218, 239
partially related denominators,
    158

part-to-part ratio, 46
part-to-whole ratio, 46
Pascal, Blaise, 28
Pascal's Triangle, 28
Pattern Blocks,
    for adding and subtracting
      fractions, 116
patterning,
    to add integers, 342
patterns,
    for numbers, 368–370
    graphing, 373–375
    in a book signature, 2
pentagon,
    tiling the plane, 267
pentagonal prism, 76 *illustration*
percent circle, 306
percents, 291
    as decimals and fractions,
      292–294
    calculating and estimating,
      297–299
    conversion from decimals and
      fractions, 406
    from dividing, 311, 312
    from multiplying, 302, 303
perfect cube, 24, 34
perfect square, 24, 34
perimeter,
    of irregular figure, 234, 235
    of rectangle, 95, 106, 216
    of square, 95, 106, 216
    of trapezoid, 226–228
Pick's Theorem, 286, 287
    *Investigation*
pictorial diagram, 85
pie chart, 195
place-value chart, 117
point on a grid, 249
polygon, 76, 112 *Investigation*,
    251
polyhedron, 76
population simulation, 432
    *Investigation*
positive integer, 328
positive number, 327
power, 23, 34
prefixes,
    in units of length, 152
primary data, 169, 208
prime number, 15, 34
prism, 76

probability,
  applications of, 420, 421
  experimental, 411–413
  theoretical, 416–418, 427
pyramid, 76

**Q**
quadrilaterals, 254
  congruent, 257
  tiling the plane, 267
quotient, 19, 150

**R**
range, 200
rate, 62–64, 69
ratios, 45, 46, 69
  applications of, 58–60
  comparing, 53–55, 69
  equivalent, 50, 51, 69
  in scale drawings, 112
    *Investigation*
  in simplest form, 51
  part-to-part, 46
  part-to-whole, 46
  terms of, 46
rectangle,
  area of, 94, 106, 216
  perimeter of, 95, 106, 216, 378
rectangular prism,
  surface area of, 97, 98, 106
  volume of, 101, 102, 106
reflection, 262
regular polyhedron, 76
related denominators, 126, 158
relative frequency, 411–413, 427
repeated addition, 141, 142
repeating decimals, 144
right isosceles triangle, 79
right triangle, 246
rotation, 262
rotational symmetry,
  in a hexagon, 252
  in a polygon, 251
rounding, 6, 7

**S**
same denominators, 158
scale, 68
scale drawing, 112 *Investigation*
scalene triangle, 246

scatter plots,
  investigating with *Fathom*,
    185–187
secondary data, 169, 208
signatures, 2
similar polygons, 112
  *Investigation*
simplest form of a ratio, 51
simulation, 432 *Investigation*
sketching objects, 78, 79, 84–86
*Skills You'll Need*
  adding and subtracting
    fractions with Pattern
    Blocks, 116
  calculating mean, median, and
    mode, 168
  classifying triangles, 246
  comparing and ordering
    decimals, 119
  constructing a triangle, 247
  converting among metric
    units, 44
  converting fractions and
    decimals to percents, 406
  divisibility rules, 9
  graphing on a coordinate grid,
    367
  greatest common factor, 42
  identifying polyhedra, 76
  lowest common multiple, 43
  mental math, 8
  mental math strategies for
    addition and subtraction,
    326
  multiplying by 0.1, 0.01, and
    0.001, 117
  multiplying by 10, 100, 1000,
    7
  operations with decimals, 118
  order of operations, 366
  perimeter and area of a
    rectangle, 216
  percent, 291
  plotting points on a
    coordinate grid, 249
  rounding, 6, 7
  using isometric dot paper to
    draw a cube, 77
  writing a fraction as a
    decimal, 290
solving equations, 390–393

spreadsheets, 193–196
square,
  area of, 95, 106
  perimeter of, 95, 106
square number, 19, 24, 34
square pyramid, 76 *illustration*
square root, 20, 34
standard form of a number, 24,
  25, 34
Statistics Canada (Stats Can), 172
stem, 180, 181
stem-and-leaf plots, 179–181
subtracting fractions, 136, 137
  using models, 132, 133
subtracting integers, 351–353,
  359
  with tiles, 346–348, 359
subtracting mixed numbers, 138
subtraction,
  mental math strategies, 326
surface area, 97, 98
  of cube, 106
  of rectangular prism, 97, 98,
    106
systematic trial,
  solving equations by, 390–393,
    398

**T**
tally chart (*see* frequency table)
temperature, 327
terminating decimals, 144
terms of a ratio, 46
tessellations, 284, 285
tetrahedron, 76
theoretical probability, 416–418,
  427
tiles,
  adding integers with, 337, 338,
    359
  subtracting integers with,
    346–348, 359
tiling patterns, 266, 267
tiling the plane, 266, 267
transformations, 261–263
  making designs with, 270–272
  using *The Geometer's
    Sketchpad*, 274–277
translation, 262
trapezoid,
  area of, 226–228, 239
  perimeter of, 226–228

tree diagram, 407, 408
trend, 186, 187
triangles,
    acute, 246
    area of, 221, 222, 239
    classifying, 246
    congruent, 255, 256, 281
    constructing, 247
    equilateral, 246
    isosceles, 246
    obtuse, 246
    right, 246
    scalene, 246
    tiling the plane, 266
triangular numbers, 30
triangular prism, 76 *illustration*

**U**

unit fraction, 130
unit rate, 62
unrelated denominators, 126, 158
upward trend, 186

**V**

variables, 94, 95
    in expressions, 378, 379, 398
vertex, 76 *illustration*
volume
    of cube, 24, 106
    of rectangular prism, 101, 102,
      106

**W**

*World of Work, The*
    advertising sales
      representative, 153
    clothes buyer, 395
    forensic graphics specialist, 88
    historian, 358
    hospital administrator, 27
    measuring for construction,
      231
    meteorologist, 183
    office space planner, 280
    race engineer, 68
    sports trainer, 316

**Z**

zero pair, 334, 335

# Acknowledgments

The publisher wishes to thank the following sources for photographs, illustrations, and other materials used in this book. Care has been taken to determine and locate ownership of copyright material in this text. We will gladly receive information enabling us to rectify any errors or omissions in credits.

## Photography

Cover: Gail Shumway/Getty Images
pp. 2–3 Ian Crysler; p. 4 (top) Photodisc; p. 4 (bottom) G.K. & Vikki Hart/Photodisc; p. 5 (top) Photodisc; p. 5 (bottom) David Thompson/Life File; p. 10 Canadian Press/Ryan Remiorz; p. 12 Corel Collection *Insects*; p. 13 Canadian Press/Harold Barkley; p. 23 Ray Boudreau; p.26 C Squared Studios/Photodisc/Getty Images; p. 27 Michael Newman/PhotoEdit Inc.; p. 28 Stefano Bianchetti/CORBIS/MAGMA; p. 32 © Comstock Images www.comstock.com; p. 39 Ray Boudreau; p. 40 Dorling Kindersley Media Library; p. 41 (top to bottom) Dorling Kindersley Media Library; John Warden/Index Stock; Photodisc/Getty Images; Don Mason/CORBIS/MAGMA; p. 52 Canadian Press/Don Denton; p. 53 Ian Crysler; p. 61 Anna Zuckerman–Vdovenko/PhotoEdit Inc.; p. 62 Ray Boudreau; p. 67 Ray Boudreau; p. 68 Canadian Press/*The London Free Press*/Christian Laforce; p. 69 Corel Collection *Classic Aviation*; p. 70 Corbis Royalty–Free/MAGMA; p. 72 (left) Ian Crysler; p. 72 (centre) Corel Collection *Working Animals*; p. 72 (right) Corel Collection *Mammals*; pp. 74–75 Gatorade® Bill Aron/PhotoEdit Inc.; CD case Photodisc; Timberland® shoes Cindy Charles/PhotoEdit Inc.; all others Ian Crysler; p. 78 Ray Boudreau; p. 80 Ray Boudreau; p.81 (left) Dadang Tri/Reuters/CORBIS/MAGMA; p. 81 (centre) James Shaffer/PhotoEdit Inc.; p. 81 (right) Corel Collection *Canoeing Adventure*; p. 82 Ray Boudreau; p. 84 Ray Boudreau; p. 85 Ray Boudreau; p. 86 Ray Boudreau; p. 87 (left) Ray McVay/Photodisc/Getty Images; p. 87 (centre) Ian Crysler; p. 87 (right) David Toase/Photodisc; p. 88 James Shaffer/PhotoEdit Inc.; p. 92 Jules Frazier; p. 93 (left column top to bottom) Ray McVay/Photodisc/Getty Images; Davies and Star/Getty Images; C Squared Studios/Photodisc/Getty Images; Ray Boudreau; p. 93 (right column, left) © Comstock Images www.comstock.com; (right) Dorling Kindersley Media Library; p. 97 Ray Boudreau; p. 101 Ray Boudreau; p. 104 Ray Boudreau; p. 106 Ray Boudreau; p. 107 (top) Ray Boudreau; p. 107 (centre) Dorling Kindersley Media Library; p. 107 (bottom) Cretas Images; p. 110 Spenser Grant/PhotoEdit Inc.; p. 111 Ray Boudreau; p. 112 Ian Crysler; p.

123 Ian Crysler; p. 127 Myrleen Ferguson/PhotoEdit Inc.; p. 131 Ray Boudreau; p. 132 Ray Boudreau; p. 135 Michael Newman/PhotoEdit Inc.; p. 136 Ray Boudreau; p. 139 Ray Boudreau; p. 144 Ray Boudreau; p. 153 Photodisc/Getty Images; p. 155 Stone Skyold/PhotoEdit Inc.; p. 156 Ray Boudreau; p. 157 Ray Boudreau; p. 162 Ray Boudreau; p. 166 Tom Stewart/CORBIS/MAGMA; p. 167 (top left) Tony Freeman/PhotoEdit Inc.; p. 167 (top right) Photodisc/Getty Images; p. 167 (bottom) Rudy von Briel/PhotoEdit Inc.; p. 174 (top) Ray Boudreau; p. 174 (bottom) Corel Collection *Birds*; p. 177 Ed Kashi/CORBIS/MAGMA; p. 179 Ray Boudreau; p. 183 Canadian Press/Jacques Boissinot; p. 185 Bettmann/CORBIS/MAGMA; p. 186 Mary Kate Denney/PhotoEdit Inc.; p. 188 D. Berry/Photo Link; p. 197 Digital Vision; p. 206 Ray Boudreau; p. 207 Ray Boudreau; p. 213 Ray Boudreau; p. 214 (top) © Comstock Images www.comstock.com; p. 214 (bottom) Dorling Kindersley Media Library; p. 215 (bottom) H. Wiensenhofer/Photo Link; p. 215 (top) royalty free; p. 217 Ray Boudreau; p. 231 Photo Researchers; p. 238 Ray Boudreau; p. 242 Robert Landou/CORBIS/MAGMA; p. 243 Ray Boudreau; pp. 244–245 Cathy Mellon Resources/PhotoEdit Inc.; p. 254 Corel Collections *Highway and Street Signs*; p. 255 Ian Crysler; p. 259 Tomas del Amo/Index Stock; p. 261 Ian Crysler; p. 268 M.C. Escher's Reptiles © 2004 The M.C. Escher Company–Baarn, Holland. All Rights Reserved; p. 269 Word&Image; p. 270 Ian Crysler; p. 273 Philip and Karen Smith/Photodisc/Getty Images; p. 276 © Comstock Images www.comstock.com; p. 279 Ian Crysler; p. 280 Mark Richards/PhotoEdit Inc.; p. 284 M.C. Escher's Fish © 2004 The M.C. Escher Company–Baarn, Holland. All Rights Reserved; p. 285 Ian Crysler; p. 287 Ian Crysler; pp. 288–289 royalty free; p. 296 Ian Crysler; p. 300 (top) Philippe Columbi/Photodisc/Getty Images; p. 300 (bottom) Damir Frkovic/Masterfile; p. 307 Canadian Press/Kevin Frayer; p. 310 Corbis Royalty–Free/MAGMA; p. 312 Canadian Press/Peterborough Examiner/Clifford Skarstedt; p. 314 Ian Crysler; p. 315 Ian Crysler; p. 316 Canadian Press/Aaron Harris; p. 324 (top) Bill Tice/MaxxImages; p. 324 (bottom) Tom Kitchin/Firstlight.ca; p. 325 Tom Bean/CORBIS/MAGMA; p. 327 Ron Watts/firstlight.ca; p. 329 Courtesy of Pier 21, National Historic Site; p. 333 J.Kobalenko/firstlight.ca; p. 334 Ray Boudreau; p. 336 Ryan McVey/Photodisc/Getty Images; p. 337 Ian Crysler; p. 343 © Digital Vision; p. 352 Ray Boudreau; p. 354 Corel Collections *Toronto*; p. 355 J. de Visser/Ivy Images; p. 356 © Stockbyte; p. 357 Ray Boudreau; p. 358 (bottom) Bettmann/CORBIS/MAGMA; p. 358 (inset) Erich Lessing/Art Resource, N.Y.; p. 363 Corel Collection *China and Tibet*; pp. 364–365 (left) Canadian Press/*Peterborough Examiner*/Clifford Skarstedt; (right top) Canadian Press/Calgary Herald/Dean Bicknell; (centre) Ray Boudreau; (bottom) David Young-Wolff; p. 376 SW Productions/Index Stock; p. 377 Ludovic Malsant/CORBIS/MAGMA; p. 380 Michael Newman/PhotoEdit Inc.; p. 381

Photodisc/Getty Images; p. 383 © Dinodia; p. 385 Canadian Press/Carl Patzel; p. 390 Michael Newman/PhotoEdit Inc.; p. 393 David Young–Wolff/PhotoEdit Inc.; p. 395 (bottom) Rob Melnychuk/Getty Images; p. 395 (inset) David Young–Wolff/PhotoEdit Inc.; p. 396 Gary Connor/PhotoEdit Inc.; p. 402 Ian Crysler; p. 403 (top) Tony Freeman/PhotoEdit Inc.; p. 403 (inset) James Schaffer/PhotoEdit Inc.; p. 404 (top) © Comstock Images www.comstock.com; p. 404 (centre) Tim Hall/Photodisc/Getty Images; p. 404 (bottom) David Young–Wolff; p. 404 (background) Dorling Kindersley Media Library; p. 405 (top) Photodisc/Getty Images; p. 405 (bottom) Michael Newman/PhotoEdit Inc., p. 405 (background) Johnathan A. Nourok; p. 409 David Zimmerman/CORBIS/MAGMA; p. 411 Ian Crysler; p. 414 Ian Crysler; p. 416 Ian Crysler; p. 417 Ian Crysler; p. 420 Ian Crysler; p. 422 Dennis MacDonald/PhotoEdit Inc.; p. 425 Ian Crysler; p. 426 Ian Crysler; p. 430 Ian Crysler; p. 432 Ian Crysler

**Illustrations**

Steve Attoe

Pierre Bethiaume

Steve MacEachern

Paul McCusker

Pronk&Associates

Michel Rabagliate

Craig Terlson